INTERNATIONAL AND COMPARATIVE CRIMINAL LAW SERIES

THE FAILURE TO PREVENT GENOCIDE IN RWANDA:

The Role of Bystanders

FRED GRÜNFELD
ANKE HUIJBOOM

Martinus Nijhoff Publishers
Leiden / Boston

Publisher's Note: Despite our efforts we have been unable to trace all rights holders to some copyrighted material. The publisher welcomes communications from copyrights holders, so that the appropriate acknowledgements can be made in future editions, and to settle other permission matters.

Library of Congress Cataloging-in-Publication Data

Grünfeld, Fred, 1949–
The failure to prevent genocide in Rwanda : the role of bystanders :
Fred Grünfeld and Anke Huijboom.
p. cm.
Includes bibliographical references and index.
ISBN-13: 978-90-04-15781-1 (alk. paper)
ISBN-10: 90-04-15781-6 (alk. paper)
Genocide—Prevention. 2. Humanitarian intervention. 3. International agencies. 4. Genocide—Rwanda—History—20th century. I. Huijboom, Anke. II. Title.

HV6322.7.G78 2007
967.57104'3l—dc22

2006048096

Koninklijke Brill NV incorporates the imprints Brill, Hotei Publishers, IDC Publishers, Martinus Nijhoff Publishers, and VSP.

Manufactured in the United States of America

CONTENTS

FOREWORD

After WWII, the international community vowed "never again"—but that promise was never kept. Since the end of WWII, the world has witnessed over 250 conflicts of an international and non-international character, as well as purely domestic conflicts and other forms of tyrannical regime victimization. The estimated casualties for these conflicts is between a low end of 70 million and a high end of 170 million. Whatever the actual figure, the numbers are mind-boggling. The lower-end estimate alone is cumulatively equivalent to the casualties of World Wars I and II. How did this happen? Possibly because it occurred one conflict at a time, with each conflict building within world consciousness a greater ability to passively withstand more human tragedies. We simply become more habituated to such conflicts and to a high number of victims much as a drug addict becomes less affected as his/her drug consumption becomes higher.

Human conscience can probably take tragedies in small doses and rationalize why it failed to act. Surely if there was an international duty to protect, some of these tragedies would either not have occurred or their consequences would have been mitigated. However, the international community has yet to reach that point.

The Failure to Prevent Genocide in Rwanda: The Role of Bystanders is about the international community's failure to act in Rwanda, and the responsibility of a few within the United Nations' system to raise the danger flag. Their actions were more consonant with the petty interests of politics than the basic needs of humanity. As to the inaction of the Security Council, it is certainly beyond rational human explanation. No one can now doubt the extent of the tragedy in Rwanda and the fact that it could have been averted with a limited military commitment, but the major capitals of the West were hardly interested in military protection for the civilian population of that country. Nearly everyone concerned within these governments and within the United Nations' system thought of their interests first, and from a very narrow and selfish perspective at that.

This book is reminiscent of Emile Zola's *J'accuse* (1894). It is a damning accusation against certain countries and against the senior officials and others who contributed to the non-action at the United Nations. Unlike Zola's denunciation, which was a journalistic human cry, this book is a historic and legal analysis of the tragic unfolding of the situation in Rwanda.

In Chapter 1 the authors document how early warnings should have been taken more seriously by the international community. Certainly no one could later argue that they were taken by surprise. Chapter 2 is an *a posteriori* confirmation of these early warnings arising out of the ICTR's interpretation and application of the Genocide Convention to the direct and public incitement to genocide that surely no one in the West should have ignored or underestimated. Chapter 3 addresses the colonial history of Rwanda showing the interaction between Hutu and Tutsi and how the Belgian colonial era there had sown the seeds of discord that later took place. That colonial history is reminiscent of what has happened in the Democratic Republic of Congo for the last 40 years; Belgian colonization had also sown the seeds of conflict in that country whose consequences are still felt.

Chapter 5 illustrates the intent by Belgium to lead a force, UNAMIR, to help stave off the forthcoming Hutu–Tutsi conflict. Belgium's awareness of the danger, however, was not shared by other Western powers with the capabilities of strengthening UNAMIR, particularly the United States and France. Chapter 6 outlines how Hutu extremism emerged and how the worst possible predictions contained in the early warnings described in Chapter 1 came to materialize in 1994. It also shows that as always, the United Nations seeks to address such tragic situations with reports until such time as the political will of the major Western powers becomes evident. In this case, there was hardly anything that needed uncovering during that period of time—particularly as of 1993—to warn of an impending tragedy.

It is pointed out in Chapter 7 that there was still a window of opportunity between November 1993 and January 1994 to stop the impending tragedy. However, the political will to act by major Western governments was still absent and senior U.N. bureaucrats were unwilling to rudely awaken these states from their self-induced states of denial. Chapters 8 and 9 describe how close the situation was to the boiling point before the widespread and systematic killing started to take place. Those who followed the situation at the United Nations and the few who read about what is known of the so-called "genocide" continued to tragically underestimate it. Canadian General Romeo Dallaire's efforts and warnings simply did not move the senior officials, nor did it move France or the United States to act. The political deadlock that ensued in New York, as described in Chapter 10, continued, notwithstanding Dallaire's strong support by Belgium who wanted to broaden UNAMIR's mandate and strengthen its force.

Chapter 12 reveals how a combination of in-country anti-Belgian sentiments and American *lassez-faire* worsened the situation. When it became clear to the Hutu side that the international community's will to intervene was lacking, the genocide began. Chapter 13 is an account of how the genocide began to unfold, Secretary-General Boutros-Ghali's efforts before the Security Council, the Belgian withdrawal of its few remaining troops for fear of being left alone to suffer the inevitable consequences, and the Security Council's decision of non-interference. If there was ever a situation where the responsibility of states was to be determined by its conscious and deliberate failure to act, this was one of them. The height of hypocrisy was reached with the unanimous adoption of Resolution 912, favoring the withdrawal of UNAMIR troops but leaving a symbolic number of peacekeepers who could do nothing to prevent the impending tragedy.

Chapter 17 describes the role of the Netherlands—to some ambiguous and not quite decisive—but still positive. Chapter 18 is probably most telling: Ten years later, governments and inter-governmental organizations, one by one, extended their apologia or regrets, as if these would be enough to alleviate their moral, historic, and legal responsibilities. The apologists include Belgium, the United States, France, the United Nations, the European Union, and the African Union. The latter, who should be most interested in what happens on its continent, is nevertheless the least effective of all political intergovernmental organizations.

As one who has observed this and other tragedies (from 1992 through 1994, I was the Chairman of the Security Council Commission investigating war crimes in the former Yugoslavia), I cannot help but think that the difference between Rwanda and other major tragedies, such as Cambodia during the Khmer Rouge killing spree that resulted in the estimated death of anywhere between 1–2 million people over the span of ten years (1975–1985), is that in this case, major powers and IGOs saw fit to express a quasi *mea culpa*. The authors conclude Chapter 18 with a hopeful section dealing with lessons learned as evidenced by the heads of states declaration at the 2005 U.N. Summit. But much as the previous apologies for the tragedy, the pious declarations of the 2005 U.N. Summit are words devoid of commitment to prevent such future tragedies.

In the Rwanda tragedy, the warnings were there, and the signs were clear. The information was available to senior U.N. officials, and the Security Council purposely looked the other way. The Security Council played the perfect role of the ostrich, and in the end, an estimated 800,000 people were killed. Ten years later, apologies were issued.

Many, like the authors and myself, believe that if such tragedies are to be instructive and the deaths not to have been for naught, then we have to establish an international legal responsibility to protect, thus converting the Security Council from the pliable club responsive to the will of its permanent members to a body that will not only selectively decide what constitutes a threat to peace and security, but that is obligated at the very least to act under certain circumstances to protect against genocide.

Considering what has been happening in the DRC and in Darfur, it is clear that the genocide in Rwanda, and for that matter the 70–170 million casualties since WWII all over the world, are not enough to displace the cynicism of *realpolitik*. How many more Rwandas will it take?

The Failure to Prevent Genocide in Rwanda: The Role of Bystanders is a documented moral cry. With hope it will instruct future generations on how to avoid such human tragedies. The authors are to be congratulated for their moral message presented in a well-documented historical/political/legal analysis of one of the worst contemporary tragedies. The book is a significant contribution to the truth about an unspeakable human tragedy.

Chicago, February 19, 2007

M. Cherif Bassiouni
Distinguished Research Professor of Law
Emeritus President
International Human Rights Law Institute
DePaul University College of Law

PREFACE

The failure to prevent the genocide in Rwanda in 1994 is the topic of this book. In particular, the research focuses on why the early warnings of an emerging genocide were not translated into early preventative action. The warnings were well documented by the most authoritative source, the Canadian U.N. peace-keeping commander Roméo Dallaire, and sent to the leading political civil servants in New York. The communications and the decisionmaking processes are scrutinized, i.e., who received what messages at what time, to whom the messages were forwarded and which (non-) decisions were taken in response to the alarming reports of weapon deliveries and atrocities. This book makes clear that this genocide could have been prevented.

Moreover, despite having the power and instruments available to prevent and stop the genocide, the policies of the third parties—the bystander states and international organizations—could even be said to have promoted it. These failures are not to be reduced to one single moment—for instance the alarming genocide fax of January—but are a pattern that can be seen over the course of several months, in which all requests for any action were prohibited by the top civil servants of the United Nations in New York. These top civil servants—Hedi Annabi, Kofi Annan and Iqbal Riza—did not inform the Security Council of these requests, and they also failed to inform the members of the Security Council of the deteriorating situation in Rwanda in the months preceding the genocide. They were predominantly focused on the impartiality of the U.N. peace-keepers to preserve and implement the Arusha Peace Accords. That is why they systematically neglected all signals that the Rwandan leadership was not implementing the agreements and installing an interim-government, but on the contrary, planning to take power for the extremists.

The ten Belgian peace-keepers were deliberately killed in order to realize the withdrawal of all peace-keepers. No enforcement power was attributed to these peace-keepers before or during the genocide. All requests from the Belgian government for the strengthening of the peace-keeping forces were also rejected by the top U.N. civil servants, whereas the robust military force of Italians, Americans, French and Belgian appeared on Rwandan territory with heavy military equipment within the first days of the genocide in order to rescue their own nationals. Although the peace-keepers were absolutely forbidden from the use of force, it was only at the moment when the Belgian U.N. commander of the capital, Kigali, was placed under the direct command of the Belgian evacuation force, changing from a Blue Helmet to a Belgian national soldier, that the use of force was allowed by Annan in his instructions from New York.

This research is based on available studies from scholars, from the inquiry commissions of the United Nations and the parliaments of Belgium and France. These data have been supplemented with studies in the archives of the Netherlands Ministry of Foreign Affairs and with interviews with key actors, such as UNAMIR Major Brent Beardsley from Canada, Colonel Luc Marchal from Belgium, the Belgian Minister of Foreign Affairs Willy Claes, the Dutch Minister of Development Co-operation Jan Pronk, the Presidential National Security Adviser in the United States Anthony Lake of the White House, the American State Department Heads of African Affairs Prudence Bushnell and of Human Rights John Shattuck, the U.N. Special Rapporteur Bacré Ndiaye from Senegal, the initiator of the Belgian inquiry commission Alain Destexhe and the American ambassador in Rwanda David Rawson. These interviews are integrated into the text of this book.

ACKNOWLEDGMENTS

In 2003 I, Fred Grünfeld, was appointed to the chair at Utrecht University on the causes of gross human rights violations. This chair is an initiative of the PIOOM (Interdisciplinary Projects on the Causes of Human Rights Violations) with a board and a board of governors for this chair. The research was done within the framework of the Netherlands Institute of Human Rights in the Law Faculty of the Utrecht University, and at the Maastricht Centre for Human Rights in the Law Faculty of the Maastricht University. Research at both institutes is embedded in the Netherlands Research School of Human Rights.

In 2003 I, Anke Huijboom, wrote my Masters thesis at Maastricht University on "Gacaca," the Rwandan local justice system. Fred Grünfeld was the supervisor of this thesis. Returning from my fieldwork for the Royal Netherlands Embassy in Rwanda in 2004, Fred asked me whether I wanted to cooperate with him in this research, which I saw as a great opportunity. For more than one and a half years, we fruitfully worked together in the research and writing of this book.

From the start, the study was financially supported by the Horstman Foundation, a foundation aimed at subsidizing studies for early warning in order to prevent the passivity of the 1930s. Its founder, Albert Horstman, a resistance fighter against the Nazis in the Second World War, warned in vain about the emerging fascism. This foundation—boarded by Isaac Heertje, Roel Klaassen and Jaap Roodenburg—subsidized personal part-time assistance over the course of four years. Thanks to this subsidy, it was possible to involve assistants at both universities, and without this support this study would never have been published.

We would like to thank Eva Rieter in particular for her research on academic literature about early warning and early action. Two student assistants helped very much at the final stage. Hayley Jordan, my best student—as Erasmus exchange student from Cambridge—in the course on the Causes of Gross Human Rights Violations at Utrecht University, revised the whole text and edited all texts over six months in 2006. Jennifer Sellin, the assistant at the Maastricht Centre for Human Rights put the manuscript in October 2006 into the right format for publication. Finalized the indexes in the beginning of 2007 and promoted this publication. Additionally, we want to thank Theo van Boven from Maastricht University who has read the manuscript and has given us very valuable comments that we greatly appreciated.

The Netherlands Institute of Human Rights (SIM) in the Faculty of Law of Utrecht University, the Maastricht Centre for Human Rights and the

Department of International and European Law at the Faculty of Law of Maastricht University were the locations in which the study was carried out. We are grateful for this support in housing, permitting sabbatical leave and traveling for research. The PIOOM board (Johan Bom, Adriaan Dorresteijn, Gerard van Lennep and Johan Scholten) and the governing board of the PIOOM chair (Cees Flinterman, Fried van Hoof, Ellie Lissenberg, Johan Scholten and Harmen van der Wilt) stimulated this research and gave their full attention to its progress over the years.

A special word of thanks goes to those who were interviewed in the course of the research, as they contributed greatly by telling us about their roles in the decisionmaking from 1993 to 1994. The Netherlands Ministry of Foreign Affairs was also very helpful in opening the archives on Rwanda for us.

Fred Grünfeld
and
Anke Huijboom

LIST OF ABBREVIATIONS

APC	Armored Personnel Carriers.
ARDHO	Association pour la Protection des Droits de l'Homme. Rwandan human rights organization.
AU	African Union.
BBTG	Broad Based Transitional Government. The BBTG was planned to be installed on January 1, 1994, but due to a political deadlock this was not possible. On January 5, President Habyarimana was sworn in, but the full installation was postponed to March 25, and then again to March 28, and then again to early April.
CCOAIB	Council representing non-governmental organizations working for development.
CDR	Coalition pour Défense de la République. The CDR was a Hutu extremist party, a splinter group of the MRND. The group had separated from the MRND, because they were of the opinion that President Habyarimana was too moderate; the leaders of the CDR were among the main organizers of the genocide.
CLADHO	Collectif des Ligues et Associations de Défense des Droits de l'Homme. CLADHO is a Coalition of Rwandan human rights organizations.
CND	Conseil National pour le Développement. The CND was the building of the National Assembly where the RPF resided since the end of December 1993.
DPKO	Division of Peace-Keeping Operations.
DNAT	French anti-terror division.
EU	European Union.
FAR/RGF	Forces Armées Rwandaises/Rwandan Government Forces. FAR/RGF was the army of the Rwandan government, Hutu dominated; the FAR/RGF was heavily involved in the genocide. The term FAR will be used throughout the book.
GA	U.N. General Assembly.
HRW	Human Rights Watch.
ICISS	International Commission on Intervention and State Sovereignty.
ICRC	International Committee of the Red Cross.
ICTR	International Criminal Tribunal for Rwanda.

IGO	Inter-governmental organization.
KIBAT	Kigali Battalion, Belgian-commanded peace-keeping force of UNAMIR.
KWSA	Kigali Weapon Secure Area. The KWSA agreement was signed on the December 23, 1993, and prescribed that all militant units were required to store all the weapons and ammunition; weapons and armed troops were only allowed to move under permission and escort of UNAMIR.
MRND	Mouvement Révolutionnaire National pour le Dévoloppement. The MRND was the political party that was founded by President Habyarimana in 1975; until the genocide in 1994, it was the ruling party; over the years the party turned into a Hutu extremist party, many of the leaders were involved in the organization of the genocide.
MDR	Mouvement Démocratique Républicain. The MDR was the largest opposition party to President Habyarimana's regime and was split into moderate and extremist parts.
NGO	Non-governmental organization.
NIC	National Intelligence Council (CIA).
NID	National Intelligence Daily.
NIE	National Intelligence Estimates.
OAS	Organization of American States.
OAU	Organization of African Unity.
PDC	Parti Démocrate Chrétien/Christian Democratic Party. The PCD was the smallest opposition party of the main four opposition parties.
PDD25	Presidential Decision Directive.
PL	Parti Liberal/Liberal Party. The liberal party was a moderate party, which had many Tutsi members. It was the opposition party that was third place out of the four main opposition parties.
PSD	Parti Social Démocrate. The Social Democratic Party was the second largest opposition party.
PG	Presidential Guard. The PG was the best trained and equipped FAR unit, also known as the "intellectuals" party. The unit was heavily involved in the genocide.
ROE	rules of engagement.
RPA	Rwandese Patriotic Army. Army of the RPF.
RPF	Rwandese Patriotic Front. The RPF was both a political and military movement, Tutsi dominated; the RPF was originally a rebel army of Rwandan refugees that had lived in Ugandan refugees camps; Paul Kagame was the leader of the RPF.
RTLMC	*Radio Télévision Libre des Milles Collines*. Independent radio station with strong extremists elements.

SC	U.N. Security Council.
SGR	Service Général Renseignement de l'Armée.
SRSG	Special Representative Secretary-General.
U.N.	United Nations.
UNDP	United Nations Development Program.
UNHCR	United Nations High Commissioner for Refugees.
UNAMIR	United Nations Assistance Mission for Rwanda.
UNICEF	United Nations Childrens Fund.
UNOMUR	United Nations Observer Mission Uganda-Rwanda.
WEU	Western European Union.

LIST OF ACTORS

Kevin Aiston	U.S. Desk officer for Rwanda.
Jean-Paul Akayesu	Former mayor of the Rwandan commune Taba; sentenced to life imprisonment by the ICTR for, among other things, genocide and crimes against humanity.
Hedi Annabi	Head of the Africa Section in the Political Division of DPKO.
Kofi Annan	U.N. Under Secretary-General in charge of peace-keeping operations. Future U.N. Secretary-General.
Colonel Théoneste Bagosora	*Chef de cabinet* of the Minister of Defense, FAR; Hutu extremist, sentenced to life imprisonment for, among other things, genocide and crimes against humanity by the ICTR.
Jean-Bosco Barayagwiza	One of the heads of the extremists party, CDR; one of the founders of the *Radio Télévision Libre des Mille Collines* (RTLMC); he was sentenced to 35 years imprisonment by the ICTR for, among other things, genocide and crimes against humanity.
Maurice Baril	Canadian Military Adviser to the Secretary-General, head of the military division of DPKO.
Brent Beardsley	Canadian Military Assistant to Major General Dallaire.
Jaques Bihozagara	RPF politician; after the genocide, he became Minister for Rehabilitation and Social Reintegration.
Augustin Bizimana	Minister of Defense; member MRND; extremist Hutu.
Pasteur Bizimungu	Senior political adviser of the RPF; president of Rwanda from July 1994 to March 2000.
Jaques Roger Booh Booh	Special Representative of the Secretary-General from November 22, 1993, until May 1994; former Minister of Foreign Affairs of Cameroon.

Boutros Boutros-Ghali	Secretary-General to the United Nations, from January 1992 until December 1996.
Alexis Brouhns	Belgian vice-permanent representative to the United Nations.
Martin Bucyana	President of the extremist party, CDR; murdered on the February 22 near Butare.
Prudence Bushnell	U.S. Deputy Assistant Secretary for African Affairs. Head of the 24-hour Task Force that led the U.S. evacuation.
General Jose Charlier	Chief of staff of the Belgian army.
Jean-Pierre Chrétien	French historian with expertise in the Great Lakes region of Africa.
Warren Christopher	U.S. Secretary of State in 1994.
Captain Frank Claes	Belgian paramilitary commando and Special Forces officer; head of the UNAMIR intelligence section.
Willy Claes	Belgian Minister of Foreign Affairs.
Richard Clarke	Special advisor to President Clinton on the National Security Council.
President William Clinton	U.S. President during the genocide in Rwanda.
Jean-Luc Dehaene	Belgian Prime Minister.
General Roméo Dallaire	Canadian Force Commander of UNAMIR; Chief Military Observer UNOMUR (October 1993–August 1994).
Captain Willem de Kant	Dutch officer who was *aid-de-camp* of General Dallaire.
Leo Delcroix	Belgian Minister of Defense.
Alvaro de Soto	Assistant Secretary-General in the U.N. Department of Political Affairs.
Alain Destexhe	Former Secretary-General of the Belgian NGO Doctors without Borders.
Lieutenant Colonel Jo Dewez	Belgian commanding officer of the second paramilitary commando unit.
K. Terry Dornbush	U.S. Ambassador to the Netherlands.
Mark Doyle	BBC reporter; the only reporter who stayed in Rwanda during the genocide.
Lucie Edwards	Canadian Ambassador.
Michel Forte	The director of the French department of Amnesty International in 1992.
Ibrahim Gambari	Nigerian Ambassador to the United Nations.
Félicien Gatabazi	Head of the Parti Social Démocrate (PSD), the second largest opposition party; killed on February 22, 1994.

Chinmaya Gharekhan	Senior Political Adviser and Special Representative of the Secretary-General on the Security Council.
Juvénal Habyarimana	President of Rwanda; Hutu, founder and head of MRND; came to power in 1973; was killed on April 6, 1994.
Karl Inderfurth	U.S. representative to the United Nations.
Jean Pierre	Informant who warned of a plan by extremists to kill Belgians peace-keepers in order to guarantee a withdrawal and who described and showed arms caches in January 1994; he was a commando and a presidential guard, chief trainer of the Interahamwe.
Abdul Hamid Kabia	Acting Executive Director of UNAMIR; U.N. diplomat for Sierra Leone.
Major General Paul Kagame	Military commander of the Rwandan Patriotic Army, the military wing of the RPF; became President of Rwanda in April 2000.
Robert Kajuga	President of the Interahamwe.
Jean Kambanda	Extremist Hutu within the MDR; Rwandan prime minister during the time of the genocide; convicted and sentenced to a life sentence by the ICTR.
Major Frank Kamenzi	RPF liaison officer to UNAMIR.
Agathe Kanzinga	Wife of President Juvénal Habyarimana.
Joseph Kavaruganda	Judge and president of the Constitutional Court; killed in the morning of April 7.
Gregoire Kayibanda	First President of Rwanda (1962–1973).
Colin Keating	Ambassador to the United Nations from New Zealand; President of the SC in April 1994.
Peter Kooijmans	Minister of Foreign Affairs for the Netherlands; U.N. Rapporteur on Torture.
Willy Kuypers	Belgian Senator.
Anthony Lake	The National Security Adviser.
José Ayala Lasso	Human Rights Commissioner.
General Jean-Claude Lafourcade	French commander of Operation Turquoise.
Lieutenant Colonel André Leroy	Commanding officer of the first Belgian paramilitary commando battalion.
Lieutenant Thierry Lotin	Belgian paramililtary commando commader of the escort guarding Prime Minister Agathe; one of the ten Belgian peace-keepers who were killed on April 7, 1994.

Ruud Lubbers	Dutch Prime Minister.
Luc Marchal	Belgian commander of the sector Kigali; Belgian contingent commander in UNAMIR.
Lieutenant Colonel Tony Marley	Political Military Adviser in the U.S. State Department and the U.S. military liaison to the Arusha process.
Jean-Jaques Maurin	French Colonel, who led the French evacuation.
Christophe Mfizi	Former senior official of the MRND.
François Miterrand	President of France from 1981 to 1995.
Sese Seko Mobutu	President of Zaire/Congo from 1965 to 1997.
George Moose	U.S. Assistant Secretary of State for African Affairs.
Justin Mugenzi	President of the Parti Liberal (PL).
Donat Murego	MDR secretary.
Yoweri Museveni	President of Uganda; head of the New Resistance party.
Mwami Musinga	King of Rwanda until 1931.
Ali Hassan Mwinyi	President of Tanzania; facilitator of the Arusha negotiations.
Ferdinand Nahimana	One of the founders of the *Radio Télévision Libre des Mille Collines* (RTLMC).
Melchior Ndadaye	Burundian President; he was killed on October 21, 1993.
Landoald Ndasingwa	Tustis head of the PL, known as Londo; Minister of Labor and Social Affairs; owner of Hotel Chez Lando; husband of the Canadian Helene Pinsky; he and his family were killed in the morning of April 7.
Bacré Waly Ndiaye	Special Rapporteur of the U.N. Commission on Human Rights on extrajudicial, summary or arbitrary executions; visited Rwanda in 1993 and spoke of a possible genocide.
Augustin Ndindiliyimana	Chief of staff of the *gendarmerie*, national police commander, member of the MRND, supporter of Habyarimana; indicted by the ICTR for, among other things, genocide and crimes against humanity; in January 2006 the trial was still pending.
Marc Nees	Belgian military intelligence officer.
Félicien Ngango	Member of the PSD, he was killed in the morning of April 7.

Hassan Ngeze	Editor-in-chief of the newspaper *Kangura*; sentenced by the ICTR for, among other things, genocide, direct and public incitement to commit genocide, crimes against humanity; in January 2006 the case was on appeal.
Mathieu Ngirumpatse	President of the MRND party; hutu extremist, indicted by the ICTR for, among other things, genocide and crimes against humanity; in January 2006 the trial was still pending.
Boniface Ngulinzira	Minister of Foreign Affairs during the Arusha negotiations, he and his family were attacked and fled their homes in the morning of April 7; he was killed during the genocide.
Jean Damascene Nizimana	Hutu hardliner who represented Rwanda in the Security Council during the genocide.
Paul Noterdaeme	Belgian representative to the United Nations.
Colonel Déogratias Nsabimana	Army Commander (FAR/RGF), who was killed in the plane crash on April 6.
Dismas Nsengiyaremye	Former Prime Minister of Rwanda, from April 1992 to July 1993, MDR party, Nsengiyaremye-led government started negotiations with the RPF on the peace treaty.
Joseph Nzirorera	Secretary-General of the MRND.
Jan Pronk	Minister for Development Cooperation in the Netherlands. Special Representative of the Secretary-General in Sudan in 2004–2006.
David Rawson	American Ambassador in Rwanda.
Filip Reyntjens	Belgian Professor of Law and Politics at the University of Antwerp, Belgium.
Iqbal Riza	Assistant Secretary-General, DPKO; diplomat from Pakistan.
Frans Roelants	Secretary-General of the Belgian Ministry of Foreign Affairs
Colonel Jean-Pierre Roman	Belgian Colonel who arrived with the Belgian evacuation forces.
Mutara Rudahigwa	Successor of King Musinga.
Enoch Ruhigira	Chef de cabinet of the President; former Prime Minister of Rwanda.
Ephrem Rwabalinda	FAR liaison to UNAMIR; killed in early July.
Major-General Fred Rwigyema	Most famous Rwandan refugee in the NRA and leader of the RPF during the 1990 invasion.

Dr. Salim Ahmed Salim	Secretary-General of the OAU.
Professor William Schabas	Director of the Irish Centre for Human Rights at the National University of Ireland, Galway; visited Rwanda in 1993; he was convinced that what was happening in Rwanda was genocide.
John Shattuck	U.S. Assistant Secretary of State for Democracy, Human Rights and Labor.
Johan Swinnen	Belgian Ambassador in Kigali from 1990 to 1994.
Strobe Talbott	U.S. Deputy Secretary of State.
Peter Tarnoff	U.S. Under-Secretary for Political Affairs.
Relus Ter Beek	Dutch Minister of Defense.
Master Corporal Philippe Troute	Dallaire's personal driver; Belgian paramilitary commando.
Faustin Twagiramungu	Prime Minister designate for the interim government; member of the MDR; became Prime Minister after the genocide.
Agathe Uwilingiyamana	Prime Minister for the interim government of the MDR; known as Madame Agathe; killed on April 7, 1994.
Major Robbert Van Putten	Dutch assistant of General Roméo Dallaire in Rwanda.
Herman Van Rompuy	Belgian Vice Prime Minister
Josephine Verspaget	Dutch member of Parliament from the Labor Party
Lieutenant Colonel Charles Vuckovic	Based at the U.S. embassy in Cameroon but also had responsibilities in Rwanda and Burundi; he arrived in Rwanda one day before the plane crash and had an evacuation plan.
Lode Willems	Cabinet chief of the Belgian Minister of Foreign Affairs.
James Woods	U.S. Deputy Assistant Secretary for African Affairs.

GLOSSARY

Akazu	Kinyarwanda for "little house;" In pre-colonial times Akazu was the name for the inner circle of the Royal Court. Later it was the name given to the inner core of Habyarimana's regime.
Inkontanyi	Kinyarwanda for "those who fight courageously." The name was given by the RPF to its soldiers; later it was generally used to indicate the RPF.
Interahamwe	Kinyarwanda for "those who attack together." Used to describe the militant youth groups of the MRND party; the Interahamwe are seen as the main perpetrators in the genocide.
Inyenzi	Kinyarwanda for "cockroach." Used by Hutu extremists to describe Tutsi.
Kangura	Kinyarwanda for "wake others up," Name of Rwandan hate newspaper.
Kinyarwanda	Native language in Rwanda, spoken by Hutu, Tutsi and Twa.

CHAPTER 1

EARLY WARNINGS AND EARLY ACTION BY BYSTANDERS

1.1 INTRODUCTION

1.1.1 Human Rights Standards

Since the Shoa (Holocaust), the *cri de coeur* of "NEVER AGAIN" is heard all over the world and is said to be for many political leaders a guideline in their political behavior. The Genocide Convention was adopted in 1948 and many human rights standards and instruments have been adopted and are supervised in many ways on a treaty basis; these human rights treaties are called as a whole the "International Bill of Rights." At the U.N. website of the High Commissioner for Human Rights some 100 of these instruments are to be found.[1] Many other human rights instruments are not treaty based but have been developed within the U.N. Commission on Human Rights in Geneva. For instance, the confidentially discussed violations in particular countries, situations where a consistent pattern of gross human rights violations is occurring and the many rapporteurs and working groups that report to the Human Rights Council, as the Commission on Human Rights was renamed in 2006.[2] Themes and particular countries may be addressed by all of these bodies. Apart from the United Nations, other systems for the protection of human rights have also developed on a worldwide specialized scale (UNESCO and ILO) and on a regional scale in Europe (EU, OSCE, CoE), America (OAS) and Africa (OAU). Nevertheless, the genocides were not halted after 1948 and took place during the Cold War in Asia (Cambodia, 1975–1979) and also after the Cold War in Africa (Rwanda, 1994, Darfur, since 2003) and Europe (Srebrenica, 1995).

---

1 See http://www.ohchr.org/english/law/index.htm.

2 On the evolution and the development of international systems for human rights protection, see Hilde Reiding, The Netherlands and the development of international human rights instruments (2007).

1.1.2 After the Cold War

This research will address the genocides that occurred after the Cold War from a perspective that considers whether these genocides could have been prevented or halted by the third parties. Only situations that followed the Cold War are selected, because during the Cold War any intervention in any other country entailed the risk of escalating into a huge scale catastrophic nuclear war between the superpowers, the United States and the Soviet Union, in that bipolar world system. This means that intervention by military means was almost precluded within the sphere of influence of the other, although there were situations of military intervention within their own "power bloc" (for example in the East—Hungary, 1956, Czechoslovakia, 1968—and in the West—Grenada, 1983, Panama, 1989). Besides, in some cases military interventions took place by making use of other countries in order to avoid a direct superpower confrontation. These so-called proxy wars were located in, for instance, Angola, the Arab-Israeli conflict and Vietnam. In some situations, even during the Cold War, some military interventions took place by one state to stop atrocities in the neighboring state (India in East Pakistan (Bangladesh, 1974), Vietnam in Cambodia, 1979, Tanzania in Uganda, 1979) that were accepted afterwards and did not lead to an increased risk of great power warfare, because these interventions did not harm the antagonistic interests of the nuclear superpowers in those days. These military interventions were not authorized by the Security Council (SC) of the United Nations. They are often called humanitarian interventions and are in fact forceful military interventions for humanitarian purposes.

After the Cold War, an optimistic view dominated situations in which any aggression could be deterred or stopped because the original U.N. collective security system could be invoked. The ideas revived of cooperation in maintaining international peace and security and with respect for human rights from 1945 in San Francisco. The United Nations was established just before the more antagonistic interests of the Soviet Union and the United States, the main allied powers in World War II, became clear and also just before the atomic bomb was dropped on Hiroshima and Nagasaki. In 1945 the original aim and spirit of the United Nations was made clear in the conference during which the Charter of the United Nations was adopted, and it is that spirit in another timeframe that received an important revival in 1990. For example, the day the Iraqi troops crossed the border of Kuwait, the Security Council decided in Resolution 660 the very same day on August 2, 1990, to qualify the situation as a breach of the peace.[3] Since then, the SC could impose its will on Iraq by taking mandatory decisions under Chapter VII of the U.N. Charter. Consequently the United Nations demanded the Iraqi withdrawal and used all means at its disposal—diplomatic and economic sanctions and military invasion—to successfully obtain

3 U.N. Doc. S/RES/660 (1990).

their objectives in this situation. This was made possible because in this situation no state exercised its veto power to block a binding decision for the military intervention. This intervention, known as operation Desert Storm, took place under the authorization of the U.N. Security Council and was led under American and British command with participation of many states, some of which were Arab.[4] The importance of the role for third parties became apparent.

1.1.3 Perpetrator—Victim—Bystander Approach

In the literature on the Shoa we observe that at different periods the roles of the victim, perpetrator or the bystander, i.e., the third party, have been addressed. The focus on the victim in memories and in the description of their fate was done by historians. Witnesses and survivors made clear under what conditions this so-called "final solution" could have taken place. The public acknowledgment of what has happened to the victims is an important aspect for society as a whole but also particularly for the victims, because it allows them to become survivors instead of continuing to be victims, which from at least a psychological point of view is an important difference. Truth telling was also one of the functions and effects of the trials of the Nazi-perpetrators with a strong impact on society. In particular, the Eichmann trial in 1961 in Jerusalem impressed many because the focus was now on how the Shoa was organized. It was not only the role of the individual perpetrator at the micro-level that was now exposed but also the role of the bureaucratic or so-called armchair perpetrator, representing the involvement of the state towards the destruction of the Jews as being a normal state activity. This was difficult to grasp.

The role of the perpetrator at many different levels is now studied, and this has led to important insights into how these atrocities could have taken place in a modern society and how the perpetrators could go on unhampered by others in the accomplishment of their genocidal crimes. The "other" is the role of the third party, the onlooker, the passenger, the bystanders at the three different levels of micro (individual), meso (society, groups in a state) and macro level (states and the international political system). In our view, the role of the bystander, particularly at the macro level, is becoming crucial, because the possibility to prevent or stop gross human rights violations is increasingly dependent on the behavior of the third party rather than the perpetrator and the victim. In short, in most circumstances in which a state is using terror to retain power, the perpetrator will continue his atrocious activities, and the victims are no longer able to prevent or stop these at that moment. The chances for peaceful change are no longer available when terror and suppression reigns.

---

4 U.N. Doc. S/RES/678 (1990).

1.1.4 Third-Party Intervention

In order to intervene effectively before or during such a period, of gross human rights violations, a thorough knowledge of the society in the target country is needed for the intervening state or the international organization. This means that we do not underestimate the worth of studies that are conducted to get an insight at different levels into the perpetrator and victim. Bob de Graaff rightly wrote that in order to understand the victim, knowledge of the perpetrator—his intentions and behavior—is needed. Getting some insight into the perpetrator makes prevention possible.[5]

Perpetrators and victims are the aims and the targets of any intervention, and it is their position that should determine whether any intervention, and with which means, is needed at a certain phase. The director of Yad Vashem, Avner Shalev, at the opening of the new Holocaust museum in Jerusalem focused on the victims and survivors.[6] Ronny Naftaniel underlined in his comment the role of the bystander "the neighbor stood silent idly by and the biggest lesson to draw from history is that hardly anybody did act when the Jews, Sinti and Roma were killed and it is precisely this passivity and inertia which threaten our societies." In this way Naftaniel shifts the attention from the victim to the bystander, whereas he underlines that the signals for the bystander are emanating from the victims.[7]

Chapter 18 addresses the responsibility to protect in general and pays attention to the different stages—before, during, after—in activities of prevention, action and rebuilding by third parties. It is the situation on the ground that should be seen as the determining factor in deciding whether or not to intervene. However, how grave such a situation may be and how much it may be realized that the situation is very serious, there is no indication that this will

---

5 Bob de Graaff (inaugural speech, April 3, 2006, Universiteit Utrecht), Op de klippen door de vaargeul? De omgang van de historicus met (genocidaal) slachtofferschap, (Steering clear of dangerous rocks: History-writing and genocidal victimhood.), p. 43 (2006).

6 Avner Shalev's Speech at the Inauguration Ceremony of Yad Vashem's new Holocaust Museum, March 15, 2005:

> The museum that we are dedicating today is a monument to those who were murdered—attempting to preserve their names, faces and identities for future generations. This museum is the authentic, personal, cry of the generation of those who can tell the story. It is their Jewish story and ours, and it is the story of the rupture and the universal eclipse of an entire world in which the perpetrator committed murder, the neighbor silently stood idly by and only the very few chose to save their fellow human beings.

7 Ronny Naftaniel, Lessen uit het verleden (Lessons from the past), Israel Nieuwsbrief, March 17, 2005.

lead to action because of the qualification of the situation. The qualification of the situation can and is measured and monitored with more or less sophisticated indicators, and this will be addressed in Section 3 of this chapter as an early warning. In other words, early warning focuses on describing the situation of the perpetrators and victims in some part of the world and bringing this to the attention of others outside that country or region. This description would include advice on how to react, i.e., policy options are included in early warnings. Whatever the "others" will do with this information was, in many cases, very disappointing in the past. They often do not react, because a reaction is not seen to be in their state or institutional interest, or because they are not compelled to react by an internal domestic pressure or an external foreign pressure, meaning that they can easily afford not to react without losing votes or international credibility or reputation. This book addresses the big problem that early warning does not automatically lead to early or any action. Afterwards, apologies are made and the "never again" *cri de coeur* is reiterated, but at the moment when decisions should be made, previous "never agains" are forgotten. The aim of this book is to address this huge problem and to fill the gap by scrutinizing the decision-making process at the international (macro) level in the bystander states and the bystander international organizations at the moment in which the warnings become known. The answer by both scholars and political leaders until now has been that the political will to act and react on this alarming information is lacking. That is correct, but, in our view, the concept of political will is too general and abstract and should be analyzed further in order to gain a real insight into why the political will was absent, at what moment, under which circumstances and for whom in the bureaucracies in an international organization or a state.

1.2 THE ROLE OF THE BYSTANDER

In all gross human rights violations and in all violent conflicts, the following three different roles can be identified: (1) perpetrator (in military conflicts often called the aggressor); (2) victim; and (3) bystander. It is difficult to clearly discern the role of the bystander from the other two roles. Moreover, any role may change over time. In this respect, it is important to distinguish the phase of the atrocities: before, during or afterwards. Often the so-called neutral and innocent bystanders during the conflict were afterwards considered to have been very helpful in continuing and performing the atrocities. The crucial question then becomes: with hindsight, is there any role of the bystander, or does this role disappear afterwards? Is the threefold distinction (perpetrator, victim, bystander) no longer tenable, and does it instead become a twofold distinction of: (1) perpetrators and collaborators with the perpetrator; and (2) victims and rescuers of the victims?

This question can be answered afterwards but not beforehand. Therefore, we have developed a working definition for the bystander as: the third party that will not act or that will not attempt to act in solidarity with the victims of gross human rights violations.[8] This means that this bystander will be evaluated afterwards as a collaborator. However there is an alternative, and that is to act or to attempt to act in solidarity with the victims of the gross human rights violations. In this case, they will be considered afterwards as the rescuers.

By not acting and pretending not to know what is happening, the bystander will, in the period since the Cold War, be categorized as a collaborator. Regarding the relevance of knowledge:

> The easiest way to become or to pretend to be a bystander has always been the lack of knowledge of what is going on or has passed. This ignorance, which is coupled with indifference towards the fate of the victims, is an important explanation for the behavior of various inactive third parties. This ignorance, which can be seen as a necessary condition to become a bystander, is deliberately promoted by the perpetrators in order to minimize the risk of getting some solidarity of third parties with the victims. The perpetrator aims to prevent that the bystander shall act on behalf of the victims.[9]

In this definition, there is no room for another category, such as the indifferent bystander and the ignorant outsider. Relevant in this regard is that the perpetrators deliberately try to keep the third party ignorant. Ignorance is thus in the interest of the perpetrators at all stages during the occurrence of gross human rights violations, because they enable the perpetrators to go on.[10] This definition is based, among others, on the work of Elie Wiesel[11] and Ervin Staub. Staub pointed to the relevant role of the bystander for any continuation or discontinuation of the ongoing atrocities. For the continuation he said: "The bystander plays a central part in the establishment and maintenance of human rights abuses. By turning away or remaining passive in the face of threats to human life, the conditions for genocide are maximized."[12] For the discontinu-

---

8 *The Role of the Bystanders in Human Rights Violations*, in, Rendering Justice to the Vulnerable. Liber Amicorum in Honour of Theo van Boven, pp. 131–143 (Fons Coomans, Fred Grünfeld, Ingrid Westendorp and Jan Willems (eds.), 2000).

9 *Id.*, p. 141.

10 *Id.*, p. 132.

11 See, in particular, Elie Wiesel, Le ville de la chance, 1962 (translated in English as: The town beyond the wall, 1964; translated in Dutch as: De stad van het geluk, 1987) and Elie Wiesel, Un Juif, aujourd-hui, 1977 (translated in English as: A Jew today, 1979; translated in Dutch as: Een Jood, vandaag, 1978).

12 Quoted in A. Austin, *Early Warning and the Field: A Cargo Cult Science?* in, Berghof Handbook for Conflict Transformation, p. 13 (2003).

ation he stated: "Bystanders can exert powerful influence . . . Even the behavior of governments can be strongly affected by bystanders—individuals, groups or other governments. Repeatedly when they faced substantial opposition, the Nazis backed away. . . . A lack of protest can confirm the perpetrators' faith in what they are doing."[13] Moreover, in almost all situations of gross human rights violations, outsiders were not totally unaware of what was happening, and clear signals were put forward to alarm the third party.[14] The information is particularly available since the end of the Cold War. In this book the test is therefore put even higher, because in this study we will not assume that clear signals of early warnings were available, but we will scrutinize each message that was made and follow the message from the sender to the receiver to investigate how the receiver of this message reacted to the message. The decisionmaking or non-decisionmaking resulting from the early warning is the focus of this research.

1.3 EARLY WARNING

Gross human rights violations never occur all of a sudden. It is not only the so-called trigger event that is seen as the immediate cause of the gross human rights violations. The trigger event may indeed lead to a disaster on an enormous scale, although the trigger event does not have that magnitude itself. For instance the assassination in the city of Sarajevo on June 28, 1914, and the shooting down of the airplane in Rwanda on April 6, 1994, were the direct triggers of World War I and the Genocide in Rwanda, but the underlying causes were already manifest a long time before. These underlying causes are to be viewed in terms of structural deep-rooted causes that can only be taken away in the long term.[15] Structural causes can be found in the relationships between gross human rights violations and poor economic development or in the linkage between gross human rights violations and non-democratic political systems. That means that more prosperity through economic advancement or a successful democratization may promote a better human rights situation. The problem however is that most gross human rights violations occur in the poorest countries and regions of the world in states that can be classified as dictatorships. To some extent, this is circular reasoning, because democracy is based

---

13 E. Staub, The roots of evil—the origins of genocide and the other group violence, p.78 (1989).

14 Samantha Power, A Problem from Hell; America and the Age of Genocide (2002).

15 These are often called the Structural Causes or Root Causes. See FEWER, Forum on Early Warning and Early Response: Conflict Analysis and Response Definition, Abridged Methodology, April 2001; Susan Ampleford, Methodology Review, Discussion Paper Country Indicators for Foreign Policy, July 2000; WANEP Preventive Peacebuilding in West Africa, October 2000, *available at* http://www.fewer.org.

on respect for fundamental human rights. The removal of these root causes is not only a very long-term process, but it also remains to be seen whether the intended consequences will indeed take place. What is more relevant, however, is that these long-term processes will not prevent the impending gross human rights violations or stop the on-going gross human rights violations.

In this research, we are primarily interested not in the immediate cause, the trigger, and not in the long-term root causes, but in the short-term accelerators or proximity causes. When these proximity causes are taken seriously by acting upon them, the conflict will not erupt. The former High Commissioner on National Minorities of the OSCE, Max van der Stoel stated: "My job is to issue early warnings to avoid action, and to take action to avoid early warnings."[16]

1.3.1 Categorizing Early Warnings on Human Rights Violations

In the period before the gross human rights violations take place, a longer development of increasing human rights violations could be observed. Limitations on freedom of speech or freedom of the press as a way of manipulating information can be a prelude to the arrest of political prisoners who, in a more severe situation, are to be tortured or extra-judicially killed. It is well-known that "where authority fails, repression begins"; this was stated by Hannah Ahrendt.[17] This has been elaborated on by Marjo Hoefnagels in her research on political violence and peace research, among others.[18] In more recent research, a decision-making model has been developed by many political scientists on the relationship between repression and conflicts. Internal and external conflicts are taken into account in order to answer the question of under what circumstances which level of repression is employed.[19]

The intensity (how often), the scope (from political opponents, via racial or religious groups to the whole population), severity (from unequal distribution of houses to extra-judicial killing) may vary, and it is this variation of the combined factors that has led to the well-known five points scale (Political Terror index from Michael Stohl at Purdue University and ranked in PIOOM

---

16 Quentin Peel, *OSCE Minorities chief aims for early action*, Financial Times (May 19, 2000), in, W.A. Kemp (ed.), Quiet Diplomacy in Action: The HCNM, p. 34 (2000).

17 Hannah Ahrendt, *What is authority*, in, Between past and future: eight exercises in political thought, (1954, reissued 1993).

18 Marjo Hoefnagels, Repression and repressive violence (1977).

19 S.C. Poe, *The decision to repress: An integrative theoretical approach to the research on human rights and repression*, in, S.C. Carey and S.C. Poe, Understanding Human Rights, pp. 16–38. See also S.C. Carey, *Domestic treat and repression: An analysis of state response to different forms of dissent*, in. S.C. Carey and S.C. Poe, Understanding Human Rights, pp. 202–220 (2004).

Human Rights and Conflict Map).[20] From all the gross human rights violations a ranking on this so-called political terror scale of the five stages (further mentioned as PIOOM level) is possible, which are not only limited to life integrity violations:

Scale Level 1: Countries live under a secure rule of law, people are not imprisoned for their views and torture is rare or exceptional. Political murders are extremely rare.

Scale Level 2: There is a limited amount of imprisonment for non-violent political activity. However, few persons are affected, torture and beatings are exceptional. Political murder is rare.

Scale Level 3: There is extensive political imprisonment, or a recent history of such imprisonment. Executions or political murders and brutality may be common. Unlimited detention, with or without trial, for political views is accepted.

Scale Level 4: The practices of Level 3 are expanded to larger numbers. Murders, disappearances and torture are a common part of life. In spite of its generality, on this level violence affects primarily those who interest themselves in politics or ideas.

Scale Level 5: The violence of Level 4 has been extended to the whole population. The leaders of these societies place no limits on the means or thoroughness with which they pursue personal or ideological goals.

When we carefully analyze the different levels, in particular, until Scale Level 4, we get an insight into the process of politicide. Politicide and genocide are defined by Harff and Gurr as:

> The promotion, execution, and/or implied consent of sustained policies by governing elites or their agents—or in case of civil war, either of the contending authorities—that result in the deaths of a substantial portion of a communal, political, or politicized communal group. In genocides, the victimized groups are defined primarily in terms of their communal characteristics whereas in politicides groups are defined primarily in terms of their political opposition to the regime and dominant groups.[21]

The killing or destruction of the group—see Genocide Convention in Section 2.1—is essential, and so we will not broaden the term as was done for instance by Baruch Kimmerling, who defines politicide as "a process that covers a wide range of social, political and military activities whose goal is to destroy the polit-

---

20 See http://www.goalsforamericans.org/publications/pioom/atf_world_conf_map.pdf.

21 Barabara Harff and Ted Robert Gurr, *Systematic Early Warning of Humanitarian Emergencies*, in, Journal of Peace Research 35(5), p. 560 (1998).

ical and national existence of a whole community of people and thus deny it the possibility of self-determination."[22] The situation in Rwanda after the plane crash started as a politicide and only after a week—in which we may notice a lack of any third-party involvement or resistance—developed into a genocide.

Each of these five situations can be clearly defined by the degree of human rights violations. Only a very limited number of civil and political human rights were incorporated into these yardsticks. It is predominantly the personal integrity rights that were included. Some tried to develop a much broader yardstick with many more civil and political rights but also including the economic, social and cultural human rights. Moreover some rights, such as children's rights and the right to education, encompass both categories (civil-political and social-economic) of human rights. The aim was to find very specific indicators to measure these concrete human rights violations. The rate of illiteracy, for instance, is a statistical fact but not a measure for the violation of the right to education as it has so often been treated in research.[23] It is not possible to name specifically the violation, for instance, of children's rights in general, but we can distinguish between child labor, street children, *"les bonnes,"* forced child labor, child soldiers, trade in children for forced labor, child prostitution, child trafficking for prostitution. These concrete violations are published yearly in state reports, the U.N. reporting system, NGO reports and can easily be used in research.

Indicators must be put into the context of early warning for concrete human rights violations. Compliance with the human rights of the International Bill of Human Rights is measured. The empirical data however, as Martin Scheinin has observed, cannot replace a normative assessment, and that is why they should be put into context.[24] These indicators will thus be related to different human rights. The realization of these human rights, both civil and political, on the one hand, and economic, social and cultural human rights, on the other

---

22 Baruch Kimmerling, Politicide; Ariel Sharon's war against the Palestinians, pp. 3–4 (2003). In his view the policy of Sharon will lead to a double politicide of both the Palestinian entity—dissolution of the Palestinian people's existence as an entity—and the Jewish entity because of undermining the moral foundations of the Jewish state.

23 See R.L. Callaway and J. Harrelson-Stephens, *The path from trade to human rights: the democracy and development detour*, in, S.C. Carey and S.C. Poe, Understanding Human Rights, pp. 87–109 (2004) and W.T. Milner and others, *Providing Subsistence Rights: Do States Make A Difference?*, in, S.C. Carey and S.C. Poe, Understanding Human Rights, pp. 110–126 (2004). See also UNDP annual reports, *available at* http://www.undp.org. Fred Grünfeld, Bookreview: Sabine C. Carey and Steven C. Poe (ed.), Understanding Human Rights Violations, New Systematic Studies, Ashgate, 2004, in, Netherlands Quarterly of Human Rights 23 no. 3, pp. 530–534, in particular p. 532 (September 2005).

24 Martin Scheinin, Improving the EU's human rights country assessment through the use of indicators, Ludwig Boltzmann Institute of Human Rights, Vienna speech at the plenary session of the COST Workshop on the Occasion of the 7th annual conference of the Association of Human Rights Institutes (AHRI) on Indicators and Monitoring

hand, is our yardstick. Making use of this yardstick as an instrument for early warning would allow interfering at an early stage. In scheme "Hurivic" in the appendix, we specify some civil and political rights and some economic, social and cultural rights. These specifications are our indicators to measure these violations at scale-point 2 of the Purdue/PIOOM scale. That is the moment for intervention, because, without any action, these violations may increase in time towards scale-points 3, 4 and 5.

1.3.2 Linking Gross Human Rights Violations to Violent Conflicts

In the research, the linkage between gross human rights violations and violent conflict has been demonstrated. Any violent political conflict leads to gross human rights violations. Not only is the right to life endangered, but as a result of warfare all human rights, both civil and political rights as well as economic, social and cultural rights, are violated.

A relationship has been made between the five-point political terror scale and the use of increasing violence in conflicts. A three-point scale is MC1, MC2 and MC3 for armed conflicts that cause (1) less than 100 deaths per year, (2) between 100 and 1,000 deaths per year, (3) more than 1,000 deaths per year. As a concrete illustration, we will refer to the situation in Georgia in the period 1992–2002 during which all three levels of violence were measured, which made it possible to relate to human rights violations that indeed increased from scale-points 2 to 5.[25]

Military Conflict	**Political terror scale PIOOM Scale**	**Civil and political rights—Freedom House scale**
MC 1 in 1996–2002	2-3	3-4
MC2 in 1992, 1994 and 1995	2-3-4	4-5
MC3 in 1993	4-5	5-5

Systems Preventive Tools for ensuring Peace and Security and Respect for Human Rights in External Policy-Making of the EU, September 8, 2006).

25 Fred Grünfeld, Vroegtijdig optreden van omstanders ter voorkoming van oorlogen en schendingen van de rechten van de mens, oratie, (Early action of bystanders to prevent wars and gross human rights violations, inaugural lecture) December 10, 2003, Universiteit Utrecht, p. 26. In the CD-Rom on Human Rights Violations in the Nineties from 1989 until 2002 in association with Jan de Vries. Data on Political Terror, Violent Conflict, Violations on 11 states in 13 years are investigated of Civil and Political Rights, Rights of the Child, Safe Working Conditions, Right to Housing and Right to Food. The states are: 1. Kenya; 2. Algeria; 3. Tunesia; 4. Mali; 5. Georgia; 6. Croatia;

The resulting warnings were assumed to be the signals for a decision for early action. In such a way, all early warnings are directed towards the third party, the bystander. This role will become increasingly important when the repression reaches PIOOM-level 3. From then on, the oppressed, i.e., the victims, are no longer able to resist or can hardly change the behavior of the perpetrator on their own. The role of the bystander is crucial. Indeed, in situations of genocide PIOOM-level 3 has already passed. It needs no explanation that in genocide we are confronted with a situation at the highest level of both violent conflicts and of gross human rights violations. Early warning in this view does not stop in simply sending the message but also entails advising how to react. It was formulated as follows: "Early warning is the collection and analysis of information about potential and/or actual conflict situations, and the provision of policy options to influential actors at the national, regional and international levels that may promote sustainable peace."[26]

In this regard, we would like to refer in particular to the publications of Harff and Gurr who have made models for early warning in which conflicts in the past and respect for minorities play an important role. They stress the following: "The point is that genocides and politicides do not just happen, they are intentional mass murders: Policy decisions must be made, actions have to be planned, strategies and tactics must be enunciated to the executioners, and international acquiescence secured."[27] The international acquiescence of genocide may cause us to shiver but it is what has happened implicitly. In the Rwandan case we will conclude that at that moment international acquiescence was likely, the *genocidaires* were strengthened in their commitment to the genocide in 1994.

The development of early warning systems is based on the "expectation that better early warning research will help give national and international officials the more reliable assessment they need for effective, proactive policymaking."[28] Harff and Gurr have applied their model with the different accelerators and decelerators on the situation in the period of 1993–1994 in Rwanda; the data for each month are presented in the following diagram.[29]

---

7. El Salvador; 8. Paraguay; 9. Thailand; 10. Sri Lanka; 10a. LTTE; 11. Israel; 11a. Occupied Territories; 11b. Palestinian Authority.

[26] See http://www.fewer.org/resources/methodology_38.html. WANEP, Preventative Peacebuilding in West Africa—West Africa Early Warning and Response Network Training Module, Accra-Ghana: WANEP 2000, p. 11.

[27] See Barbara Harff and Ted Robert Gurr, *Systematic Early Warning of Humanitarian Emergencies,* in, Journal of Peace Research 35(5) pp. 568–569 (1998).

[28] *Id.*, p. 572.

[29] Figure 1 from: Barbara Harff and Ted Robert Gurr, *Systematic Early Warning of Humanitarian Emergencies*, in, Journal of Peace Research 35(5) p. 571 (1998), Sage Publications. Reproduced with permission from Matthew Lambert from Sage Publications Ltd.

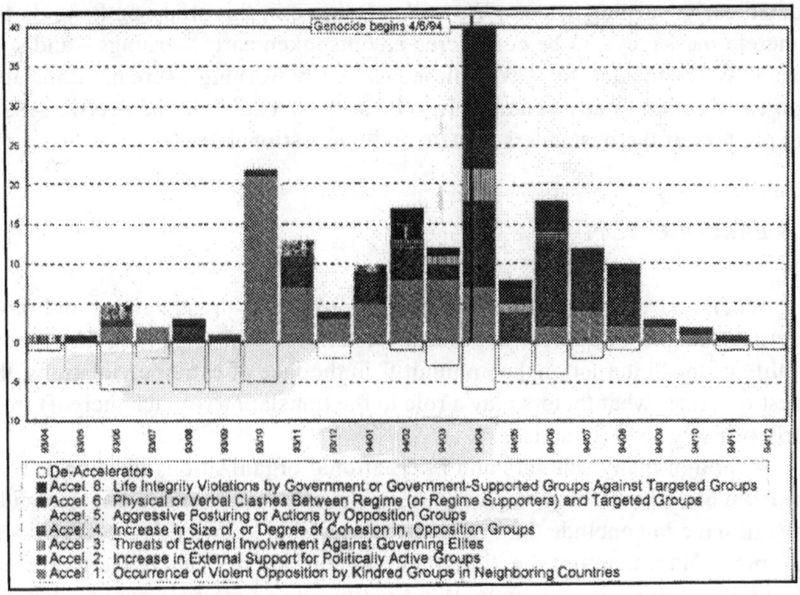

The observation afterwards that the warnings were not heeded and that the political will to act was lacking leads them to question whether and how early warning research might overcome this problem.[30] The more we have studied this subject, the more we are convinced that this is not the right question and that it is pointless to put energy into developing more sophisticated and perhaps better early warning systems. The early warning, as we will demonstrate in this study, is good, reliable, outspoken, clear, policy oriented, etc. What is lacking today is not a reliable early warning system but action based on this warning. Early warning is based on two assumptions. These are:

> 1. That empirical theory and evidence on ethno-political warfare and genocide and politicide are good enough to identify sites of potential future episodes. That is why we can identify high-risk situations and provide analytical tools that make it possible to track the escalation or de-escalation of these situations;
> 2. [I]f researchers can forecast more accurately the sites ad sequences of crisis escalation, policy-makers will be more likely to act early than late.[31]

In reality, this second assumption is not fulfilled. That is why we will not continue in this study with the refinement of indicators in developing a more sophis-

30 *Id.*, p. 571.
31 *Id.*, p. 552.

ticated early warning system. We will scrutinize in this study on Rwanda the concrete messages—to be considered as outspoken early warnings—and subsequently ask the questions why these clear early warnings were not translated into early action or any action. It is to be seen as a study in the decision-making process of the bystanders at state and international level.

1.4 EARLY ACTION

When and why do states and inter-governmental organizations and other international players decide to act and when not to act? Assuming the responsibility of the "international community" in the face of extreme violations, the question arises what factors play a role in the translation (or lack thereof) from early warning to early action.

Although many scholars and international organizations have dealt with the issue of early warning of gross human rights violations including genocide, we still have to conclude that, despite the available knowledge on early warning, more often than not the "international community" has failed to prevent or put a halt to such violations. What is the role of international bystanders (states, international organizations and non-governmental organizations) in the face of gross human rights violations? Generally speaking, it is not early warning that is lacking, but early action. "The challenge, therefore, lies in organizing and interpreting that information for action in an accelerated decision-making process where only small windows of opportunity exist for the implementation of preparedness and preventive measures."[32] Recently the high level panel on Threats, Challenges and Change appointed by the U.N. Secretary-General once more emphasized the importance of institutional and organizational changes to be able to take early action.[33] We will deal with this report in Chapter 18.

A preliminary survey shows that the available literature on early action and international response to ongoing or impending gross human rights violations is rather limited. The normative assumption that the world community should intervene to put a stop to genocide and other gross human rights violations is mainly followed by a discussion of the legal status of humanitarian intervention with or without a Security Council mandate. Legal literature is available on international responsibility and the modern interpretation of non-interference in internal affairs, national sovereignty and non-intervention in the context of human rights violations.

---

32 J.N. Clarke, *Early warning analysis for humanitarian preparedness and conflict prevention*, in, Journal of Humanitarian Assistance, January 24, 2004.

33 Report of the Secretary-General's high-level panel on threats, challenges and change, A more secure world: our shared responsibility, December 2, 2004, U.N. Doc. A/59/565.

The literature often deals with what would be the most effective type of early action, once the decision is made that such action is to take place. It examines past actions for effectiveness. Obviously this question is linked to that of what blocks or triggers early action, but it still examines urgent situations from a different angle.[34]

Nevertheless, the realization that early action might actually prevent gross human rights violations mainly takes the form of discussing methods for early warning and adding that early action should follow.[35] It stops short of examining factors explaining (lack of) early action. Thus, the questions *what* should be done to prevent conflict (including gross human rights violations) and *when* would be the right moment to intervene, from the perspective of the effectiveness of the intervention, are dealt with more often than the questions when and how international actors come to decide to intervene. With regard to specific situations, such as the genocides in Rwanda and Bosnia, reports have indeed been made about the roles of third states and international organizations. The approaches in the literature seem to navigate between "it should work" and "it is not going to work." Not many analyses of the roles of the various players in the decision-making processes of governments and IGOs are available as yet, explaining the when, where and how of (early) intervention or the lack thereof, including the responses of individual players to early warnings.

In short, the main question is: why did states and international organizations not intervene to stop the escalation?

This is exactly the question we will address in this study. Realizing that early warning—in any form, whether it is simple or very sophisticated—is not enough, because it will not automatically generate the spillover effect from early warning to (early) action. That is why we have focused our research on this point: The bridge or gap between early warning and early action. This is also why we analyze the decisionmaking precisely before the genocide in Rwanda took place in order to analyze why the genocide was not prevented and how the decision-making was conducted during the genocide in order to analyze the passivity that did not lead to action to stop the genocide.

---

34 See also Ulf Engel and Andreas Mehler, Closing the gap between early warning and early action: applying political science to violent conflicts in Africa, p. 23 (2000), on three case studies to underline the domestic situation.

35 L. Feinstein and A-M Slaughter, A duty to prevent, Foreign Affairs January/February 2004.

CHAPTER 2

THE TRIBUNAL'S INTERPRETATION AND IMPLEMENTATION OF THE GENOCIDE CONVENTION

The first person in history to plead guilty to acts of genocide before an international tribunal was Jean Kambanda, the Rwandan Prime Minister at the time of the genocide.[1] He admitted before the International Criminal Tribunal for Rwanda (ICTR) to having contributed to "a widespread and systematic attack against the civilian population of Tutsi, with the purpose to exterminate them."[2] Following his guilty plea, he was sentenced to life imprisonment for "genocide, conspiracy to commit genocide, direct and public incitement to commit genocide, complicity in genocide and crimes against humanity."[3]

Responding to the killing of 800,000 Tutsi, the Security Council, acting under Chapter VII of the U.N. Charter, created the International Criminal Tribunal for Rwanda. The Tribunal was established to prosecute persons responsible for the genocide and other serious violations of international humanitarian law committed in Rwanda between January 1 and December 31, 1994. Article 2 of the ICTR Statute deals with "genocide." This article is identical to Articles 2 and 3 of the 1948 Genocide Convention.[4] The ICTR has been able to deliberate in an extensive way on the exact meaning of this article.

Two cases that have had an important influence on the interpretation of the

---

1 Prosecutor v. Kambanda, Case No. ICTR-997-23-S, Judgment and Sentence, September 4, 1998 (hereinafter referred to as the Kambanda case); CNN, U.N. tribunal to give first verdict on Rwanda genocide, September 1, 1998, *available at* http://www.CNN.com.

2 In November 1994 the Security Council adopted a resolution to establish an International Tribunal to prosecute those responsible for the Rwandan genocide. Officially called Statute of the International Criminal Tribunal for the Prosecution of Persons Responsible for Genocide and Other Serious Violations of International Humanitarian Law Committed in the Territory of Rwanda and Rwandan Citizens Responsible for Genocide and Other Such Violations Committed in the Territory of Neighboring States, between January 1, 1994 and December 31, 1994. U.N. Security Council Resolution 955, November 8, 1994, U.N. Doc. S/RES/955 (1994).

3 Kambanda case, paragraph 39.

4 The fact that the statute deals with "genocide" in Article 2, while for example the Statute of the International Criminal Tribunal for the former Yugoslavia (ICTY) deals with "genocide" in Article 4, may indicate that the ICTR places more emphasis on the crime of genocide. The difference is also reflected in the charges of the defen-

concept of genocide by the ICTR will be discussed in this chapter.[5]

2.1 THE 1948 CONVENTION DEFINITION OF GENOCIDE

Articles 2 and 3 of the Convention on the Prevention and Punishment of the Crime of Genocide from December 9, 1948, read as follows:[6]

> *Article 2:*
> Genocide means any of the following acts committed with intent to destroy, in whole or in part, a national, ethnical, racial or religious group, as such:
> (a) Killing members of the group;
> (b) Causing serious bodily or mental harm to members of the group;
> (c) Deliberately inflicting on the group conditions of life calculated to bring about its physical destruction in whole or in part;
> (d) Imposing measures intended to prevent births within the group;
> (e) Forcibly transferring children of the group to another group.
>
> *Article 3:*
> The following acts shall be punishable:
> (a) Genocide;
> (b) Conspiracy to commit genocide;
> (c) Direct and public incitement to commit genocide;
> (d) Attempt to commit genocide;

---

dants. Before the ICTR, the defendants were charged systematically with the crime of genocide, while before the ICTY the focus was placed more upon crimes against humanity. Machteld Boot, Genocide, Crimes against Humanity, war crimes, Nullum Sine lege and the subject matter jurisdiction of the International Criminal Court, pp. 243–244 (2002) (hereinafter Boot); Guémaël Mettraux, International Crimes and the ad hoc tribunals, pp. 206–209 (2005) (hereinafter Mettraux).

5 Giving an insight into the interpretation of the concept of genocide by the ICTR, only two cases will be dealt with here: The Prosecutor v. Akayesu, Case No. ICTR-96-4-T (hereinafter the Akayesu case) and The Prosecutor v. Ferdinand Nahimana, Jean-Bosco Barayagwiza and Hassan Ngeze, Case No. ICTR-99-52-T (hereinafter the Nahimana case). The concept of genocide was however dealt with in many more cases before the ICTR. See the Cases of "Kayishema," "Ruzindana," "Rutaganda," "Bagilishema," "Kristic," "Musema," "Gacumbitsi" and "Muhimana," *available at* http://www.ictr.org.

6 Convention on the Prevention and Punishment of the Crime of Genocide, adopted by Resolution 260 (III) A of the United Nations General Assembly on December 9, 1948, entered into force January 12, 1951, *available at* http://www.ohchr.org/english/law/genocide.htm.

(e) Complicity in genocide.

These two articles are at the core of the International Tribunal for Rwanda; together they form Article 2 of the Statute of the ICTR. Article 1 of the Statue states: "The International Tribunal for Rwanda shall have the power to prosecute persons committing genocide as defined in paragraph 2 of this article or of committing any of the other acts enumerated in paragraph 3 of this article."[7] Thus, as early as Article 2 of the Statute, the content of "genocide" is dealt with, demonstrating the importance of the concept for the Tribunal.

The Genocide Convention was not only inspired and drafted by Raphael Lemkin, but he also did his utmost for the adoption by the General Assembly of this Convention. He selected the word genocide, which is derived from the Greek *"geno"* which means race or tribe and from the Latin *"cide"* from *"caedere,"* which means killing.[8]

Another important article of the Convention that refers in particular to the role of third parties in the case of genocide is

> *Article 8:*
> Any Contracting Party may call upon the competent organs of the United Nations to take such action under the Charter of the United Nations as they consider appropriate for the prevention and suppression of acts of genocide or any of the other acts enumerated in Article 3.

Later in this book, we will investigate the way in which other states and the United Nations may or may not have made use of this possibility in the Convention to take action. We will now take a closer look at the precise implementation of the definition of genocide by the Tribunal. We will consider the broad definition taken by the Tribunal by considering the case of a conviction for incitement to genocide based on a speech. We will then turn our specific attention to issues related to early warning, namely the condemnation of the mass media's role during the months preceding the genocide, which amounted to a conviction for genocide.

---

7 For the Statute of the ICTR, see http://www.ictr.org.

8 Samantha Power, "A problem from hell:" America and the age of genocide, p. 42 (2003). See, in particular, her chapters 3 *"The Crime With a Name"* pp. 31–45, 4 *"Lemkin's Law"* pp. 47–60 and 5 *"A Most Lethal Pair of Foes"* pp. 61–85.

2.2 THE RWANDA TRIBUNAL'S DEFINITION OF GENOCIDE

2.2.1 Akayesu's Hate Speech: Direct and Public Incitement to Genocide

In the first and probably most historic judgment by the ICTR, the former mayor of the Rwandan Taba-commune, Jean-Paul Akayesu was convicted of genocide.[9] This was the first conviction for genocide following the signing of the Genocide Convention in 1948. In its judgment, the ICTR gave a detailed description of the different elements of genocide and defined the punishable acts related to genocide as "conspiracy to commit genocide," "direct and public incitement to commit genocide," "attempt to commit genocide" and "complicity in genocide." Here we will discuss Akayesu's conviction for direct and public incitement to genocide, which was a revolutionary decision for the ICTR.[10]

The first aspect that made the decision revolutionary was the fact that the conviction was based on a speech given by Akayesu on April 19, 1994.[11] In this speech, during a gathering in Taba, Akayesu urged the population to eliminate "the sole enemy," the accomplices of the "Inkotanyi." The ICTR ruled that Akayesu's speech was understood by the community as a call to kill the Tutsi population and that Akayesu himself was aware of the impact of his statements.[12] The tribunal ruled that there was a "causal relationship" between Akayesu's speech and the killings of the Tutsi minority.[13]

A second important aspect of Akayesu's conviction for incitement to genocide was the Tribunal's views on the question of whether this crime should be punished even in cases where the incitement had been unsuccessful. The ICTR ruled that genocide is such a serious crime that direct and public incitement to commit such a crime must be punished, even where such incitement fails to produce the result expected by the perpetrator.[14]

---

9 Akayesu case, Judgment and Sentence, September 2, 1998. Judgment of the Appeals Chamber was made on June 1, 2001).

10 Akayesu case, the verdict. See http://www.ictr.org.

11 Akayesu case, paragraphs 709, 710, 672–675.

12 Akayesu case, paragraphs 333–347, 673, 709.

13 There needed to "be proof of a possible causal link," which, according to the Tribunal, was fulfilled through the "causal relationship" between Akayesu's speech and the killings of the Tutsi minority. See Akayesu case, paragraphs 349, 362; W.A. Schabas, Genocide in International law, the crimes of crimes p. 384 (2000) (hereinafter Schabas, 2000); W.A. Schabas, *The International Criminal Tribunal for Rwanda 1994–1999*, in, Annotated leading cases of International Criminal Tribunals pp. 546–549 (André Klip and Göran Sluiter (eds.), 2001).

14 Akayesu case, paragraphs 549–562. Not only did the Tribunal give an exhaustive explanation of the definition of genocide with regard to "direct and public incitement to commit genocide," the Tribunal also gave a broad explanation of the definition

2.2.2 *Hate Propaganda by Radio RTLMC and the Newspaper,* Kangura: *Genocide*

Another case in which the Tribunal gave an extensive legal analysis of the concept of genocide is the case against Ferdinand Nahimana, Jean-Bosco Barayagwiza and Hassan Ngeze; the so-called "Media-case." In this case, the ICTR had to deal with the question of whether the media's free expression had developed into genocide. At the Nuremberg Tribunal, there had been two cases in which the Tribunal had decided upon the role of the media in relation to massive violations of international humanitarian law, but there had been no cases since.[15]

In this case, Ferdinand Nahimana and Jean-Bosco Barayagwiza, the two founders of the extremist radio station *Radio Télévision Libre des Mille Collines* (RTLMC), and Hassan Ngeze, the editor-in-chief of the hate-inciting newspaper *Kangura*, were convicted of genocide for their role in the radio broadcasts and newspaper issues.[16] Before ruling upon the responsibility of the accused

---

of genocide. The Tribunal considered "rape" to be a form of genocide, because rape constitutes "serious bodily or mental harm." The Tribunal noted that because the rapes were committed only against Tutsi women, this resulted in "physical and psychological destruction of Tutsi women, their families and their communities." See Akayesu case, paragraphs 721 and 731–733.

15 The two cases before the Nuremberg Tribunal dealing with media use of hate speech in connection with massive violations of international humanitarian law were the so-called *Streicher* and *Fritsche* cases. Julius Streicher founded and edited *Der Stürmer* [The Attacker], the Nazi anti-Semitic weekly newspaper with a distribution of 500,000 copies in 1937. He was convicted of crimes against humanity at the Nuremberg war crimes trial and executed in October 1946. In the *Streicher* case, the Nuremberg Tribunal did not explicitly note a direct causal link between Streicher's publications and specific acts of murder, but the judgment characterized his work as a poison "injected in to the minds of thousands of Germans which caused them to follow the National Socialists' policy of Jewish persecution and extermination." Fritsche was Head of the Radio Section of the Propaganda Ministry during the Second World War. Fritsche, who was charged with incitement as a crime against humanity, was acquitted by the International Military Tribunal, because he "had not had control over the formulation of propaganda policies." Walter Laqueur (ed.), The Holocaust Encyclopedia, pp. 613, 614 (2001); see also Gregory S. Gordon, *"A War of Media, Words, Newspapers, and Radio Stations"—The ICTR Media Trial Verdict and a New Chapter in the International Law of Hate Speech,* in, Virginia Journal of International Law 45 pp. 139–98 (2004) (hereinafter Gordon).

16 The three were also convicted for direct and public incitement to commit genocide, conspiracy to genocide, extermination and persecution as crimes against humanity. See Nahimana case (Case No. 96-11) paragraphs 946–1088, the Barayagwiza case (Case No. 97-19), and Ngeze case (Case No. 97-27). All got life imprisonment. All three cases, under Case No. 99-52, are now—since December 3, 2003—pending in the Appeals Chamber.

for genocide, the Tribunal had an in-depth look at the RTLMC broadcasts and issues of *Kangura*.

According to the Tribunal, *Kangura's* article "The Appeal to the Conscience of the Hutu" and the therein included "Ten Commandments" published in December 1990, conveyed "contempt and hatred for the Tutsi ethnic group, and for Tutsi women in particular as enemy agents, and called on readers to take all necessary measures to stop the enemy, defined as the Tutsi population."[17] The so-called "Ten Commandments" instructed:

(1) Every Hutu male should know that Tutsi women, wherever they may be, are working in the pay of their Tutsi ethnic group. Consequently, shall be deemed a traitor:
   (a) Any Hutu male who marries a Tutsi woman;
   (b) Any Hutu male who keeps a Tutsi concubine;
   (c) Any Hutu male who makes a Tutsi woman his secretary or protégée.
(2) Every Hutu male must know that our Hutu daughters are more dignified and conscientious in their role of woman, wife and mother. Are they not pretty, good secretaries and more honest!
(3) Hutu women, be vigilant and bring your husbands, brothers and sons back to their senses.
(4) Every Hutu male must know that all Tutsis are dishonest in their business dealings. They are only seeking ethnic supremacy. "RIZABARA UWARIRAYE" (Only he who spent a sleepless night can talk about the night). Shall be consequently considered a traitor, any Hutu male:
   (a) Who enters into a business partnership with Tutsis;
   (b) Who invests his money or State money in a Tutsi company;
   (c) Who lends to, or borrows from, a Tutsi;
   (d) Who grants business favors to Tutsis [granting of import licenses, bank loans, building plots, public tenders. . .].
(5) Strategic positions in the political, administrative, economic, military and security domain should, to a large extent, be entrusted to Hutus.
(6) In the Education sector, (pupils, students, teachers) must be in the majority Hutu.
(7) The Rwandan Armed Forces should be exclusively Hutu. That is the lesson we learned from the October 1990 war. No soldier must marry a Tutsi woman.
(8) Hutus must cease having any pity for the Tutsi.

---

17 According to the Tribunal, this article summoned the Hutu to "wake up," to "cease feeling pity for the Tutsi," to "take all necessary measures to deter the enemy from launching a fresh attack." Furthermore, the article warned that the enemy was "still there, among us" and waiting "to decimate us." The article ended with the so-called "Ten Commandments."

(9) The Hutu male, wherever he may be, should be united in solidarity and be concerned about the fate of their Hutu brothers. The Hutus at home and abroad must constantly seek friends and allies for the Hutu Cause, beginning with their Bantu brothers. They must constantly counteract Tutsi propaganda. The Hutu must be firm and vigilant towards their common Tutsi enemy.

(10) The 1959 social revolution, the 1961 referendum and the Hutu ideology must be taught to Hutus at all levels. Every Hutu must propagate the present ideology widely. Any Hutu who persecutes his brother for having read, disseminated and taught this ideology shall be deemed a traitor.

This cartoon originally appeared in January 1992 (No. 16), in a moderate, "democratic" paper, *Rwanda Rushya*, as ridicule of the extremism of ideologues like Hassan Ngeze, who was the producer of *Kangura*. It depicts Ngeze being psychoanalyzed by the democratic press. Ngeze says, "I am sick Doctor." The Doctor asks, "What is your ailment?" Ngeze replies, "The Tutsis . . . Tutsis . . . Tutsis!"[18]

Furthermore, the Tribunal found that other editorials and articles echoed the contempt and hatred demonstrated in the "Ten Commandments" and were intended "to fan the flames of ethnic hatred, resentment and fear against the Tutsi population and Hutu political opponents who supported the Tutsi ethnic group." The Tribunal judged that the cover of *Kangura* No. 26 of November 1991 (see the illustration below), promoted violence by conveying the message that the "machete should be used to eliminate the Tutsi, once and for all."

---

18 See http://www.onemancult.com/rwanda/rwandaprop2.html.

According to the Tribunal, this was a call "for the destruction of the Tutsi ethnic group as such."[19]

Cover of *Kangura* No. 26, December 1993: This allusion to the revolution for independence in 1959 (i.e., the *muyaga*) appeared on the cover of *Kangura* in December 1993 (No. 26). The heading to the right of "SPECIAL" reads: "Tutsi: Race of God!" The inscription to the right of the machete asks, "What weapons will we use to win over the inyenzi (cockroaches) for good? What if the 1959 revolution was brought back in order to beat the Tutsi inyenzi?" The man photographed is Dominique Mbonyumutwa, a Hutu under-chief (sous-chefs) in the Gitarama prefecture whose death, supposedly caused by an attack of a Tutsi mob, was influential in sparking Hutu mobilization and the movement by force for independence.[20]

According to the ICTR, RTLMC's broadcasts "engaged in ethnic stereotyping in a manner that promoted contempt and hatred against the enemy," which was defined as the Tutsi ethnic group. The broadcasts called for the extermination of the Tutsi. Both before and after April 6, RTLMC broadcasted names of Tutsi individuals, their families and Hutu political opponents who supported the Tutsi ethnic group. In some cases, these persons were subsequently killed. According to the Tribunal, a "specific causal connection" between the RTLMC broadcasts and the killing of these individuals was established.[21]

The cartoon below appeared on the cover of *Zirikana* in March 1993 (No. 6). Rwandan Patriotic Front (RPF) insurgents have captured a family of three Hutus. The soldier in the foreground is cutting the throat of a baby, after slicing off its hands and lower legs. He announces, "This piece of meat is very small.

19 Nahimana case, paragraphs 950, 136–188.

20 See http://www.onemancult.com/rwanda/rwandaprop11.html.

21 Nahimana case, paragraphs 949, 342–619.

You and your wife will eat the arms and legs while we will take the liver and chest, O.K.?" The mother screams in horror. The RPF soldier in the background asks, "Mam, what's your problem? You didn't give yourself to us. Here we share everything, right?" The caption on the bottom left reads, "The RPF democracy in full function: equal shares for all."[22]

One of the important aspects of this case is the ICTR's judgment on the required "causation" with respect to the media. The Tribunal decided that "the nature of media is such that causation of killing and other acts of genocide will necessarily be effected by an immediately proximate cause in addition to the communication itself." However, as the Tribunal stated, "this does not diminish the causation to be attributed to the media," or "the criminal accountability of those responsible for the communication."[23] In other words, the ICTR decided that those in control of the media are responsible for its consequences, and if these consequences comprise genocide, those in control are responsible for genocide. With respect to this case, the Tribunal decided that there was a causal relationship: the killing of Tutsi civilians had resulted, at least in part, from the message of incitement to ethnic killings that was clearly and effectively disseminated through RTLMC and *Kangura* before and after April 6, 1994.[24] The two cases set out above have shown that the International Tribunal for Rwanda has given a very wide interpretation to the concepts of genocide and direct and public incitement to genocide, by which the definition seems to have broadened. In the Appeals Chamber of the ICTR in 2007 the defense argued

---

22 See http://www.onemancult.com/rwanda/rwandaprop12.html.

23 Nahimana case, paragraphs 952, 953.

24 Nahimana case, paragraphs 952–953. For more information, see Gordon.

that the definition of incitement has been expanded beyond the existing international law. Whereas the prosecutor argued that incitement was synonymous with instigation, he stated that there is no actual need for the crime to occur in the case of "incitement to commit genocide."[25]

Another important aspect of this "media-case" is that the three accused were largely held accountable for their role in the media *prior* to the genocide. In order to make a judgment with regard to Hasan Ngeze, the editor in chief of *Kangura*, the Tribunal looked into the content of issues of *Kangura* published *before* the start of the genocide.[26] Furthermore, the verdict of genocide was largely founded on the article "The Appeal to the Conscience of the Hutu" and the therein included "Ten Commandments," which were published in December 1990, and on the cover of *Kangura* No. 29, published in November 1991.[27] In their verdict on Barayagwiza's case, the ICTR explicitly noted that he was held responsible for genocide for his active role *before* the start of the genocide and his failure to intervene after the start of the genocide.[28] Making a judgment in Nahimana's case, the Tribunal admitted that Nahimana was less actively involved in RTLMC after April 6, 1994, the moment when the broadcasts intensified and called explicitly for the extermination of the Tutsi population, but according to the Tribunal, the programming of RTLMC after April 6, was built on the foundations created *before* that date. As the Tribunal stated, after April 6, RTLMC did "what Nahimana wanted it to do."[29] For these reasons, the Tribunal held Nahimana responsible for genocide.

It was in the International Criminal Tribunal for Rwanda that convictions were based on genocide for the first time in history. The hate speeches broadcasted on the radio and printed in newspapers were addressed during the trials, and it was concluded that the people responsible for hate propaganda broadcasted or published *prior* to the genocide, but functioning as an incentive to genocide, must be held responsible for genocide. Such incitements to hate and to kill an ethnic group were clear "early warnings" of the genocide that followed, and, in retrospect, these radio broadcasts and newspaper articles have been considered as such. The judgment makes clear that these "early warnings" can fall under the concept of genocide. Though at the time they were neglected by the bystanders, after the genocide they were taken extremely seriously by the court, as these early warnings were classified as genocide.

---

25 See Press Release, ICTR/INFO-9-2-510.EN, Arusha, January 19, 2007: Appeals Chamber Concludes Hearing in the Media Case, *available at* http://69.94.11.53/default.htm.

26 Nahimana case, paragraphs 122–257, 950. Note: *Kangura's* first issue was published in May 1990 and its last in 1995; during the genocide, no issues were published: *Kangura* No. 59, published in March 1994, was followed by No. 60 in September 1994. Nahimana case, paragraph 122.

27 Nahimana case, paragraphs 950, 977A.

28 Nahimana case, paragraph 973.

29 Nahimana case, paragraph 974.

CHAPTER 3

RWANDAN HISTORY

3.1 GERMAN COLONIAL RULE

Germany did not play a very active role in the negotiations for the Arusha Peace Accords, though it was Germany who had arrived in Rwanda as the first colonial power exactly 100 years before.[1]

During the division of Africa among the European powers in 1884, Rwanda was ascribed to Germany and consequently Count von Gützen went to the African country known as "Ruanda." The Germans were amazed by Rwanda's well-organized and structured monarchy. In pre-colonial times Rwanda was already a highly controlled and hierarchical country. The structure was based on divisions between *Province, District, Hill* and *Neighborhood levels*. For every level, a chief was appointed who ruled that sector.[2] The Rwandan population was divided into three groups: The Twa, who compromised only 1 percent of the population, the Hutu, who were the vast majority, and the Tutsi who made up 17 percent of the population. These groups could, however, not be seen as different tribes; they spoke the same language, shared the same religion, told the same myths and lived in the same places, but they did have different appearances. The Twa were pygmies and thus very small, the Hutu had typical Bantu features: They were broadly built and short, and the Tutsi were taller and thinner with sharp, angular features.[3] The monarchy was Tutsi, as were most of the

[1] Germany functioned, together with Belgium, France and the United States, as an observer state during the peace process, meaning that they were present at several sessions. Howard Adelman and Astri Suhrke, Early warning and conflict management genocide in Rwanda, p. 12 (1995); Joel Stettenheim, *The Arusha Accords and the failure of international intervention in Rwanda*, in, Words over war: Mediation and arbitration to prevent deadly conflict, p. 17 (M.C. Greenberg, et al. (eds.), 2002) (hereinafter Stettenheim).

[2] Linda Melvern, A People Betrayed. The Role of the West in Rwanda's Genocide, pp. 7–8 (2000) (hereinafter Melvern, 2000); Linda Melvern, Conspiracy to Murder. The Rwandan Genocide, pp. 7–8 (2004) (hereinafter Melvern, 2004).

[3] There is no consensus among historians and anthropologists on the origins of the divisions between Hutu and Tutsi. Many anthropologists are of the opinion that the

king's army and the provincial, hill and district chiefs.[4] The neighborhoods were mostly run by Hutu who obeyed the orders of those above them in the hierarchy, thus predominantly Tutsi. The Germans, who were only present in a very small number, followed a policy of indirect rule and allowed Rwanda's monarchy to continue. German colonial rule continued the Tutsi dominance and reinforced the position of power of the Tutsi's.[5]

3.2 BELGIAN COLONIAL RULE

The German rule in Rwanda was taken over by the Belgians after the First World War. From 1926 Belgium began to implement their colonization policy. The Belgian policy measures reinforced further the Tutsi dominance in the authoritative functions and supremacy over the Hutu population in daily life.

The above-mentioned provincial, hill and district chiefs under the original Rwandan regime were merged into one, and these new positions were almost always given to Tutsis. One chief only, often a Tutsi, now controlled the rural Hutu who, under the previous system, had been able to maintain some influence by manipulating the chief of one level against the chief of another level.[6] The result of the Belgian rule was therefore that the Hutu were systematically removed from positions of power.

A second Belgian policy measure was the introduction of new rules regarding land division, which meant that "the state" could gain control of the traditional Hutu landholdings in the Northwest and the Southwest of the country.[7] Since the Tutsi were those holding the positions of "chief" in "the state," it was the Tutsi who gained power over these landholdings.[8] Another development that accelerated the supremacy of the Tutsi over the Hutu was the foundation of the privatization rules. In this context too, it was predominantly the Tutsi who gained from these rules; because they were closest to the people in political control in

---

distinction is caused by a difference in class or caste. The Tutsi are said to originate from the northern part of Africa and have migrated south. For more information, *see* Gerard Prunier, The Rwanda Crisis: History of a Genocide (1959–1994), p. 12 (1995) (hereinafter Prunier); Antoine Lema, African divided: the creation of Ethnic Groups, p. 53 (1993) (hereinafter Lema); Peter Verlinden, Hutu en Tutsi, Eeuwen strijd, p. 27 (1995) (hereinafter Verlinden); Alison Des Forges, Leave None to Tell the Story, Genocide in Rwanda, pp. 32–33 (1999) (hereinafter Des Forges).

4 The word Hutu means "servant" or "subject," and the word Tutsi means "those rich in cattle."

5 Prunier, pp. 24–45; Verlinden, pp. 34, 37.

6 Prunier, p. 27.

7 For more information, see Prunier, pp. 27–28.

8 For more information, see Prunier, pp. 27–28.

governmental service, they therefore gained control in the public administration of these previously private, mostly Hutu-owned lands.[9] Furthermore, the Hutu were excluded from higher education, which was education mostly necessary for careers in positions of public authority.[10]

3.2.1 Belgian Introduction of Identity Cards

As a result of the favoring rules regarding administrative posts and education for Tutsi, the Belgians needed to know who was a Tutsi and who was not. Therefore, in 1933, all Rwandans were given an identity card by which they were classified as Hutu, Tusti or Twa.[11] Depending on their appearance, looking like a Tutsi, Hutu or Twa, they were classified as belonging to one group or the other. As a result of inter-marriages that in certain parts of Rwanda were very common, it was impossible to divide many Rwandans into certain groups on the basis of their physical features alone. Wealth could also be a decisive factor in gaining one identity card or another. People who had a lot of money or many cows were often able to obtain a Tutsi card. The cards caused discrimination against the Hutu population in all aspects of daily life, which forced hundreds of thousands of Hutu to flee to neighboring countries.[12]

Whether the European colonization incited the violence between the Hutu and Tutsi, eventually leading to the genocide, is highly debated among critics. However, Prunier has formulated the following generally agreed view: "Rwanda was definitely not a land of peace and bucolic harmony before the arrival of the Europeans, but there is no trace in its pre-colonial history of systematic violence between Tutsi and Hutu as such."[13] Colonial rule vested feelings of superiority in the Tutsis. Destexhe has summarized the colonial rule as follows: "Thus, in short, if the categories of Hutu and Tutsi's were not actually invented by the colonizers, the policies practiced by the Germans and Belgians only served to exacerbate them. They played an essential role in creating an ethnic split and ensured that the important feeling of belonging to a social group was fuelled by ethnic, indeed racial, hatred."[14]

---

9 Prunier, p. 28.

10 Des Forges, p. 35.

11 Des Forges, p. 37.

12 Melvern, 2004 p. 6; Des Forges, p. 37.

13 Prunier, p. 39.

14 Alain Destexhe, Rwanda and Genocide in the Twentieth Century, p. 41 (1996) (hereinafter Destexhe).

3.3 HUTU DOMINANCE AFTER INDEPENDENCE

The killing of hundreds of thousands of Tutsi in the genocide of 1994 constituted by far the worst massacre between Hutu and Tutsi in Rwandan history. However, this massacre was certainly not the first.

Under pressure of the U.N. Trusteeship Council, the Belgians started to slowly increase the number of Hutu in positions of public authority during the 1950s. More Hutu were placed in important administrative positions and admitted to education. Despite this first initiative, the process did not go fast enough for the Hutu. To end their subjugated position under the Tutsi elite, the Hutu started a violent political combat in 1957. A Hutu mobilization published a "manifesto" calling for majority rule and emancipation. They encouraged the belief that the Tutsi were not Rwandans but invaders from the North who had gained power and enslaved the Hutu.[15]

In 1959, following a number of incidents, grave violence of the Hutu against the Tutsi broke out.[16] The Hutu, who had gained more control over the last years, started to hunt down the Tutsi minority. The violence spread rapidly from one hill to another. How many people were killed is unclear. Different estimates have been made, but it is clear that thousands of Tutsi fled.[17] A special U.N. mission to Rwanda came back with a report talking about "Nazism against Tutsi minorities" and "artificially engineered hostility between the ethnic groups that led to the murder of around 2,000 people."[18] Despite the ongoing violence, local elections were held in June and July 1960, which resulted in a victory for the Parmehutu party.[19]

---

15 Since 1945 the United Nations has been focused on the Belgian role in Rwanda. Belgium was criticized for their causation of the predominant status of the Tutsi population. Between 1948 and 1962, the U.N. Trusteeship Council sent five visiting missions to Rwanda, all of whom produced very critical reports. Belgium then started, though very slowly, to introduce electoral procedures. Melvern, 2000 p. 13; Prunier, pp. 41–52. In 1957 the U.N. Trusteeship Council published a report that stated that it found "little hope for rapprochement between the races." The report called upon the Belgians to replace the Tutsi authorities with Hutu. Melvern, 2000 p. 13; Prunier, pp. 41–52.

16 In 1959 the Tutsi king, Mutara Rudahigwa, who had always tried to keep the situation calm, died in mysterious circumstances. The Tutsi elite blamed the Belgians and the Hutu extremists. His half-brother, Kigeri Ndahindurwa, who was influenced by the most conservative Tutsi group, succeeded the King. In November 1959, a Hutu leader was attacked by several Tutsi, which led to an eruption of violence. Prunier, pp. 48–49; Verlinden, p. 81 states that 160,000 Tutsis fled to neighboring countries.

17 Dozens of Tutsi petitions were sent to the United Nations stating that the killings had been planned and organized. Melvern, 2004 p. 7; Prunier, p. 51.

18 GA Res. 1743 (XVI) (A/5126) May 30, 1962, Question of the Future of Ruanda-Burundi. For more information, see Melvern, 2004 p. 7.

19 Parti du Mouvement de l'Emancipation Hutu was a Hutu party that called for the end of the Tutsi colonisation before ending the Belgian colonization. Prunier, p. 51; Melvern, 2000 pp. 14, 240. For more information, see Prunier, pp. 49–59.

On July 1, 1962, Rwanda became independent. The Hutu Gregoire Kayibanda won the presidential election with a large majority, and he immediately abolished the monarchy. Kayibanda is understood as the founding father of "Hutu nationalism."[20] He installed a quota system providing that only 9 percent of Tutsi were allowed access to education and employment. Many Tutsi were thrown out of their jobs. Hutu students started to check the bloodlines of students to see whether someone was Hutu or Tutsi. Lists of Tutsi students were put up on the wall. During the first years of Kayibanda's rule, the thousands of Tutsi living in neighboring countries, who were denied entry to Rwanda, tried to fight their way back into Rwanda. These invasions led to reprisals by the Hutu authority on the Tutsi still living within Rwanda.[21] The only Tutsi attack that seriously threatened Kayibanda's regime took place in December 1963.[22] As a result, Kayibanda started a campaign to kill the Tutsi, starting with the elimination of political opponents. An estimated 10,000 Tutsi were killed between December 1963 and January 1964.[23] In 1964 Kayibanda spoke the words: "if the Tutsi ever seek to obtain political power again they will find that the whole Tutsi race will be wiped out." There was total impunity for the perpetrators of these killings.[24] Des Forges states that 20,000 Tutsis were killed and 300,000 were made refugees.[25]

With Juvénal Habyarimana's coup, Kayiabanda was removed in July 1973. Habyarimana was the most senior officer in the army. He was welcomed by the Tutsi population because he promised to unite the country, and indeed under his rule violence against the Tutsi ceased, and peace and stability arrived in Rwanda. However, this stability came with the price of living in a totalitarian regime. Rwanda became a strict one-party country.[26] Habyarimana's party, the Mouvement Révolutionnaire National pour le Développement (MRND), was the only party allowed, and everyone, including babies, had to be a member. Despite the termination of the violence, the Tutsi were still being discriminated against. Habyarimana kept the identity card and the quota system for education. However, compared to Kayibanda's regime, life for the Tutsi minority was now livable. Some Tutsi had even managed to become prosperous businessmen, but the "unspoken rule" stated: "Stay out of politics: that is Hutu preserve."[27]

---

20 Melvern, 2000 pp. 17–18; Melvern, 2004 pp. 8–10; Prunier, p. 57.

21 Kayibanda used the horrific events in Burundi in 1962, where an estimated 200,000 Hutu were killed, to wash out the Tutsi population. Melvern, 2000 p. 21; Melvern, 2004 p. 10.

22 Around 1,500 men recruited from the refugee camps in Burundi tried to oust Kayibanda, but failed. Prunier, pp. 56–57.

23 Melvern, 2004 p. 8; Prunier, p. 56.

24 Peter Uvin, Aiding Violence, The Development Enterprise in Rwanda, p. 37 (1998) (hereinafter Uvin).

25 Des Forges, p. 40.

26 Des Forges, p. 40; Melvern, 2004 p. 11; Prunier, pp. 75–77.

27 Melvern, 2004 p. 12.

There was only one Tutsi minister, two Tutsi parliament members out of 70 and one Tutsi officer in the army.[28]

3.4 TUTSI-RPF INVASION IN 1990

During the 1980s, the second generation of Tutsi refugees in the neighboring countries started to organize themselves. For a great number of years, the refugees had been stateless; they did not have full rights of settlement and were denied entry to Rwanda.[29] How many Rwandan Tutsi were living in exile has never been clear; according to Habyarimana, 200,000 Rwandans were living in the neighboring countries, while in 1990 the United Nations High Commissioner for Refugees (UNHCR) came up with an estimation of 900,000 refugees. The young Rwandan refugees living in Uganda positioned themselves within the Ugandan National Resistance Army (NRA) led by Museveni.[30] At the time that the NRA took force in 1986, a quarter of the 14,000 soldiers were Rwandan refugees.[31] They had even been able to obtain high positions as leading commanders and officers within the NRA. These Rwandan NRA soldiers created the RPF, both a political and military party, and decided to return to Rwanda.[32] On October 1, 1990, the RPF violently invaded Rwanda and a three-year civil war began. The invaders consisted of more than 4,000 second-generation refugees who had fled the country between 1957 and 1963. The RPF consisted of well-trained and experienced troops. The leader was the most famous Rwandan refugee in the NRA, Major-General Fred Rwigyema.[33]

Immediately after the RPF invasion, the French government quickly came to the aid of the Rwandan army of only 5,200 troops.[34] On October 4, 1990, 150 French parachutists arrived.[35] Prunier asks the very pertinent question "what

---

28 *Id.*

29 In 1986 Rwanda announced that the country was too small for the refugees to return back to Rwanda.

30 For more information, see Prunier, pp. 70–74.

31 After his victory, Museveni began a military recruitment campaign, which increased the number of Rwandans in the NRA drastically. During the coming years the Rwandan refugees would gain more and more military expertise. See Prunier, pp. 70–74.

32 There was growing resentment in Uganda of the Rwandan refugees; later it was decided that they were even precluded from owning land, an extra stimulation for the Rwandans to return to Rwanda. Prunier, pp. 70–74.

33 The RPF demanded democracy and an end to the ethnic division and identity cards. He was killed on the second day of the invasion, and his death caused tremendous fears among the RPF.

34 President Mitterrand heard about the invasion as he was flying home from Oman to Paris. After a short conversation with his Minister of Defense, he ordered the dispatch of troops to help the small Rwandan army of only 5,200 troops. Prunier, p. 100.

35 Prunier, p. 101.

could have caused Paris to send troops to a distant African country in order to protect a faltering dictatorship from an attack launched by its own refugee population trying to return home by force?" He adds that there is no easy answer.[36] Over the years, France had replaced Belgium as Rwanda's most important ally. France wanted Rwanda to become part of its "French family," a group of states aimed at maintaining the protection of the French language. Rwanda was of the highest importance because it was situated between French and English-speaking regions of Eastern Africa.[37]

The French parachutists were followed by 400 Belgian paratroopers, but the Belgians soon found themselves forced to withdraw because Belgian national law forbids the country taking part in civil wars. Zaïre, under President Mobutu, also sent in a few hundred troops. To gain more international support, Habyarimana faked an RPF attack on Kigali on the night of October 4–5. Thousands of shots were fired. Habyarimana's plan was successful; during the next few days, France sent in hundreds more troops.[38] Thanks to the help of France, the Forces Armées Rwandaises (FAR) recovered and was able to fight back. It was perceived as an attack on a Francophone state. France, under the presidency of Mitterand, supported Habyarimana with more than 1,000 soldiers and trained the army and the militia.[39] The widely believed fake attack was used by the authorities to start a campaign saying that the Tutsi still living in Rwanda were "accomplices" of the RPF invaders. The Minister of Defense called upon the population to "track down and arrest the infiltrators." A wave of arrests followed, by which around 10,000 people got arrested.[40] People were told to burn the houses of the "inyenzi"—cockroaches—the Tutsi and to kill them. Civilian massacres spread over the hills, and soon it became clear that the people arrested were not supporters of the RPF but educated Tutsi and moderate Hutu.[41]

The RPF invasion ended with a ceasefire and on October 30. The Rwandan government announced that the war was over, but the civil war would last for another three years. The RPF had crossed back to neighboring countries or taken refuge in the Northern part of Rwanda, in the Volcano Mountains, where many of them died because of the unbearable conditions.[42]

Thanks to the leadership of Jean Paul Kagame, the RPF was able to recover, rearm and regroup itself.[43] At the time of the invasion, Kagame had been in the United States for military training. He came back to Rwanda and within a few

---

36 Prunier, p. 102. See also Prunier, p. 107.

37 Melvern, 2000 p. 24; Prunier 103–107; Stettenheim, p.16. For more information, see Melvern, 2004 pp. 24–36.

38 Prunier, pp. 100–102.

39 Prunier, pp. 105, 107, 113, 149; Des Forges, p. 118.

40 Prunier, p. 109.

41 Prunier, p. 108.

42 Melvern, 2004 p. 16.

43 The former leader, Major-General Fred Rwigyema, had died. Prunier, p. 114.

months he was able to give the army direction, discipline and a strategy.[44] Kagame had fled from Rwanda as a young Tutsi boy in 1959 and served for years as an assistant director of military intelligence in the NRA. He was seen as an intelligent, determined man and a true leader. As soon as January 1991, the RPF attacked a prison in the Northwestern town of Ruhengeri, which held some 1,000 prisoners. Kagame succeeded in freeing the prisoners, but, as a result, a new wave of killings on the Tutsi population in the Northwestern part of the country erupted. In the years to follow, the RPF undertook a series of incursions, all of which met with counter-pressure and killings by the Rwandan army.[45]

After the ceasefire of October 1990, two more ceasefires would follow, one in February 1991 and one in March 1991, which was consequently amended on September 16, 1991, and again on July 12, 1992.[46] All agreements were signed after new violence had broken out. In 1992 the negotiations for the Arusha Peace Accords finally started, and the first protocol of the agreement was signed.[47] Despite these ceasefires and negotiations, the real intentions of Habyarimana and his MRND were observed to be far different.[48]

3.5 CONCLUDING OBSERVATIONS

We may conclude from this chapter that the German and Belgian colonial rule reinforced the dominant position of the Tutsi minority in Rwanda. Because of this colonial rule, they maintained political power. This was reversed after the *coup d'état* and independence in the 1960s. The superiority of the Tutsis totally ended after the independence of Rwanda. After this point many Tutsis were killed and forced to flee to neighboring countries. A huge Tutsi population lived outside the country (particularly in Uganda) and aimed to recover their position of power in Rwanda. The period between 1991 and 1993 were the years in which Hutu extremism laid the foundations for the genocide in 1994. In Chapter 6 we will elaborate on this Hutu extremism.

---

44 Melvern, 2004 p. 16; Prunier, pp. 114–120.

45 Prunier, p. 120; Melvern, 2004 pp. 16, 17; Melvern, 2000 p. 39.

46 Tor Sellström and Lennart Wohlgemuth, The International Response to Conflict and Genocide: Lessons from the Rwanda Experience, paragraph: The Arusha Process (1996); Melvern, 2000 p. 39.

47 The Arusha Peace Accords would, in the end, consist of the "Peace Agreement," the "Ceasefire Agreement" and five additional Protocols. See Chapter 4 for The Neutral International Force.

48 Des Forges, p. 96; Prunier, p. 16.

CHAPTER 4

UNDERMINING UNAMIR

4.1 THE ARUSHA PEACE ACCORDS

It was a triumph for international diplomacy when on August 4, 1993, the Arusha Peace Accords between the Rwandan government and the Rwandan Patriotic Front (RPF) were signed. After one year of negotiations and three years of war, the parties agreed upon the power sharing agreement. Through external pressure, the two parties had come to the conclusion of the Peace Agreement, which made it a true victory for foreign diplomacy.[1] All regional states[2] had been involved: the Organization of African Unity (OAU) had led the negotiations, and Western states had observer status[3] or monitored the negotiations from their embassies in Tanzania.[4]

The peace agreement provided for the so-called Broad Based Transitional Government (BBTG) that would hold power for 22 months at the most, after which elections would follow. This interim government would consist of 21 ministers. The Mouvement Révolutionaire National pour le Développement (MRND) and the RPF would each have five ministers and the Mouvement Démocratique Républicain (MRD), the largest opposition party, would have four ministers of which one would be the prime minister during the transition. Faustin Twagiramungu would hold this position. The other seven ministerial posts were to be divided among the rest of the parties. The fear for dominance by one party or another was demonstrated by the voting system, which required a majority of two-thirds for decisions, meaning 14 votes in favor.[5]

1 Linda Melvern, A People Betrayed. The Role of the West in Rwanda's Genocide, pp. 52–53 (2000) (hereinafter Melvern, 2000); Linda Melvern, Conspiracy to Murder. The Rwandan Genocide, p. 59 (2004) (hereinafter Melvern, 2004).

2 Melvern, 2000 p. 52; Burundi, Zaire, Senegal and Tanzania.

3 *Id.* France, Belgium, Germany and the United States.

4 *Id.* Britain, Canada, the Netherlands and the EU.

5 Gerard Prunier, The Rwanda Crisis: History of a Genocide (1959–1994), pp. 192–194 (1995) (hereinafter Prunier).

It is argued by some that the failure of Arusha lies in the fact that extremists were not represented in the Peace Accords.[6] The hardliners within the MRND and the new grouping of extremists in the Coalition pour Défense de la République (CDR) did not have any power within the transitional institutions. There had been difficult discussions about whether to include or exclude the CDR from the negotiations. The RPF was strictly opposed to the inclusion of the CDR saying that this party was the "fascist separation fraction of the MRND." France and Tanzania supported Habyarimana who was in favor of the inclusion of the CDR. According to the President, the only way to control the CDR was by having them represented in the government. Even the British and American diplomats tried to convince Paul Kagame, the leader of the RPF forces, however unsuccessfully. Some critics saw Arusha as "a conquest for the RPF;" the CDR was excluded from any position in the interim government, and the RPF

[6] Organization of African Unity (OAU) report, paragraph 8.9; Tor Sellström and Lennart Wohlgemuth, The International Response to Conflict and Genocide: Lessons from the Rwanda Experience, p. 44 (1996) (hereinafter Sellström); Prunier, p. 193; Melvern, 2000 p. 54; Joel Stettenheim, *The Arusha Accords and the failure of international intervention in Rwanda*, in Words over war: Mediation and arbitration to prevent deadly conflict, p. 18 (M.C. Greenberg et al. (eds.), 2002) (hereinafter Stettenheim).

and the MRND, who had been the ruling party over the last two decades, were equally represented.[7]

The cartoon above appeared in the magazine *Kangura* in October 1993 (No. 51, p. 14).[8]

Another agreement of Arusha was the inclusion of the military branch of the RPF in the national army, the Forces Armées Rwandaises (FAR). The division would be 60 percent governmental troops and 40 percent RPF troops and an equal division in the officer corps.[9] Arusha called for an International Neutral Force to help ensure its implementation. The RPF wanted the French troops to withdraw and wanted them to be replaced by a U.N. force.[10] The U.N. force had to provide security and supervise the installment of the transitional government, the demobilization of combatants, the creation of a new army and preparations for national elections.[11]

Up until that moment, the OAU had overseen the peace negotiations, but it was the United Nations that would play this peace-keeping role, through the Arusha peace agreement between the parties, and their explicit demand for an international force "under the responsibility and command of the United Nations."[12] This peace-keeping operation was seen as a rather simple operation to implement the agreement and install the interim government.[13] A reconnaissance mission from the United Nations was sent to Rwanda in order to prepare for the decisionmaking with regard to the peace-keeping force and to

---

7 Melvern, 2000 p. 54; OAU report, paragraph 8.9; Sellström, p. 44; Prunier p. 193.

8 The man in fatigues is Paul Kagame, who was the leader of the Rwandan Patriotic Front (RPF). The man extending his hand was the President of Rwanda, Juvénal Habyarimana. The caption on the left reads, "They say that Kagame would refuse to shake the hand of a Hutu." Kagame says, "Let it be known that I cannot shake a Hutus hand." The sign "Kinihira" signifies a neutral "buffer zone" in Rwanda that was brokered between the RPF and Habyarimana at the U.N.-sponsored Arusha Peace Accords in the summer of 1993. See http://www.onemancult.com/rwanda/rwandaprop3.html. See also http://www.onemancult.com/rwanda/rwandaprop14.html.

9 Melvern, 2000 p. 53; for more information, see Prunier, pp. 159–173.

10 Prunier, p. 194.

11 The United Nations and Rwanda, 1993–1996.

12 U.N. Doc. A/48/824—S/26915, December 23, 1993, U.N. Doc. S/26488, Report of the Secretary-General on Rwanda, September 25, 1993 (hereinafter A/48/824—S/26915), Protocol of Agreement between the Government of the Rwandese Republic and the Rwandese Patriotic Front on the Integration of the Armed Forces of the two parties.

13 United Nations, Report of the Independent Inquiry into the Actions of the United Nations during the 1994 Genocide in Rwanda, December 15, 1999, Ingvar Carlsson, Han, Sung-Joo, Rufus, M. Kupolati, U.N. Doc. S/1999/1257, p. 6 (hereinafter Carlsson Report, S/1999/1257).

formulate the mandate and the rules of engagement for this operation. In Chapter 5 we will continue with the reconnaissance mission and installment of the United Nations Assistance Mission for Rwanda (UNAMIR).

4.2 THE MISSION OF THE NEUTRAL INTERNATIONAL FORCE IN THE ARUSHA PEACE AGREEMENT

The Arusha Peace Accords consisted of a Peace Agreement, a Ceasefire Agreement and five additional Protocols.[14] The mandate of this Neutral International Force was laid down in Article 54 of the Protocol of Agreement between the Government of the Republic of Rwanda and the Rwandese Patriotic Front on the Integration of the Armed Forces of the two parties. The article reads as follows:[15]

> *Article 54: Missions*
> The Neutral International Force shall have the following missions:
> A. Overall Mission:
> The Neutral International Force shall assist in the implementation of the Peace Agreement, more especially through the supervision of the

---

14 The Peace Agreement consisted of the following documents:

1. Peace Agreement between the Government of the Republic of Rwanda and the Rwandese Patriotic Front, signed on August 4, 1993.
2. The N'Sele cease-fire agreement between the Government of the Rwandese Republic and the Rwandese Patriotic Front, signed on September 16, 1991, and on July 12, 1992.
3. Protocol of Agreement between the Government of the Rwandese Republic and the Rwandese Patriotic Front on the rule of law, signed on August 18, 1992.
4. Protocols of Agreement between the Government of the Rwandese Republic and the Rwandese Patriotic Front on Power-Sharing within the framework of the BBTG, signed on October 30, 1992, and on January 9, 1993.
5. Protocol of Agreement between the Government of the Rwandese Republic and the Rwandese Patriotic Front on the repatriation of Rwandese refugees and the resettlement of displaced persons, signed on June 9, 1993.
6. Protocol of Agreement between the Government of the Rwandese Republic and the Rwandese Patriotic Front on the Integration of the Armed Forces of the two parties, August 3, 1993.
7. Protocol of Agreement between the Government of the Rwandese Republic and the Rwandese Patriotic Front on the Integration of the Armed Forces of the two parties on miscellaneous issues and final provisions, signed on August 3, 1993.

See Letter from the representative of the United Republic of Tanzania to the U.N. Secretary-General, December 23, 1993, A/48/824—S/26915.

15 A/48/824—S/26915.

implementation of the Protocol of Agreement on the Integration of Armed Forces of the two parties as well as the provision of all kinds of assistance to the competent authorities and organs.

B. Security Missions:

1. *Guarantee the overall security of the country* [emphasis added] and especially verify the maintenance of law and order by the competent authorities and organs.
2. Ensure the security of the distribution of humanitarian aids.
3. Assist in catering for the security of civilians.
4. *Assist in the tracking of arms caches* [emphasis added] and neutralization of armed gangs throughout the country.
5. Undertake mine clearance operations.
6. Assist in the recovery of all weapons distributed to, or illegally acquired by the civilians.
7. Monitor the observance by the two parties of modalities for the definite cessation of hostilities, provided for in the Peace Agreement.

C. Missions of Supervising the Process of Formation of the National Army:

1. Undertake the demarcation of the Assembly Zones and identify places for the establishment of Assembly and Cantonment points.
2. The Neutral International Force shall be responsible for the preparation of Assembly and Cantonment points. It shall take in and manage all the equipment and financial resources required for the performances of that duty.
The military barracks may serve as Assembly or Cantonment points, on the condition that the two parties be informed. These camps shall be subjected to the monitoring of the Neutral International Force and the requirements of the other Assembly or Cantonment points.
3. Determine security parameters for the City of Kigali, in line with the objective of making it a neutral zone.
4. Supervise:
   - Operations for the disengagement of forces, especially the movement of troops towards Assembly points, and servicemen moving to the Cantonment points for purposes of depositing heavy weapons;
   - the transformation of military barracks into Assembly or Cantonment points;
   - verifications following these operations.

> 5. Ensure that rules of discipline by servicemen inside and outside assembly points are observed.
> 6. Cross-check inventories of armament and ammunitions of the two parties and monitor operations for the separation of heavy from light weapons.
> 7. Keep watch on cantonment points and participate in the guard of the light weapons and ammunition magazines located in Assembly points.
> 8. Supervise operations for the identification of the military personnel, to be carried out in the various Assembly points.
> 9. Supervise operations for the supplies to the troops in the Assembly points, it being understood that the supplies shall be confined to non-lethal items.
> 10. Participate in the program designed for the training of members of the New Armed Forces and cater for the security of Training Centers.
> 11. Supervise the operations for the demobilization of servicemen and gendarmes not eligible to constitute the new Armed forces.
> 12. Assess the status of implementation of the formation process and make recommendations to the broad based transitional Government and the Command Council of the National Gendarmerie.

We may conclude that the parties of the Arusha Peace Agreement were very much aware of possible pitfalls, and they have taken these into account in a detailed way for the proposed military force to keep the peace.

4.3 THE UNAMIR MANDATE

According to the Arusha Accords, this Neutral International Force had to be established by September 10, 1993. It would be on October 5 when the Security Council decided upon the installment of the U.N. Assistance Mission to Rwanda, which would assist in the installation of the Broad Based Transitional Government.[16] The mandate of UNAMIR was laid down in point 3 of Security Council Resolution 872:[17]

> [The Security Council] [D]ecides that, drawing from the Secretary-General's recommendations, UNAMIR shall have the following mandate:
> (a) *To contribute to the security of the city of Kigali* [italics added] inter alia within a weapons-secure area established by the parties in and around the city;

---

16 Carlsson Report, S/1999/1257, p. 31.

17 U.N. Doc. S/RES/872 (1993).

(b) To monitor observance of the cease-fire agreement, which calls for the establishment of cantonment and assembly zones and the demarcation of the new demilitarized zone and other demilitarization procedures;
(c) To monitor the security situation during the final period of the transitional government's mandate, leading up to the elections;
(d) To assist with mine clearance, primarily through training programs;
(e) To investigate at the request of the parties or on its own initiative instances of alleged non-compliance with the provisions of the Arusha Peace Agreement relating to the integration of the armed forces, and pursue any such instances with the parties responsible and report thereon as appropriate to the Secretary-General;
(f) To monitor the process of repatriation of Rwandese refugees and resettlement of displaced persons to verify that it is carried out in a safe and orderly manner;
(g) To assist in the coordination of humanitarian assistance activities in conjunction with relief operations;
(h) To investigate and report on incidents regarding the activities of the gendarmerie and police.

In general, the basic understanding for peace-keeping is that the parties, or at least the party in which territory the forces are located, are welcoming these military and are positive about their continuation, because they will improve security and help to promote a peace agreement. When the consent is no longer available, the forces will be removed, as happened on the request of the President of Egypt, Gamal Abdel Nasser, in May 1967. The problem—already observed in 1967—however is that when the troops are removed, there is no longer a buffer between the parties, and war will be the result. For this reason we may very well understand the dominating principle in the United Nations that impartiality and the non-use of force should be respected all the time, in particular by the forces themselves.

4.4 DIFFERENCES BETWEEN THE ARUSHA ACCORDS AND THE UNAMIR MANDATE

The Arusha Peace Accords asked for an International Neutral Force that would "guarantee the overall security of the country" and would "assist in the tracking of arms caches," but the mandate of UNAMIR—as laid down in the Security Council resolution—only stated that UNAMIR would "*contribute* to the *security* of the *city*." With this provision, the Security Council has devalued the mandate, because: Firstly, under this mandate UNAMIR was only allowed to *contribute* to the security, while Arusha asked for a force that would *guarantee* the security. Secondly, Arusha's request to guarantee the security of the *country* was now limited to the security of *Kigali inter alia, within a weapons-secure area established by the parties in and around the city*. Thirdly, the UNAMIR mandate did not provide for the possibility to search for arms, while Arusha had asked for a force that would *assist in the tracking of arms caches*.

Why did the Security Council adopt a mandate that was far weaker than that which was asked for by Arusha? In his report to the Security Council about the establishment of UNAMIR, dated September 24, 1993, the Secretary-General proposed a mission to Rwanda with a mandate in line with the Arusha Accords. The Secretary-General wrote that the Mission would assist "in the recovery of arms" and "in maintaining general security in the country, particularly in Kigali."[18]

The Belgian Senate writes that the weak mandate is said to be the result of the U.N. Secretariat, which was of the opinion that the mandate as described in Arusha was unfeasible.[19] The Belgian Senate adds that the United States and Russia were also against such a broad mandate.[20] Willy Claes, the former Belgian Minister of Foreign Affairs, declared before the Senate:

> During the discussion, the permanent members of the Security Council wanted to limit the mandate as much as possible. The Americans, Russians, Chinese and British were very reticent. I think it would have been an illusion to attempt to convince them to broaden the mandate. In any case, I was never asked to plead for an improvement of the mandate, because nobody saw the necessity thereof. We have not undertaken steps. If we had done so, we would undoubtedly have met with a categorical refusal by the permanent members.[21]

A telex sent from the Belgian delegation in New York to the Ministry of Foreign Affairs in Brussels on August 9, 1993, stated: "The secretariat underlines that one of the principle tasks of the reconnaissance mission is to develop a 'realistic and practicable mandate,' in view of the reticence of the USA, the UK and Russia." The telex adds: "As a consequence, there could well be a big difference between what the two parties have demanded in their initial request of the 14th of June to the Secretary General and the final mandate of the Neutral Intervention Force."[22]

---

18 U.N. Doc. S/26488, pp. 5, 7 and 9.

19 Sénat de Belgique, Commission d'Enquête parlementaire concernant les événements au Rwanda, Sénat de Belgique, session de 1997–1998, 6 décembre 1997, Rapport fait au nom de la commission d'enquête par MM Mahoux et Verhofstadt, p. 230 (hereinafter Belgian Senate).

20 Belgian Senate, p. 230; Hearing Cools, BV, BCR, April 29, 1997, pp. 406, 407.

21 Belgian Senate, p. 231; Hearing Claes, BV, BCR, March 5, 1997, p. 88.

22 Telex New York 93/01336, August 9, 1993; Belgian Senate p. 231. Translated from French into English. Original text: "Le secrétariat souligne qu'une des tâches principales de la mission de reconnaissance est de mettre au point un 'mandat réaliste et

Willy Claes testified that "his services" never mentioned the "hollowing of the mandate" compared to the mandate as it was foreseen in the Arusha Accords.[23] According to the Belgian Senate, no efforts were made by Belgium to get "a stronger mandate" or "a mandate that was as strong as possible." The Belgian Senate writes that Alexis Brouhns, the Belgian Vice Permanent Representative at the United Nations at the time, declared that he did not receive any instructions to use the Belgian key position as UNAMIR's backbone to make the Belgian participation dependent on several conditions.[24] According to the Belgian Senate, Brouhns' words were confirmed by Willy Claes and Lode Willems, the Minister's Chef de Cabinet.[25]

4.5 THE RULES OF ENGAGEMENT AND THE OPERATIONAL PROCEDURE

The mandate as set out in the SC resolution was further defined in specific regulations. The two most important regulations were the rules of engagement (ROE) and the "operational procedure for the establishment of the weapon-free zone in Kigali."[26]

4.5.1 The Rules of Engagement

The rules of engagement (ROE) of peace-keeping missions comprise a total of commands, prohibition rules and directions for the U.N. blue-helmets. The

---

praticable' vu la retenue des U.S., de U.K. et de Russie . . . 'Par conséquent, il pourrait bien y avoir une grande différence entre ce que les deux parties ont demandé dans leur requête initiale du 14 juin au secrétariat général et le mandat final de la Force d'intervention neutre' ."

23 Belgian Senate, p. 231; Hearing Claes, BV, BCR, March 5, 1997, p. 87.

24 Belgian Senate, p. 231; Hearing Brouhns, BV, BCR, February 28, 1997, p. 50.

25 Belgian Senate, p. 231; Hearing Claes, BV, BCR, March 5, 1997, pp. 84, 88 and Mr. Willems, March 18, 1997, p. 186.

26 Translated from French into English. Originally called: "Procédure opérationnelle pour l'établissement da la zone de consignation d'armes de Kigali." The Regulations that defined the mandate were: The Directive opérationnelle No.2: Dispositions réglementant l'ouverture du feu (provisoires) du 19 novembre 1993 (the operational Directive No.2: Measures regulating the opening of fire (provisional) of November 19th, 1993); the instructions à tout personnel de la minuar autorisé de port d'armes et munitions (the instructions to all UNAMIR personnel authorized to carry arms and munitions); the Directives de la Minuar pour le comportement des militaires aux points de contrôle (the UNAMIR Directives for the behaviour of soldiers at control points); Procédure opérationnelle pour l'établissement de la zone de consignation d'armes de Kigali (Operational procedure for the establishment of a weapon-free zone in Kigali).

rules tell them at what time and in what manner they can resort to force and from who they will get the needed permission to act. These rules have to be made when implementing the mandate. In general it is not the Security Council who draws up the ROE but the Force Commander in cooperation with the commanders of the troop-contributing countries. In the case of UNAMIR, it was indeed Lieutenant General Roméo Dallaire and the Belgian military, being the largest contributor of troops, who were involved in drawing up the ROE.[27]

On November 23 Dallaire sent the rules of engagement for approval to U.N. headquarters. The headquarters, however, never responded to his request.[28] According to U.N. military adviser Maurice Baril, the headquarters did not have a formal procedure for the approval of draft ROE at that time. The Carlsson Report records that the Force Commander must have considered the Rules "as approved" when no reply was received; Carlsson adds that it was "reasonable of Dallaire to do so."[29]

In his draft, Dallaire had deliberately included Paragraph 17, which widened Dallaire's scope to make use of military force in cases of crimes against humanity. Such a paragraph was very unusual for a traditional peace-keeping mission.[30] Paragraph 17 stated:

> Crimes against Humanity: Ethnically or politically motivated criminal acts may also be committed during this mandate and will morally and legally require UNAMIR to use all available means to put an end to them. Examples: Executions, attacks or displaced persons or refugees, ethnic riots, attacks on demobilized soldiers, etc. On such occasions, UNAMIR military personnel will follow the ROE outlined in this directive, in support of UNCIVPOL and local authorities or in their absence, UNAMIR will take the necessary action to prevent any crime against humanity.[31]

---

27 Belgian Senate, p. 232.

28 Carlsson Report, S/1999/1257, p. 35.

29 *Id.*

30 Roméo Dallaire, Shake Hands with the Devil, The Failure of Humanity in Rwanda, pp. 71, 72 (2004) (hereinafter Dallaire); Carlsson Report, S/1999/1257, p. 35.

31 ROE—Directive opérationnelle No.2: dispositions réglementant l'ouverture du feu (provisoires) du 19 novembre 1993, see Sénat de Belgique, Commission d'Enquête parlementaire concernant les événements au Rwanda, (Commission of parliamentary enquiry concerning the events in Rwanda), session de 1997–1998, 6 décembre 1997, Rapport fait au nom de la commission d'enquête par MM Mahoux et Verhofstadt, Annexes p. 93 (hereinafter Annex Belgian Senate). Translated from French into English. Original text: "Crimes contre l'humanité: Des actes criminels motivés ethniquement ou politiquement peuvent également être perpétrés pendant ce mandat et demanderont moralement et légalement que la Minuar utilise tous les moyens disponibles pour y mettre fin. Exemples : Exécutions, attaques ou personnes déplacées ou réfugiés, émeutes ethniques, attaques contre des soldats démobilisés, etc. A ces occasions, le personnel militaire de

The ROE would turn out to be very limiting and restrictive.[32] With the exception of legal self-defense, the ROE prescribed that in the case of incidents, arms could only be used after permission had been gained, and depending on the type of force, this permission had to be gained from the Commander of KIBAT, the Commander of the Sector Kigali or from the Force Commander himself. Despite the fact that after April 6 the genocide broke loose, the possibilities to use force created by Paragraph 17 were never used.

4.5.2 *The Operational Procedure for the Establishment of the Weapon-Free Zone in Kigali*[33]

Another important set of rules for the implementation of the mandate was the so-called "operational procedure for the establishment of the weapon-free zone in Kigali."[34] These rules defined UNAMIR's most important assignment, namely the creation of the so-called Kigali Weapon Secure Area (KWSA). After long negotiations, in which both Dallaire and Luc Marchal, the Belgian commander in UNAMIR, participated, the Operational Procedures were accepted by the FAR and the RPF on the night of December 23–24, 1993.[35] The rules defined the means that could be used to create the KWSA, such as "Control Points," "Roadblocks," "Searches," "Military Patrols."[36]

One of the most important rules laid down in the Operational Procedure was the so-called "Searching and Scouring."[37] The Operational Procedure stated the following about "Searching and Scouring:" "UNAMIR could be led to organizing a search operation with a view to searching for arms, munitions and explosives. A preliminary authorization from the headquarters of UNAMIR is necessary to execute such an operation. This operation will be done in liaison with the gendarmerie and the local police and it should be done with sufficient

---

la Minuar suivra les ROE élaborées dans cette directive, en appui de la POLCIV UN et des autorités locales ou en leur absence, la Minuar prendra l'action nécessaire pour empêcher tout crime contre l'humanité."

32 See also the conclusion of the Ad Hoc Commission, see Annex Belgian Senate, p. 52.

33 Translated from French into English. Originally called: "Procédure opérationnelle pour l'établissement da la zone de consignation d'armes de Kigali."

34 Translated from French into English. Originally called: Procédure opérationelle pour l'établissement de la zone de consignation d'armes de Kigali. See Annex Belgian Senate, p. 102.

35 Belgian Senate, p. 233.

36 Translated from French into English. Originally called: "Points de Contrôle," "Barrages Routiers," "Perquisitions," "Patrouilles."

37 Translated from French into English. Originally called: "Ratissages et Fouilles."

38 Translated from French into English. Original text: "La Minuar peut être amenée à organiser une opération de fouille en vue de rechercher des armes, munitions

forces and funds."[38]

This rule shows that the language used in the Operational Procedure was in itself already very much limiting UNAMIR's possibilities, and, with that, UNAMIR's mandate was drifting even further away from the mandate as foreseen by Arusha. There could have been some leeway, were the rules to be subjected to a broad interpretation. But, as will be seen in the following chapters, the rules were interpreted very strictly. In creating the Weapons Secure Area, UNAMIR was restricted to "helping," "participating" and "cooperating with the local authorities." UNAMIR was not allowed to act alone in dismantling the arms caches, a limitation that would prove to be a great hindrance in carrying out the mandate.[39]

We may conclude that one important factor in the failure to prevent genocide in Rwanda was already made in the making of a far weaker mandate, lacking the use of force instruction that was requested, needed and proposed by the Rwandan parties of the peace agreement.

---

et explosifs. Une autorisation préalable du Quartier Général de la Minuar est nécessaire pour exécuter une telle opération. Cette opération se fera en liaison avec la gendarmerie et la police locale et elle doit être faite avec des forces et des réserves suffisantes." Procédure opérationelle pour l'établissement de la zone de consignation d'armes de Kigali. See Annex Belgian Senate, p. 102, point 11.

[39] See Chapters 8 and 11.

CHAPTER 5

THE INSTALLMENT OF UNAMIR WITH BELGIAN PARTICIPATION

5.1 THE PREPARATION BY THE RECONNAISSANCE MISSION

On August 8, 1993, Lieutenant General Roméo Dallaire received a phone call from his executive assistant Major Brent Beardsley to tell him that something unexpected had happened: The Arusha Peace Accords had been signed.[1] By this time Dallaire was already deeply involved in Rwanda. He was the commander of the U.N. Observer Mission Uganda-Rwanda (UNOMUR) that had started two months earlier. UNOMUR was a deployment of military observers to monitor the border between Rwanda and Uganda and verify that no military assistance was being provided across it.[2]

Under the Arusha Agreement, an International Neutral Force had to be established by September 10, which was only five weeks away. The United Nations had to look into the Agreement and assess whether or not a U.N. peacekeeping mission to Rwanda would be plausible.[3] On August 17 Dallaire and Beardsley, both French-speaking Canadians, were sent to Rwanda to spend two weeks on a reconnaissance, or so-called "technical" mission, to investigate whether a U.N. mission would be possible.

---

1 Frontline interview with Dallaire, Autumn 2003; Linda Melvern, A People Betrayed. The Role of the West in Rwanda's Genocide, p. 52 (2000) (hereinafter Melvern, 2000); Roméo Dallaire, Shake Hands with the Devil, The Failure of Humanity in Rwanda, pp. 52–53 (2004) (hereinafter Dallaire).

2 UNOMUR was deployed on the Ugandan side of the border between Uganda and Rwanda. Its mandate was to monitor the border "to verify that no military assistance reaches Rwanda, focus being put primarily in this regard on transit or transport, by roads or tracks which could accommodate vehicles, of lethal weapons and ammunition across the border, as well as any other material which could be of military use." The mission was installed in accordance with Security Council Resolution 864, June 22, 1993; S/1993/864, See http://www.un.org/Depts/dpko/dpko/co_mission/unomur.htm; Dallaire, pp. 42–53.

3 Frontline interview with Dallaire, Autumn 2003; Dallaire, pp. 52–53.

Before being sent off, Dallaire and Beardsley were clearly notified that if they were to recommend a U.N. mission it would be subject to strict limitations. It was to be a low-budget operation; the mission had to be "small, cheap and fast."[4] The common request from the Rwandan government and the RPF was a mission of 4,260 troops.[5] However, Dallaire and Beardsley knew beforehand that the chance of getting this many troops was extremely low.[6] Before leaving, General Dallaire was told, "don't bring in a request for anything more than 2,500, it won't be approved." Years later, Beardsley said "it was a situation called situating the estimate; you make the plan before you do the plan."[7]

The technical mission gave Dallaire and Beardsley a clear picture of the two military sides. Regarding the Rwandan Government Forces (FAR), Habyarimana's national army, they noticed a difference between the Presidential Guard and the Commandos, on the one hand and the recruited units, on the other. The Presidential Guard and the Commandos were proud and committed, whereas the recruited troops lacked such motivation and pride. The army of the RPF, the Rwandan Patriotic Army (RPA), was disciplined and well structured. The soldiers were well led, well trained and very motivated. The officers, though very young, knew how to handle their troops. The reconnaissance mission observed that the lack of logistical support was the RPF's only limitation.[8] The division in the number of troops was estimated to be 40,000 FAR troops to 15,000 of the RPF.[9]

Dallaire deeply regretted that it was only on the very last day of the reconnaissance mission that he was finally able to meet with President Habyarimana. This lack of interest alarmed Dallaire.[10] Dallaire had extensive consultations with the German, Belgian, American and French diplomats, all arguing that the

---

4 Interview with B. Beardsley, June 6, 2005; Frontline interview with Dallaire, Autumn 2003; Dallaire, pp. 55–56.

5 United Nations, Report of the Independent Inquiry into the Actions of the United Nations during the 1994 Genocide in Rwanda, December 15, 1999, Ingvar Carlsson, Han, Sung-Joo, Rufus, M. Kupolati, U.N. Doc. S/1999/1257, p. 7 (hereinafter Carlsson Report, S/1999/1257).

6 Interview with B. Beardsley, June 6, 2005.

7 *Id.*; Frontline interview with Beardsley, November 15, 2003; Dallaire, p. 56.

8 Frontline interview with Dallaire, Autumn 2003.

9 Filip Reyntjens, L'Afrique des Grands Lacs, en crise: Rwanda, Burundi: 1988–1994, p. 255 (1994) (hereinafter Reyntjens); Gerard Prunier, The Rwanda Crisis: History of a Genocide (1959–1994), p. 193 (1995) (hereinafter Prunier).

According to Prunier both were low. The Secretary-General wrote in his report that the Rwandan government had declared that it had a force of an effective strength of 23,100 personnel deployed largely in the northern part of the country and in the Kigali area, and that the RPF had declared itself to have a force of a strength of approximately 20,000 personnel. The Secretary-General reported furthermore that the *Gendarmerie* was made up of 6,000 personnel. See U.N. Doc. S/26488, paragraph 27, p. 6.

10 Dallaire, pp. 76–77; Frontline interview with Dallaire, Autumn 2003.

United Nations had to get on the ground as soon as possible, but none of them gave an in-depth analysis of the current situation. Nor did any of them come forward with troops; on the contrary most of them worried about the potential size and costs.[11] When Dallaire left Rwanda after 12 days, he was sure that Rwanda needed a peace-keeping mission, and due to the political uncertainty, the mission had to get on the ground as soon as possible.[12] There was no question that the mission would be a classic peace-keeping mission under the so-called Chapter VI 1/2 of the U.N. Charter. A peace-keeping mission is, for the diplomatic ends of Chapter VI, a pacific settlement with military means of soldiers with a limited mandate of impartiality, based on consensus of the parties concerned and the use of force only for self-defense. The alternative was a mission under Chapter VII, but Dallaire knew that no nation in the Security Council would be prepared to make such a mandatory decision for an enforcement mission.[13] Dallaire: "If I had suggested a Chapter VII mission I would have been on a one way flight back to Ottawa (Dallaire's hometown). Chapter VI was the only option we had."[14] As we have seen in Section 4.5.1, it was for this reason that Dallaire would add paragraph 17 to his ROE; a paragraph that widened his scope to use military force. According to Dallaire, by introducing this paragraph they "were breaking new ground."[15]

As explained above, before the start of the reconnaissance mission, Dallaire was told that only a small mission would be accepted; the Western diplomats he met during his technical mission confirmed this presumption. The decisive restriction on the size of the mission was "money." The American Congress was highly concerned about the mounting American share of peace-keeping costs. From 1992 to 1993 the costs had increased by 370 percent.[16] Thus, the American position was that the job should be done with a minimal force.[17] The first proposal of the U.S. delegation to the United Nations was to send a mission of 500

---

11 Dallaire, p. 62.

12 Dallaire, pp. 77–83.

13 Chapter VII means in imposing mandatory decisions with economic (Article 41) or military means (Article 42).

14 Dallaire, p. 72.

15 Dallaire, pp. 71–72. For an overview of the Mandate provided for in the Arusha Accords, the Mandate in the final U.N. resolution and the ROE, see Chapter 4.

16 The increased activities of U.N. peace-keeping forces after the end of the Cold War had led to a dramatic increase in U.S. contributions, from U.S. $29–47 million in 1985–89, to U.S. $460.4 million in 1993. Under later adopted PDD 25, the costs of all Chapter VII operations plus those in which U.S. troops were involved would be charged to the Pentagon's budget; see Howard Adelman and Astri Suhrke, Early warning and conflict management genocide in Rwanda, p. 25 (1995) (hereinafter Adelman); Jeremy Rosner, The New Tug-of-War. Congress, the Executive Branch and National Security. pp. 65–91 (1995) (hereinafter Rosner); Dallaire, pp. 84–90.

17 Dallaire, p. 84.

troops to Rwanda, because "of the expected easiness of the operation."[18] France was also of the opinion that a small force would be sufficient and proposed a mission of 1,000 troops.[19] In the opinion of Beardsley, there was no will for this mission. Two previous reconnaissance missions had been done, one led by Colonel Ross from Canada, who estimated a requirement of 8,000 troops, and another led by Maurice Baril, the Candian Military Adviser to the Secretary-General, who recommended a force of 5,000.[20] When Beardsley and Dallaire were sent on a reconnaissance mission, they "were told beforehand not to request more than 2,500, because otherwise it will not be approved. We were constantly told: keep it small, keep it cheap and keep it fast."[21]

Back in New York, the report of the reconnaissance mission was first interpreted and modified by the Department of Peace Keeping Operations (DPKO) and then by the Secretary-General into a version that would be presented on September 24 to the Security Council.

With the knowledge that only a small mission would be approved, Dallaire and Beardsley proposed a maximum force of 4,500 troops and added that they were willing to do the job with a minimum viable force of 2,500. In the words of Beardsley, "when we did an honest evaluation in Rwanda we came up with 5,500 troops, but we knew only 2,500 would be approved by the Security Council."[22]

In his report to the Council, the Secretary-General recommended a force of only 2,548 troops. According to Adelman, with this low number of troops, the Secretariat was already anticipating that this was the maximum number of troops that the Security Council would approve.[23] Ever since, Dallaire is haunted by the questions: "Did I compromise too much?" "Did I want the mission so badly that I took an unacceptable risk?"[24] Years later he said that if he had known about the previously published human rights reports, he would have insisted on a larger force.[25]

Eleven days later, on October 5, 1993, the Security Council unanimously adopted Resolution 872 by which UNAMIR was established.[26] As already described in Chapter 4, there was an important difference between the proposal

---

18 Dallaire, p. 84; Adelman, p. 25.

19 Adelman, p. 25.

20 Interview with B. Beardsley, June 6, 2005.

21 *Id.*

22 *Id.*; Carlsson Report, S/1999/1257, p. 32; Adelman, p. 25.

23 U.N. Doc. S/26488, paragraph 41, p. 9; Adelman, p. 25.

24 Dallaire, p. 82.

25 Scott Straus, Remember Rwanda, Dallaire pleads "Absolutely unacceptable to forget slaughter of 800,000 people," *Globe and Mail*, Toronto, February 27, 1998.

26 U.N. Doc. S/RES/872 (1993). The Council's resolution was adopted two days after the Battle of Mogadishu (Battle of the Black Sea), which was fought between forces of the United States against Somalian guerilla fighters on October 3, 1993, in the Black Sea district of Mogadishu, Somalia.

of the Secretary-General and the final Security Council resolution, which defined the UNAMIR mandate.[27] The most important difference concerned UNAMIR's competence to search for arms. In compliance with the Arusha Agreement, the Secretary-General had proposed that UNAMIR "would assist in the recovery of arms," but this element was absent in the final U.N. resolution. The resolution stated instead that UNAMIR would "contribute to the security of the city of Kigali inter alia within a weapons-secure area established by the parties in and around the city."[28] This difference was to have grave consequences for the fulfillment of the mission when UNAMIR soldiers were explicitly prohibited by New York to clear the arm stocks.

Following the Security Council resolution, Dallaire was appointed as the Force Commander of UNAMIR on October 18. He was known as a principled soldier and a dynamic and charismatic commander. Most importantly, he was experienced in U.N. missions. He had been a brigade commander in Cambodia and Bosnia.[29]

5.2 BELGIAN PARTICIPATION

5.2.1 The Only Western Country Willing to Participate

Despite the fact that it was going to be a small mission of only 2,548 troops, there was doubt over where these troops would be coming from. Belgium was the only Western state that offered to provide troops. However, as it is U.N. doctrine that former colonial powers do not participate in peace-keeping missions to the respective countries, the Belgian offer was seen "a mixed blessing."[30] Another Western state that offered to provide troops was France, but their offer was immediately declined because the RPF was strictly opposed.[31]

Dallaire wondered why no other Western countries stepped forward to offer troops. Dallaire: "this was supposed to be a straight-forward little Chapter VI mission." Dallaire was told that the countries were "peacekeepinged out"; however, at the same time, troops were being sent off to Somalia and the Balkans.[32] During his reconnaissance mission, Dallaire had heard other reasons from the

---

27 For an overview of the differences between the Mandate as set out in the Arusha Agreement, in SC Resolution 872, in the rules of engagement developed by Dallaire and in the Operational Procedures, see Chapter 4.

28 U.N. Doc. S/26488; U.N. Doc. S/RES/872.

29 He was appionted as Force Commander on October 18, and on January 1, 1994, he was promoted to Major-General.

30 Interview with B. Beardsley, June 6, 2005; Dallaire, p. 89; Prunier, p. 194; Melvern, 2000 p. 82.

31 Melvern, 2000 p. 82.

32 Dallaire, p. 89.

Western diplomats: "Rwanda was on nobody's radar as a place of strategic interest." Furthermore, Dallaire suspected that "powerful nations" like France, the United Kingdom, China, Russia and the United States had a far better idea of the "threats of the successes of Arusha" than the rest of the countries.[33]

5.2.2 Belgium Explicitly Requested by the United Nations to Participate

Dallaire writes that "despite continued efforts of DPKO, out of all developed nations, only the Belgians still wanted to sign up," hereby suggesting that DPKO tried everything to find a substitute for the Belgian participation and was left with no choice but to accept its offer.[34] But is this true? Did DPKO consider the Belgian participation as the only plausible option?

As early as August 1993, even before the adoption of the Security Council resolution on the establishment of UNAMIR, the U.N. Secretariat asked Belgium to offer troops. Claes, the former Belgian Minister of Foreign Affairs stated:

> The participation of Belgium was a direct result of an explicit request of the Secretary General himself. Ghali contacted me about it personally during a Yugoslavia conference in London. He told me "look, I am of the opinion that you with your Africa experience, a small country that cannot be suspected of any imperialistic aims, could participate."[35]

Claes' words are confirmed by the testimonies given before the Belgian Senate. Delcroix, the former Belgian Minister of Defense, told the Senate that he had already been informed of the informal request from the Secretariat by the second half of August 1993. Delcroix explained that he was informed of this request by the Belgian Ministry of Foreign Affairs.[36] The Prime Minister Dehaene also told the Senate that the first contacts between the Secretary-General and the Belgian Minister of Foreign Affairs concerning the Belgian participation were made in August 1993.[37]

From the investigation of the Senate, it has become clear that Belgium received an official informal request from the United Nations to participate in

---

33 Dallaire, pp. 89, 90.

34 Interview with B. Beardsley, June 6, 2005; Dallaire, p. 89; Prunier, p. 194; Melvern, 2000 p. 82.

35 Interview with W. Claes, January 13, 2006.

36 Sénat de Belgique, Commission d'Enquête parlementaire concernant les événements au Rwanda, Sénat de Belgique, session de 1997–1998, 6 décembre 1997, Rapport fait au nom de la commission d'enquête par MM Mahoux et Verhofstadt, p. 176 (hereinafter Belgian Senate); Hearing Delcroix, p. 96, BV, BCR, March 5, 1997.

37 Belgian Senate, p. 176; Hearing Dehaene, p. 103, BV, BCR, March 5, 1997.

UNAMIR on September 8, 1993.[38] Before the Senate Cools, the Belgian primary secretary of the permanent representation to the United Nations declared that Belgium was the first country to be asked. The Senate concluded that Belgium was recommended to be the Western provider of troops because of its traditional bond with Rwanda, the positive achievements of Belgium in previous peace-keeping missions and because both the RPF and the Rwandan government had insisted hereon.[39] Colonel Engelen told the Senate: "To my knowledge, the initiative to send Belgian paras was definitely coming from the U.N. Major Martin has informed me personally. He told me that Belgium received the absolute priority because it was the only country upon which everybody agreed." Engelen added that the request was "informal but powerful."[40]

In the interview with Claes, he explained that the Belgian history with Rwanda and the financial aspects of a Belgian participation caused a certain hesitance towards Boutros-Ghali's request; nevertheless Claes assured Boutros-Ghali that he would discuss the issue in the Belgian Cabinet.[41] As promised, on September 10 Claes informed the Council of Ministers of the U.N. request to send 800 Belgian troops to Rwanda. During a debate one week later, it was decided that "in principle," Belgium could participate in the mission.[42] Three days after Resolution 872 was adopted, the Belgian Council of Ministers officially decided to deliver troops. The decision was announced informally to the U.N. Secretariat in order to secure a formal request from the United Nations to Belgium to participate in the mission. Thus, on October 14, the United Nations then made its official formal request to the Belgian government to deliver 800 troops.[43] The Belgian Council of Ministers decided furthermore to send a Belgian reconnaissance mission to Rwanda.[44] The mission took place from October 25–31.[45] It was on November 19 that the Council of Ministers officially decided to send 370 troops to Rwanda, which could expand to a maximum of 450.[46] According to the Belgian Ad Hoc group, the Belgian decision to contribute to UNAMIR was not unexpected. During the peace negotiations Belgium had advocated the deployment of an international power to implement the Arusha Accords. Hence, when the Arusha Accords included the deployment of a "neutral international force," Belgium was willing to help implement the Arusha Accords by participating in this mission.[47] Another reason for Belgium to par-

---

38 Belgian Senate, p. 176.

39 *Id.*; Hearing Cools, BV, BCR, February 28, 1997, p. 47.

40 Belgian Senate, p. 176; Hearing Engelen, BV, BCR, April 16, 1997, p. 287.

41 Interview with W. Claes, January 13, 2006.

42 *Id.*; Belgian Senate, p. 177.

43 Belgian Senate, p. 179.

44 Belgian Senate, pp. 178, 179.

45 Belgian Senate, p. 180.

46 Belgian Senate, pp. 182, 183.

47 On April 7, 1994, just after the death of the ten Belgians, the Prime Minister

ticipate was the fact that Belgium's participation would have a "reassuring effect" on the Belgian expatriates in Rwanda.[48] In our interview with Claes, he denied that this had played any role in the Belgian decision-making process.[49] Furthermore, General-Lieutenant Charlier argued in a note sent to the Minister of Defense on October 15 that the Belgian participation in UNAMIR would be a reason to refuse the request to prolong the presence of the Belgian troops in Somalia.[50] Charlier's statement was confirmed by Dehaene. When the Belgian Senate asked Dehaene about the elements that had played a role in the decision-making process on the Belgian participation in Rwanda, he confirmed that the presence in Somalia had to be ended.[51]

In short, Belgium was deliberately selected by the United Nations from the beginning to participate. Belgium made no pre-conditions for its participation.

5.2.3 Belgian Awareness of the Danger of Participating in UNAMIR

When asked whether the anti-Belgian feelings were already present before November 19, the date when the Council of Ministers decided to send troops to Rwanda, Claes told us that they were not: "At that moment? Absolutely not. Rumours had been heard . . . that the President and the people close to him were not very enthusiastic . . . about the Belgian participation. A check was done which proved the opposite; the President himself said, you are welcome. That is the principle on which we started."[52]

Nevertheless we have discovered that before November 19, some telexes had already been sent between the Belgian Ministry of Foreign Affairs, the

---

confirmed once more that the implementation of the Arusha Accords was the most important reason for Belgium to contribute to the mission. Parliamentary Proceedings of the Belgian Senate, Meeting of 22 April 1994. Sénat de Belgique, Commission d'Enquête parlementaire concernant les événements au Rwanda, (Commission of parliamentary enquiry concerning the events in Rwanda), session de 1997–1998, 6 décembre 1997, Rapport fait au nom de la commission d'enquête par MM Mahoux et Verhofstadt, Annexes, p. 15 (hereinafter Annex Belgian Senate). On September 29 Claes sent a letter to the American Minister of Foreign Affairs asking for a quick deployment of this neutral force. According to the Ad Hoc group it was the Somalia debacle that caused the Americans to have doubts about a new peace-keeping mission in Africa. Annex Belgian Senate, p. 15.

[48] Additional information note of September 28, 1993, from the Belgian Intelligence Service (SGR), documents SGR No. 7140 and further; Annex Belgian Senate, p. 15.

[49] Interview with W. Claes, January 13, 2006.

[50] Belgian Senate, p. 179; Annex Belgian Senate, pp. 14, 15.

[51] Belgian Senate, p. 179: Note 4; Hearing Dehaene, BV, BCR, Senaat, March 5, 1997, p. 103.

[52] Interview with W. Claes, January 13, 2006.

Ministry of Defense and the Belgian embassy in Kigali that spoke about the anti-Belgian climate in Rwanda.[53] On November 5 the Belgian embassy informed the Ministry of Foreign Affairs by fax of the reservations of the MRND to the Belgian participation.[54] Exactly one week later, on November 12, the embassy gave a detailed description of the anti-Belgian climate within the CDR, the MRND and certain parts of the MRD.[55] That same day, the embassy informed the Ministry of a letter that was sent to the U.N. Secretary-General. The letter, which was not signed, had the title: "No Belgian troops in Rwanda." In this letter, the Belgian participation was heavily criticized.[56]

A week before the Council of Ministers would decide upon the Belgian participation, a limited committee of ministers came together to discuss the issue. In preparation for this meeting, the committee received different documents of the Ministry of Defense, some of them dealing with the risks of the Belgian participation.[57] The report of the Belgian reconnaissance mission noted in November 1993 that they became aware of actions by Hutu extremist movements against the participation of Belgium in UNAMIR. These extremists made

---

53 According to the Ad Hoc group, it was during the decision-making process, specifically between the signature of the Arusha Accords on August 4 and the Belgian decision to participate in UNAMIR on November 19, that the anti-Belgian climate developed. Besides that, the Ad Hoc group stated that the anti-Belgian climate was not completely new: in February 1993 two Belgian diplomats in Kigali were threatened and when RTLMC was founded in April 1993, anti-Belgian propaganda started not long afterwards. At the end of September, the Belgian embassy was still positive about the Rwandan response to Belgium's participation. On September 27, the embassy sent a telex to the Ministry of Foreign Affairs emphasizing the credits that Belgium would have in Rwanda. The telex stated: "The Belgian participation, it states here, is wished for unanimously by the Rwandan regime and the population" (Translated from French into English, original text: "La participation Belge, y déclarait-on, est souhaitée unanimement par le régime Rwandais et par la population.") Telex No. 975, September 27, 1993, from the Belgian embassy in Kigali to the Ministry of Foreign Affairs in Brussels. Annex Belgian Senate, pp. 15–16.

At the end of October the Belgian embassy reported to the Ministry of Foreign Affairs in Brussels that Belgian school children had been harassed. Telex No. 1057, October 22, 1993, from the Belgian embassy in Kigali to the Ministry of Foreign Affairs in Brussels. Annex Belgian Senate, pp. 15–16.

54 Telex No. 1106, November 5, 1993, from the Belgian embassy in Kigali to the Ministry of Foreign Affairs in Brussels. Annex Belgian Senate, pp. 16–17.

55 Telex No. 1128, November 12, 1993, from the Belgian embassy in Kigali to the Ministry of Foreign Affairs in Brussels. Annex Belgian Senate, p.17.

56 From whom the letter came is unknown. Fax No. 259, November 12 from the Belgian embassy in Kigali to the Ministry of Foreign Affairs in Brussels. Annex Belgian Senate, p.17. Translated from French into English. Original title: "Pas de troupes Belges au Rwanda."

57 Annex Belgian Senate, p.17

use of the press and at least one independent radio station.[58] A telex from the reconnaissance mission to Evere, Belgium, home of the Operation Center of the Belgian Army, stated: "We are waiting for the five days following the demonstrations directed . . . against the participation of Belgium in UNAMIR."[59] Another note spoke about expected "provocation by extremist Hutu movements."[60] One of these examples is the following cartoon of December 1993.[61]

[58] JSO-P033578, see also Evere No. 21634. Annex Belgian Senate, p. 17. Translated from French into English. Original text: "Il est fait état d'actions de mouvements extrémistes HUTU, notamment contre la participation de la BELGIQUE à l'UNAMIR. . . . Ces mouvements disposent d'organes de presse et d'au moins une radio libre."

[59] JSO-P033578; see also Evere No. 21634. Annex Belgian Senate, p. 17. Translated from French into English. Original text: "Nous attendons pour les cinq jours qui viennent des manifestations dirigées . . . contre la participation de la Belgique à l'UNAMIR."

[60] File of November 10, 1993, sent from the General staff to the Ministry of Defense for a limited minister committee (JSO-P 033578). Annex Belgian Senate, p. 17. Translated from French into English, original text: "Provocations de la part des mouvements extrémistes hutus."

[61] This cartoon of Belgian soldiers with Tutsi women was published in the mag-

On November 12 Belgian Ambassador Johan Swinnen informed his Ministry of a meeting with President Habyarimana about the anti-Belgian climate. During the meeting, Habyarimana argued that the MRND was not against the Belgian participation but that he and the MRND advocated a more balanced composition. The President opted for a French participation. Furthermore, he mentioned that the average Rwandan still had some "bad memories" about the Belgian policy in 1990.[62] A briefing sent from the Belgian general intelligence service to Evere on November 18 gave a summary of the views of the different Rwandan political parties and Habyarimana on the Belgian participation in UANMIR.[63] According to the briefing, the MRND resisted the Belgian participation, because it suspected Belgium of being biased and pro-RPF. The main reason for this opinion was the Belgian refusal to deliver weapons in 1990.

On November 19, the day that the Belgian Council of Ministers decided to send troops to Rwanda, Claes sent a cable to Swinnen. According to the Ad Hoc group, Claes' words showed that he was aware of the continuing anti-Belgian atmosphere and the danger it could create for the Belgian peace-keepers. Claes added that the anti-Belgian climate should end: "I therefore ask you to intervene without delay with the authorities . . . so that they may prohibit any provocative speech by any of the parties. As far as we are concerned, this is vital for our compatriot blue-helmets."[64]

The foregoing shows that, when deciding to participate in UNAMIR, Belgium was aware of opposing opinions within the different political parties as to the Belgian participation.

5.3 COMPOSITION OF THE PEACE-KEEPING FORCE AND ITS RESOURCES

Being the only Western provider of troops, the Belgian contingent was assumed to be the best-trained, best-equipped and best-disciplined one. They were indeed the best-trained and best-equipped troops, but they were far from

---

azine *Power* in December, 1993 (No. 2, p. 12), *available at* http://www.onemancult.com/rwanda/rwandaprop6.html.

62 With 1990, Habyarimana meant the moment that the fighting between the FAR and the FPR started. The Belgians left Rwanda and refused to deliver the planned weapons. Annex Belgian Senate, p. 18.

63 Documents of the Belgian Intelligence Service No. 7260. The summary is based on the aforementioned telexes, 1106, 1126, 1128, 1130 and 1135. Annex Belgian Senate, p. 19.

64 Annex Belgian Senate, p. 19. No cable-number mentioned in the Annex of the Belgian Senate. Translated from French into English. Original text: "Je vous prie dès lors d'intervenir sans délai auprès des autorités . . . pour qu'elles fassent interdire tout discours provocateur des partis quels qu'ils soient. En ce qui nous concerne, cela est capital pour nos compatriotes casques bleus."

the best-disciplined ones. Many of the Belgian soldiers came straight from Somalia where they had completed a Chapter VII mission. They brought a very aggressive attitude, which would cause many problems to the mission.[65] Apart from Belgium, other states, such as Bangladesh, Ghana, and Tunisia, also contributed with peace-keepers. The 900 Bangladeshi troops, including soldiers, medical personnel, logisticians and military police, were poorly trained, had little to no experience and had nothing but their personal weapons and kit.[66] The 800 Ghanaian troops were very well trained and disciplined, but they also lacked equipment; they arrived without a single vehicle.[67] For the organization and composition of UNAMIR, see Annex 2.

The first troops arrived in November 1993 and, by the end of December, nearly 1,300 peace-keepers were deployed. The so-called "phase two deployment of peacekeepers" took place in the beginning of 1994 when another 1,000 blue helmets came to reinforce the mission. This reinforcement brought UNAMIR to the mandated 2,548 in February 1994.[68]

As soon as the first troops arrived, it became even more evident that Rwanda was only of minor interest to the super-powers in the Security Council. The mission was haunted by endless administrative and resource problems. It never received the equipment that was authorized, and its budget was, like any U.N. mission, subjected to the lengthy U.N. decision-making process and was only formally approved on April 4, 1994.[69] This resulted in numerous shortcomings in personnel, equipment and ammunition.[70] There should have been 22 armored

---

65 The first Belgian contingent was everything but disciplined and would have to be displaced by another. This second Belgian battalion, which replaced the first Belgian battalion, was very motivated, disciplined and well-trained. Dallaire, pp. 84, 106, 113; Interview with B. Beardsley, June 6, 2005.

66 United Nations, The United Nations and Rwanda, 1993–1996, p. 28 (1996) (hereinafter U.N., the United Nations and Rwanda); Dallaire, p. 124. As soon as the Bangladeshi and Belgian troops were established in Kigali, the 600 to 700 French troops withdrew, by which Operation Noroit was ended. The first objective of UNAMIR was to move the RPF battalion into Kigali, to counter-balance the Rwandan Army. Furthermore, some RPF civilian leaders were escorted to Kigali. The RPF contingent was quartered at the imposing national parliament building. As Alison des Forges said, "a reasonable choice . . . but it underlined how much the old regime had lost to the newcomers." Alison Des Forges, Leave None to Tell the Story, Genocide in Rwanda, p. 141 (1999) (hereinafter Des Forges).

67 Melvern, 2000 p. 86.

68 SC Resolution 872, U.N. Doc. S/RES/872 and the report of the Secretary-General, U.N. Doc. S/26488, provided for the "phased deployment of UNAMIR." *See* U.N. Doc. S/26488, point 40, p. 8. The Ghanaians were part of this second phase and arrived in February 1994. U.N., the United Nations and Rwanda, p. 28; Melvern, 2000 p. 89.

69 Adelman p. 26; Melvern, 2000 p. 85.

70 *Id.*

personnel carriers (APCs) and eight military helicopters to provide for the "quick reaction capability." However, none of these eight military helicopters ever arrived, and it was only in March 1994 that eight APCs arrived, of which only five were useful.[71] With only a small civilian police unit and the lack of a human rights cell, the mission was unable to investigate violent incidents happening throughout the country. For the first months, most of Dallaire's time was spent on administrative and logistical matters. In the words of Dallaire: "I spent most of my time fighting the heavy mechanical U.N. system with all its stupidity . . . we would order torches, and after a long delay they would arrive without batteries . . . seeing to the most immediate needs stopped us from seeing what was reserved for us in the future."[72]

5.3.1 No U.N. Intelligence Unit

One of the gravest deficiencies was the lack of an intelligence cell that gathered information about the political and military developments. Dallaire deplored this shortcoming to U.N. headquarters and requested provision of an intelligence unit, but his requests were denied. According to U.N. headquarters, such an "intelligence-gathering capability" was contrary to peace-keeping policy.[73] He forwarded this view to Luc Marchal, who asked Dallaire any intelligence function.[74] Because Dallaire's information was far too limited, he circumvented U.N. headquarters and appealed directly to the Belgian Military Intelligence, the so-called Service Général Renseignement de l'Armée (SGR), resulting in the creation of a "two-person cell" that reported to UNAMIR headquarters and to the Belgian military headquarters in Evere. Eventually the cell had five informants who were paid a small amount for their information. The cell was run by lieutenant Mark Nees who belonged to KIBAT, the Belgian-commanded peace-keeping force of UNAMIR. Dallaire thus gathered his intelligence through the Belgian military information office, which produced "daily situation reports" that were sent to him and to New York.

---

71 *Id.*

72 Jaques Castonguay, Les Casques Bleu au Rwanda, p. 141 (1998). Translated from French into English. Original text: "J'ai passé la plus grande partie de mon temps à combattre la mécanique lourde de l'ONU avec ses stupidités . . . On commandait des lampes de poche, par exemple, et après long délai on les recevait mais sans batteries . . . Les besoins immédiats nous empêchaient de voir ce que nous réservait l'avenir."

73 Melvern, 2000 p. 91.

74 Luc Marchal, Aan de poorten van de Rwandese hel: getuigenis van een peacekeeper, pp. 141–142 (2001).

5.4 CONCLUDING OBSERVATIONS

The installed peace-keeping mission was, in all aspects, too weak. The Rwandan parties concerned requested 4,260 troops, and the U.N. specialists agreed that at least at 5,000 were needed, yet only troops of 2,500 were authorized by the Security Council. These soldiers were very badly equipped, and only the Belgians were well trained and had good equipment available. However, the Belgians, because of their colonial history and the bad behavior of the Belgian soldiers, were hated among the population. In this way, getting rid of the peace-keepers was therefore facilitated by the *genocidaires*.

CHAPTER 6

EARLY WARNING OF ATROCITIES IN 1991–1994

6.1 HUTU EXTREMISM EMERGES

Strengthened by the RPF invasion, opponents of Habyarimana's regime started to pressure the regime to allow new political parties into the system. Through this pressure and pressure from donor countries, it was in June 1991 that Habyarimana legalized the political parties.[1] Within just a few months, there were 15 parties competing with Habyarimana's Mouvement Révolutionaire National pour le Développement (MRND). The most threatening party was the Mouvement Démocratique Républicain (MDR). The MDR was the successor of MDR-Parmehutu, the party of Rwanda's first President Kayibanda. Half of the MDR members originated from Kayibanda's traditional stronghold, Gitarama and Ruhengeri. Some MDR members were former members of the MRND, had personal fights with Habyarimana and wanted to oust the party.[2]

Other smaller parties that came into existence and would play a role in the immediate future were the so-called intellectuals' party, the Parti Social Démocrate (PSD), with some popularity in the south, the Parti Libéral (PL), which enjoyed some support from business people, and consequently from the Tutsi group, and the Parti Démocrate Chrétien (PDC).

The opposition wanted Habyarimana to accept a coalition in which they would share power, and in April 1992 Habyarimana had to accept such a coalition. Except for the very small parties, all parties were represented. Habyarimana kept his position as President, and nine out of 19 Ministers stayed with the MRND, but the position of Prime Minister went to the MDR.[3]

---

1 Linda Melvern, A People Betrayed. The Role of the West in Rwanda's Genocide, p. 36 (2000) (hereinafter Melvern, 2000); Linda Melvern, Conspiracy to Murder. The Rwandan Genocide, p. 23 (2004) (hereinafter Melvern, 2004); Gerard Prunier, The Rwanda Crisis: History of a Genocide (1959–1994), pp. 121–126 (1995) (hereinafter Prunier).

2 Filip Reyntjens, L'Afrique des Grands Lacs, en crise: Rwanda, Burundi: 1988–1994, p. 106 (1994) (hereinafter Reyntjens); Melvern, 2004 p. 23; Prunier, p. 124.

3 Agathe Uwilingiyimana, member of the MDR, got the position as minister of primary and secondary education. She immediately abolished the quota system; access

The share in power with opposition parties reinforced the Hutu extremism, which was shown in the creation of the radical Hutu racist party, the Coalition pour la Défense de la République (CDR). The party stated that "no party, no institution, no person had been able to defend the interests of the majority [the Hutu] publicly and consistently" and therefore they had to take their fate into their own hands.[4] The CDR criticized the MRND and Habyarimana himself for being too soft towards the RPF and the opposition parties. In the following cartoon President Habyarimana is depicted in native garb dancing and announcing an extract from one of his speeches to the MRND Congress: "I am the invincible one who vanquished the rebels and the traitors. WEEEEEEEEE." The Congress responds, "Bravo, Bravo." A common Rwandan radio listener listens to the broadcast of Habyarimana and is skeptical, saying, "This man is really exceeding his limits. While the population is being decimated by mines, he is making a self-applauding speech."[5]

But despite the harsh criticism, the CDR and the MRND often collaborated. According to Des Forges, some observers have concluded that this racist anti-Tutsi party—CDR—existed merely to announce the views that were held

to higher education would be decided on merit alone. As a result, armed men beat her up in her home. Thousands of students and mothers demonstrated in support of her new policy. On April 7, 1994, Rwandan army soldiers killed her. See Reyntjens, pp. 115–116.

4 Reyntjens, p. 127.

5 See http://www.onemancult.com/rwanda; This cartoon was published in the newspaper *Le Soleil* on May 12, 1992.

by the MRND but too radical for them to proclaim openly. This new party, which was established one month after the creation of the coalition government, was not represented in the coalition.[6] However, their influence was nevertheless felt, as the authorities took heed of their extremist views out of fear of losing power to new opposition parties. The major influential and, in particular, most extreme racist political party in the government, the MRND, hindered public meetings of other political parties and accepted that its own members were engaged in disrupting demonstrations. The party not only tolerated but even encouraged the MRND supporters assaulting members of the opposition and burning down and plundering their houses.[7]

As shown above, the emerging violence was not only against members of the political opposition, but there was also growing evidence of Hutu extremism against the Tutsi minority. The human rights violations ranged from hate propaganda to discrimination, violence and killings of Tutsi and moderate Hutu. The MRND developed their youth group, known as the Interahamwe, into a real militia.[8] Members received military training, initially to handle weapons, but soon they were also taught to kill. This was all made possible by the import of arms in this period. For instance, the official French arms exports in the period between 1990 and 1994 was 137 million French francs, the licenses for these exports were obtained from the Ministry of Defense.[9] It has been estimated that France sent for $6 million in 1991–1992 and for $4 million in 1993, besides an arms deal with a French company of $12 million took place in May 1993, but these arms never arrived, according to Melvern.[10]

6.1.1 *Military Attacks in 1991–1993*

In January 1991, as a reprisal for the RPF attack on the prison, killings started in the Northwestern part of Rwanda and spread throughout the region. According to Prunier, the systematic killings stopped in mid-March, but sporadic killings continued until June 1991. Between 300 and 1,000 people were killed.[11] In November 1991 the Interahamwe was engaged in Tutsi killings in

---

6 Alison Des Forges, Leave None to Tell the Story, Genocide in Rwanda, p. 53 (1999) (hereinafter Des Forges); Prunier, p. 128; Melvern, 2004 pp. 51, 52.

7 Des Forges, p. 55; Prunier, pp. 121–126.

8 During 1992 and 1993, attacks by Interahamwe took some 200 lives and injured scores of people in different communities. See Human Rights Watch, Beyond the Rhetoric: Continuing Human Rights Abuses in Rwanda, pp. 6–10 (1993) (hereinafter HRW, 1993).

9 Assemblée Nationale du France, Rapport d'information, Mission d'information sur le Rwanda, No. 1271, December 15, 1998, p. 180.

10 Melvern, 2004 pp. 58–59.

11 Prunier, p. 136.

Muambi, which is positioned east of Kigali.[12] Moreover, numerous houses were looted and destroyed, and livestock was stolen. Bugesara, a region in the Southeast of Rwanda with a high Tutsi population, was subjected to massacres several times. First, in October 1991, 28 Tutsi men were taken; eight of them never returned. In February 1992 another five civilians were taken, returning only after pressure from human rights organizations.[13] In March 1992 Bugesara was subjected to the most violent massacre, in which the Interahamwe, local authorities and armed forces were engaged.[14]

On March 3 a news item on Radio Rwanda spoke of the Tutsi planning to kill the Hutu. The local authorities were called upon to "clear the bush," so to kill the Tutsi. The following day, killings started and subsequently 300 people were murdered and some 1,500 Tutsi fled.[15]

6.1.2 Reaction by Bystander States in Spring 1992

The massacre was acknowledged by foreign diplomats, and they began to act. Canadian and U.S. ambassadors went to Habyarimana to express their concern. George Martres, the French ambassador, refused to join them. Habyarimana trivialized the killings as self-defense. The Belgian ambassador to Rwanda, Johan Swinnen, got in contact with Brussels and stated that the Interahamwe had taken part in carefully planned killings in Bugesara.[16] Three months later, on June 4, 1992, Michel Forte, the director of the French department of Amnesty International, said on the French radio that the people responsible for the massacres were soldiers who had been helped by the Rwandan authorities. He added that these people should be held accountable; otherwise the horrors would be repeated.[17] It is important to note that in spring 1992 the bystander-states Canada, the United States, France, Belgium and the NGO Amnesty International put the killings of the Tutsis in Rwanda on their agenda and held the Rwandan government responsible and accountable for these atrocities.

---

12 Melvern, 2004 p. 45; One person was killed, tens were wounded and hundreds displaced; André Guichaoua, (ed.), Les Crisis Politiques au Burundi et au Rwanda, p. 267 (1995).

13 Melvern, 2004 p. 26. The HRW reports do not specify which organizations, but upon reading the Amnesty International report, it appears likely that they were involved: "In May 1992 Amnesty International was still trying to ascertain the truth of government claims that the 'disappeared' had been freed and not killed." Amnesty International, Rwanda, Persecution of Tutsi minority and Repression of Government critics 1990–1992, p. 4 (1992) (hereinafter Amnesty International, 1992).

14 Melvern, 2000 p. 46; Prunier, p. 137.

15 Melvern, 2000 p. 45; Melvern, 2004 p. 27; Prunier, p. 137.

16 Melvern, 2000 p. 45; Melvern, 2004 p. 27; Prunier, p. 137.

17 Melvern, 2004 p. 27.

6.1.3 *Violence Continues During Arusha Peace Negotiations 1992–1993*

Half-way through 1992, the violence in Rwanda increased. Grenades were thrown into crowds in Kigali, there was a bomb explosion and reports of Tutsi killings outside Kigali started to come in. The country was in total chaos.[18] The Arusha Peace Accords consisted of a Peace Agreement, a Ceasefire Agreement and five additional Protocols that were progressively signed from 1992 until August 1993.[19] But Habyarimana's intentions during the peace process were anything but sincere; an attitude that is manifested in the following behavior, which we now will put forward.

This cartoon was published in the newspaper *Kamarampaka* on April 7, 1993 (No. 15, p. 14). The headline reads, The inkotanyi (RPF insurgents) have left their mark on Ruhengeri. The inscriptions on various victims read CDR, MRD and MNRD, respectively. These were the three key extremist political parties that were influential in aggrandizing power and propagating the genocide.[20]

The day after the first protocol was signed, on August 18, 1992, Habyarimana announced that he would not allow the negotiators to *"lead our*

---

18 Melvern, 2000 p. 46; Prunier, pp. 141–144.

19 See Chapter 4.

20 See http://www.onemancult.com/rwanda/rwandaprop13.html.

country into an adventure it [the country] would not like" [emphasis added].[21] Three days later, supporters of the MRND and the CDR killed dozens of Tutsi and members of the opposition.[22] The protocol on power-sharing that was signed on October 30, 1992, was denounced as a *"scrap of paper"* [emphasis added].[23] At the end of December 1992, the MRND and the CDR called the Accords *"a plan for treason"* which *"we must prepare to defeat"* [emphasis added].[24] In January 1993 the Rwandan government and the RPF agreed upon the third part of the Arusha Accords that dealt with the political arrangements for the transitional government. However, at the same time, the Secretary-General of the MRND and Habyarimana himself *"denounced the Accords again"* [emphasis added].[25] To disrupt the peace process, the MRND and the CDR massacred some 300 people living in Ruhengeri and Gisenyi in the last days of January 1993.[26]

A sudden and extremely violent attack by the RPF followed; hundreds of people were killed, and thousands of people fled the country. The executions are not very well documented; estimations of the number of killings vary between 50 and 200.[27] The RPF proceeded up to 23 kilometers from Kigali. It was France that, by sending in new troops, prevented the RPF from taking the capital. Habyarimana was so shocked by the attack that now he called for a return to the Arusha negotiations.[28] The return to the negotiation table was welcomed outside Rwanda.

6.2 REPORTS FROM DIPLOMATS TO THE OUTSIDE WORLD

As Arusha was being negotiated and the foundations for the transitional government were being laid down, the situation on the ground was characterized by grave violence. The foreign diplomats observed this violent development and reported home. A lot of information was shared between the United States, Belgium, Germany and France.[29] As will be seen below, the amount of information received by the diplomats in Kigali about the highly complex and critical situation in Rwanda increased drastically at the end of 1992 and the beginning of 1993.

---

[21] Des Forges, p. 96; Prunier, p. 16; U.N. Doc. A/48/824—S/26915, December 23, 1993, U.N. Doc. S/26488, Report of the Secretary-General on Rwanda, September 25, 1993 (hereinafter A/48/824—S/26915).

[22] Des Forges, p. 96; Prunier, p.161.

[23] Reyntjens, pp. 204–205; Prunier, pp. 162–163, 171.

[24] Des Forges, p. 96.

[25] Reyntjens, p. 205.

[26] Melvern, 2004 p. 39.

[27] Prunier, p. 175.

[28] Melvern, 2004 p. 38; Prunier, pp. 173–179.

[29] Howard Adelman and Astri Suhrke, Early warning and conflict management genocide in Rwanda, pp. 16, 27 (1995) (hereinafter Adelman).

In the years preceding the genocide, the diplomatic community in Rwanda, the officials engaged in the Arusha negotiations and the officials abroad dealing with Rwanda knew or should have known about the existence of the "Akazu," a close network of Hutu extremists that had its own death squad. The Akazu originated from the well-established Hutu family of Habyarimana's wife, Agathe Kanzinga.[30] The most important people of Akazu were Habyarimana's three brothers-in-law, Protais Zigiranyirazo, Colonel Pierre-Célestin Rwagafilitia and Séraphin Rwabukumba. The Akazu consisted of a personal network, called *"Réseau Zéro,"* and had contacts within local councils, prefectures, Rwandan embassies and with many senior civil servants and military officers.[31]

As early as 1991, an intelligence assessment, written by a French agent, identified an inner circle of power that was ruled by Agathe and her family. According to the agent, the inner circle had the objective of retaining power; any form of negotiation or attempt to impose democracy would provoke their resistance, and in their reaction they would spread fear. This analysis was sent to the various donor states.[32]

That same year, Jean-Pierre Chrétien, a French historian with expertise in the Great Lakes region of Africa, "warned" that the racist atmosphere in Rwanda had not come into existence after the RPF-invasion of 1990 but that this ideology had been there for decades. Chrétien wrote that the Rwandan import of weapons had to be stopped; otherwise the country would become a "powder keg."[33]

In the spring of 1992 Johan Swinnen, the Belgian ambassador to Rwanda, reported to his ministry in Brussels about the existence of a "secret group" that was "planning the extermination of the Tutsi."[34] According to the Belgian Senate, Swinnen sent three faxes to Brussels dealing with the existence of "this group."[35]

---

30 Prunier, p. 85. Akazu means "The little house," the word was used in pre-colonial times for the inner circles of the Royal household.

31 Melvern, 2000 pp. 42–43; Melvern, 2004 pp. 27–32.

32 Adelman, p. 16; Melvern, 2000 p. 43.

33 J.-P. Chrétien, Le défi de l'ethnisme: Rwanda et Burundi, 1990–1996, p. 136 (1997) (hereinafter Chrétien, 1997).

34 Sénat de Belgique, Commission d'Enquête parlementaire concernant les événements au Rwanda, Sénat de Belgique, session de 1997–1998, 6 décembre 1997, Rapport fait au nom de la commission d'enquête par MM Mahoux et Verhofstadt, pp. 493–495 (hereinafter Belgian Senate).

35 The Belgian Senate did not get permission to search the documents of the Belgian Ministry of Foreign Affairs from before the Arusha Accords. Nevertheless, the Senate was able to inspect several of these documents. After intervention of the Belgian Court, the Senate was allowed to do a house search at the Ministry. The Senate does not describe the content of the first two faxes. Nevertheless, the Senate noted that the first fax was titled "Subject: Disturbance in Rwanda—Actional terrorplan" and the second fax was titled "Subject conversation with X." This might also be the reason that the Senate did not see all three faxes, but only the last one. Belgian Senate, p. 493.

The third fax, titled "Subject: Rwanda—Disturbance Bugesera," was sent by Swinnen on March 27, 1992. In this fax, Swinnen explained that he had received a copy of an anonymous pamphlet with a members list of a "secret group which is planning the extermination of Tutsi of Rwanda to resolve once and for all, in their own way, the ethnic problem and the crush to internal Hutu opposition."[36] Swinnen wrote "as you see this list corresponds exactly with the names that X gave me several weeks ago, even the order of rank is identical." Swinnen added that, like Mister X, the pamphlet stated that the responsibility of Habyarimana was definite. According to Swinnen, the pamphlet pointed at the Gendarmerie-school in Ruhengeri and the MRND-militia as the executors of the "extermination plan."[37] Hence, in the beginning of 1992 ambassador Swinnen had a conversation with a certain Mr. X about the existence of a "secret group" that was planning the extermination of the Tutsi in Rwanda, and, not much later, Swinnen received an anonymous pamphlet about its existence. Mr. X and the pamphlet listed exactly the same members of this group. All alarm bells should have rung loudly after receiving this fax from the involved Belgian ambassador in particular in response to the use of the words "extermination," *"résoudre définitivement"* (final solution), "*problème ethnic*" and *"écraser l'opposition"* (trample all opposition). These wordings resemble the Nazi language of 50 years before.

The Belgian Senate notes that the Belgian government was also in possession of a document from inside the Rwandan Ministry of Defense. This document described all Tutsi in and outside Rwanda as the "principal enemy" and it described all people helping these principle enemies as "the supporters." The scope of the targeted group of enemies was thus broadened, encompassing, for instance, the moderate Hutu's and all other internal and external players, including the peace-keepers. The document was sent to "all sector commanders" in Rwanda including the staff of the *gendarmerie* on September 21, 1992.[38]

In December 1992, the Belgian Professor in African Law and politics and specialist on Rwanda, Filip Reyntjens, identified the existence of the death squad of Akazu. He and Senator Willy Kuypers gave a press conference in the Senate in Brussels arguing that the death squad had been engaged in the killings in Bugesara in March 1992[39] The information released before the Senate included the names of many Akazu members, including the three brothers of Agathe, members of the presidential guard and the head of military intelligence. Some of the names that were listed would later turn out to be the organizers of

---

36 Belgian Senate, p. 493. Translated from French into English, original text: "Etat-major secret chargé de l'extermination des Tutsis au Rwanda afin de résoudre définitivement, à leur manière, le problème ethnique au Rwanda et d'écraser l'opposition Hutue intérieure."

37 Belgian Senate, p. 494.

38 Belgian Senate, p. 495.

39 In their comments, Reyntjens and Kuypers were supported by the Belgian lawyer Johan Scheers. Des Forges, p. 44, note 16; Melvern, 2004 p. 27.

the genocide. Colonel Bagosora, for example, was mentioned by Reyntjens and would years later be convicted of crimes of genocide by the International Criminal Tribunal for Rwanda (ICTR).[40]

Christophe Mfizi, a former senior official of the MRND, sought the international press in August 1992 to draw attention to the power of Akazu in Rwanda. His open letter, describing the activities of the so-called *"Réseau Zéro,"* which was in essence the Akazu, was published in France.[41] He spoke about the infiltration of "the network into all areas of Rwandan society" and stated that the group held power by "inciting racism and regional division."[42]

Half a year later, another article dealing with the existence of Akazu was published in the French newspaper *Libération.* The journalist wrote that for the last two years, France had been supporting a regime in Rwanda that was organizing the extermination of the Tutsi minority and that death squads from a *"Réseau Zéro"* were undertaking a genocide against this minority.[43]

6.3 REPORTS FROM HUMAN RIGHTS ORGANIZATIONS

In the years before the genocide of 1994, non-governmental organizations (NGOs), like aid agencies and human rights organizations, became increasingly active in Rwanda. They reported on the massacres in different parts of the country and the involvement of the military and local officials.[44] According to Melvern, this information does not seem to have been shared with the Western diplomats negotiating Arusha.[45]

In May 1992 Amnesty International released a report dealing with the persecution of the Tutsi minority and government opponents between 1990 and 1992.[46] The report stated very clearly that the Rwandan government officials and members of the security forces were guilty of serious human rights violations mostly against the Tutsi minority. The report talked about "extrajudicial execution of more than 1,000 Tutsi since 1990, widespread torture and other forms of ill-treatment of detainees, dozens of disappearances, and the impris-

---

40 For the Bogasora judgment, see http://www.ictr.org. For more information about the Akazu Judgment, see Melvern, 2000 pp. 42–43; Melvern, 2004 pp. 27–32.

41 Reyntjens, pp. 189, 190; Melvern, 2000 p. 42, note 7; Christophe Mfizi, "Le Resau Zéro," Lettre Ouverte a Monsieur le president du Mouvement Républicain National pour la Démocrati et le Développement (MRNDD), Editions Uruhimbi, BP 1067, Kigali, Rwanda, 1992. In which paper his letter was published is unknown by the authors.

42 Melvern, 2000 pp. 42–43.

43 According to Melvern, the article was published In *Libération* on February 9, 1993. Melvern, 2000 pp. 43–44.

44 According to Melvern, in 1993 there were 39 NGO's active in Rwanda. Melvern, 2000 p. 55.

45 Melvern, 2000 p. 55.

46 Amnesty International, 1992.

onment, mostly without charge or trial, of more than 8,000 people."[47] The report added that the impunity of the perpetrators of the human rights violations "seemed to have encouraged others to carry out further abuses."[48]

In January 1993 a coalition of Rwandan human rights associations appealed to international human rights organizations to create a commission to investigate the situation in Rwanda. Ten experts from the organizations Human Rights Watch (HRW), Africa Watch, the International Federation of Human Rights, the Inter African Union of Human Rights and the International Center of Rights of the Person and of Democratic Development formed the International Commission.[49] This commission spent three weeks in Rwanda, interviewing witnesses, victims and family and collecting testimonies about the events over the preceding two years. The report was published early in 1993 and talked about government-supported massacres against the Tutsi, the killings of at least 2,000 Tutsi and the detention of more than 10,000 Tutsi and moderate Hutu. The commission argued that the highest level of authority, including President Habyarimana, was accountable for the human rights violations committed by soldiers, militia and civilians.[50]

The press release issued by the Commission at the conclusion of its visit was entitled "Genocide and War Crimes in Rwanda."[51] But subsequently, after deliberations within the commission, a more equivocal position was taken. The final report said that there were some who considered "acts of genocide" had been committed, but it did not take a firm position on this point. One of the people who was strictly opposed to using the word "genocide" was the representative of HRW. According to him, it was too stringent to argue that the events in Rwanda amounted to genocide. But William Schabas, the representative of the International Center of Rights of the Person and of Democratic Development, was convinced that what was happening in Rwanda did fulfill the criteria of Article 2 of the Genocide Convention of 1948.[52] According to him, the intent to destroy the Tutsi as a group was evident and amounted to genocide. The commission report was widely circulated, but the international attention was minimal. Only from the Belgian side was some reaction on the report shown; the

47 Amnesty International, 1992, pp. 2, 6, 7, 11.

48 Amnesty International, 1992, pp. 2, 3.

49 Federation of International des Droits de l'Homme, Report of the International Commission into Human Rights Abuse in Rwanda, p. 51 (1996) (hereinafter Fédération Internationale des Droits de l'Homme, 1996).

50 Fédération Internationale des Droits de l'Homme, 1996.

51 Adelman, p.17; Melvern, 2000 p. 56.

52 Professor Schabas was a delegate of the investigation commission; he was the representative of the International Center of Rights of the Person and of Democratic Development in Montreal, Canada. Schabas has confirmed this text in his e-mail to Fred Grünfeld on September 30, 2006.

Belgian government consulted its ambassador, Johan Swinnen, for information.[53] Bacré Waly Ndiaye, U.N. Special Rapporteur on Extrajudicial, Summary or Arbitrary Executions, referred to the commission report in his own report.

6.4 REPORT FROM THE U.N. SPECIAL RAPPORTEUR ON EXTRAJUDICIAL EXECUTIONS

Bacré Waly Ndiaye, who was the U.N. Special Rapporteur on Extrajudicial, Summary or Arbitrary Executions, talked explicitly about a "possible genocide." He conducted an investigation mission to Rwanda from April 8–17, 1993, after he was informed of allegations of violations of the right to life. Moreover, he was asked to participate in the above-mentioned NGO commission of ten experts, an invitation he could not accept because of his position as Special Rapporteur. However, as Special Rapporteur he could take the initiative to start his own enquiry in Rwanda. Because of the gravity of the situation he encountered in Rwanda, he submitted a 36-page addendum to his main report in which he gave a detailed explanation of his mission.[54]

In this addendum, the Special Rapporteur wrote that the "inter-communal violence" indicated "very clearly that the victims of the attacks, Tutsis in the overwhelming majority of cases, have been targeted solely because of their membership of a certain ethnic group, and for no other objective reason." He added that genocide might therefore be committed in these cases.[55] Concerning the massacres, Ndiaye wrote that "time and time again government officials were involved either directly by encouraging, planning, directing or participating in the violence, or indirectly through incompetence, negligence or deliberate inaction."[56] Ndiaye spoke about the use of the media to spread "unfounded rumors and exacerbating ethnic problems."[57]

In an interview with the former Special Rapporteur in the spring of 2005, he said: "I felt, I saw, I knew this is making a difference on the basis of birth and not on the basis of political motivations or power-politics . . . this is not politicide this is genocide . . . but nobody believed it." The word genocide had come into existence 50 years before and was linked to the Second World War. His choice to use the word genocide was therefore regarded as "inappropriate." Furthermore, using the word "genocide" would threaten the Arusha Accords, which were most important and needed to be maintained.[58] He was pressured to change his report and to delete the references to genocide, but he decided

53 Adelman, p. 18; Melvern, 2000 p. 56. According to Melvern, France dismissed the massacres as rumours.

54 E/CN.4/1994/7/Add. 1.

55 E/CN.4/1994/7/Add. 1, paragraph 79, p. 23.

56 E/CN.4/1994/7/Add. 1, paragraph 28, p. 10.

57 E/CN.4/1994/7/Add. 1, paragraph 56, p. 17.

against it. He wrote of what he had encountered, and according to him that was genocide.[59]

Ndiaye's report was published in August 1993 and in February 1994 it was formally tabled during the 50th session of the Commission of Human Rights.[60] But his story was paid no attention at all in August 1993, nor in February 1994, two months before the genocide. There is no indication that the U.N. Center of Human Rights or any other part of the United Nations made it its task to ensure that the report was impressed upon senior U.N. decisionmakers. Nor is there any indication that senior decisionmakers dealing with Rwanda were aware of the report.[61] In the interviews with former officials, we have asked whether they knew about Ndiaye's report. The U.S. officials, who should have been aware of Ndiaye's report, told us that they were not: John Shattuck, U.S. Assistant Secretary of State for Democracy, Human Rights and Labor, was unaware of the report; as were Anthony Lake, the U.S. National Security Adviser, and Prudence Bushnell, the U.S. Deputy Assistant Secretary for African Affairs.[62] The Belgian Minister of Foreign Affairs at the time, Willy Claes, said in the interview with him that he had not been informed of the report either.[63]

However, when on April 6 the plane was shot down, Ndiaye knew exactly what was about to happen: "This was the work of the extremists, planning to kill all those who were mentioned on the death-lists. This was the start of genocide."[64]

6.5 HUMAN RIGHTS WATCH WARNINGS IN 1993 AND 1994

Human Rights Watch released two reports dealing with the critical situation in Rwanda: one in June 1993 and the other in January 1994.[65] The report of June 1993 was in line with the previous findings of Amnesty International and the International Commission. The report described the continuing human

---

58 Interview with B.W. Ndiaye, May 25, 2005.

59 *Id.*

60 E/CN.4/1994/7/Add. 1.

61 Interview with B.W. Ndiaye, May 25, 2005; United Nations, Report of the Independent Inquiry into the Actions of the United Nations during the 1994 Genocide in Rwanda, December 15, 1999, Ingvar Carlsson, Han, Sung-Joo, Rufus, M. Kupolati, U.N. Doc. S/1999/1257, p. 3 (hereinafter Carlsson Report, S/1999/1257); E/CN.4/1994/7/Add. 1.

62 Interview with P. Bushnell, May 27, 2005; Interview with J. Shattuck, May 26, 2005; Interview with A. Lake, May 21, 2005.

63 Interview W. Claes, January 13, 2006.

64 Interview with B.W. Ndiaye, May 25, 2005.

65 HRW, 1993; Human Rights Watch, Arming Rwanda: The Arms Trade and Human Rights Abuses in the Rwandan War, (1994) (hereinafter HRW, 1994).

rights abuses in Rwanda since October 1990. All Tutsi and Rwandans labeled as RPF "accomplices" lived in constant insecurity, liable to attack in their homes or abuse on the streets. HRW held the armed forces accountable for bomb and grenade attacks, rape, killings, beatings, arbitrary arrests and distributing guns to the civilians. Like the International Commission, HRW concluded that local and central authorities directed the massacres on Tutsi and held Habyarimana accountable.[66]

The second report of HRW, published two and a half months before the outbreak of the genocide, was called "Arming Rwanda." The report gave an in-depth view of the influx of weapons from foreign countries into Rwanda. Since the invasion of the RPF in 1990, Rwanda had been a very impoverished country, unable to meet its human needs. The report showed that Rwanda nevertheless devoted its scarce resources to the accumulation of a wide range of arms. In March 1993, Rwanda and Egypt entered into a $6 million arms sale, made possible by a bank guarantee of the French National Bank, Credit Lyonnais. The purchase included automatic rifles, mortars, long-range artillery, shoulder-fired rocket launchers, munitions and landmines. Representatives from France and Egypt declined to comment, but the Rwandan Minister of Defense confirmed the existence of the transaction.[67] South Africa was also found to be involved in arms deals with Rwanda. HRW obtained an invoice of a $5.9 million arms purchase, by which Rwanda in 1992 received a wide range of South African light arms machine guns and ammunition.[68] On the involvement of France, the report stated: "France, in particular, has played a large, but not completely defined, role in arming and supporting Rwanda's military. France has either supplied or kept operational most of the heavy guns, artillery, assault vehicles and helicopters used by Rwanda in the war" and "deployed up to 680 troops during the Rwandan war."[69]

---

66 HRW, 1993.

67 HRW, 1994, pp. 14–15.

68 This arm's deal was in contravention with the U.N. Security Council Resolution 558 of December 13, 1984, which opposed importation of weapons from South Africa; HRW, 1994, p. 16.

69 Sources had been telling HRW that the French troops did also take a direct role in the conflict, which would go far beyond the French mandate to protect the lives and ensure evacuation of French expatriates. However, France denied that its forces had a direct role in the fighting; HRW, 1994, p. 16. Not only did international human rights organization report about the developing threats in Rwanda, but also many national organizations wrote about the massacres happening throughout the country in 1993.

6.6 AMERICAN WARNINGS—CIA—IN 1993 AND 1994

Prior to the genocide, the CIA published two reports that dealt with the grave and imminent violence in Rwanda and possible consequences thereof. A CIA study in January 1993 spoke of the "likelihood of large-scale ethnic violence" and a report in December 1993 talked about 40 million tons of small arms that had been transferred from Poland to Rwanda via Belgium.[70]

In October 1993 the CIA's National Intelligence Council (NIC) also predicted that the chances of renewed conflict in Rwanda remained high. The NIC comprises national intelligence officers who cover regional, functional and transnational issues and reports.[71] NIC's main products are the National Intelligence Estimates (NIE), which predict "events." In October 1993 an NIE official stated that "Africa will continue to generate humanitarian emergencies on an unparalleled scale." Concerning the situations in Liberia and Rwanda, the NIE predicted that "chances of renewed conflict in both countries remain high."[72]

In January 1994, three months before the start of the genocide, the CIA handed a desk-level analysis over to the State Department, which said that "if hostilities would resume half a million people would die . . . the Arusha Accords would fail and massive violence would break out."[73]

6.7 HATE PROPAGANDA IS REPORTED AS EARLY WARNING

Integral parts of the hate propaganda against the Tutsi minority were the hate-citing radio broadcasts and newspaper articles. *Kangura*, the most racist newspaper in Rwanda, started publishing four years before the outbreak of the genocide and became more violent in its expressions towards April 1994.[74] The

---

70 Samantha Power, A problem from hell: America and the age of genocide, p. 338 (2003) (hereinafter Power, 2003).

71 These issues and reports are sent to the Director of Central Intelligence (DCI), James Woolsey.

72 Doc. NIE 93–36, October 1993; see http://www2.gwu.edu/~nsarchiv/NSAEBB/NSAEBB117/Rw36.pdf.

73 Power, 2003 p. 338; Melvern, 2000 p. 91; Des Forges, p. 159, note 77: Human Rights Watch interview, Washington, December 8, 1995. It was only after the end of the genocide that UNAMIR received the information from these reports.

74 The first issue of the *Kangura* newspaper was published in May 1990 and the last in September 1995. During the genocide, no issues were published; *Kangura* No. 59, published in March 1994, was followed by No. 60 in September 1994. From February 1991 all *Kangura* covers were titled "Ijwi Rigamije Gu*Kangura* No Kurengera Rubanda Nyamwinshi" meaning "The Voice that Awakens and Defends the Majority People." The Prosecutor v. Ferdinand Nahimana, Jean-Bosco Barayagwiza and Hassan Ngeze, Case No. ICTR-99-52-T paragraph 136 (hereinafter the Nahimana case). Chrétien gives a comprehensive list of newspapers, along with their political tendencies, and describes

hate radio, *Radio Télévision Libre des Milles Collines* (RTLMC) would displace *Kangura* and other journals in 1993 as the "voice of extremism."[75] Marc Nees, who worked as a Belgian military intelligence officer in Rwanda from November 1993 to March 1994, said in his testimony before the Belgian Senate: "I am convinced that if we could have stopped RTLMC we would have had more chance to prevent the genocide, or at least to limit it."[76]

6.7.1 *Hate Newspaper* Kangura

Immediately after the RPF invasion of October 1990 *Kangura* started its attacks on the RPF and the Tutsi. *Kangura* was very well known both within and outside the country.[77] The newspaper had two versions, one in Kinyarwanda and one in French.[78] Its importance was also shown by the strong support of powerful government and military officials. *Kangura* was financed by people at the highest levels of the Habyarimana regime.[79] *Kangura*, meaning "wake others up," promoted a Hutu nation by inciting ethnic hatred and violence.[80] In December 1990, *Kangura* published an article titled "Appeal to the Conscience of the Hutu" which included the so called "Ten Commandments."[81] The article and the "Ten Commandments" portrayed the Tutsi as the enemy, as evil, dishonest and ambitious. The commandments were "inflammatory rules to create divisiveness and resentment and hatred for the Tutsi ethnic group, and for Tutsi women in particular as enemy agents."[82] The Commandments insisted on the need to maintain "Hutu purity and to avoid pollution from the Tutsi."[83]

---

the following others as being also "extrémiste du hutuisme": Intera, Echo des Mille Collines, La Medaille Nyiramacibiri, *Kangura* International, Interahamwe, Ikinani and Power-Pawa. Others linked to "Hutu Power" were: Umuranga Magazine (Indépendant puis Hutu Power), Ijambo (Mod. puis "Hutu Power"), Ijisho Rya Rubanda (Libertaire puis "Hutu-Power"), Ijabo (Hutuisme), Dusana Sane Imitima Tudahushun (Hutu Power), Jyambere (Hutuisme), Zirikana (Hutu Power—CDR), Paix et Democratie (Modéré, puis "Power"), Le Courrier du People (MDR "Hutu Power"). Chrétien, 1997 pp. 383–386.

75 Nahimana case, paragraphs 342, 488.

76 Translated from Dutch into English. Marc Nees was an intelligence officer of KIBAT I from November 1993 to March 1994. See Hearing with luitenant Nees, BV, BCR, Senate, p. 122; Belgian Senate, p. 599. Belgian General Uytterhoeven, who visited Rwanda in February 1994, strongly believes that the activities of RTLMC were one of the main causes of the killings. See Hearing with General-Major Uytterhoeven, BV, BCR, Senate, p. 366; Belgian Senate, p. 599.

77 Nahimana case, paragraph 122.

78 Nahimana case, paragraph 123.

79 Chrétien, 1997 p. 45; Nahimana case, paragraphs 122–130.

80 Chrétien, 1997 pp. 45–50.

81 See Section 2.2.2.

82 *Kangura*, No. 6, December 1990; Nahimana case, paragraphs 138–159, 950.

83 Nahimana case, paragraphs 138–159, 950; Chrétien, 1997 p. 16; Prunier, p. 166.

Kangura spread the notion that "the Tutsi were preparing a genocidal war against the Hutu that would leave no survivors" and that "the RPF wanted to re-establish the Tutsi monarchy and enslave the Hutu."[84] Despite the fact that some 70 percent of the Rwandan population was illiterate, the news of *Kangura* spread rapidly through the country.[85] The people learned about the articles by hearing from others and they were all able to understand the cartoons accompanying the texts.[86] Throughout the years, *Kangura* became more violent and started to include direct verbal attacks on the Tutsi.[87] *Kangura*'s issue of February 9, 1991, said: "Let us learn about the inkontanyi [RPF supporters] and let us exterminate every last one of them."[88] An article in March 1993 stated: "A cockroach gives birth to a cockroach . . . the history of Rwanda shows us clearly that a Tutsi stays always exactly the same, that he has never changed . . . the inyenzyi [cockroaches] who attacked in October 1990 and those of the 1960s are linked . . . their evilness is the same."[89] *Kangura* was the most infamous hate-citing newspaper, but it was certainly not the only one. Of the 42 journals that were founded in 1991, 11 newspapers were linked to Akazu, which had the consequence that they at least contained "racist elements."[90]

It must be noted that we have not been able to find responses of the diplomatic community in Rwanda to the *Kangura* newspaper—neither on specific hate-citing articles like the "Ten Commandments," nor on the role of *Kangura* in particular.

---

84 Chrétien, 1997 p. 45; Melvern, 2004 p. 50.

85 Melvern, 2004 p. 50.

86 Chrétien, 1997 p. 50.

87 Chrétien, 1997 p. 45.

88 Chrétien, 1997 p. 156; Melvern, 2004 p. 50.

89 Chrétien, 1997 p. 156; Melvern, 2004 p. 50. Inyenzi is Kinyarwanda for "coackroach," a term used by Hutu extremists to describe Tutsi.

90 Chrétien, 1997 p. 45. On December 17, 1993, *Le Flambeau*, described as an "opposition journal" published an article entitled "The Fatal Day" that stated that plotters within the MRND and CDR were seeking a "final solution" that was comparable to Hitler's final solution. The article mentioned that "political adversaries and defenseless populations" were going to be slaughtered. According to the article "about 8,000 Interahamwe" were "sufficiently trained and equipped by the French army await the signal to begin the assassinations among the residents of the city of Kigali and its surroundings." The article is quoted in African Rights, *Rwanda: Death, Despair and Defiance*, in, Review of African Political Economy 61, pp. 471–472 (1994). Although 42 journals could be said to have incited genocide (see Chrétien, 1997 particularly at pp. 383–386), the only journal that was involved and put on trial at the ICTR in Arusha was the most well known *Kangura*. No convictions have been made for other journals.

6.7.2 Hate Radio Mille Collines

In July 1993 the Hutu extremists founded *Radio Télévision Libre des Mille Collines*, which would turn out to be the most effective method to spread their hate propaganda. On July 8, at the time that the Arusha Accords were being concluded, the Hutu hardliners broadcast their first radio program. Until then there had been only one radio station, National Radio Rwanda, a formal station that broadcasted the ideas of MRND and President Habyarimana himself. As a result of the coalition government in April 1992, the MRND had to share the station with the opposition parties. This development caused the Hutu hardliners to decide to set up their own radio station: RTLMC.[91]

Because of its informal style, with lively pop music and street language, the station attracted a vast and diverse audience within just a few weeks. There were lengthy interviews, and listeners were invited to call in and to express their opinions. Like *Kangura*, RTLMC was financed by Hutu extremists. All members of Akazu were shareholders of RTLMC, with Habyarimana being the largest one.[92] In a number of ways the hate radio was linked to Radio Rwanda and the MRND regime: RTLMC was allowed to broadcast on the same frequencies as the National Radio, RTLMC drew personnel from Radio Rwanda and RTLMC used equipment belonging to government ministries.[93]

The purpose of the radio was to set up a campaign to demonize the Tutsi and spread an anti-Arusha and anti-Tutsi message throughout the country. Nahimana, who years later would be convicted of genocide for his role in RTLMC,[94] was the brain behind the radio station. He was the one who planned the news bulletins to create fear and incite the massacres. Throughout the months, the anti-Tutsi propaganda became more evident and began to call for massacres and to list people who deserved to die and should be exterminated.[95] As the months passed and UNAMIR was fully established, RTLMC also started to instigate hate against UNAMIR and particularly against the Belgian peacekeepers.[96]

---

91 Soon after its invasion, the RPF set up its own radio station, Radio Muhabura, but the station was unable to broadcast throughout the whole country. In December 1993 Radio Rwanda agreed to let the RPF participate in its broadcasts. However, when the genocide started in April, the decision was still not implemented. Some 29 percent of all households had a radio in 1991, but through the government policy of distributing radios throughout the country, the percentage was a lot higher by the start of the genocide in 1994. The exact percentage is unknown. Des Forges p. 68; Chrétien, 1997 pp. 57, 74; Nahimana case, paragraphs 342, 488.

92 Nahimana case, paragraphs 342–344; Melvern, 2000 p. 71; Des Forges, p. 69.

93 Chrétien, 1997 p. 70.

94 See Section 2.2.2.

95 Chrétien, 1997 p. 45.

96 Belgian Senate, pp. 592–599.

According to Adelman, both Western and African diplomats "tended to dismiss" the hate media, because it was "so explicit and literal."[97] Adelman quotes the Canadian ambassador Lucie Edwards in saying:

> The question of Radio Mille Collines propaganda is a difficult one. There were so many genuinely silly things being said on the station, so many obvious lies, that it was hard to take it seriously. It was like relying on the National Enquirer, a supermarket tabloid, to determine your policy in outer space. Nevertheless, everyone listened to it, I was told by Tutsis (sic), in a spirit of morbid fascination and because it had the best music selection.[98]

Among the Western diplomats in Kigali, the Belgian ambassador Swinnen seems to have been the one who took the inflammatory broadcasts most seriously. According to David Rawson, the U.S. ambassador to Rwanda, the United States did not want to take action because they believed in the freedom of speech.[99] According to Bushnell, during the genocide, her department "wanted very much" to stop the radio broadcasts, but they were told "it was against international law." Bushnell: "I almost hit the ceiling, this is how frustrating it was."[100] According to Melvern, the French ambassador, Marlaud, was also against taking action.[101]

Johan Swinnen on the other hand, warned Brussels many times of the danger of RTLMC. Years later, Swinnen declared before the Belgian Senate:

> we did not have the needed manpower at the embassy to listen to all the broadcasts of RTLMC or to translate them. In the beginning, RTLMC was broadcasting only 1 to 2 hours a day in French. At a certain moment I gave the order to listen to the broadcasts more often. Many broadcasts were taped and I exhaustively reported to Brussels about the content of the broadcasts.[102]

When, on November 26, 1993, RTLMC called for the first time for the assassination of opposition leaders, more explicitly the extermination of the Prime Minister Agathe Uwilingiyamana and Prime Minister-designate Twagiramungu, Johan Swinnen reported this information to his ministry in Brussels immediately.[103] In the following months, RTLMC became more violent in its broad-

97 Adelman, p. 17.

98 Adelman, p.17, note 37: "Communication to the authors, October 27, 1995."

99 Melvern, 2000 p. 71.

100 Interview with P. Bushnell, May 27, 2005.

101 Melvern, 2000 p. 71.

102 Translated from Dutch into English. Belgian Senate, p. 505; Hearing Swinnen, BV, BCR, Senate, p. 143.

103 Belgian Senate, p. 599; Sénat de Belgique, Rapport du Groupe Ad Hoc Rwanda

casting.[104] At the end of the year, Swinnen was aware of the fatal influence of the radio.[105] In January 1994 Swinnen pointed out that RTLMC was interlinked with the extremist party, the CDR.[106] When the Belgian Minister of Foreign Affairs, Claes, visited Rwanda in February 1994, he was notified by several "representatives of the international community" that RTLMC was being run by Habyarimana's brother-in-law, who was one of the most important members of Akazu.[107] Before the Belgian Senate, the former Belgian Minister of Defense, Leo Delcroix, said that he had strong presumptions that President Habyarimana was a shareholder of RTLMC.[108] In a telex sent on the first of February 1994, Swinnen informed his ministry that the inflammatory language of the station was an increasingly important factor in the destabilization of the country.[109] Exactly one month later, on March 1, Swinnen sent another fax that was even more clear about the devastating expressions of RTLMC. He wrote: "Inflammatory declarations call for the hatred—and even extermination—of the other ethnic component of the population."[110]

Many warnings and very serious signals of a worsening situation with a possibility of consequential atrocities were made in the years preceding the genocide. State and non-state actors informed others, but no action for any prevention was undertaken, and—as we will see in the next chapters—the early warnings made public in this chapter were easily forgotten in the following months, from December 1993 up to April 1994.

We have observed many very clear early warnings from divergent sources. Various NGOs, such as Amnesty International, Human Rights Watch and also an International Commission of Human Rights Organizations, were very clear, concrete and outspoken. The same can be said of the Special Rapporteur of the United Nations; he clearly concluded that not politicide but genocide was already taking place in 1993. No one paid attention inside and outside the United Nations to his very reliable report. Moreover ambassadors, ministers and other diplomats from Canada, the United States, France and Belgium made these serious early warnings public. No one reacted to these outspoken warnings.

A La Commission des Affairs Etrangeres, Sénat de Belgique, 7 janvier 1997, p. 70 (hereinafter Belgian Ad Hoc Group).

104 Belgian Ad Hoc Group, p. 70.

105 *Id.*; Hearing Swinnen, BV, BCR, Senate, p. 139; Belgian Senate, p. 604.

106 Hearing Swinnen, BV, BCR, Senate, p. 136; Belgian Senate, p. 607. It is not stated explicitly in the Senate documents to whom Swinnen has "pointed" this out, but it is probable that it was to the Ministry of Foreign Affairs.

107 Belgian Senate, p. 607; Hearing Claes, BV, BCR, Senate, p. 303.

108 Belgian Senate, p. 607; Hearing Delcroix, POR, Senate, pp. 801–802.

109 Belgian Senate, p. 595; Belgian Ad Hoc Group, p. 51.

110 Translated from French into English. Original text: "Des déclarations inflammatoires appelant à la haine—voire même l'extermination—de l'autre composante ethnique de la population." Belgian Senate, p. 600; Belgian Ad Hoc Group, p. 78.

CHAPTER 7

EARLY WARNINGS FROM NOVEMBER TO JANUARY

7.1 A VIOLENT START FOR UNAMIR

During his first weeks on the ground, it became clear to General Roméo Dallaire that this was not going to be a classic peace-keeping mission that was installed with the full consent of parties who were committed to the peace agreement.[1] Dallaire:

> Rumors with regard to the extremists having signed under duress started to come out. The presence of the militias or, let put it this way, the youth movements . . . were become more vociferous and more brazen. . . . The tone of what was happening was shifting from evident goodwill to an atmosphere that was less than stable, or less than solid. We were starting to get a whiff of the complexities that might be ahead.[2]

The mission started off with the assassination of the Burundian President Ndadaye. Exactly one day before Dallaire's arrival in Kigali, on October 21, the Burundian President was killed. Ndadaye had been elected only four months earlier. He was a Hutu and symbolized the unity between the Hutu and the Tutsi. The violence that broke out was terrible: between 35,000 and 50,000 Burundian Tutsi and Hutu were killed. The events had enormous consequences for Rwanda. The assassination gave a propaganda boost to the Hutu extremists in Rwanda, who claimed that the assassination was part of a wider plan to eliminate the Hutu. MRND and CDR officials claimed that Major General Paul Kagame, military commander of the Rwandan Patriotic Army, the military wing of the RPF, had plotted the assassination.[3] During a rally in Kigali, a few days after

---

1 Frontline interview with Dallaire, Autumn 2003.

2 *Id.*

3 Gerard Prunier, The Rwanda Crisis: History of a Genocide (1959–1994), pp. 201–206 (1995) (hereinafter Prunier). Many critics see this event as a decisive factor for the following tragedy in Rwanda. Organization of African Unity, The Preventable Genocide of the International Panel of Eminent Personalities to Investigate the 1994

Ndadaye's death, politicians of the MRND and the CDR together with opposition-hardliners asserted that Kagame had planned the assassination, and that he had lied when he signed the Arusha Agreement. The MRD member Karamira, who had always been a moderate, shouted to the crowd that the "enemy" was amongst the people. Karamira: "We are not simply heating heads by saying we have plans to work . . . We cannot sit down and think that what happened in Burundi will not happen here . . . All Hutu are one power."[4] Besides this emerging hate propaganda, Rwanda had to deal with an enormous refugee flow. An estimated 300,000 Burundian refugees sought exile in Rwanda.[5] Another consequence of the assassination was a shift of the international attention to the situation in Burundi.[6]

As soon as Dallaire hit Rwandan soil, alarming messages started coming in. In Rukara, an area in which Hutu and Tutsi had always lived together, the Hutu youth began to separate themselves into "youth wings." They organized demonstrations against the Tutsi and Hutu opposition, and some of the "youth wings" were taught to shoot.[7] David Waller, who was a specialist in this region working for Oxfam, warned that "the Rwandan society was now more violently divided against itself than at any time since independence." Waller spoke of an "unchartered abyss of anarchy and violence."[8]

The middle of November saw the appearance of a number of reports of shooting and killing around the country.[9] A series of killings took place in the Northern communities of Rwanda; all victims were Hutu. On the night of November 17–18 massacres took place in five different locations. The killings were very well planned. The victims were men, women and children. Most of the adults among the victims were associated with the ruling MRND party. The killings immediately led to an explosion of RTLMC broadcasts accusing the

---

Genocide in Rwanda and Surrounding Events, p. 57 (2000) (hereinafter OAU Report); Alison Des Forges, Leave None to Tell the Story, Genocide in Rwanda, pp. 137–138 (1999) (hereinafter Des Forges); See also Ian Linden, The Churches and genocide: Lessons from Rwanda, p. 28 (1995) (hereinafter Linden); and René Lemarchand, Burundi: Ethnic Conflict and Genocide, (1995) (hereinafter Lemarchand, 1995).

4 Prunier, pp. 201–206; Linda Melvern, A People Betrayed. The Role of the West in Rwanda's Genocide, p. 84 (2000) (hereinafter Melvern, 2000); Des Forges, p. 138. Froduald Karramira was the vice-president of the MRD. The court of Kigali convicted him of genocide on September 15, 1997; he was publicly executed on April 24, 1998. Many critics see the assassination of Ndadaye as a decisive factor for the following tragedy in Rwanda. See also Linden; Lemarchand, 1995.

5 Melvern, 2000 p. 84; Prunier, pp. 201–206.

6 Interview with P. Bushnell, May 27, 2005.

7 Melvern, 2000 p. 88.

8 *Id.*

9 Roméo Dallaire, Shake Hands with the Devil, The Failure of Humanity in Rwanda, p. 115 (2004) (hereinafter Dallaire).

RPF.[10] The CDR also reacted fiercely; they issued a press release calling for the resignation of President Habyarimana and Prime Minister Uwilingiyimana if they failed to react to the massacres. If the President and Prime Minister did not react, they would be considered to be "accomplices" of the RPF. The CDR added that the "majority population had to be ready to neutralize by all means its enemies and their accomplices."[11] On November 24 another report of killings came in. In Mutura "a number of Hutu" had been murdered, together with six children. One boy of eight and five girls aged between six and 14 had been strangled to death. The girls had all been gang raped.[12]

In both massacres, UNAMIR was unable to discover the perpetrators of the killings. Because all victims were Hutu, the hard-liners saw this failure as "proof" that UNAMIR was biased against the regime. RTLMC used the two massacres to provoke hate against the RPF and to depict UNAMIR as supporters of the RPF. In the ICTR judgment in the Nahimana case, the following is put forward: "The suggestion that UNAMIR General Dallaire had a relationship with the Tutsi, expressed in the cartoons as one of sexual intimacy, echoes the articles in Kangura accusing Dallaire of favoring the Tutsi."[13] In particular in *Kangura* No. 56, he is shown with his arms around two women, one of whom is kissing him. The title reads: "General Dallaire and his army fell prey to the traps of the femmes fatales."[14] Jean Kambanda testified for the Tribunal that the cartoon was to show how women had corrupted the UNAMIR head who was there to oversee peace and the implementation of the Arusha Accords. He said this and other cartoons in *Kangura* portrayed Tutsi women as spies.[15]

---

10 Melvern, 2000 p. 88; Des Forges p. 143; Sénat de Belgique, Rapport du Groupe Ad Hoc Rwanda A La Commission des Affairs Etrangeres, Sénat de Belgique, 7 janvier 1997, pp. 67, 74 (hereinafter Belgian Ad Hoc Group).

11 Melvern, 2000 p. 89; Des Forges, p. 144, note 9: Communiqué du CDR, signed by Martin Bucyana, Kigali, November 23, 1993.

12 In the literature, different figures are given regarding the date and number of the killings. The figures in our text are based upon Dallaire's book, Shake Hands with the Devil, pp. 115–116. *See* further: Des Forges, p. 144; Melvern, 2000 p. 87–88. Des Forges speaks about the killing of "more than a dozen on the 29th-30th of November," Melvern speaks about the killing of "25 adults and 9 children on the 29th of November," Dallaire speaks about the killing of "a number of Hutu and 6 children on the 24th of November."

13 Prosecutor v. Nahimana, Barayagwiza, and Ngeze, Case No. 99-52-T Judgment and Sentence, December 3, 2003, p. 211.

14 Translated from the French: "Le général Dallaire et son armée sont tombés dans le piège des femmes fatales."

15 Prosecutor v. Nahimana, Barayagwiza, and Ngeze, Case No. 99-52-T Judgment and Sentence, December 3, 2003, p. 210.

In an encoded cable to New York on January 6 Dallaire described the massacres and set out UNAMIR's efforts regarding the inquiries. He told New York that in his estimation, the massacres were well organized, that the perpetrators were well motivated and prepared to conduct murders. Dallaire stated:

> The manner in which they were conducted, in their execution, in their coordination, in their cover-up, and in their political motivation, lead us firmly to believe that the perpetrators of these evil deeds were well-organized, well-informed, well-motivated and prepared to conduct premeditated murder. We have no reason to believe that such an occurrence could not and will not be repeated again in any part of this country where arms are prolific and ethnic tensions are prevalent.[16]

In the same telex, Dallaire asked for reinforcements, but instead he received the second deployment of peace-keepers that would only expand the mission to 2,548 troops.[17] After the CDR had threatened both the President and the Prime Minister a few days before, RTLMC called for the assassinations of the Prime Minister, Madame Agathe Uwilingiyimana (often known as Madame Agathe), and Prime Minister-Designate Twagiramungu. On November 26 Ambassador Swinnen reported this to his Ministry in Brussels.[18]

On the same day, Swinnen reported to Brussels that a Belgian Red Cross truck had been accidentally hit by a mine. However, an investigation by UNAMIR

---

16 Melvern, 2000 p. 88, note 26: UNAMIR, Code cable January 6, 1994.

17 Melvern, 2000 pp. 88, 89.

18 Sénat de Belgique, Commission d'Enquête parlementaire concernant les événements au Rwanda, (Commission of parliamentary enquiry concerning the events in Rwanda), session de 1997–1998, 6 décembre 1997, Rapport fait au nom de la commission d'enquête par MM Mahoux et Verhofstadt, Annexes, p. 70 (hereinafter Annex Belgian Senate).

a few days later proved that the truck was targeted deliberately. The mine had been operated from a distance, most likely by Hutu soldiers of the FAR.[19] The violence was understood as a direct attack on the Belgians. A second "incident" involving the Belgians occurred when FAR soldiers assaulted two missionaries, because they were thought to be Belgian. When it became clear the missionaries were not Belgian, they were released. Ambassador Swinnen reported to the Ministry of Foreign Affairs about the two anti-Belgian incidents and added that a MRND-minded journal *Kamarampaka* had given plain criticism of the Belgian peace-keepers.[20] The journal called upon the Hutu "to be categorically opposed to the Belgians guarding the town of Kigali."[21] In April 1993 this journal published a cartoon in which the Tutsi demonization (FPR) and Hutu victimization (CDR, MRD and MNRD) in this propaganda are depicted.[22]

On the first day of the new month, the Rwandan human rights organization Association pour la Protection des Droits de l'Homme (ARDHO) published a report discussing more than a dozen attacks on Tutsi throughout November.[23] According to the report, the assailants had declared "this population is an accomplice of the Inkotanyi because it is mostly Tutsi and its extermination would be a good thing for them."[24] On December 1, the Belgian embassy forwarded this information to its Ministry of Foreign Affairs. Two days later the embassy sent another fax arguing that it was a "plausible hypothesis" that the violence in the second half of the month of November, particularly the attack on the Belgian Red Cross truck and the killings in Ruhengeri and Mutara, was the work of the CDR and MRND groups, with the aim of jeopardizing the

---

19 The road where the accident happened was under control of the FAR. Whether people got killed or injured in the accident and, if so, how many, is not said in the documents of the Belgian Senate. Telex No. 1190, November 26, 1993; Telex No. 1192, November 29, 1993; Annex Belgian Senate, p. 20.

20 This newspaper is listed by the UNHCR as an example of extremist media which defends hatred and ethnic fundamentalism. UNHCR, Fiche Pays: Rwanda, January 2006. Part VII, p.1.

21 Translated from French into English. Original text: "de s'opposer catégoriquement à ce que les Belges gardent la ville de Kigali." Telex Nos. 1190, 1192 and 1196, November 26, 29 and 30, 1993; Annex Belgian Senate, p. 20; Des Forges, p. 144.

22 This cartoon was published in the newspaper *Kamarampaka* on April 7, 1993 (No. 15, p. 14). The headline reads: The inkotanyi (Rwandan Patriotic Front (RPF) insurgents) have left their mark on Ruhengeri. *See* http://www.onemancult.com/rwanda/rwandaprop13.html.

23 The areas in which these attacks took place were Birenga, Rutonde, Muhazi, Kayonza, Kigarama, Glkomero, Bicumbi, Ngenda, Nyamata. Annex Belgian Senate, p. 44.

24 Translated from French into English. Original text: "Cette population est complice des Inkotanyi, car essentiellement Tutsi et que son extinction serait une bonne affaire pour eux." Annex Belgian Senate, p. 44; Belgian Ad Hoc Group, p. 70; Des Forges, p. 145.

Arusha Accords.[25] On December 13 Swinnen informed his Ministry again of dozens of incidents of ethnical killings throughout the country.

7.2 THE MACHIAVELLI PLAN

December would pass with far less violence than November, but early warnings about future massacres would be all the more present.[26]

On December 3 Dallaire received the most serious and threatening warning of that month. He received a letter from a number of senior officials of the FAR. In the letter, the senior officials, who remained anonymous, explained that they had recently separated from a group of military officials from Habyarimana's "home region," because they were filled "with revulsion against these filthy tactics" of this group. The letter warned about the ideas and plans of Habyarimana, who was being supported by this particular group. It spoke of a certain "Machiavelli plan" and elaborated upon the killings in Kirambo, Mutura and Ngenda, stating: "Other massacres of the same kind are being prepared and are supposed to extend to all of the regions of the country, commencing with the regions said to have a strong concentration of the Tutsi ethnic group."[27] The letter warned furthermore of the assassination of opposition leaders including the Prime Minister-designate Faustin Twagiramungu and Félicien Gatabazi, who was head of the Parti Social Démocrate (PSD), the second largest opposition party.[28]

On February 22, 1994, one and a half months before the start of the genocide, Félicien Gatabazi was indeed killed, which increased the reliability of the above-mentioned information.

---

25 Fax No. 278, December 1, 1993; Annex Belgian Senate, p. 44; Telex No. 1212, December 3, 1993; Annex Belgian Senate, p. 45. The fax underlined that it was a hypothesis and not a "definite conclusion."

26 December started however with an attack by armed "assailants" on a UNAMIR patrol in the Northern part of Rwanda. Telex No. 1219, December 3, 1993; Annex Belgian Senate, p. 25; Belgian Ad Hoc Group, p. 37.

27 Translated from French into English. Original text: "d'autres massacres du genre sont en train de se préparer et devront s'étendre sur toutes les régions du pays à commencer par les régions dites à forte concentration de l'ethnie Tutsi." Anonymous letter to Monsieur le Commandant de la Mission des Nations Unies pour l'assistance au Rwanda, of December 3, 1993 (Confidential source), the letter is reprinted in André Guichaoua, (ed.), Les Crisis Politiques au Burundi et au Rwanda, p. 654 (1995) (hereinafter Guichaoua).

28 Faustin Twagiramungu was appointed to be the Prime Minister during the BBTG period. Anonymous letter to Monsieur le Commandant de la Mission des Nations Unies pour l'assistance au Rwanda, of December 3, 1993 (Confidential source), the letter is reprinted in Guichaoua, p. 654; Annex Belgian Senate, p. 47; Melvern, 2000 p. 89; Des Forges, p. 145; OAU Report, p. 58.

29 Melvern, 2000 p. 89.

In addition to Dallaire, all diplomatic missions also received a copy of the letter.[29] Halfway through December, Swinnen forwarded the information to his Ministry, with an accompanying note in which he even stated the identity of the highly placed officers.[30]

7.3 ANNOUNCEMENTS ON THE DISTRIBUTION OF ARMS

According to its mandate, UNAMIR had to contribute to the security of Kigali, which was to be a weapons-free zone. Before UNAMIR could fulfill this task, all parties had to agree upon the so-called Kigali Weapons Secure Area (KWSA) agreement. After long deliberations the KWSA agreement was signed on December 24, and thereby the weapons-free zone went into effect.[31] Under the agreement, each party had to secure its weapons and was only allowed to move its arms and its armed troops with permission and under escort of the peace-keepers.[32]

In reality the KWSA agreement was a farce. At the moment of signature, arms were already being distributed to the militia, a practice that was only going to continue on an expanding scale.[33] Marc Nees, a Belgian intelligence officer, learned as early as November 1993 about the distribution of arms. On November 5 Habyarimana had chaired a meeting where the decision was made "to distribute grenades, machetes and other weapons to the Interahamwe and CDR's youth groups." The objective of the distribution of arms was "to kill Tutsi and other Rwandans who are in the cities and who do not support them [Interahamwe and CDR]."[34]

On December 27, three days after the conclusion of the KWSA agreement, the Belgian intelligence reported on a meeting of military commanding officers who ordered the supply of light arms, ammunition and uniforms to Hutu extremists. The report noted: "The Interahamwe are armed to the teeth and on alert. Many of them have been trained at the military camp in Bugesera. Each of them has ammunition, grenades, mines and knives. They have been trained to use guns that are stockpiled with their respective chiefs. They are all just waiting for the right moment to act."[35]

---

30 Annex Belgian Senate, p. 47.

31 Luc Marchal, Aan de poorten van de Rwandese hel: Getuigenis van een peace-keeper, pp. 63–68 (2001) (hereinafter Marchal); Dallaire, pp. 124–126.

32 Dallaire, pp, 124–125; Belgian Ad Hoc Group, p. 83.

33 This chapter deals with reports regarding the distribution of arms of December and the beginning of January. See Chapter 10 for the distribution of arms in February, March and April.

34 Belgian Ad Hoc Group, p. 70; Des Forges, p. 143.

35 Des Forges, p. 146, note 22: Walter de Bock, Belgische "Wijkagenten" zagen voorbereiding genocide, *De Morgen*, November 4, 1995, p. 5.

Throughout December announcements on the distribution of weapons started to be made in public journals. The journals *Le Flambeau* and *Kiberinka* reported that during a meeting of the General Staff of the FAR, it was decided to distribute grenades, weapons, machetes and other weapons to the Interahamwe and the CDR.[36] The newspapers noted: "The goal [of the conference] was to tell the officers of the necessity of convincing the troops so that they would fight against the Inkotanyi and the Belgians."[37] This is evidence of a purposeful decision to use weapons from the army against the Tutsi and the Belgians. Later that month, *Le Flambeau* published an article in which it discussed a plan called *"la solution finale,"* which dealt with the training of paramilitias.[38]

Ten days later, the bishop and clergy of a diocese in the Northern part of the country issued a press report speaking about the distribution of weapons in their parish. The bishop and clergy asked the Rwandan authorities to explain for what use these were intended.[39]

Local NGOs also started issuing publications about the distribution of arms and calling for the disarmament of the militia. On December 8 a coalition of several Rwandan human rights organizations, CLADHO (Collectif des Ligues et Associations de Défense des Droits de l'Homme), made an announcement in which UNAMIR was informed about the increasing ethnic and political violence that was caused by a "Machiavelli plan" of "certain civil and military authorities" and by "a fascist media propaganda by certain public and private media . . . orchestrated by groups paid by the real holders of power." Habyarimana must take responsibility, CLADHO stated, "in order to put an end to the extermination of a human group in which an organization of killers who seem to benefit from the protection or complicity of certain authorities is engaged." In the announcement CLADHO warned and "vigorously challenged the international community to protest against the trivialization of the crime in Rwanda."[40]

---

36 *Le Flambeau* published this information on December 6, and *Kiberenka* published the same information a few days later.

37 Translated from French into English. Original text: "Le but [de la conférence] était de dire aux officiers la nécessité de convaincre les troupes pour qu'ils combattent les Inkotanyi et les Belges." Annex Belgian Senate, pp. 27, 39. According to the articles, a meeting was held on November 21 where the General Staff had decided upon the distribution of arms.

38 Annex Belgian Senate, pp. 43, 48. The article was published in *Le Flambeau* on December 17, 1993.

39 Des Forges, p. 146, note 23: Msgr. Wenceslas Kalibushi and priests of Kibuye and Gisenyi, Communiqué de Presse, December 28, 1993.

40 Translated from French into English. Original text: "Certaines autorités civiles et militaires'and by 'une propaganda médiatique fasciste par certains medias publics et privés (. . .) orchestrée par des groupes à la solde des tenants réels du pouvoir." . . . "interpelle vigoureusement la communauté internationale pour qu'elle s'élève contre toute la banalisation du crime au Rwanda." See des Forges, p. 146, note 19: CLADHO, Memorandum Adressé à la Minuar et aux Missions Diplomatiques en Rapport avec les Tueries en Cours dans le Pays, December 8, 1993; Annex Belgian Senate, pp. 47–48.

On January 31 UNAMIR received a second memo from this Coalition, now asking to "immediately disarm the militia." A third request from CLADHO, asking for disarmament, followed on March 24.[41] Besides UNAMIR, all diplomatic missions received CLADHO's memorandum of December 8. Whether the embassies also received the latter two memos is unknown. What is known is that the Belgian embassy received all three memos and forwarded all of them to the Belgian Ministry of Foreign Affairs.[42]

CLADHO was not the only coalition of NGO's asking for disarmament. The Consultative Council of Organizations Supporting Grass-roots Initiatives issued a press release on December 17 in which they called for the disarmament and dismantling of the militia.[43] On January 8 the association Professional Women United, together with the council representing non-governmental organizations working for development (CCOAIB) and CLADHO, issued a declaration in which they appealed to the Rwandan and international leaders to implement Arusha rapidly and called upon politicians and the media to stop inciting hatred. The declaration noted that they "condemned unreservedly" the distribution of weapons by those who "provoke a civil war."[44]

7.4 KNOWLEDGE OF THE DISTRIBUTION OF ARMS

The telex communication of the Belgian embassy to its Ministry in Brussels makes it clear that Belgium was very well informed about the weapon distribution and the training of the militia. On December 3 a telex was sent from the embassy to the Belgian Ministry of Foreign Affairs in which three training camps were identified.[45]

Belgium was also informed of the two above-mentioned articles published in *Le Flambeau* and *Kiberinka*. The first article, speaking of the distribution of weapons to the Interahamwe and the CDR, published in both *Le Flambeau* and *Kiberenka*, was sent by UNAMIR to Evere (Operation Center of the Belgian Army) on December 19, 1993.[46] The second article, published only in *Le*

---

41 Annex Belgian Senate, pp. 56, 58.

42 Annex Belgian Senate, pp. 47–48, 56, 58.

43 Des Forges, p. 146, note 20: Consultative Council of Organizations Supporting Grass-roots Initiatives (Conseil de Concertation des Organisations d'Appui aux Initiatives de Base, CCOAIB), Communiqué de Presse, December 17, 1993.

44 Des Forges, p. 149, note 34: Pro-Femmes Twese Hamwe, CLADHO, CCOAIB, "Declaration des Collectifs Relative au Retard de la Mise sur Pied des Institutions de Transition Definies dans l'Accord de Paix d'Arusha," January 8, 1994 (CLADHO).

45 According to the telex, the camps were used by the presidential guard for the training of youth groups to take part in "rafles" in Kigali. All three camps were situated in the capital. Telex No. 1214, December 3, 1993; Annex Belgian Senate, p. 42; Belgian Ad Hoc Group, p. 65.

46 On December 22 this article in *Le Flambeau* was sent again by UNAMIR to Evere. Annex Belgian Senate, pp. 27, 39.

Flambeau and speaking of *"la solution finale,"* was sent from the Belgian embassy in Kigali to the Belgian Ministry of Foreign Affairs on December 23.[47]

The Belgian embassy informed the Belgian Ministry of Foreign Affairs of all three announcements of CLADHO. On December 13 the Belgian embassy informed the Belgian Ministry of Foreign Affairs of CLADHO's announcement—dated December 8—in which UNAMIR was informed of the increasing ethnic and political violence and was asked to disarm the militia.[48] On February 4 the Belgian embassy informed its Ministry in Brussels about CLADHO's memo to UNAMIR—dated January 31—with its request to immediately disarm the militia.[49] And on April 6 the Belgian embassy informed its Ministry in Brussels about CLADHO's memo—dated March 24—with another request for disarmament.[50]

In a telex of December 27, Ambassador Swinnen reported to his Ministry on rumors that weapons were being distributed to the local authorities.[51] In a telex two days later, he reported about his meeting with Prime Minister, Madame Agathe, who said that the intelligence service of her department could not rule out that the Ministry of Defense distributed weapons.[52] On January 5 Swinnen reminded his Ministry of Foreign Affairs of the dissemination of weapons by saying: "I remind you in addition of the information relating to the distribution of arms in certain regions of the country attributed to presidential mobility."[53] Three days later, he confirmed once again that weapons were being distributed to the population.[54]

The foregoing shows that Belgium was already highly aware of the distribution of arms amongst the militia by December and the beginning of January. The exact knowledge of the other diplomatic missions regarding the distribution of weapons is unknown. Taking note of the intensive contact between the different diplomatic missions, the amount of warnings that the Belgian embassy received, the publication about the distribution of arms in public journals and the warnings of NGO's, it is highly likely that other missions were also perfectly aware.

---

47 Annex Belgian Senate, pp, 43, 48.

48 Telex No. 1236, December 13, 1993; Annex Belgian Senate, pp. 47, 48.

49 Annex Belgian Senate, p. 56.

50 Annex Belgian Senate, p. 58.

51 Telex No. 1272, December 27, 1993; Annex Belgian Senate, p. 40.

52 Telex No. 1276, December 29, 1993; Annex Belgian Senate, p. 40.

53 Translated from French into English. Original text: "Je vous rappelle par ailleurs les informations relatives à la distribution d'armes dans certaines régions du pays attribuée à la mouvance présidentielle." Telex No. 5, January 4, 1994, Annex Belgian Senate, p. 40.

54 The ambassador confirmed to his Ministry that weapons were distributed to the people by the presidency. Telex No. 20, January 8, 1994; Annex Belgian Senate, p. 40.

7.5 INABILITY TO INSTALL THE BROAD BASED TRANSITIONAL GOVERNMENT (BBTG)

At the end of December, with the KWSA agreement signed and the Kigali battalion of Belgian and Bangladeshi peace-keepers in place, it was UNAMIR's next task to assist in the establishment of the RPF in Kigali.[55] On December 28 the Belgian peace-keepers escorted the RPF leaders and 600 of its soldiers from their base in the Northern part of the country to their new headquarters in Kigali. The difficult and dangerous task was completed without incident. In Kigali, the RPF was based in the imposing national parliament building, the Conseil National de Développement (CND). This static and impressive building underlined the loss of the old regime to the RPF.[56]

With the three future RPF ministers, Jaques Bihozagara, Paul Kagame and Pasteur Bizimungu present in Kigali, the transitional government could be installed as planned on January 1.[57] However, at the beginning of the month, due to incessant debates on the appointment of ministers on the side of the opposition parties and the MRND, there was still no consensus on the cabinet.[58]

On December 31 the installment was postponed to January 5, 1994. But on January 5 there was still no consensus. On that day, Special Representative of the United Nations Secretary-General (SRSG) Jaques-Roger Booh Booh was therefore only able to swear in President Habyarimana. The installation of the actual cabinet and with that the transfer of power was postponed to February 14.[59] By then the installment was postponed again to February 23, then to March 25, then to March 28, and finally to the beginning of April.[60]

As was stipulated in Security Council Resolution 872 on the establishment of UNAMIR, the Security Council would review the situation in Rwanda to ensure that progress was made in implementing the Arusha Accords.[61] On

---

55 Marchal, pp. 68–78.

56 Dallaire, pp. 126–127.

57 Prunier, pp. 204, 205; Frontline interview with Beardsley, November 15, 2003.

58 Furthermore, Habyarimana, supported by the Hutu hardliners of the MDR and the Parti Libéral (PL), launched several challenges to the interpretation of the Accords. One of the challenges was the proposal to get the CDR a seat in the transitional government. For more information, see Filip Reyntjens, L'Afrique des Grands Lacs, en crise: Rwanda, Burundi: 1988–1994, pp. 17–18 (1994) (hereinafter Reyntjens); Des Forges, p. 141; Prunier, pp. 204, 205; Frontline interview with Beardsley, November 15, 2003; Melvern, 2000 p. 90.

59 Dallaire, pp. 138, 139.

60 Booh Booh had arrived in Rwanda on November 23. The dates detailing the failure to install the transitional government are mentioned in the Second Progress Report of the Secretary-General, March 30, 1994, U.N. Doc. S/1994/360. See furthermore Reyntjens, pp. 17–18; Des Forges p. 141; Prunier, pp. 204, 205; Frontline interview with Beardsley, November 15, 2003. See Chapter 10.

61 See U.N. Doc. S/RES/872 point 2.

January 6, the day after the failure to install the BBTG, the Security Council conducted its first assessment of the mission. The Council decided to deploy the troops designated for "Phase Two" of the mission, even though the official condition for this second phase—the installation of the BBTG—had not been met.[62] In a fax dated January 6, General Dallaire had requested additional troops to prevent the violence from spreading over to Burundi and Southern Rwanda, but the Security Council denied his request and stressed "that continued support for UNAMIR depended on full and prompt implementation of the Accords."[63] The intelligence that UNAMIR was about to receive in the following week would prove that "full and prompt implementation of Arusha" was far from the plan of the Hutu extremists.

7.6 THE FIRST VIOLENT DEMONSTRATION

The numerous warnings on the distribution of arms made Luc Marchal and Dallaire decide upon the seizure of weapons. On January 3 Belgian peace-keepers under the command of Marchal confiscated hidden stocks of arms, ammunition and explosives.[64] A few days later, a Belgian intelligence report showed that this seizure had led to serious unrest among certain Rwandan officials. Marc Nees received a letter from an informant reporting about a meeting at the MRND-headquarters on January 7 in order to avoid future seizure of weapons.[65] The officials attending this meeting were General Augustin Ndindiliyimana, National Police Commander, Mathieu Ngirumpatse, President of the MRND-party, Colonel Nsabimana, Army Chief of Staff, Augustin Bizimana, Minister of Defense, Robert Kajuga, President of the Interahamwe and several agents of the secret police. The officials decided to move all hidden arms to new locations and to store weapons at the homes of army officers "loyal to the MRND." Furthermore, they decided to start a campaign to disrupt relations between the

---

62 Des Forges, p. 148, note 31: Anonymous, "Chronology-Rwanda," Draft document by U.N. staff member not otherwise identified, March 16, 1994 (confidential source). U.N. Doc. S/26488, the report of the Secretary-General on which Resolution 872 regarding the establishment of UNAMIR was based, states in point 40, p. 8: "Phase 1 . . . would end on D-Day, the day on which the transitional Government is installed in Kigali." See Chapter 10.

63 Melvern, 2000 pp. 88–89; Des Forges, p. 148, note 30: General Dallaire to U.N., New York, Code Cable MIR 39, January 6, 1994 (confidential source).

64 Later the Belgian peace-keepers were forced to return the weapons to the Rwandan Army; see Des Forges, p. 147, note 27: Document 6, Belgian Military Intelligence, January 8, 1994 (confidential source).

65 The meeting had taken place on January 7, and the Belgian intelligence report was published the day after. Annex Belgian Senate, p. 32; Des Forges, p. 149, note 33: Document 6, Belgian Military Intelligence, January 8, 1994.

Rwandan police and UNAMIR and to cause troubles between the Rwandan population and the Belgian peace-keepers.[66]

The following day a violent demonstration took place before the CND building of the RPF. There were hundreds of demonstrators, armed with machetes and sticks. Several civilians were assaulted and vehicles were attacked. The rally was very well planned and led by the Interahamwe and soldiers of the Presidential Guard.[67] The Interahamwe shouted anti-Belgian slogans, which were taken over by the crowd.[68] The UNAMIR officers decided not to intervene, because this kind of situation fell under the responsibility of the National Police. Furthermore, the peace-keepers fundamentally lacked the training and equipment to act. The National Police, however, did nothing to intervene; they only stood by and watched.

At that moment Dallaire and Marchal understood the demonstration as an attempt to prevent the future installment of the BBTG, but they were about to find out that the real aim of the rally was far more serious.[69]

The situation was deteriorating at the end of 1993. No progress was made with the implementation of the peace agreement, whereas the installation of the transitional government was postponed. The massacre in the neighboring country Burundi and the continuing and increasing scale of killings in Rwanda worsened the situation. In particular, the elaborated plans to assassinate the political opposition and to provoke unrest in combination with the distribution of weapons were alarming signals. Many early warnings by states and NGOs were forwarded, and these messages were received on almost a daily base at the Belgian Ministry of Foreign Affairs.

---

[66] Annex Belgian Senate, pp. 32, 41; Des Forges, p. 149, note 33: Document 6, Belgian Military Intelligence, January 8, 1994.

[67] The Belgian ambassador wrote to his Ministry that the Interahamwe was supported during the demonstration by "véhicules officiel," Telex No. 21, January 10, 1994. Marchal reported to Evere that the manifestation was organized by parties "de la mouvance Présidentielle," Report of January 9, 1994 of the Commander Sector Kigali, Marchal to Evere. Annex Belgian Senate, p. 39; Interview with L. Marchal, January 21, 2005; Marchal, pp. 110, 111.

[68] Marchal, pp. 110–111.

[69] Melvern, 2000 pp. 89–90; Annex Belgian Senate, p. 39; Marchal, p. 110. See Chapter 13.

CHAPTER 8

THE GENOCIDE FAX AND THE PROHIBITION FROM U.N. HEADQUARTERS TO ACT

8.1 MARCHAL MEETS INFORMANT JEAN PIERRE

January 10, 1994, was the date on which UNAMIR received the most important warning about the unfolding genocide.

Faustin Twagiramungu, the Prime Minister-designate, had insisted on a private meeting with General Roméo Dallaire, Canadian Force Commander of UNAMIR, for the afternoon of Monday, January 10. He told Dallaire about an informant from inside the Interahamwe who wanted to inform UNAMIR of highly important intelligence.[1]

On the evening of that day, the informant, code-named Jean Pierre, met with Colonel Luc Marchal. Jean Pierre explained that it was his job to monitor the general security within the MRND, that he had to make sure that the different "cells" throughout Kigali were supplied with weapons and that he was a trainer of the militia. He added that he received his orders directly from Mathieu Ngirumpatse, the president of the MRND. He explained his reason for unfolding his story to UNAMIR by saying: "As long as it is about warfare with the RPF I have no feelings . . . But since I have been asked to localize and to make an inventory of all Tutsi in Kigali, I realize innocent people will be killed . . . As my own mother is Tutsi, you understand I cannot agree with what is happening."[2]

The story that followed was most extraordinary and went beyond anything that Marchal could have imagined.[3] After two hours of talking, Marchal and Jean-Pierre decided to stay in contact through the Belgian Captain Frank Claes who had been present at their meeting.[4] Marchal went straight to the residence

---

1 Roméo Dallaire, Shake Hands with the Devil, The Failure of Humanity in Rwanda, p. 141 (2004) (hereinafter Dallaire).

2 Interview with L, Marchal, January 21, 2005; Luc Marchal, Titel, Aan de poorten van de Rwandese hel: Getuigenis van een peacekeeper, pp. 133–136 (2001) (hereinafter Marchal).

3 Interview with L. Marchal, January 21, 2005; Marchal, pp. 133–136.

4 Frank Claes was a Belgian para-commando and Special Forces Officer, head of UNAMIR intelligence section.

of the Force Commander where he shared the story with Dallaire and Brent Beardsley.[5]

Astonished by Marchal's information, Dallaire decided to immediately send a fax to General Baril, the Military Adviser to the Secretary-General of the United Nations and head of the military division of the Department of Peace-Keeping Operations (DPKO). He decided to inform Special Representative of the Secretary-General (SRSG), Jaques Roger Booh Booh, the next morning. For more than two hours Dallaire and Beardsley puzzled on the exact wording of the fax. On the night of January 10–11 they sent their carefully worded fax, now known as "The Genocide Fax," to New York.[6]

8.2 THE GENOCIDE FAX

The fax was titled "Request for protection informant." Dallaire commenced the cable by saying that he was put in contact with a "very, very important government politician," a top-level trainer in the cadre of the Interahamwe-armed militia of the MRND.[7]

Dallaire explained in this fax that the informant had been in charge of the demonstrations a few days before, which had been aimed at targeting the deputies of the opposition parties and the Belgian soldiers. The fax stated that the demonstrators hoped to provoke the RPF to fire upon the demonstrators and provoke civil war. Deputies were to be assassinated upon entry or exit from the Parliament. Belgian troops were to be provoked, and if Belgian soldiers were restored to force, a number of them were to be killed, thus guaranteeing Belgian withdrawal from Rwanda.[8]

The cable continued by saying that the Interahamwe had trained 1,700 men in the camps of the FAR, split into groups of 40 throughout Kigali. The informant had been ordered to register all Tutsi in Kigali, which he expected to be for their extermination. He argued that his personnel were able to kill 1,000 Tutsi in 20 minutes.[9] The informant was prepared to identify major arms caches throughout Rwanda, containing at least 135 weapons, but he wanted passports and protection for his wife and children.[10]

In the concluding paragraphs Dallaire stated: "It is our intention to take action within the next 36 hours." The Force Commander recommended that the informant was given protection and was evacuated out of the country. He added

---

5 Interview with L. Marchal, January 21, 2005; Marchal, pp. 133–136.

6 Dallaire, pp. 145–146.

7 Code Cable, January 11, 1994, from Dallaire to Baril, point 1. For the original fax, see Annex 3.

8 Code Cable, January 11, 1994, from Dallaire to Baril, point 2.

9 Code Cable, January 11, 1994, from Dallaire to Baril, points 5 and 6.

10 Code Cable, January 11, 1994, from Dallaire to Baril, point 8.

that the possibility of a trap was not fully excluded. Dallaire ended the cable with the motto: "Where there's a will, there's a way, let's go."[11]

In his book Dallaire explains that he had chosen to formulate the fax in these words because he wanted New York to realize that "even though he wanted to move quickly, he was not blind to the possibility that this could be a well-laid trap." Furthermore, he wanted to make clear that he did not ask for permission to seize weapons, but that he was informing New York of his plan.[12] According to Beardsley, Dallaire was not asking for permission, but he was saying: "This is what I intend to do and I've got 36 hours. We're conscious that this could be a set-up. This guy may be too good to be true and they're setting us up to do something, but what we will do is, we will confirm." Beardsley: "We expected to use that period [36 hours] for reconnaissance and confirmation. Then, within 36 hours, we wanted to hit at least four of those arms caches simultaneously, to knock the Interahamwe off balance and knock the extremists off balance, to capture these weapons, to expose this Interahamwe and extremist element to the nation."[13] But, as will be seen below, the U.N. main decisionmakers would not allow them to do that.[14]

8.3 THE RECIPIENTS OF THE FAX

By sending the fax to the Military Adviser Maurice Baril, Dallaire was breaking with the usual protocol. The official operating procedure was to send all communication-matters between the Force Commander and DPKO through the U.N. political civil servant, SRSG Booh Booh.[15] According to Dallaire he was opening a line of communication in an area where "he had no authority to do so."[16] In the Frontline interview, Dallaire explained why he had chosen to operate in this way:

> In normal procedures the Force Commander, who is the number two, doesn't send operational or new actions that are going to be taken directly to the Military Adviser of the Secretary General [Baril]. In this case [Baril] was a very good friend . . . [He was a] Canadian who had been there already for a year. . . . The workings with Jacques Roger Booh Booh had become very strained. . . . So when I got that information, it was late at night and [Booh Booh] wasn't keen on being dis-

---

11 Translated from French into English. Original text: "Peux ce que veux, allons-y." Code Cable, January 11, 1994, from Dallaire to Baril, points 9, 10, 11, 13.

12 Dallaire, pp. 145, 146.

13 Frontline interview with Beardsley, November 15, 2003.

14 See Section 8.4.4.

15 Dallaire, p. 145.

16 *Id.*

> turbed. . . . So I sent it directly, because it was a military operation, to [Baril]. Now that is not the formal way of doing it. But I sent it to him because I needed him to move it fast in the U.N. headquarters.[17]

These words show that the importance of the information and the urgency of the situation caused Dallaire to choose to operate through a more "direct-line," but at the same time he stuck to a merely "military approach." Dallaire did not consider sending the fax directly to the main political decisionmakers. The Carlsson Report criticizes him for this choice. The Report states that the information of the fax, particularly the information regarding the extermination of the Tutsi, was so important that it should have received the "highest priority and highest attention," meaning that Dallaire should not have sent the fax *only* to Military Adviser Baril. According to the Carlsson Report: "The cable clearly warranted immediate attention of—at the very least—the Under-Secretaries General for Peacekeeping Operations [Annan and Riza] and Political Affairs [Goulding]."[18]

Nonetheless, after Baril had received the fax, the information was immediately shared with Kofi Annan and Iqbal Riza of the political department of DPKO and with Hedi Anabi of the Department of African Affairs. However, though Annan and Riza received the fax at this point, they informed neither the Secretary-General nor the Security Council.

The Carlsson Report criticized Annan and Riza as well for not giving the fax the "highest priority and highest attention." The Carlsson Report stated that the cautious instructions that Annan and Riza sent to Booh Booh and Dallaire following the fax show that they did realize the significance of the fax.[19] Instructing Booh Booh and Dallaire to inform the heads of missions of France, Belgium and the United States was, according to Carlsson, not enough: "The seriousness of the threats in the cable justified informing the Council as whole. At the very least the Security Council should have been informed when UNAMIR reported in early February that the President had done nothing to act on the information and that the situation on the ground was deteriorating."[20]

The foregoing shows that the Carlsson Report criticized Dallaire as well as Annan and Riza for not giving the fax the "highest priority and highest attention." It must, however, be said that the criticism of Annan and Riza was not very much underlined. Firstly, the Carlsson Report did not criticize Annan and

---

17 Frontline interview with Dallaire, Autumn 2003.

18 United Nations, Report of the Independent Inquiry into the Actions of the United Nations during the 1994 Genocide in Rwanda, December 15, 1999, Ingvar Carlsson, Han, Sung-Joo, Rufus, M. Kupolati, U.N. Doc. S/1999/1257, p. 33 (hereinafter Carlsson Report, S/1999/1257).

19 Carlsson Report, S/1999/1257, p. 33; see the next paragraph, for the instructions that Annan and Riza sent to Booh Booh and Dallaire.

20 Carlsson Report, S/1999/1257, p. 33. See the next paragraph for this instruction.

Riza explicitly for the failure to inform the Secretary-General. Secondly, by saying that the Security Council "should at the very least have been informed in early February," Carlsson weakened the report's criticism of Annan and Riza's inaction immediately after receiving the fax. This fax that warned of the extermination of the Tutsi should (in our opinion) have been shared *immediately* with both the Security Council and Secretary-General—an aspect that should have been more underlined in the Carlsson Report.

As we have observed, Dallaire and Beardsley made the deliberate choice to send the fax directly to the top level of the military side of the United Nations (Baril) and not to the top political officials United Nations (Riza, Annan and Annabi). Declining to involve Booh Booh is also consistent with this way of thinking along the hierarchical lines of the military side of the United Nations. Baril was, for Beardsley and Dallaire, not only fellow military but also a fellow Canadian. The confidentiality of this highly qualified information could best be kept by transmitting the message to the trustworthy high-ranking U.N. military official, Baril. Moreover, Beardsley and Dallaire were most interested in starting a military operation—hitting the arms caches—within 36 hours. The content of the fax was nevertheless forwarded directly by Baril to Riza, Annan and Annabi. Thus, the top level of the political United Nations was informed, and they had the opportunity to inform the highest political echelon at the level of (Under-) Secretary-General. We now know that this was not done.

Although the recipients of the fax were aware of the highest urgency, we have to realize that the label of the fax "request for protection informant" was not alarming in itself, though the content of the fax "ability to kill thousands Tutsi in twenty minutes" was much more so. As we will observe, it was indeed perceived as such, because the message was not neglected, nor was it underestimated. They did not see the message as "crying wolf," because they responded immediately as we will see in the next section.

8.4 THE INSTRUCTIONS FOLLOWING THE GENOCIDE FAX

8.4.1 The First Response from Annan and Riza to Booh Booh

Annan and Riza's first reaction to Dallaire's fax was a cable on January 11 entitled "Immediate and Only."[21] The cable was not sent to Dallaire but only to SGSR Booh Booh. According to the cable, the information received was "a

21 Carlsson Report, S/1999/1257, p. 11. The cable came from Annan and was signed off by Riza. In his Frontline interview, when Riza was asked who made the decisions following the genocide fax, he answered: "I was in charge of the mission and I decided on what instructions were sent. Those were the instructions that went under my signature, yes." Frontline interview with Riza.

cause of concern but full of inconsistencies." Headquarters stated: "No reconnaissance or other action, including response to request protection, should be taken by UNAMIR unless clear guidance is received from Headquarters."[22]

8.4.2 The Direct Reaction from Booh Booh to New York

On the same day, January 11, Booh Booh replied by fax to New York, in which he emphasized that Faustin Twagiramungu had been very clear to Dallaire by saying that he had "total, repeat total confidence in the veracity and true ambitions of the informant." Booh Booh noted that the informant had only between 24 and 48 hours before he had to distribute the arms. Furthermore, the SRSG requested guidance on the overall situation and specifically on the request for protection of Jean Pierre. Booh Booh ended his fax by saying that Dallaire was willing to "pursue the operation in accordance with military doctrine with reconnaissance, rehearsal and implementation using overwhelming force. Should at any time during reconnaissance, planning or preparation, any sign of a possible contravening or possibility of an undue risky scenario present itself the operation would be called off."[23]

8.4.3 New York's Reaction to Booh Booh and Dallaire

Headquarters responded immediately.[24] This time the fax was sent to Booh Booh, as well as Dallaire. The cable contained strong and clear language: seizure of weapons went beyond the mandate of Resolution 872. Therefore, they could not agree with the proposed operation.[25] Instead, Booh Booh and Dallaire received instructions to make a *démarche* to President Habyarimana. They had to inform him of the activities of the Interahamwe and the training and deployment of subversive groups, which was a clear violation of Arusha and the Kigali Weapon Secure Area (KWSA) agreement. Headquarters noted that Booh Booh and Dallaire had to assume that Habyarimana was not aware of these activities. At the same time, they had to insist that the President take immediate action and that he inform UNAMIR within 48 hours of the steps that he had taken, including the recovery of arms. The cable continued by saying that before Dallaire and Booh Booh were to meet the President, they first had to notify the ambassadors of Belgium, France and the United States and ask them to make similar *démarches*. Furthermore, headquarters noted that the Security Council

22 Carlsson Report, S/1999/1257, p. 11.

23 *Id.*; Samantha Power, A problem from hell: America and the age of genocide, p. 344 (2003) (hereinafter Power, 2003).

24 Carlsson Report, S/1999/1257, p. 11; Dallaire, pp. 146–147. Again, the cable came from Annan and was signed off by Riza.

25 Carlsson Report, S/1999/1257, p. 11; Dallaire, pp. 146, 147.

was not yet going to be informed but that if any violence occurred "the information on the militia would have to be brought to the attention of the Council." The cable concluded with the statement: "The overriding consideration is the need to avoid entering into a course of action that might lead to the use of force and unanticipated repercussions."[26]

8.4.4 Communications Between Dallaire and New York

The cable made Dallaire furious and frustrated. Not only was he not allowed to prevent a catastrophe by confiscating the arms, for transparency reasons he even had to inform Habyarimana. Dallaire tried to convince headquarters of the need for military action. He made many phone-calls arguing the necessity of arms raids.[27] He pleaded that he "had to do this" and that if they did not seize the arms caches, these weapons would be used against them. The answer from headquarters was consistently "No" to all the requests from UNAMIR in Rwanda.[28]

8.4.5 Dallaire's Vain Attempts to Influence Booh Booh

Dallaire made attempts to convince Booh Booh, who had the authority to appeal directly to the Secretary-General, who in turn had the power to change the decision of DPKO. Booh Booh, however, decided to follow the instructions from New York. Dallaire wrote in his book that the failure to persuade New York to act on Jean Pierre's information still haunts him today.[29]

8.5 ARMS RAIDS AND THE SCOPE OF RESOLUTION 872's MANDATE

Security Council Resolution 872 stated that UNAMIR would "contribute to the security of the city of Kigali inter alia within a weapons-secure area established by the parties in and around the city."[30] The proposed arms raids had to fall under this provision. As we have already seen in Chapter 4, the Security Council had deliberately agreed upon a weaker mandate for UNAMIR than was foreseen in the Arusha Accords.[31] The UNAMIR mandate no longer encom-

---

26 Carlsson Report, S/1999/1257, p. 11; Dallaire, pp. 146, 147; Philiph Gourevitch, The Genocide Fax, The New Yorker, May 11, 1998, pp. 43–46.

27 Dallaire, pp. 146, 147; Marchal, p. 138.

28 Power, 2003 pp. 344–345.

29 Dallaire, pp. 147–148.

30 U.N. Doc. S/RES/872.

31 See Chapter 4 for a comparison between the Arusha Accords, the SC Resolution 872 and the Rules of Engagement of the mission.

passed a security guarantee for the whole country, plus the provision for the assistance in the tracking of arms caches was deleted.[32] This explains why the Carlsson Report did not criticize the Secretariat for their restrictive interpretation, which stated that the raids fell outside the mandate.[33]

The rejection from headquarters of Dallaire's proposal to seize arms was based on the conviction that raids on arm caches fell outside the mandate of Resolution 872, though the views upon this question differed widely. Annan, Riza, Baril and Annabi firmly believed that the raids fell outside the mandate.[34] U.N. Secretary-General Boutros Boutros-Ghali and Booh Booh both decided to go along with the decision of Annan and Riza.[35] On the opposite side, there were the two men in the field, Dallaire and Beardsley, who were both convinced that arms raids did fall within the mandate.[36] In our view, this different opinion was based on the rules for the operational procedure that they made in December 1993. In Section 4.5.2 we have elaborated on this, and we have underlined that the search for arms, munitions and explosives was clearly included.

In the Frontline interview, Riza stated that they (the Secretariat) did not allow the Force Commander to go ahead with the raids on arms caches, because they had to go by the mandate that was given by the Security Council. According to him, the decision not to seize weapons was not a mistake: "Dallaire was asking to take such risks going outside his mandate. And we said no." Beardsley, in his interview with Frontline, said:

> We just saw it well within our mandate. The Arusha peace agreement had called for the mutual international force—us—to recover illegal weapons; it had authorized us to do that. The mandate that we had told us to contribute to the security of the city of Kigali. In our rules of engagement, we had anticipated the recovery of illegal weapons . . . So when the answer came back in a few hours saying, "Absolutely no

---

32 See Section 4.2 and Article 54, point B.

33 Carlsson Report, S/1999/1257, pp. 33–34.

34 Carlsson Report, S/1999/1257, pp. 33–34; Dallaire, pp. 147–148.

35 Carlsson Report, S/1999/1257, pp. 33–34; Dallaire, pp. 147–148. On January 14 Boutros Ghali had a conversation with Booh Booh in which the Secretary-General confirmed the decision of his subordinates. According to Des Forges, the decision of the Secretary-General was made out of fear that an escalation would "force UNAMIR into a peacemaking rather than a peacekeeping role." See Alison Des Forges, Leave None to Tell the Story, Genocide in Rwanda, p. 154 (1999). The Belgian ambassador testified before the Belgian Senate that: "He [Boutros-Ghali] was concerned about the serious political repercussions that such an action [confiscation of arms] would cause and therefore before beginning such an operation, there must be serious reflection. . . . That is why New York insists on inquiries and measures from Habyarimana's side." See Sénat de Belgique, Rapport du Groupe Ad Hoc Rwanda A La Commission des Affairs Etrangeres, Sénat de Belgique, 7 janvier 1997, p. 86.

36 Carlsson Report, S/1999/1257, p. 33.

way, you're going way beyond your mandate," we were totally stunned by that.[37]

The Carlsson Report stated however that the Secretariat should have chosen a different approach throughout the months of January and February. As a result of the continuing distribution of arms, Dallaire kept on asking for arms raids, but the Secretariat turned down all Dallaire's requests by using the same argument that the seizure of arms fell outside the scope of the mandate.[38] The Carlsson Report stated that at that moment the Secretariat should have brought the issue of the weakness of the mandate before the Security Council with the request to rectify it. There is no proof that the Secretariat did so.[39]

8.6 CONCLUSIONS ON THE U.N. POLITICAL LEADERSHIP OF ANNAN, RIZA AND ANNABI

Some argue that the inaction of U.N. headquarters can (partly) be justified by the fact that these kind of faxes are received all the time by DPKO.

Marley, Lieutenant Colonel of the U.S. military liaison to the Arusha process, said in the Frontline interview: "I tended to discredit the accuracy of the information [in Dallaire's fax] itself, as I believe others did, because we had heard allegations of genocide, or warnings of genocide, pertaining to Rwanda dating back at least to 1992. So we'd heard it before."[40]

Boutros-Ghali said in his interview with Frontline:

> In retrospect, this telegram had an importance—but we received hundreds of telegrams giving information—that there will be an assassination of Mr. So-and-So, that there are arms which have been discovered. We had this in Salvador . . . in Guatemala, or in Nicaragua, et cetera. Retroactively, everybody paid attention to this telegram, but we practically receive tens of telegrams of this kind every day.

When Frontline asked Annan how he judged headquarters' response to Dallaire's fax in retrospect, he answered: "In fact, [Dallaire] had sent other messages, where sometimes he questioned that 'Somebody came and gave me this information. I don't know how sincere it is, whether I am being manipulated or not.'"[41]

---

37 Frontline interview with Beardsley, November 15, 2003.

38 On January 22, February 2, February 15, February 27 and March 15, Dallaire asked to be allowed to seize arms. See Section 11.1. Dallaire requests again to seize arms.

39 Carlsson Report, S/1999/1257, pp. 33–34.

40 Frontline interview with Marley.

41 Frontline interview with Annan, February 17, 2004.

It must be acknowledged that many threatening faxes are received by DPKO. It must also be acknowledged that Dallaire's fax did not warn explicitly of an unfolding genocide, but he did warn of "significant killings and massacres."[42] As Carlsson stated correctly, the fax "indicated the existence of a plan to exterminate the Tutsi."[43] A fax containing such an explicit and serious warning is highly exceptional, even within DPKO, and should have been treated differently to all others received.

Destexhe, the former Secretary-General of the Belgian NGO Doctors without Borders said in our interview with him: "[The argument that many of these faxes are received] is ridiculous because nobody can find any telex like this. I don't think there is a single other one where you speak about killing 1000 people every 20 minutes, so this fax is really unique."[44] In hindsight, Riza admitted that the wording of this fax was different to others. In his interview with Frontline, he said: "There are a number of cables that we get of this nature, but not of this magnitude, not with such dire predictions."[45]

Not only the wording of the fax, but also the highly tense political and security situation in Rwanda should have triggered the Secretariat to act. The Secretariat should have interpreted the fax in the light of the pre-existing warnings and intelligence. As shown above, the intelligence and signals regarding the threatening security situation were numerous: the peace-keeping mission had started with the massacres throughout November, RTLMC and newspapers were citing racism against the Tutsi, UNAMIR had received intelligence on Habyarimana's "Machiavelli plan" and newspapers and human rights organizations had been publishing reports about the distribution of arms ordered by Habyarimana and targeting the Inyenzi and the Belgians, and, above all, the U.N. Special Rapporteur Ndiaye had published a report talking explicitly of a possible genocide. All these signals and the existing intelligence corresponded with Dallaire's fax.

The explicit and serious warning set out in the fax, together with highly tense political and security situation in Rwanda, should have led to a far more adequate response from U.N. headquarters. Instead, the Security Council was not even informed of this early warning, no decision-making process based upon it could therefore follow and early action to prevent the genocide was precluded.

In our view, it is important not to concentrate on just one moment in assessing the reaction from New York to the events in Rwanda. It was not only the fax of January 10 but also the repeated requests based upon the increasing tensions in Rwanda that were all turned down by the U.N. political leadership—Riza, Annan and Annabi. They have been condemned in the Carlsson Report because of the pattern of neglecting all these requests. We agree with this con-

---

42 Frontline interview with Dallaire, Autumn 2003.

43 Carlsson Report, S/1999/1257, p. 33.

44 Frontline interview with Destexhe, April 22, 2005.

45 Frontline interview with Riza.

clusion of the Carlsson Report, because the continuing refusal of Annan, Riza and Annabi to approve any early action to prevent the atrocities is extremely concerning. The signals from UNAMIR in Rwanda were not ignored, but the early warnings that were received were not translated into any early action, nor were the signals and requests for action forwarded to the U.N. Security Council. The withholding of this information from the members of the Security Council by the U.N. bureaucracy precluded any Security Council decision in this field.

CHAPTER 9

THE NEGATIVE RESPONSE OF NEW YORK AND CAPITALS IN THE WEST TO THE DETERIORATING SITUATION

9.1 FOLLOWING THE INSTRUCTIONS AFTER THE GENOCIDE FAX

Failing to convince the Secretariat, General Roméo Dallaire was forced to abide by the instructions received.

Dallaire and Jacques Roger Booh Booh had to make a *démarche* to President Habyarimana, in which he was informed of the information received and asked to take action within 48 hours. Furthermore, they had to inform the heads of the missions of the United States, Belgium and France of Jean Pierre's story and ask them to make a similar *démarche*.[1]

On January 13 Booh Booh cabled Kofi Annan outlining these undertaken activities. He informed New York that the heads of missions had expressed serious concerns about the information and that they would inform their governments.[2] In his book, Dallaire explains that none of the ambassadors seemed to be surprised by Jean Pierre's story, which according to Dallaire meant that the information was merely a confirmation of what the ambassadors already knew. Dallaire had asked the ambassadors to find sanctuary for Jean Pierre and his family, but they had all refused.[3]

Booh Booh's cable continued by describing the meeting with President Habyarimana on January 12. The Special Representative to the Secretary-General (SRSG) noted that the President had denied knowledge of the activities of the militia and had agreed upon an investigation, the findings of which he would make available to UNAMIR. When Dallaire and Booh Booh had raised the issue of the harassment of UNAMIR personnel and the violence of Rwandans "all belonging to one specific group" during the demonstration of April 8, the

1 Roméo Dallaire, Shake Hands with the Devil, The Failure of Humanity in Rwanda, p. 149 (2004) (hereinafter Dallaire); United Nations, Report of the Independent Inquiry into the Actions of the United Nations during the 1994 Genocide in Rwanda, December 15, 1999, Ingvar Carlsson, Han, Sung-Joo, Rufus, M. Kupolati, U.N. Doc. S/1999/1257, p. 11 (hereinafter Carlsson Report, S/1999/1257).

2 Carlsson Report, S/1999/1257, p. 12.

3 Dallaire, p. 148.

President had answered that he was unaware of the demonstration.[4] A cable of February 2 from Booh Booh to Annan would show that Habyarimana never informed UNAMIR of the promised investigation.[5] This inaction on the side of Habyarimana would put the credibility and reliability of Habyarimana further at stake, but this warning was not taken seriously by New York.

Lastly, Booh Booh's cable mentioned that Habyarimana had asked Booh Booh and Dallaire to inform the President of the MRND, Mathieu Ngirumpatse (Jean Pierre's boss). Following this request, the SRSG and the Force Commander met with Mathieu Ngirumpatse and Joseph Nzirorera, the Secretary-General of the MRND. Booh Booh explained that both deputies had denied that the MRND or its militia were involved in the alleged activities. The fax stated that "the president of the MRND seemed unnerved and is reported to have subsequently ordered an accelerated distribution of weapons." In a final comment, Booh Booh wrote that the feedback from the meetings showed that both Habyarimana and the MRND officials were "bewildered by the specificity of the information."[6]

9.2 THE RESPONSE OF THE HEADS OF MISSIONS OF FRANCE, BELGIUM AND THE UNITED STATES TO THE FAX OF DALLAIRE

On January 13 ambassador Swinnen sent a fax to the Belgian Ministry of Foreign Affairs in which he described Jean Pierre's information.[7] Having set out Jean Pierre's story, the ambassador wrote: "This information confirms what was already believed or presumed."[8] Swinnen added: "All this cannot simply be ignored."[9] Swinnen mentioned that Booh Booh had asked the heads of mis-

---

4 Dallaire, pp. 148–149; Carlsson Report, S/1999/1257, p. 12.

5 Carlsson Report, S/1999/1257, p. 12. See Section 11.1.

6 Carlsson Report, S/1999/1257, p. 12; Alison Des Forges, Leave None to Tell the Story, Genocide in Rwanda, p. 152 (1999) (hereinafter Des Forges), note 43: Fax from Jacques-Roger Booh-Booh and General Dallaire to DPKO, U.N., January 13, 1994 (confidential source).

7 The information that Swinnen sent to Brussels was identical to the information that Dallaire had sent to New York. Telex No. 32, January 13, 1994, of the Belgian embassy Kigali to the Ministry of Foreign Affairs in Brussels; Sénat de Belgique, Commission d'Enquête parlementaire concernant les événements au Rwanda (Commission of parliamentary enquiry concerning the events in Rwanda), session de 1997–1998, 6 décembre 1997, Rapport fait au nom de la commission d'enquête par MM Mahoux et Verhofstadt, Annexes, p. 27 (hereinafter Annex Belgian Senate).

8 This proves that Dallaire's understanding that Jean Pierre's story was merely a confirmation for the heads of missions of France, Belgium and the United States was correct, at least for Belgium. Annex Belgian Senate, p. 27.

9 Telex No. 32, January 13, 1994, of the Belgian embassy Kigali to the Ministry of Foreign Affairs in Brussels; Annex Belgian Senate, p. 27.

sion to make an immediate *démarche* to the President and ended his fax with a request for instructions.[10] The same day, the Belgian Ministry of Foreign Affairs gave permission to make a *démarche* to President Habyarimana together with their French and American colleagues.[11]

As scheduled, on January 14 the three ambassadors met with President Habyarimana. This meeting was initially planned to temper the objections against the installation of the Broad Based Transitional Government (BBTG) and to express concern about the implementation of the Arusha Accords.[12] Now it could be used to make a *démarche* to the President. Judging by the Belgian telex-communication, however, it becomes clear that the *démarche* made was very weak.[13] The ambassadors did not discuss the information from Jean Pierre explicitly, and the plan to wound and kill the Belgian peace-keepers was only mentioned in a very indirect way.[14] Reporting upon the meeting, Swinnen wrote to the Belgian Ministry of Foreign Affairs: "Our statement regarding the security was repetitive and strong[ly] underlined."[15] Subsequently he asked whether a specific *démarche* was still necessary. He stated: "Regarding the strong emphasis that [in the meeting with the President] was put on the security aspects (the activities of the Interahamwe and the weapon distribution) the question arises whether a specific démarche, especially because Habyarimana showed understanding, [is still necessary]." Swinnen added that Paris had reacted "restrictively" towards the idea of a specific *démarche*.[16] The next day, January 15, Swinnen informed the Ministry of Foreign Affairs that the three ambassadors

---

10 Telex No. 32, January 13, 1994, of the Belgian embassy Kigali to the Ministry of Foreign Affairs in Brussels; Annex Belgian Senate, p. 27.

11 Annex Belgian Senate, p. 29.

12 Telex No. 41, January 14, 1994, of the Belgian embassy in Kigali to the Ministry of Foreign Affairs in Brussels; Annex Belgian Senate, p. 28.

13 Telex No. 41, January 14, 1994, of the Belgian embassy in Kigali to the Ministry of Foreign Affairs in Brussels; Annex Belgian Senate, p. 28; Belgian Ad Hoc Group, p. 41; United Nations, The United Nations and Rwanda, 1993–1996, p. 32 (1996) (hereinafter U.N., the United Nations and Rwanda).

14 Telex No. 41, January 14, 1994, of the Belgian embassy in Kigali to the Ministry of Foreign Affairs in Brussels; Annex Belgian Senate, p. 28. According to Des Forges, the ambassadors did not say anything specific about the information of Jean Pierre in their meeting with the President because the "French opposed doing so." *See* Des Forges, p. 154, note 49: According to the report of the French National Assembly, the three diplomats made a *démarche* to Habyarimana "in the same sense"—but not identical to—that of the U.N. representatives (Booh Booh and Dallaire). Assemblée Nationale, Mission d'information commune, Enquête, Tome I, Rapport, p. 203.

15 Telex No. 41, January 14, 1994, of the Belgian embassy in Kigali to the Ministry of Foreign Affairs in Brussels; Annex Belgian Senate, p. 28; Belgian Ad Hoc Group, p. 41; U.N., The United Nations and Rwanda, p. 32.

16 Telex No. 41, January 14, 1994, of the Belgian embassy in Kigali to the Ministry of Foreign Affairs in Brussels; Annex Belgian Senate, p. 28.

of France, the United States and Belgium had decided not to make another *démarche* to the President but that they would follow the information of Jean Pierre very closely.[17] In the same fax Swinnen pointed once again to the possibility that President Habyarimana "as many assert" was in control of what is called "a Machiavelli Plan."[18] In another fax of January 15 the Belgian embassy wrote to the Ministry of Foreign Affairs in Brussels that: "UNAMIR has sufficient proved information now regarding the existence of at least four weapon depots. The most important 'cache' is the headquarters of MRND in the Kimihurura area. The informant showed several dozen weapons to an African UNAMIR officer who was especially appointed by Dallaire to accompany the informant." The fax stated that "according to the informant the destabilization plan is very well organized, the Interahamwe operates throughout numerous cells and have been ordered to localize the Tutsi." The fax continues by saying that UNAMIR is inclined to conduct investigation operations as soon as possible, "because it knows that the weapons will disappear in the coming days in the direction of the Interahamwe and the civilian population." The fax mentioned that New York decided to postpone the dismantling of weapons, which meant that the distribution would continue in the coming days "with all risks that are attached to this regarding the destabilization of the country."[19]

We may conclude that it is highly remarkable that the three ambassadors, who were asked by Booh Booh and Dallaire to make a *démarche* to President Habyarimana, made just this weak *démarche* during a scheduled meeting. The inactivity in the follow-up of Jean Pierre's story was considered to be especially striking for ambassador Swinnen. First of all, it was Belgian peace-keepers that according to Jean Pierre were to be wounded or killed as part of a plan. Secondly, the Belgian ambassador seemed to be very aware of the dangerous situation. As seen above, he wrote to the Ministry of Foreign Affairs that Jean Pierre's story was a "confirmation of what was already expected" and that this information "could not be ignored."[20] Thirdly, in the same fax as that in which Swinnen informed his Ministry that no specific *démarche* would be made, he wrote that Habyarimana was said to be in control of the so-called "Machiavelli Plan." Lastly, Swinnen was not hindered by his Ministry of Foreign Affairs; he had received permission to make a *démarche*.[21]

Swinnen's notion of the dangerous situation and the possibility of the involvement of Habyarimana were at odds with the decision not to make a spe-

---

17 Telex No. 44, January 15, 1994, of the Belgian embassy in Kigali to the Ministry of Foreign Affairs in Brussels; Annex Belgian Senate, p. 28.

18 See Section 7.2 for the "Machiavelli Plan."

19 See Telex No. 45, January 15, 1994, of the Belgian embassy in Kigali to the Ministry of Foreign Affairs in Brussels; Annex Belgian Senate, pp. 28–29. See also Section 11.2.

20 Telex No. 32, January 13, 1994, of the Belgian embassy Kigali to the Ministry of Foreign Affairs in Brussels; Annex Belgian Senate, p. 28.

21 Annex Belgian Senate, p. 29.

cific *démarche*. An explanation lies most likely in the French rejection of a firm response towards Habyarimana. According to Des Forges, it was due to French opposition that the three ambassadors did not say anything specific about the information of Jean Pierre in their meeting with the President.[22] According to Swinnen, it was France which had reacted "restrictively" towards the idea of a specific *démarche*.[23]

9.3 JEAN PIERRE PROVES HIS STORY BUT IS DENIED ASYLUM

As stated above, the ambassadors had refused to give Jean Pierre and his family sanctuary.[24] In the name of Dallaire, Marchal repeated the request to ambassador Swinnen, but the official reaction of Belgium was that no asylum could be allowed, in order to remain neutral.[25] In response to the refusal, Swinnen sent a fax to the Ministry of Foreign Affairs in Brussels in which he suggested an investigation into whether Jean Pierre could be taken by a U.N. service into Tanzania or Kenia.[26] Whether a response to this suggestion was ever received is unknown.

In the meantime, Marchal had his second meeting with Jean Pierre. Marchal told him that proof was needed to sustain his story. That same day, Jean Pierre showed the Senegalese Captain Deme an arms cache in the basement of the MRND headquarters. Jean Pierre, who told the guards at the MRND headquarters that his companion was an African friend, had no problems showing Deme around. Afterwards Jean Pierre escorted Captain Claes and Captain Deme throughout the city for two hours, in which he identified more weapons depots. At the end of the meeting, Jean Pierre urged UNAMIR to take prompt action, because the weapons would soon be distributed. With this new information Dallaire hoped to convince New York that action was needed, but headquarters did not change its opinion.[27] A few days later, Jean Pierre told Captain Claes that the weapons had indeed been distributed.

Now that the weapons had been spread amongst the people, and Jean Pierre was unable to get asylum, Marchal realized that further contact with Jean Pierre

---

22 Des Forges p. 154.

23 See Telex No. 41, January 14, 1994, of the Belgian embassy in Kigali to the Ministry of Foreign Affairs in Brussels; Annex Belgian Senate, p. 28.

24 Dallaire, p. 148.

25 Interview with L. Marchal, January 21, 2005.

26 Annex Belgian Senate, p. 77; Telex No. 45, January 15, 1994, of the Belgian Embassy in Kigali to the Belgian Ministry of Foreign Affairs.

27 Luc Marchal, Aan de poorten van de Rwandese hel: Getuigenis van een peacekeeper, p. 139 (2001) (hereinafter Marchal); Des Forges, p. 153, note 46: Service de Police Judiciaire auprès de la Justice Militaire, En cause de Dewez Joseph et Marchal Luc, Annexe A/6 au PV No. 1210 du 6/11/95.

was pointless.[28] He could not offer him any guarantees, and the official contact with Jean Pierre was therefore ended. Throughout January UNAMIR did stay in sporadic contact with Jean Pierre, but at the end of the month Jean Pierre broke all communication.[29] Jean Pierre disappeared at the end of January, and up to this day it is not clear what happened to him, although Rawson was of the opinion that he finally got out of the country to Kenya.[30] Claes also holds the opinion that he was moved from Rwanda to another African country.[31]

---

28 Marchal, pp. 140, 141.

29 Dallaire writes in his book that thanks to Jean Pierre UNAMIR had "all the information to confirm that a well-organized conspiracy consisted in the country to destroy the Arusha Accords, by all means necessary." Dallaire pp. 150–151.

30 Interview D. Rawson, May 26, 2005.

31 Interview W. Claes, January 13, 2006.

CHAPTER 10

DETERIORATING SECURITY IN RWANDA AND THE NEGATIVE RESPONSE FROM NEW YORK FROM JANUARY UP UNTIL MARCH

10.1 POLITICAL DEADLOCK IN THE ARUSHA PEACE AGREEMENTS

The installation of the transitional government was originally planned for December 31, 1993, but the ceremony did not take place. The installation was postponed and would be postponed another five times. Eventually the government would not be installed before the outbreak of the genocide.

On December 31 the installment was postponed to January 5, 1994. On January 5 only President Habyarimana was sworn in.[1] Due to a lack of consensus on the appointment of the ministers, the installment of the rest of the cabinet was postponed until February 14. By that date, the installment was postponed again to February 23, then to March 25, then to March 28 and finally to the beginning of April.[2]

Discussing the political deadlock in his second progress report of March 30, the U.N. Secretary-General, Boutros-Ghali, argued that during the previous months, his Special Representative Booh Booh (SRSG) had expressed his

---

[1] The difficulties existed especially within the Liberal Party (PL) and the Mouvement Démocratique Républicain (MRD) regarding the lists of their representatives to serve as ministers in the Broad Based Transitional Government (BBTG) and as deputies in the Transitional National Assembly. Furthermore, Habyarimana, supported by the Hutu hardliners of the MRD and the PL, launched several challenges to the interpretation of the Accords. One of the challenges was the proposal to give the Coalition pour Défense de la République (CDR) a seat in the transitional government. For more information, see Filip Reyntjens, L'Afrique des Grands Lacs, en crise: Rwanda, Burundi: 1988–1994, pp. 17–18 (1994) (hereinafter Reyntjens); Alison Des Forges, Leave None to Tell the Story, Genocide in Rwanda (1999) (hereinafter Des Forges); Gerard Prunier, The Rwanda Crisis: History of a Genocide (1959–1994), p. 204 (1995) (hereinafter Prunier); Frontline interview with Beardsley, November 15, 2003.

[2] Repeated here from Section 7.5.

concern over the delay in the installment of the various political leaders. Boutros-Ghali further stated that Booh Booh had urged Habyarimana and other leaders continuously to "expedite action for the establishment of the transitional government." The Secretary-General argued furthermore that he himself spoke to Habyarimana on a number of occasions by telephone and that he had written him to convey his strong expectations, as well as the international community's expectations, that the transitional government should be promptly established.[3]

This research will disclose that in the contacts between the Secretary-General with both the SRSG and President Habyarimana about the political deadlock and the failure to install the government, Boutros-Ghali's response consisted mainly of a threat to withdraw UNAMIR when no improvement was seen. This was exactly what the extremists wanted to hear.

In this chapter we will substantiate this observation with an explanation of the events in Rwanda and the subsequent reactions of U.N. headquarters in New York during the months of January, February and March 1994.

10.2 JANUARY 1994

In the second half of January, the security situation deteriorated rapidly. More violent demonstrations took place, and armed mobs started to riot in the streets of Kigali.

On January 14 Booh Booh informed Secretary-General Boutros-Ghali by telephone that the two parties in Rwanda had so far failed to respect the agreement to establish the transitional government. Booh Booh stated that he was trying to find a solution together with the ambassadors of France, Belgium, the United States and Tanzania. Boutros-Ghali asked Booh Booh to meet Habyarimana to express his concern about the situation and to explain that each day of delay might cost the United Nations many thousands of dollars, because the troops would be obliged to remain available for a long time and that for this reason delays would cause problems with the Security Council.[4] Whether or not Booh Booh delivered this message to Habyarimana is unknown to the authors.

However, when the Secretary-General received a phone call from Habyarimana that very same day, he got the opportunity to speak to the President himself. The file of the telephone conversation states that:

---

3 U.N. Doc. S/1994/360, Second progress report of the Secretary-General on UNAMIR for the period from December 30, 1993, to March 30, 1994, paragraph 8, p. 2 (hereinafter S/1994/360).

4 United Nations, Report of the Independent Inquiry into the Actions of the United Nations during the 1994 Genocide in Rwanda, December 15, 1999, Ingvar Carlsson, Han, Sung-Joo, Rufus, M. Kupolati, U.N. Doc. S/1999/1257, pp. 12, 13 (hereinafter Carlsson Report, S/1999/1257).

> The Secretary General assured the President that the U.N. trusted his leadership and asked him to do his best to resolve the problem. The Secretary General argued that unless there was progress the U.N. would be obliged to withdraw its presence. The President responded that this would be a disaster for his country. He promised that he would do his best and that he would meet the ambassadors again the following week.[5]

By telling Habyarimana bluntly that if there was no progress, UNAMIR would have to withdraw itself, Boutros-Ghali was probably giving the extremists the response that they had hoped for.

On January 16 some 5,000 MRND supporters came together at the Nyamirambo stadium. It was a calm demonstration that passed without incident. However, as UNAMIR discovered a few days later, the meeting had been used to distribute weapons amongst the people. One of the people that gave a speech during the gathering was Justin Mugenzi, leader of the Hutu Power Section of the Liberal Party. In his speech, Mugenzi referred to the ethnic divisions in Rwanda.[6] It was only a few days later that assassins tried to kill him.[7]

On January 21 a crowd, armed with machetes, gathered in front of the Conseil National de Développement (CND) building and was yelling at the RPF guards. Brent Beardsley, Canadian Military Assistant to General Roméo Dallaire, who realized that the situation could easily escalate, decided to intervene. He ordered the RPF not to respond to the provocation and to stay in their compound. Together with Dallaire's personal driver, Master Corporal Troute, Beardsley went into the crowd. At the center of the mob they found a man and a pregnant woman on the ground, both heavily wounded by the crowd. By threatening with their rifles, Beardsley and Troute were able to get the two civilians into safety.[8] This kind of violence in which innocent Tutsi civilians were attacked had rarely been seen up to this point, but it would soon become a common scene in the streets of Kigali.

The next day, machete and club-carrying youth had blocked all major intersections in Kigali.[9] The situation developed into a violent demonstration.

---

5 Carlsson Report, S/1999/1257, pp. 12, 13.

6 Des Forges states in her book that Justin Mugenzi, president of the PL, "played on" the ethnic divisions, but the authors do not know what the exact background of this statement was. Des Forges, p. 155.

7 Linda Melvern, A People Betrayed. The Role of the West in Rwanda's Genocide, p. 96 (2000) (hereinafter Melvern, 2000); Des Forges, p. 155, note 55: Marchal, "Considerations relatives," p. 14; Annexe A/7 au PV no. 1210 du 6/11/95 du Service de Police Judiciaire auprès de la Justice Militaire; Des Forges, p. 156, note 59: Anonymous, "Rwanda, Chronology." Who the assassins that tried to kill him were is unknown.

8 Roméo Dallaire, Shake Hands with the Devil, The Failure of Humanity in Rwanda, pp. 157–158 (2004) (hereinafter Dallaire).

9 *Id.*, pp. 159, 160; Melvern, 2000 p. 96.

UNAMIR decided to leave the situation up to the *gendarmerie*. It turned out to be a wise decision: Jean Pierre told Captain Frank Claeys that this demonstration had been another attempt by the extremists to entice the Belgian peacekeepers to use force.[10] As a result of this demonstration, Dallaire asked headquarters for a broader mandate on January 22.[11] Whether U.N. headquarters responded to Dallaire's request is unknown.

On January 24 Booh Booh complained to the press that weapons were being distributed from arms caches around Kigali and even inside the town.[12] On January 27 Boutros-Ghali wrote to Habyarimana to convey his strong expectations, as well as the international community's expectations, that the transitional government was going to be promptly established.[13]

Approaching the end of the month, the violence in Kigali increased.[14] Machete-carrying mobs attacking Tutsi started to turn up all over the city.[15] The Interahamwe rioted in the streets.[16] Major Frank Kamenzi, the RPF liaison officer to UNAMIR, was attacked with a grenade. Another grenade was thrown into UNAMIR's headquarters. Luckily there were no casualties. More grenades were thrown at the CND building.[17] According to Luc Marchal, January was a period of intimidation, theft, aggression, violence and murder.[18]

---

10 Dallaire, pp. 159–161. Dallaire gives a lengthy description of the demonstration on January 22 and does not speak of a demonstration on January 23. Melvern, on the other hand, speaks of a demonstration on the 23rd during which 47 people were killed. Melvern does not speak of a demonstration on January 22. Therefore, it may be that they are, in fact, speaking of the same demonstration. Melvern, 2000 p. 96; Dallaire, pp. 159–161.

11 Des Forges, part warnings. note 62: Anonymous, "Rwanda, Chronology." According to Melvern, Dallaire's request was made one day later, on January 23. Melvern, 2000 p. 96.

12 Howard Adelman and Astri Suhrke, Early warning and conflict management genocide in Rwanda, p. 28 (1995).

13 S/1994/360, paragraph 8, p. 2.

14 Luc Marchal, Aan de poorten van de Rwandese hel: Getuigenis van een peacekeeper pp. 151, 152 (2001) (hereinafter Marchal).

15 Dallaire, pp. 158, 159.

16 Des Forges, p. 157, note 65: Anonymous, "Rwanda, Chronology."

17 Marchal, pp. 151, 152; Des Forges, p. 158, note 69: Anonymous, "Rwanda, Chronology."

18 Marchal, pp. 150–152. On February 3 officers of the general staff in Evere (Operation Center of the Belgian Army) informed the Belgian Ministry of Foreign Affairs that they suspected the grenade attacks in Kigali to be the result of "an organized plan." Sénat de Belgique, Rapport du Groupe Ad Hoc Rwanda A La Commission des Affairs Etrangeres, Sénat de Belgique, 7 janvier 1997, p. 71 (hereinafter Belgian Ad Hoc Group). How many people were wounded or killed throughout the month of January is unknown.

This critical security situation caused Booh Booh and Dallaire to send a cable to Kofi Annan in New York on February 3.[19] They wrote that the security situation was deteriorating on a daily basis. The fax stated:

> Increasingly violent demonstrations, nightly grenade attacks, assassination attempts, political and ethnic killings, and we are receiving more and more reliable and confirmed information that the armed militias of the parties are stockpiling and may possibly be preparing to distribute arms to their supporters. If this distribution takes place, it will worsen the security situation even further and create a significant danger to the safety and security of U.N. military and civilian personnel and the population at large.[20]

According to the Carlsson Report, by sending this fax, "UNAMIR sought the guidance and approval of headquarters to commence deterrent operations."[21] Following this request, Dallaire's mandate was broadened a little. Dallaire got permission to assist the Rwandan authorities in recovering weapons, but he did not get the authorization to conduct such operations alone. U.N. headquarters stated: "UNAMIR's role . . . should be limited to a monitoring function."[22]

10.3 FEBRUARY 1994

In the first two weeks of February, the security situation was relatively quiet. The date for the installment of the government was getting closer, and

---

19 According to the Carlsson Report, Booh Booh sent the fax on February 2. According to Dallaire, he sent the fax on February 3. The text of Booh Booh's fax, which as cited in the Carlsson Report, contains the same elements as the text of Dallaire's fax cited in his book. In Dallaire's book, it is said that Booh Booh responded positively to his fax and that Booh Booh sent the fax to New York. Des Forges and Melvern speak of a fax from Dallaire on February 3 in which the same information is also cited. For this reason, it is assumed that the two faxes (Booh Booh's fax of February 2, which is cited in the Independent Inquiry, and Dallaire's fax of February 3 are the same). It seems that Dallaire wrote the fax that was sent by and with the approval of Booh Booh to New York. The text of this footnote is also in Section 11.1.

20 Carlsson Report, S/1999/1257, p. 13. According to Carlsson, Booh Booh sent this report on February 2, and according to Melvern, Dallaire sent this report on the 3rd. See Melvern, 2000 p. 99; see Section 11.1.

21 Carlsson Report, S/1999/1257, p. 13.

22 Dallaire states in his book that he received an answer from headquarters, but he does not give a specific date when he received this answer. It seems that he received the response fairly quickly, on February 3 or 4. Dallaire, pp. 167; Des Forges, note 82: Anonymous, "Rwanda, Chronology." See more in Section 11.1.

renewed attention was paid to the political situation.[23] Political negotiations took place in several so-called "all-party meetings." These meetings were organized by Booh Booh and took place at the UNAMIR headquarters in Kigali.[24] The meetings aimed at getting a consensus of the representatives of different parties within the transitional institutions.[25] At the last "all-party meeting" before the planned ceremony on February 14 the MRND suddenly did not turn up, and no final decision could be made on the different ministerial posts.[26] At the swearing-in the following day—February 15—none of the parties was present. On February 15 UNAMIR continued to express concern about the security situation in a meeting with ambassadors in Kigali from Belgium, France, Germany and the United States.[27]

In mid-February the Security Council gave a presidential statement about the deteriorating security situation in Rwanda. The Security Council reminded parties of their obligation to respect the Kigali Weapon Secure Area (KWSA) agreement.[28] The Council's statement was handed over to Habyarimana February 19, which would be the last day before grave violence erupted again.[29] The week of February 20–26 would become the most violent week in the approach to the genocide, characterized by many political murders.

On February 20 the MRD held a meeting at the Nyamirambo stadium. When the gathering began, the Interahamwe had surrounded the building, making it almost impossible for the MRD to get to the stadium. As soon as Prime Minister Agathe Uwilingiyamana, member of the MRD, arrived, the crowd started throwing stones. Belgian peace-keepers escorting Madame Agathe had to fire 63 shots in the air in order to free themselves.[30] The *gendarmerie* was finally able to get the situation under control, but not before at least five people had been killed.[31] That night, assailants tried to kill Prime Minister-desig-

---

23 The newly set date for the installment of the government was February 14.

24 The meetings took place on February 7, 10 and 13. S/1994/360, paragraph 12, p. 3.

25 According to Marchal, the date was set for February 15. Dallaire, p. 178.

26 The idea was raised to swear-in those ministers upon whom everyone had decided. The newly installed government would then be able to decide upon these last positions that were left unfulfilled. This way, the PL would have more time to resolve its internal problems and to join those institutions later. However, the PL and the MDR did not want to go ahead with this idea. They argued that all outstanding problems should first be resolved before proceeding to set up the BBTG; see S/1994/360, paragraph 12, p. 3 and Dallaire, pp. 178, 179.

27 Carlsson Report, S/1999/1257, p. 13.

28 The statement was made on February 17. Presidential Statement S/PRST/1994/8; Carlsson Report, S/1999/1257, p. 14.

29 Carlsson Report, S/1999/1257, p. 14.

30 Belgian Ad Hoc Group, p. 38; Dallaire, p. 186.

31 Marchal, p. 156.

nate Faustin Twagiramungu, member of the MRD. Twagimurungu was able to escape, but one of his bodyguards was killed in the attack.[32]

The following day, February 21, the CDR organized a demonstration. Hutu extremists blocked the center of Kigali, and CDR demonstrators burst into Madame Agathe's office, where they took several hostages. After a few hours of negotiating, UNAMIR and the *gendarmerie* were able to release them.[33] That evening, the Minister of Public Affairs, Félicien Gatabazi, who was head of the PSD party and a prominent Hutu moderate, was shot dead. The media of the extremists reacted by "spinning headlines in which the killing of Gatabazi was celebrated as a victory."[34]

On February 23 extremists and moderates alike went out into the streets.[35] In Kigali, UNAMIR and the *gendarmerie* were able to keep the situation under control. In Gatabazi's home town, Butare, however, very violent demonstrations took place. In this violence, PSD supporters killed the head of the extremist party CDR, Martin Bucyana.[36] This resurgence of violence, in which two prominent political leaders, Félicien Gatabazi and Martin Bucyana, were murdered, worsened the overall political climate.[37] We must remind ourselves here of the letter that Dallaire had received from high-ranking military officers December 3.[38] The letter spoke of a "Machiavelli plan" and predicted the killing of both Twagiramungu and Gatabazi. By now, Twagimarungu had been the victim of an attempted murder and Gatabazi had been killed. The installation of the interim government was planned to take place February 23, the day after Gatabazi's death. Due to a sudden outbreak of violence in Kigali, the installation was postponed.[39]

In the face of the deteriorating political and security situation, the Secretary-General called President Habyarimana on February 24. Boutros-Ghali stressed the need for urgent action to end the political stalemate and to proceed with the establishment of the transitional institutions. Furthermore, he warned the President that the "international community" would not take responsibility if the situation were to explode.[40] A few days later, Boutros-Ghali received a special envoy of Habyarimana, the Minister for Transport and Communications.

---

32 Dallaire, p. 187.

33 Dallaire, pp. 187, 188; Marchal, p. 156.

34 Daillaire, p. 188.

35 *Id.*

36 Melvern, 2000 p. 100.

37 S/1994/360, paragraph 13, p. 3.

38 See Section 7.2.

39 See Second Progress Report of the Secretary-General on the United Nations Assistance Mission in Rwanda which states that during negotiations that took place on the 16th and the 18th an agreement was reached to postpone the installment to February 23. S/1994/360.

40 United Nations, The United Nations and Rwanda, 1993–1996 p. 34 (1996) (hereinafter U.N., The United Nations and Rwanda); S/1994/360, paragraph 14, p. 4.

In this conversation, Boutros-Ghali stressed again the need to end the political impasse and threatened once more to withdraw UNAMIR if no progress was achieved. The Secretary-General emphasized the "competing priorities of the U.N." and added that UNAMIR could be withdrawn within 15 days.[41]

On February 23, as soon as the death of Bucyana became known in Kigali, a wave of violence spread through the city. Hysterical and violent civilians, mostly armed with machetes, went out into the streets.[42] UNAMIR did not use force, because Dallaire was convinced that by doing so the situation would only escalate. Prime Minister Uwilingiyamana went on the National Radio to appeal for calm and a curfew was introduced from 7 o'clock in the evening until 5 o'clock in the morning.[43] Due to the clearly anti-Tutsi character of the violence, Tutsis started to seek shelter at churches, UNAMIR and the CND building.[44]

On the day that Bucyana was killed, an RPF convoy was escorted by Belgian peace-keepers from Mulindi to Kigali.[45] The convoy was initially planned to be escorting the RPF leadership, but because of the dangerous situation, Major General Paul Kagame had forbidden the leadership to go, so the convoy proceeded without them.[46] The extremists, however, were unaware of Kagame's decision, so, to them, the convoy supposedly carrying the RPF leadership was an interesting target.[47] Late at night, when the convoy entered Kigali, it was attacked by the Interahamwe and the presidential guard.[48] The Belgian peace-keepers were able to escape, leaving the RPF behind. When they realized the RPF had not been able to follow them, they did not return. Instead they headed for safety for themselves. As soon as the message of the attack on the convoy was received at the CND building, the RPF burst out of their compound, crossing the city to rescue their comrades. In the ambush a civilian and an RPF soldier died, and a U.N. military observer was wounded, but the convoy was released.[49]

According to Dallaire, he had ordered the Belgian peace-keepers not to return to Kigali that night and to stay in Mulindi until the "all-clear was given," but the Belgians had deliberately disobeyed his order and risked returning to Kigali after dark. Marchal, who also discussed the issue in his book, did not

---

41 Carlsson Report, S/1999/1257, p. 15; S/1994/360, paragraph 14, p. 4.

42 Marchal, pp. 156, 157.

43 Dallaire, pp. 188–189; Marchal, pp. 156, 157.

44 Marchal, pp. 157–158.

45 Because of the long distance between Mulindi and Kigali, the convoy would arrive after dark.

46 According to Dallaire, it was a regular convoy: The RPF returned from its headquarters where they had picked up firewood, food and mail. Dallaire, pp. 191–192.

47 Melvern, 2000 pp. 100–101; Belgian Ad Hoc Group; Des Forges, p.164, note 100: Anonymous, "Chronology-Rwanda."

48 Marchal, p. 157; Dallaire, p. 192.

49 Belgian Ad Hoc Group, p. 38; Dallaire, p. 192; Marchal, p. 157.

talk about a "disobeyed order of the Belgian peacekeepers."[50] According to Dallaire, the incident put so much shame on the Belgian forces that it was "never expunged."[51] The situation made Kagame realize "how little help the U.N. peacekeepers would provide in an emergency."[52] This event had an important impact on Kagame's view of the possible role of bystanders in order to help and rescue the victims of the violence and atrocities in Rwanda.

In response to the grave violence of the previous days, Dallaire sent a report to the headquarters on February 23 saying that all information was pointing to death squad target lists and planning of civil unrest and demonstrations. He wrote: "Time does seem to be running out of political discussions as any spark on the security side could have catastrophic consequences."[53] The following day, Booh Booh informed the Secretariat that circulating reports indicated that "the violence of the last few days might have been ethnically motivated and directed against the Tutsi minority. In view of Rwanda's long and tragic history of ethnic conflict, the possibility of ethnically motivated incidents is a constant threat, especially during moments of tension, fear and confusion." He added: "UNAMIR, however, did not have conclusive or compelling evidence that the events of the past days were either ethnically motivated or provoked ethnic consequences or reactions."[54] That same day, Boutros-Ghali telephoned President Habyarimana. He stressed the need for urgent action to end the political stalemate and to proceed with the establishment of the transitional institutions.[55] He did not disclose any fear of emerging gross human rights violations at that time.

In the following days, 35 people were killed and 150 people were wounded. Most of the victims were Tutsi and moderate Hutu.[56] According to Belgian officers, the situation at the end of February was "explosive," about which they could do little as a result of the limited mandate.[57] In his book Dallaire wrote, in hindsight, that by this point, all possible doubts were gone: "The poison of

---

50 Marchal, pp. 156–157; Dallaire pp. 191–192.

51 Melvern, 2000 p. 101.

52 Melvern, 2000 p. 101, note 3: Interview, Major-General Paul Kagame, Kigali, October 1997.

53 Carlsson Report, S/1999/1257, p. 14.

54 Carlsson Report, S/1999/1257, p. 14. Equally, according to the record of a meeting with the Ambassadors of Belgium, France and the United States on March 2, Dallaire discounted suggestions that the recent killings in Kigali might have been ethnically motivated.

55 U.N., The United Nations and Rwanda, p. 34; S/1994/360, paragraph 14, p. 4.

56 Dallaire, p. 189; Melvern, 2000 p. 101.

57 Belgian Ad Hoc Group, p. 38; Sénat de Belgique, Commission d'Enquête parlementaire concernant les événements au Rwanda, (Commission of parliamentary enquiry concerning the events in Rwanda), session de 1997–1998, 6 décembre 1997, Rapport fait au nom de la commission d'enquête par MM Mahoux et Verhofstadt, Annexes, p. 26 (hereinafter Annex Belgian Senate).

ethnic hatred had been well-stirred and was about to boil over."[58] The violence started to decrease by February 26, but the Tutsis, who still felt terribly unsafe, tried to find sanctuary. UNAMIR opened two centers in Kigali where they could seek protection.[59]

10.4 MARCH 1994

The violent month of February was followed by a relative calm month.[60] March was dominated by developments on the political front; political negotiations were taking place more than ever.[61] Expectations were raised, but, as the month proceeded, the political developments were dragged into a political deadlock. When the installation of the transitional government failed, the security situation started to deteriorate once again. However, the security situation would remain far more "peaceful" than in the previous months.

In March, one negotiation meeting after another took place, preparing for the installment of the transitional government on the newly set date of March 25. At the beginning of the month, all signs were positive, but serious complications soon started.[62]

The first obstacle was the failure to reach an agreement on the appointment of ministers on the side of the Liberal Party (PL). The second problem was that Habyarimana insisted on the inclusion of the CDR in the transitional government.[63] Surprisingly, Habyarimana received support from all foreign diplomats and the SRSG. Suddenly the President and the extremists were relieved of international pressure, and it was the RPF that was pressured to compro-

---

58 Dallaire, p. 189.

59 Belgian Ad Hoc Group, pp. 71–72. On February 27 Dallaire informed the Secretariat of his intention to redeploy two companies, a small command group and a logistics component of the Ghanaian contingent in the DMZ to Kigali to take over guard duties there as a temporary measure until the situation in the capital stabilized. Dallaire emphasized the urgency of the operation, stating that "the present serious increase in terrorist actions combined with the serious decrease in gendarmerie and UNAMIR reaction capability could lead to an end to the peace process." Carlsson Report, S/1999/1257, p. 14; Marchal, pp. 157–158.

60 The security situation in March was far more stable than in the previous months. Marchal, pp. 166–167.

61 According to Marchal, it was a surrealistic atmosphere: "Everything was quiet, while all the problems that led to the violence at the end of February were still present." Of course, the violence of February still had its impact. Many of the moderate politicians received death threats; five of them were under permanent protection of UNAMIR. Marchal pp. 166–167.

62 Dallaire, p. 210; Marchal, p. 162.

63 Dallaire, p. 210; Marchal, p. 165.

mise.[64] Both the RPF and Habyarimana sought the support of Mwinyi, the President of Tanzania, the facilitator of the Arusha Agreement, to arbitrate a solution. Mwinyi sent his minister of foreign affairs, Joseph Rwegaseria, to negotiate the situation.[65] But Rwegaseria did not deal with the problem of the inclusion of the CDR. At the end of his visit, he stated that the stumbling block of putting the transitional government in place revolved around the internal problems within the PL. He argued that this power struggle was unacceptable, because it had no legal basis within the framework of the Arusha Agreement. He said that the proposed composition of the transitional government was within the prerogative of the prime minister's designate, Twagimarungu, as long as he respected the lists of ministers proposed.

On March 18 Twagimarungu read out the final lists of ministerial candidates on the National Radio. He assured the people that nothing could now prevent the government from being installed. The following day, Madame Agathe read out the list of the names of the deputy-ministers. Habyarimana was very displeased with the lists and went on the National Radio to castigate the Prime Ministers for not consulting him before they had made the lists public. Furthermore, he told Twagimarungu that the CDR should be represented in the Broad Based Transitional Government (BBTG).[66]

On March 25 the government was not installed. Due to the unsolved dispute on the lists of participants and the participation of the CDR, the RPF refused to attend.[67] On March 28 another attempt failed.[68] With these two failures, Rwanda was back in its political impasse.[69]

---

64 At the end of March, after the installation of the government had failed twice, the Kigali diplomatic corps, Papal Nuncio and Booh Booh endorsed the President's proposal that "all parties acknowledged in Arusha should be included in the BBTG." This meant, in fact, that they supported Habyarimana's idea to have the CDR represented in the BBTG. Together with all representatives of the Great Lakes Region, they signed a joint declaration. Habyarimana had succeeded in isolating the RPF, who became the sole part holding up the peace process by opposing the CDR inclusion. In his book, Dallaire describes the situation as a trap organized by Habyarimana: "All the diplomats with Booh Booh in the lead accepted Habyarimana's gambit." See Dallaire, pp. 210, 212.

65 Dallaire, p. 210; Marchal, pp. 162–163.

66 Furthermore, Habyarimana told Twagiramungu that he had received complaints from members of the PL on the choice of the minister of Justice. The President told the Prime Ministerial designate to continue the negotiations with the PL. Dallaire, p. 211.

67 Marchal, p. 165.

68 Dallaire, pp. 210, 211; Marchal, pp. 165, 166.

69 In the light of the highly sensitive political situation at the end of March, Booh Booh's decision to spend the Easter weekend with Habyarimana at one of his residences was highly remarkable. Dallaire and Abdul Hamid Kabia, acting Executive Director of UNAMIR, who were both very disturbed by Booh Booh's decision, tried to convince him that the RPF, as well as the moderates, would question his impartiality. Booh Booh answered that he would use the visit to gain inside intelligence. Furthermore, he argued

When the Secretary-General presented his second progress report to the Security Council on March 30, he explained that the transitional government had not been set up as a result of the inability to agree on the relevant modalities, including the lists of members.[70] Interestingly enough, the Secretary-General hardly paid any attention to Habyarimana's will to include the extremist party CDR into the BBTG, which had been unacceptable to the RPF.

Throughout the month of March, the worst incidents consisted of the murder of two influential moderates, the sister of Enoch Ruhigira and her husband.[71] Furthermore, an attack on Hotel Chez Lando injured eight people.[72] On the last day of the month, assailants killed Alphonse Ingabire (known as Katumba), the operational head of the CDR. Militia of the CDR killed a member of the PSD and wounded three others.[73]

10.5 APRIL 1994

Situated in this political impasse, Rwanda entered the month of April. On April 2 "Radio Rwanda" broadcasted an interview with Booh Booh in which he threatened, once more, a "U.N. pull-out." He said the Security Council was going to review UNAMIR on April 5, but the progress towards peace had been "rather pathetic."[74]

From April 3–5 and from April 7–8 RTLMC broadcasted a prediction that the RPF would do "a little something with its bullets and grenades." It seemed that Hutu extremists were accusing Tutsi. The prediction increased fears in an already tense situation. Some people who felt at risk sent their children away from Kigali, while others took refuge in places thought to be safe havens.[75]

The German ambassador, speaking for the European Union, expressed on April 3 his concern about increasing insecurity, proliferation of weapons and

---

that because he had known Habyarimana since he was Minister of Foreign Affairs of Camaroon, he could "penetrate Habyarimana's intentions." Booh Booh insinuated that Kabia's and Dallaire's misgivings were the result of an imperfect understanding of Francophone Africa. As had been expected on the first Easter day, formal protests started coming in from the RPF questioning the SRSG's impartiality.

[70] S/1994/360.

[71] Ruhigira was Cabinet-chef of the President and former Prime-Minster of Rwanda.

[72] Dallaire, p. 212. Ruhigira's sister and husband were killed on March 15, and Chez Lando was attacked on March 19.

[73] Des Forges, note 134: Société Civile, c/o Centre Iwacu, "Déclaration de la Société Civile au Rwanda dans sa réunion du 31 mars 1994."

[74] Summary of world broadcasts/ AL/1962 A/3. April 4, 1994.

[75] Des Forges, note 137: RTLMC, April 3, 1994, recorded by Faustin Kagame (provided by Article 19).

the unacceptable role of some media. He suggested that continued support depended on implementing the Accords.[76]

At a party on April 4, to celebrate the national day of Senegal, Colonel Théoneste Bagosora told people that "the only plausible solution for Rwanda would be the elimination of the Tutsi." Dallaire, Booh Booh, Marchal and Shariyah Khan, adviser to Booh Booh, were present at the party. Furthermore Bagosora told Marchal that if the RPF attacked successfully, the Rwandan forces had plans for guerrilla warfare against them.[77]

In an interview with Linda Melvern, a Polish peace-keeper recalled that some Tutsi were going to sleep in churches out of fear of an attack. He said: "Genocide hung in the air."[78]

Four days later at 8:23 p.m., the plane with President Habyarimana was shot down and all hell broke loose. In the morning of April 7, Annan got a call from Kigali that at least three, probably more, peace-keepers had been killed. Soon it was confirmed that the number was ten.[79]

10.6 CONCLUDING OBSERVATIONS

In the first three months of 1994 the situation deteriorated in all aspects in Rwanda. No progress was made in the political negotiations to install a moderate cabinet. Extremists gathered more and more influence and destabilized the situation both on the political and security fields. Violence between both ethnic groups led to killings in February. UNAMIR was hardly able to act and was deliberately provoked. The RPF leader, Kagame, concluded following an incident of February 23 that he could no longer count on the peace-keepers for the safety of his Tutsi people. On the other hand, the mitigating effect of UNAMIR on the violent atmosphere was floored by the top U.N. officials in New York when they underlined that UNAMIR could be withdrawn if Habyarimana did not stop the unrest in the country. The changing attitude of Habyarimana—increasingly under the influence of extremists—was not observed, and he was thus trusted too much.

The reaction from New York towards these events in this period was a continuing compulsion to proceed with the peace process; all pressure from New York was placed directly on President Habyarimana. The ultimate threat given by New York to Habyarimana was a possible withdrawal of UNAMIR. All inter-

---

76 Prunier, p. 209.

77 Belgian Ad Hoc Group, p. 79.

78 Interview Stefan Stec, The Hague, October 1995, in, Melvern, 2000 p. 108.

79 Sénat de Belgique, Commission d'Enquête parlementaire concernant les événements au Rwanda, (Commission of parliamentary enquiry concerning the events in Rwanda), session de 1997–1998, 6 décembre 1997, Rapport fait au nom de la commission d'enquête par MM Mahoux et Verhofstadt, p. 523.

actions between the Rwandan President and New York were characterized by two aspects. The first aspect was the trust in the head of the Rwandan government, holding him accountable for the situation in the country. The second aspect was the trust in the progress of the peace process. Everything was based on both the Arusha Agreement and the classic peace-keeping force, UNAMIR, which was the only means of achieving the implementation of the Accords. From this perspective, the U.N. reluctance to act is easy to understand.

CHAPTER 11

REQUESTS FROM DALLAIRE AND FROM BELGIUM TO NEW YORK FOR A STRONGER AND FIRMER BROADENED MANDATE FOR UNAMIR

In the previous chapter we dealt with several warnings of the degenerating situation in Rwanda. In this chapter we will elaborate on two very concrete requests to New York to change and broaden the mandate of UNAMIR. The changing security situation in Rwanda required UNAMIR's mandate to be altered, or it would become impossible for UNAMIR to fulfill its mission any longer. The difference from Chapter 10 is that we will now deal with very clear and concrete requests that were rejected by U.N. headquarters in New York. We will first present the request from UNAMIR Force Commander General Roméo Dallaire to seize arms (Section 11.1). The request had been rejected explicitly from mid-January until mid-March by U.N. headquarters not less than six times. Secondly, we will put forward the requests from the Belgian government for a robust mandate for the peace-keepers (Section 11.2).

11.1 DALLAIRE'S REQUESTS TO SEIZE ARMS

After Jean Pierre had come forward, General Dallaire immediately asked headquarters, on January 11 to authorize the seizure of weapons. However, as we have elaborated on in Section 8.4, headquarters decided that very same day that the seizure of arms was not allowed. According to headquarters, UNAMIR's mandate was too limited—*(January 11, Rejection One)*. As will be seen below, Dallaire did not give up. Throughout the months of January, February and March he kept asking to seize arms.

Dallaire's next request came on January 22 following a violent demonstration the day before. Dallaire sent a fax to New York in which he asked for a broader mandate so that he could seize weapons. Unfortunately his request was refused again[1]—*(January 22, Rejection Two)*.

Another, very strongly worded request followed in the first week of February.

---

1 Alison Des Forges, Leave None to Tell the Story, Genocide in Rwanda (1999) p. 157, note 62: Anonymous, "Rwanda, Chronology" (hereinafter Des Forges). According to Melvern, Dallaire's request was made one day later, on January 23. Linda Melvern,

SRSG Jacques Roger Booh Booh sent a cable to Kofi Annan stating that the security situation was deteriorating on a daily basis.[2] The fax spoke of:

> Increasingly violent demonstrations, nightly grenade attacks, assassination attempts, political and ethnic killings, and we are receiving more and more reliable and confirmed information that the armed militias of the parties are stockpiling and may possibly be preparing to distribute arms to their supporters. If this distribution takes place, it will worsen the security situation even further and create a significant danger to the safety and security of U.N. military and civilian personnel and the population at large.

The fax continued by saying that there were indications that the FAR was preparing for a conflict; they were stockpiling ammunition and attempting to reinforce positions in Kigali:

> We can expect more frequent and more violent demonstrations, more grenade and armed attacks on ethnic and political groups, more assassinations and quite possibly outright attacks on UNAMIR installations and personnel . . . Each day of delay in authorizing deterrent arms recovery operation will result in an ever deteriorating security situation and may if the arms continue to be distributed result in an inability of UNAMIR to carry out its mandate in all aspects.

The conclusion of the fax was that determined and selective deterrent operations were necessary "targeting confirmed arms caches and individuals known to have illegal weapons in their possession." According to the fax, operations would not only *fulfill the requirements of the mandate* in recovering illegal arms,[3] but they would also ensure the safety and continued operation of U.N. personnel and facilities in Rwanda.[4]

The fax was very clear: Due to the threatening situation, UNAMIR sought

---

A People Betrayed. The Role of the West in Rwanda's Genocide, p. 96 (2000) (hereinafter Melvern, 2000).

2 United Nations, Report of the Independent Inquiry into the Actions of the United Nations during the 1994 Genocide in Rwanda, December 15, 1999, Ingvar Carlsson, Han, Sung-Joo, Rufus, M. Kupolati, U.N. Doc. S/1999/1257, p. 13 (hereinafter Carlsson Report, S/1999/1257).

3 It is highly remarkable that, in this fax of February 2, Booh Booh argued that deterrent operations would *fulfill* the mandate, while on February 15 Booh Booh sent a fax to Claes in which he emphasized the strict limitations of the mission in emphasizing the limited scope of the UNAMIR mandate.

4 *See* Carlsson Report, S/1999/1257, p. 13; Roméo Dallaire, Shake Hands with the Devil, The Failure of Humanity in Rwanda, p. 167 (2004) (hereinafter Dallaire); Des Forges, p. 160, note 81: General Dallaire to U.N., New York, Code Cable MIR 267, February 3, 1994 (confidential source).

the guidance and approval of headquarters to commence deterrent operations. According to the Carlsson Report, Booh Booh sent the fax on February 2. Dallaire writes in his book that he sent the fax on February 3. The text of Booh Booh's fax, which is cited in the Carlsson Report, contains the same elements as the fax that is cited in Dallaire's book. In Dallaire's book, it is said that Booh Booh responded positively to his fax and that he (Booh Booh) then sent the fax to New York. Des Forges and Melvern speak about Dallaire's fax as well. According to them the fax was sent on February 3. For this reason, it is assumed that the two faxes (Booh Booh's fax of February 2, which is cited in the Carlsson Report, and Dallaire's fax of February 3, which is cited in Dallaire's book, Melvern's book and Des Forges' book) are the same. It seems that Dallaire had written the fax, which was sent by and with the approval of Booh Booh to New York.

Headquarters responded to Booh Booh and Dallaire's fax by broadening the mandate very slightly. The Force Commander was given permission to assist the Rwandan authorities in recovering weapons, but he did not get the authorization to conduct such operations alone. The wording of the fax was:

> We are prepared to authorize UNAMIR to respond positively on a case by case basis to requests by the government and the RPF for assistance in illegal arms recovery operations. It should be clearly understood however that while UNAMIR may provide advice for the planning of such operation, it cannot—repeat—cannot take an active role in their execution. UNAMIR's role . . . should be limited to a monitoring function—*(February 2, Rejection Three)*.

Dallaire, who had expected that the strongly worded fax would have convinced headquarters, was deeply shocked by the instructions in this answer.[5] He continued to press for permission to take a more active role in deterrent operations. The Secretariat, however, maintained its narrow interpretation of the mandate, stating that UNAMIR could only support the efforts of the *gendarmerie*[6] *(Mid-February, Rejection Four)*.

---

5 Dallaire, p. 167; Des Forges, p. 160, note 82: Anonymous, "Rwanda, Chronology." Dallaire and Des Forges do not give a date on which the Force Commander received the reply from headquarters, but it seems that the reply was received quickly, on February 3 or 4.

6 Dallaire, p. 180. In contradiction to Dallaire, the Secretariat argues that Dallaire did not come back to the issue of a more active role after he had received the authorization to help local authorities to collect arms and dismantle weapons stocks. Sénat de Belgique, Commission d'Enquête parlementaire concernant les événements au Rwanda, (Commission of parliamentary enquiry concerning the events in Rwanda), session de 1997–1998, 6 décembre 1997, Rapport fait au nom de la commission d'enquête par MM Mahoux et Verhofstadt, Annexes, p. 56 (hereinafter Annex Belgian Senate).

Later that month, between February 20–26, the security situation deteriorated rapidly. Violent demonstrations took place, anti-Tutsi violence spread throughout Kigali and several prominent political leaders were killed. Following the violence, on February 27, Dallaire once again sought approval to seize weapons.[7] This time, headquarters answered that he should concentrate on the installment of the new transitional government[8] *(February 27, Rejection Five).* On March 15 Dallaire sought permission once more to confiscate the weapons, but again his request was turned down[9] *(March 15, Rejection Six).*

11.1.1 Failure of U.N. Top Officials

The foregoing shows that Dallaire filed at least six official requests for authorization for a seizure of weapons and that all were turned down by arguing that the mandate was too limited: on January 11 and 22, on February 2, in mid-February, on February 27 and on March 15. We have shown that at least six requests and six rejections of these requests, encompassing at least 12 messages, were communicated in the course of these two months. All were directed to New York to obtain the requisite permission to act, and the content of all the requests by their own U.N. peace-keepers was to fulfill their mandate with a deterrent recovery operation. Every time these requests were rejected by the top officials—Hedi Annabi, Kofi Annan and Iqbal Riza—and never did they put discussion of these requests onto the agenda of the Security Council. The members of the Security Council were thus never informed and had no opportunity to decide whether or not to act. They were deliberately kept ignorant by these top officials. This is why, in our opinion, these top officials were to blame for the emerging catastrophes. It was no longer the whole Untied Nations or the whole Security Council but particularly these three top officials who did not respond in the way that should be expected from a top official at the United Nations. All three have since continued fine careers, becoming the Secretary-General of the United Nations (Annan), the Under-Secretary-General of the United Nations (Riza) and the deputy Secretary-General (Annabi). Our evaluation does not differ very much from the conclusions of the Carlsson Report, but the conclusions of the Carlsson Report were never followed up with any consequences.

---

[7] In that same fax, Dallaire requested reinforcements of 150 soldiers. Des Forges, p. 164, note 101: Anonymous, "Rwanda, Chronology."

[8] Des Forges, p. 164, note 101: Anonymous, "Rwanda, Chronology."

[9] Dallaire's request included again a reinforcement of 150 soldiers. Walter De Bock and Gert Van Langendonck, Legerstaf wist alles over nakende genocide Rwanda, *De Morgen*, November 4, 1995, p. 6. It was April 1 when the first deterrent raid on suspected arm caches had been done. UNAMIR troops provided the security cordon, and the *gendarmerie* conducted the actual search. No arms were found; the plan had leaked, and the weapons had been moved. Dallaire, p. 215.

The Carlsson Report did not criticize in particular the Secretariat for its decision, made immediately after the information received by Jean Pierre that the seizure of weapons fell outside the mandate.[10] The report did, however, criticize the Secretariat for sticking to this decision when Dallaire continued to ask for authorization throughout the months of January, February and March. According to the Carlsson Report, when Dallaire repeated his requests over and over again, the Secretariat should have brought the issue of the weakness of the mandate before the Security Council with the request to rectify it. But as the inquiry stated, there is no proof that the Secretariat did so.[11] Despite the fact that Belgium asked the Secretariat of U.N. headquarters for a firmer mandate for UNAMIR—as we will see in the next section—they never asked to put this issue and request onto the agenda of the Security Council.[12]

It is this pattern of neglect, by these top U.N. officials, of the very serious warnings from the very trustful source, their own UNAMIR peace-keeping Force Commander that is the most horrifying aspect of this period before the genocide.

11.2 BELGIUM ASKS FOR A MORE ROBUST ROLE FOR UNAMIR

Belgium was the only country that acknowledged the weakness of UNAMIR's mandate and advocated stronger powers. When New York argued that deterrent operations were not possible due to the limited scope of the mandate, Belgium argued for a broader mandate. When it became apparent that certain countries would not agree with a broader mandate, Belgium tried to enforce UNAMIR under the present mandate. Ambassador Swinnen was the first to advocate this firmer mandate, followed by the Belgian Ministers of Foreign Affairs and Defense. The United States and Great Britain seem to have been the strongest opponents of a broader mandate.

On January 15, just after Jean Pierre had come forward, Ambassador Swinnen reported to the Belgian Ministry of Foreign Affairs that UNAMIR had to act soon, because, otherwise, the arms would be distributed to the Interahamwe and other civilians. The ambassador expressed the opinion that if Dallaire were to cooperate with the *gendarmerie*, the regulations permitted UNAMIR to seize arms. Swinnen added that Dallaire would not do so without specific instructions from headquarters. According to the ambassador, Secretary-General Boutros-Ghali had given instructions not to seize weapons the previous day. Swinnen's point of view was that the Secretary-General was afraid of an esca-

---

10 See Chapters 8 and 9.

11 Carlsson Report, S/1999/1257, pp. 33–34. The inadequacy of the mandate was discussed in a broader manner in Chapters 4 and 8.

12 Interview with W. Claes, January 13, 2006.

lation that could turn the mission into an enforcement force instead of peacekeeping mission.[13]

A few days later, the Belgian embassy sent a telex to the Ministry of Foreign Affairs in Brussels reporting that the head of the Rwandan Army had declared: "The Rwandan authorities have asked UNAMIR and the GD (Gendarmerie) to proceed to actions aimed at dismantling these groups."[14]

As seen above, on January 22 Dallaire sent another request to New York in which he asked for a broader mandate so that he could seize arms. Two days after his request was turned down, Swinnen wrote to his Ministry of Foreign Affairs that it was impossible for UNAMIR to act under its present mandate. He added that UNAMIR's mandate should be broadened, or the troops should be withdrawn.[15] A few days later, Luc Marchal endorsed Swinnen's statement. He sent a report to the Operation Center of the Belgian Army in Evere, in which he explained that it was impossible for UNAMIR to act effectively. Marchal underlined his statement with the example that after 924 mobile patrols, 320 foot patrols and the establishment of 306 checkpoints, UNAMIR had collected only nine weapons.[16]

On January 28 the general intelligence service of the Belgian Ministry of Defense sent a briefing to Evere emphasizing the powerlessness of the mission: "The problem is that UNAMIR's control of traffic and movement of arms is very difficult to realize . . . The U.N. is still not ready to authorize more severe actions by UNAMIR in this domain either."[17] On February 3 Swinnen sent a

---

[13] Telex No. 45, January 15, 1994, Belgian Embassy Kigali to the Ministry of Foreign Affairs in Brussels; Sénat de Belgique, Rapport du Groupe Ad Hoc Rwanda A La Commission des Affairs Etrangeres, Sénat de Belgique, 7 janvier 1997, p. 86 (hereinafter Belgian Ad Hoc Group); Annex Belgian Senate, p. 54.

[14] Translated from French into English. Original text: "Les autorités Rwandaises ont demandé à la Minuar et à la GD (Gendarmerie) de procéder à des actions visant à démanteler ces groupes." Telex No. 63, January 20, 1994, of the Belgian Embassy in Kigali to the Ministry of Foreign Affairs in Brussels; Annex Belgian Senate, p. 54.

[15] Telex No. 69, January 25, 1994, of the Belgian Embassy Kigali to the Ministry of Foreign Affairs in Brussels; Annex Belgian Senate p. 55; Belgian Ad Hoc Group, p. 87. The same is more or less repeated on January 27 in Telex No. 78; see Annex Belgian Senate, p. 55.

[16] Report of January 30, 1994, from Marchal to Evere, documents SGR No. 1867 and documents Evere No. 1626; Belgian Ad Hoc Group, p. 88; Sénat de Belgique, Commission d'Enquête parlementaire concernant les événements au Rwanda, (Commission of parliamentary enquiry concerning the events in Rwanda), session de 1997–1998, 6 décembre 1997, Rapport fait au nom de la commission d'enquête par MM Mahoux et Verhofstadt, p. 56 (hereinafter Belgian Senate); Luc Marchal, Aan de poorten van de Rwandese hel: Getuigenis van een peacekeeper p. 152 (2001) (hereinafter Marchal). This report did not correspond with a report sent by Marchal only a few days before. In Telex No. 64, January 23, 1994, from the Belgian Embassy in Kigali to the Ministry of Foreign Affairs in Brussels, it is said that Marchal was relatively satisfied with the procedures regarding the confiscation of weapons in Kigali. See Annex Belgian Senate p. 54.

[17] Annex Belgian Senate, p. 55. Translated from French into English. Original

report to his Ministry of Foreign Affairs in which he called UNAMIR a "powerless instrument." He wrote that it was very urgent that the distributions of arms were halted and that the existing stocks were dismantled. Swinnen cited Marchal in saying: "In any case, it cannot go on like this anymore."[18] In a report informing the Ministry of Foreign Affairs a few days later, Swinnen wrote: "Faced with the violence of the militia and the young people of CDR, the non-intervention of UNAMIR seems like a confession of powerlessness. In the opinion of certain officers, the searching of arms depots and the disarmament of the militia is becoming more pressing."[19]

Throughout the month of February, the Belgian Minister of Foreign Affairs, Willy Claes, took up a more active role regarding the mission in Rwanda and started advocating a broader mandate.

On February 11 Claes sent a fax to Boutros-Ghali concerning the security situation and the mandate of UNAMIR. He warned the Secretary-General that Rwandan leaders had admitted that "a prolongation of the current political deadlock could result in an irreversible explosion of violence." He expressed his appreciation for the instructions from the Secretary-General to Booh Booh to push harder for the installation of the transitional government. Furthermore, he stated that UNAMIR had to undertake firmer action, or the mission might find itself unable to continue at all.[20]

The *first message* from Brussels to New York dealing with the Belgian requests for a broader mandate was the letter from Claes to the Secretary-General on *February 11*. On February 11 Claes sent a letter to the Secretary-General in which he endorsed Dallaire's requests for a broader mandate.[21] According to

---

text: "Le problème du Ctl par l'UNAMIR du trafic et des Mov d'armes est très difficile à réaliser. . . . L'ONU n'est pas encore prête non plus à autoriser des actions plus sévères de l'UNAMIR dans ce domaine."

18 Telex No. 99, February 3, 1994, of the Belgian Embassy in Kigali to the Ministry of Foreign Affairs in Brussels; Annex Belgian Senate, p. 56. That same day officers of the general staff of the Ministry of Defense in Evere informed the Ministry of Foreign Affairs that they were of the opinion that the grenade attacks, which had taken place in Kigali, were the result of "an organized plan." Belgian Ad Hoc Group, p. 71; Annex Belgian Senate, p. 56.

19 Translated from French into English. Original text: "Face aux violences des milices et des jeunes CDR, la non-intervention de l'UNAMIR apparait comme un aveu d'impuissance. De l'avis de certains officiers la recherche des dépôts d'armes et le désarmement des milices s'imposent." Telex No. 109, February 7, 1994, of the Belgian Embassy in Kigali to the Ministry of Foreign Affairs in Brussels.

20 Belgian Senate, p. 242. In the U.N. Independent Inquiry the date given is February 14, 1994.

21 Belgian Senate pp. 342, 392; Carlsson Report, p. 13. According to the Belgian Senate, Claes wrote the Secretary-General on February 11, and according to Carlsson he wrote Boutros-Ghali on February 14.

22 Dallaire, p. 180.

Dallaire, this Belgian request was a result of the "persuasive discussions" Marchal had with the Belgian authorities.[22]

Claes wrote in his letter to the Secretary-General, in which he asked for a strong deterrent force, that he feared that if they do not succeed in halting the negative developments, UNAMIR would be hindered in continuing to proceed with its basic assignment, important support in the implementation of the Arusha Accords.[23] It is clear, and it is now also viewed by Dallaire and by Carlsson, that Claes indeed asked for a broader mandate for UNAMIR that was able to deter and thus stop the increasingly dangerous situation.[24]

A few days later, the Belgian representative to the United Nations, Paul Noterdaeme, responded to the fax of Claes. He informed the Belgian Ministry of Foreign Affairs of the Secretariat's reaction.[25] Noterdaeme stated:

> The first reaction [of the secretariat] . . . was rather perplexed . . . General Dallaire had already gotten the authorization to help local authorities to collect arms and dismantle weapons stocks. . . . Dallaire has not come back to the issue of a more active role, although the week before he had said he would make some concrete proposals.[26]

This was the answer on February 14 from New York to the first message from Brussels.

The *second message* dealing with this issue was a cable from New York to Dallaire dated *February 15*. On February 15 New York sent a cable to Dallaire

---

23 In Dutch he said: "Niettemin valt te vrezen, dat als we er niet in slagen de negatieve ontwikkelingen een halt toe te roepen, UNAMIR verhinderd zal worden om haar basisopdracht naar behoren voort te zetten, te weten belangrijke steun te bieden bij de uitvoering van de vredesakkoorden van Arusha. Ik kan u verzekeren dat de Belgische regering van haar kant President Habyarimana en de andere Rwandese politieke verantwoordelijken ertoe blijft aanzetten om de onvermijdelijke compromissen te aanvaarden." And in French he has said before this quote: "Il me parait cependant que cette accentuation du profil de l'ONU au niveau politique devrait aller de pair avec une attitude plus dissuasive de la Minuar sur le plan de la sécurité. . . . Il est à craindre néanmoins qu'à défaut d'enrayer l'évolution négative à laquelle nous assistons, la Minuar pourrait se trouver dans l'impossibilité de poursuivre valablement sa mission." In the United Nations, the United Nations and Rwanda, 1993–1996, (1996) the letter was dated March 14, 1994, see p. 244. Report of the Belgian Senate, p. 242 and the Belgian Ad Hoc Group, p. 89 date the letter to February 11.

24 Claes said in Flemish that he favored a "ontradende houding van de UNAMIR," which means "a reluctant attitude," but in the French wording, he is clear, "une attitude plus dissuasive de la Minuar," which means a real deterrent force (in French: force de dissuasion) that should have been translated in Dutch as "een afschrikkingsmacht."

25 Telex of February 14, 1994, of Noterdaeme to the Ministry of Foreign Affairs in Brussels.

26 Annex Belgian Senate, p. 56.

in which they explained that the Belgian Minister of Foreign Affairs had, in a letter to the Secretary-General, endorsed Dallaire's call for deterrent operations.[27] Dallaire was very relieved that he had somebody on his side who might be able to persuade New York to give him greater leeway.[28] In this cable Dallaire was asked to respond to the letter that the Secretary-General had received from Claes. Following this request, Dallaire drafted a cable in which he underlined the concerns of the Belgian Minister. Furthermore, he added public security measures to his existing plans for arms recovery operations. With regard to headquarters' permission to "support operations of local authorities," Dallaire wrote that these authorities did not have the resources to conduct search operations.[29] Booh Booh responded positively to Dallaire's draft cable, which Dallaire thought was going to be sent to both headquarters and Claes, being the *third and the fourth message*. Dallaire would later find out, however, that Booh Booh sent Dallaire's cable only to Annan. Booh Booh's fax to Claes was different than the one sent to Annan. Even more striking is that the content differed on an essential aspect. Dallaire wrote that Booh Booh, in his reply to Claes, "downplayed the information we [UNAMIR] had gathered on the distribution of weapons and training of recruits for the militias and he emphasized in the strongest terms the strict limitations on the mission."[30] The faxes from Dallaire and Booh Booh to both headquarters and Claes were also sent on *February 15*.[31]

The *fifth message* in this respect was a cable from U.N. headquarters (Annabi and Annan) to UNAMIR in Kigali. This cable, which was drawn up with the advice of Annabi, was received by Dallaire on *February 17*. Annan stated:

> UNAMIR cannot and probably does not have the capacity to take over the maintenance of law and order in or outside Kigali. Public security and the maintenance of law and order is the responsibility of the author-

---

27 Dallaire p. 180.

28 *Id.*

29 *Id.*

30 *Id.*

31 Dallaire writes, in his book, that after he had received the fax from New York on February 15 (informing him about Claes' fax to the Secretary-General), he "quickly drafted" a "reply-fax" that was sent by Booh Booh and himself to New York. Dallaire adds that they received a reply from New York to their fax two days later. Carlsson writes that Dallaire wrote a fax to New York on February 15 and that New York replied, no date is mentioned about the reply from New York. But the reply from New York, as mentioned in Dallaire's book and in the Carlsson Report, contain the same elements. For this reason we conclude that Dallaire and Booh Booh wrote New York on February 15 and that a reply was received on February 17. Carlsson Report S/1999/1257, p. 14; Dallaire, p. 180; Des Forges, p. 162, note 89: Anonymous, "Rwanda, Chronology."

> ities. It must also remain their responsibility, as is the case in all other peacekeeping operations.[32]

He added: "As you know, resolution 792 [sic] (1993) only authorized UNAMIR to contribute to the security of the city of Kigali, i.e., within a weapons secure area established by repeat by the parties."[33]

When Claes visited Rwanda at the end of February, he was shocked that the authorities did not even try to hide the weapons; they were openly distributed among the people.[34] In a fax on February 24 Claes wrote a letter to Noterdaeme about the need to strengthen UNAMIR's mandate. (This is the *sixth message*, from Brussels to New York on *February 24*.) The fax included the following points:

> Under the present mandate UNAMIR cannot carry out a strong maintenance of public order. . . . *If in any case the situation were indeed to deteriorate and the UNAMIR orders mentioned above remain in force, public opinion would never tolerate having Belgian peacekeepers remain passive witnesses to genocide and having the U.N. do nothing.* [emphasis added] . . . UNAMIR should play a more active role and raise its profile to reinforce the credibility of the international community. The question is whether this is possible without a new mandate from the Security Council. If strengthening UNAMIR requires a new mandate . . . there would be problems given the current policy of the U.S. At this point, an extension of the operation (peacekeepers, funding) appears excluded for them. . . . It will be extremely important to see how the action can be reinforced under the present mandate (including Austrian peacekeepers? More decision-making powers for Dallaire? Temporary deployment of peacekeepers from other operations in the region?) and how to effectively increase diplomatic and political pressure.

Claes stated that the foregoing points should be taken into consideration for possible new steps.[35]

With this fax, Claes indicated that the present mandate was too weak, but because the United States would oppose a new one, it should be seen whether

32 Dallaire pp, 180–181.

33 Carlsson Report, S/1999/1257, p. 14; Dallaire pp. 180–181. According to the Carlsson Report, Annan spoke about Resolution 792, while the resolution dealing with the mandate of UNAMIR was Resolution 872, October 5, 1993. SC Resolution 792 is a resolution of November 30, 1992, about Cambodia. It is being assumed that either the Independent Inquiry has cited Annan incorrectly, or Annan made a mistake when he mentioned the resolution.

34 Melvern, 2000 pp.103–104.

35 Annex Belgian Senate, p. 56.

the action could be enforced under the present mandate. By using the word "genocide," he showed that Belgium was aware of the critical security situation and the possible explosion of violence. In the interview, however, he did not remember to employ the word "genocide" in this message on February 24.[36]

Having discussed Claes' fax with the Secretary-General and "principal members' of the Security Council, Noterdaeme replied to the Ministry of Foreign Affairs.[37] He stated that the enlargements of the troops and the the mandate were unlikely. The United States and Great Britain opposed an enlargement for "financial reasons" and because "the operation was undertaken under Chapter VI of the U.N. Treaty." He added that Dallaire could help Rwandan authorities to plan and carry out the elimination of weapons stocks and that he could do this in a visible way.[38]

Léo Delcroix, the Belgian Minister of Defense, visited Rwanda in March. Informing the Ministry of Foreign Affairs of this visit, he indicated that he was aware of the difficulties and the dangers connected to the mandate. Anticipating the fact that the United Nations would have to decide upon UNAMIR's mandate on April 5, Delcroix gave a few possibilities to amend the mandate. He

---

36 Interview with W. Claes January 13, 2006.

37 In the Annex of the Report of the Belgian Senate, it is said that Noterdaeme discussed the issue with the "secretariat and prominent members of the Security Council." Out of minutes of a coordination meeting between the Belgian Ministries of Foreign Affairs and Defense on March 3, it appears that "secretariat" meant the Secretary-General himself. The minutes stated:

> [The Belgian delegation to the U.N.] intervened with the Secretary General to examine with him the means of reinforcing the authority of UNAMIR, at this stage within the framework of the existing mandate. Dallaire is aware of the necessity of carrying out this enforcement. 200 Ghanaian Blue-helmets should be redeployed in the demilitarized zone at Kigali in order to allow the Belgian Blue-helmets to better use their skills in the matter of mobility.

Translated from French in English. Original text:

> [The Belgian delegation to the U.N.] est intervenu auprès du Secrétaire général pour examiner avec lui les moyens de renforcer l'autorité de la Minuar, à ce stade dans le cadre du mandat existant. Dallaire est conscient de la nécessité de procéder à ce renforcement. 200 Casques bleus ghanéens devraient être redéployés de la zone démilitarisée à Kigali pour permettre aux Casques bleus belges de mieux utiliser leurs avantages en matière de mobilité.

See Annex Belgian Senate, p. 57. It is unknown which countries are meant by the "principal members."

38 Annex Belgian Senate, p. 57; Belgian delegation to the United Nations to the Ministry of Foreign Affairs in Brussels, answer on telex of February 24, 1994. Belgian Senate, p. 394.

spoke of "more freedom of movement" and "more persuasive action."[39] In the next section we will see whether the weakness of the mandate was put forward by the Secretary-General to the members of the Security Council when they discussed the continuation of UNAMIR on April 5, two days before the genocide erupted.

11.3 CONCLUSION

In the three months preceding the genocide, the UNAMIR commander asked at least six times for a stronger mandate to seize the hidden arms. All these requests were rejected. This would be understandable had the Security Council concluded, for example, that a broadening of the mandate would have endangered the peace-keeping force or the situation in the country. However, this was not the case, because none of these requests and none of these rejections were tabled on the agenda of the Security Council. The members of the Security Council were never informed of these requests from the peace-keeping force, and they had no opportunity to decide whether to act. The top officials—Annan, Annabi and Riza—lacking any democratic legitimization, deliberately kept the members of the Security Council ignorant. We do not know whether the Security Council members would have taken decisions and, if they had, what kind of decision these would have been. Instead they missed the opportunity to react to the alarming signals. It is this pattern of neglect, by these top U.N. officials, of the very serious warnings from the very trustful source, their own UNAMIR peace-keeping force commander that is the most horrifying aspect of this period before the genocide.

Belgium was fully informed of the deteriorating situation and requested the strengthening of the mandate. It was Belgium that acted and asked the Secretary-General urgently to allow UNAMIR to undertake firmer action. Five messages followed this request in February. The message from Minister Claes

---

39 Telex No. 209, March 15, 1994, of the Belgian Embassy in Kigali to the Ministry of Foreign Affairs in Brussels; Annex Belgian Senate, p. 57. In minutes of a coordination meeting between the Belgian Ministries of Foreign Affairs and Defense on March 17, it is mentioned that the Rwandan police requested themselves for a broader UNAMIR mandate. The minutes noted: "The Rwandan police wish for a modification of the UNAMIR mandate which would permit these to show more firmness and to intervene on their own initiative. The police considers itself to be incapable of facing up alone to the role which has been entrusted to them by the Arusha accords." Translated from French into English. Original text: "La gendarmerie Rwandaise souhaite une modification du mandat de la Minuar qui permette à celle-ci de faire preuve de davantage de fermeté et d'intervenir d'initiative. La gendarmerie s'estime elle-même incapable de faire face seule au rôle qui lui a été confié par les accords d'Arusha." Minutes of the coordination meeting of the Belgian Ministries of Foreign Affairs and Defense on March 17, 1994; Annex Belgian Senate, p. 58.

to Secretary-General Boutros-Ghali on February 11 was that a strong deterrent force was needed to stop the increasingly dangerous situation. Dallaire was asked by New York to write a response to Claes in Brussels. Dallaire appreciated very much that at least some diplomatic support was given to his request. He wrote a reply, but the answer that was sent to Brussels by Booh Booh was a distortion of his original reply, emphasizing the limitations of the mission and downplaying the information on illegal weapons distribution and the recruitment and training of the militias. The original letter, without the distortion, was sent by Booh Booh only to New York where Annan again answered that UNAMIR was not allowed to undertake firmer action.

At the end of February, after a visit to Rwanda, during which Claes witnessed the very bad situation, he again made an appeal to Boutros-Ghali to raise the profile of UNAMIR, with more power in order not to "remain passive witnesses to genocide." This message was also not forwarded to the Security Council members. The top officials of the United Nations only answered that the United Kingdom and the United States would oppose any enlargement. These anticipatory expectations determined their behavior. The top officials are however to blame, in our view, for their behavior in not forwarding all these requests to the most authoritative organ of the United Nations, the Security Council.

CHAPTER 12

UNAMIR: ITS MANDATE AND THE OFFENDING BELGIAN ROLE

12.1 SC RESOLUTION 909, APRIL 5, 1994: A POSSIBILITY TO BROADEN THE UNAMIR MANDATE

UNAMIR had been established on October 5, 1993, for a period of six months, which meant that the Security Council had to decide upon the future of the mission on April 5, 1994.[1]

In preparation for this decision, the Secretary-General presented his second "progress report" to the Council on March 30.[2] It was a very optimistic report saying that the "parties demonstrated that they remained committed to the peace process." The Secretary-General recommended an extension of the mandate for another six months. But he did not propose a broader or firmer mandate. He did not even mention the problems relating to the limited size of the mandate, nor did he mention the numerous requests of General Roméo Dallaire for a firmer mandate. Throughout the months of January, February and March, the issue of the weakness of the mandate was not once brought to the Security Council, and when the Council now had to decide upon the mandate, the Secretary-General still failed to bring the issue to the Council's attention.

So it came that on April 5, 1994, two days before the outbreak of the genocide, the Security Council unanimously adopted Resolution 909, which contained

---

1 To emphasize the necessity of maintaining and strengthening the mandate of UNAMIR, Rwandan human rights associations appealed to the Security Council "to maintain and reinforce" the mission. The organizations stated that a withdrawal "would be interpreted as abandoning the civilian population to the worst of calamities." Alison Des Forges, Leave None to Tell the Story, Genocide in Rwanda (1999) (hereinafter Des Forges), p. 171, note 134: Société Civile, c/o Centre Iwacu, "Déclaration de la Société Civile au Rwanda dans sa réunion du 31 mars 1994."

2 U.N. Doc. S/1994/360, Second progress report of the Secretary-General on UNAMIR for the period from December 30, 1993, to March 30, 1994 (hereinafter S/1994/360).

the same limited mandate.[3] The discussion of UNAMIR's mandate would get a whole new impetus after the start of the genocide only two days later.

12.2 THE AMERICAN ATTITUDE TOWARDS PEACE-KEEPING IN 1994

Somalia has always played a prominent role in the American attitude towards UNAMIR. Despite the horrific events of October 3, 1993, in Somalia, in which American soldiers were dragged through the streets of Mogadishu, the United States voted in favor of the UNAMIR resolution only two days later. What was the reasoning behind the U.S. decisions in relation to UNAMIR? Two interpretations of the American role are heard most often. The first interpretation reflects the opinion that the Americans have always been reluctant about UNAMIR. After Somalia, the Republican Party wanted the United States to get less involved in the peace-keeping missions of the United States, which was shown in the development of the Presidential Decision Directive 25 (PDD25), a formal U.S. peace-keeping doctrine. The directive was developed by the special assistant of President Clinton to the National Security Council, Richard Clarke. When finished, the PDD25 gave 16 factors that policymakers had to consider when deciding whether to support peace-keeping activities or not. According to many critics, the directive was aimed to "kill peacekeeping missions." Despite the fact that the directive was only released on May 3, 1994, it had a great influence on the minds of the U.S. officials involved in the shaping of policy in Rwanda.[4] Boutros-Ghali has always been of the opinion that:

> According to this document, the United States will not get involved in any peacekeeping operation unless there is a demand of the true pro-

---

[3] The resolution extended the mandate until July 29, 1994, and provided for the possibility of a review after six weeks if the political deadlock continued. The Independent Inquiry stated that the "key members" of the Council were "reluctant to accept such a long mandate extension." United Nations, Report of the Independent Inquiry into the Actions of the United Nations during the 1994 Genocide in Rwanda, December 15, 1999, Ingvar Carlsson, Han, Sung-Joo, Rufus, M. Kupolati, U.N. Doc. S/1999/1257, p. 15 (hereinafter Carlsson Report, S/1999/1257). Only the proposal of the Secretary-General to increase the number of civilian police was accepted; see S/1994/360, paragraph 38 and U.N. Doc. S/RES/909 (1994), point 5. What seems to have been on the mind of the members of the Security Council, is shown by paragraph 9 of the resolution: "The Council reiterated its request to the Secretary General to continue to monitor the size and cost of UNAMIR to seek economies." U.N. Doc. S/RES/909 (1994), point 9.

[4] "The Clinton Administration's Policy in Reforming Multilateral Peace Operations," Presidential Directive 25, May 3, 1994; Samantha Power, A problem from hell: America and the age of genocide, pp. 341–342 (2003) (hereinafter Power, 2003).

> tagonists of the dispute; unless there is a peace; unless we know how many months we will need the presence; and unless it will be in the interest of the United States. So practically, it was a return to the [non-intervention] policy of the United States.

According to Boutros-Ghali, PDD25 showed the opinion of the United States that even if they would not be sending American blue helmets, indirectly they would always be involved, both on a financial and on a military basis, and, in case of emergency, they would be called upon to help out.[5]

According to the second interpretation, Clinton was in need of a successful peace-keeping operation after Somalia. He needed to persuade Congress that peace-keeping did matter and was capable of working, and, in doing so, a rather positive policy towards the United Nations could continue.[6] Viewing Rwanda as a simple, classical peace-keeping operation, keeping the peace by implementing the agreement in a short period of time, Clinton defended this peace-keeping operation.

Both interpretations are reflected in practice. The second interpretation made the start of UNAMIR with the approval of the United States possible, but the first interpretation explains in some way the weak role of the United States. when they became aware of the first problems and no longer insisted on any continuation.[7] In an interview with Anthony Lake, the American National Security Adviser, he stressed the first interpretation to understand American foreign policy under Clinton at the start of UNAMIR.[8] Other civil servants from the State Department underlined the impact of the new peace-keeping directive (PPD25) on the American policy during the genocide in Rwanda.[9]

12.3 CONTINUING ANTI-BELGIAN FEELINGS

In Section 5.2 we described the Belgian participation at the explicit request of the Secretary-General and the Belgian authorities' reluctance to play a role. Moreover, we dealt with the role of former colonial powers in peace-keeping missions in general, and in UNAMIR in particular. We also explained that the Belgian ambassador in Rwanda was aware of the anti-Belgian feelings within a section of the Rwandan population. There had already been rumors and criticisms of the Belgian participation in UNAMIR. And as soon as the Belgian troops hit Rwandan soil, a real anti-Belgian climate started to develop. In the

---

5 Frontline interview Boutros-Ghali, January 21, 2004.

6 Howard Adelman and Astri Suhrke, Early warning and conflict management genocide in Rwanda (1995).

7 See Chapters 13 and 16 for a further deliberation on this point.

8 Interview with A. Lake, May 21, 2005.

9 Interviews with J. Shattuck, May 26, 2005, and P. Bushnell, May 27, 2005.

months leading to the genocide, hatred of the Belgians and threats against them became more and more apparent. The question is whether Belgium was aware of the serious danger towards the Belgian Blue Helmets. In the Belgian telex communication, the issue became more prominent as time proceeded.

A telex sent by Willy Claes to the embassy on November 30, in which he gave a full summary of the anti-Belgian incidents of the last weeks, showed that the minister was aware of the anti-Belgian climate.[10] A synthesis report from the embassy in the first week of December stated that the Rwandan authorities hardly did anything to inhibit the anti-Belgian climate. Ambassador Johan Swinnen wrote: "In my opinion, I must however deplore that neither the leaders of the MRND nor the President of the Republic made positive and corrective public propositions to allow ambiguity to be removed (and the impression of double entendre) and to create a more peaceful climate in the country."[11] On December 8 Swinnen had a meeting with President Habyarimana in which he asked him for more positive public statements about the efforts of the international community and of Belgium in particular. Positive statements from Habyarimana could counter the smear campaign against Belgium.[12] In the same month, UNAMIR sent a very clear report to the Belgian intelligence service talking about the "existence of an alarming anti-Belgium atmosphere." The report added: "People tell us that they are being intimidated and threatened because they are pro-Belgium."[13]

---

[10] Sénat de Belgique, Commission d'Enquête parlementaire concernant les événements au Rwanda, (Commission of parliamentary enquiry concerning the events in Rwanda), session de 1997–1998, 6 décembre 1997, Rapport fait au nom de la commission d'enquête par MM Mahoux et Verhofstadt, Annexes, p. 21 (hereinafter Annex Belgian Senate). A briefing from the general intelligence service that was sent to Evere stated that the animosity regarding the Belgian participation was continuing. Briefing of November 26 from the general intelligence service of the Belgian Ministry of Defense to Evere. Annex Belgian Senate, pp. 19–20.

[11] Translated from French into English. Original text: "De mon coté, je dois cependant déplorer que ni les dirigeants du MRND ni le président de la République ne tiennent publiquement des propos positifs et correctifs permettant de lever l'ambiguïté (et l'impression de double langage) et de rendre le climat plus serein dans le pays." Telex No. 1229, December 8, 1993 of the Belgian embassy in Kigali to the Ministry of Foreign Affairs in Brussels. Annex Belgian Senate, p. 21.

[12] Swinnen informed his Ministry by fax of this conversation. Telex No. 1231, December 8, 1993, of the Belgian embassy in Kigali to the Ministry of Foreign Affairs in Brussels. The Ugandese press spoke as well about the unwanted presence of Belgium by the Rwandans. Different articles were sent from the Belgian Intelligence Service to Dallaire. Documents Belgian Intelligence Service (SGR), No. 1243. Annex Belgian Senate, p. 22.

[13] Report of December 29 from the Belgian Intelligence Service to Evere, Doc. 1319. Annex Belgian Senate, p. 21. In a briefing of UNAMIR to Evere on December 29 the atmosphere was called anti-Belgian. Doc. SGR No. 1316, Annex Belgian Senate, p. 22.

January was the month that Jean Pierre came forward and told UNAMIR about extremists who were planning to wound or kill Belgian peace-keepers to guarantee a Belgian withdrawal. Belgium's response to this great and imminent threat seems to have been fairly limited.

According to the Belgian Ad Hoc Group, the Belgian embassy sent only three faxes to the Ministry of Foreign Affairs in Brussels that mentioned this plan to kill Belgian peace-keepers.[14] Moreover, the Ad Hoc Group concluded that in these three faxes only a few words were devoted to this plan. On January 13 the Belgian embassy in Kigali sent a cable to the Ministry of Foreign Affairs in Brussels that spoke of a meeting of the ambassadors with SRSG Jacques Roger Booh Booh and Dallaire. During the meeting, the ambassadors were informed of Jean Pierre's story, including the plan to kill the Belgians.[15] On January 14 the embassy informed the ministry that an ambassadors delegation, including Swinnen, met with President Habyarimana. This telex showed, however, that the ambassadors mentioned the plan to kill the Belgians only in an extremely indirect way to President Habyarimana.[16] On January 15 the embassy informed the Ministry that the three ambassadors of France, Belgium and the United States had decided not to make a special *démarche* to Habyarimana about the information received from Jean Pierre.[17] The Ad Hoc Group concluded, furthermore, that the Belgian Ministry of Foreign Affairs only sent one fax to the embassy in Kigali in which the plan to kill the Belgians was mentioned.[18] One week after Jean Pierre had come forward, the Belgian telexes no longer spoke of the plan to kill the Belgians. According to the authors, four faxes, in which the plan to kill the Belgians was mentioned, only in an indirect way, together with the lack of a specific *démarche*, was a rather poor response to this great and imminent threat.

On January 20 Paul Noterdaeme informed the Ministry of Foreign Affairs in Brussels that he had told Iqbal Riza of the Belgian fears about the security situation in Rwanda and more specifically of the security situation of the Belgian troops.[19] On January 22 Luc Marchal forwarded a letter to Evere (Operation

---

14 Annex Belgian Senate, pp. 28–29. Telex No. 32, January 13, 1994, of the Belgian embassy in Kigali to the Ministry of Foreign Affairs in Brussels; Telex No. 41, January 14, 1994, from the Belgian embassy in Kigali to the Ministry of Foreign Affairs in Brussels; Telex No. 44, January 15, 1994, from the Belgian embassy in Kigali informs the Ministry of Foreign Affairs in Brussels.

15 Telex No. 32, January 13, 1994, of the Belgian embassy in Kigali to the Ministry of Foreign Affairs in Brussels.

16 Telex No. 41, January 14, 1994, from the Belgian embassy in Kigali to the Ministry of Foreign Affairs in Brussels.

17 Telex No. 44, January 15, 1994, from the Belgian embassy in Kigali informs the Ministry of Foreign Affairs in Brussels.

18 Telex No. 32, January 13, 1994, from the Ministry of Foreign Affairs in Brussels to the Belgian embassy in Kigali.

19 Cable of January 20, 1994, from Noterdaeme to the Ministry of Foreign Affairs in Brussels. Annex Belgian Senate, p. 30.

Center of the Belgian Army). The letter was originally sent from the Interahamwe to Booh Booh and spoke about virulent attacks on the Belgian troops.[20] Three days later, Swinnen reported to the Ministry of Foreign Affairs about his meeting with MDR secretary Donat Murego, who was known to be an extremist Hutu. According to Murego, it was Habyarimana and the MRND who incited hatred against the Belgians. Murego added that the Interahamwe would start a civil war and that they would play on the Belgium animosity.[21]

Throughout February, reports on the anti-Belgium feeling were continuously sent between the Belgian institutions.[22] On February 6 UNAMIR informed Evere that it had stopped the checkpoints from operating, because many of the incidents at the checkpoints were not the result of the Belgian peace-keepers "but the result of a . . . will to seek incident with Belgian militaries." In another note, Marchal informed Evere that he stopped the checkpoints from operating because they"[m]ade me fear of a deliberate will to trigger incidents with the soldiers of the Belgian Detachment."[23] On February 7 Lieutenant Marc Nees informed Marchal that the anti-Belgian feeling should not be seen as a result of the behavior of the Belgians but as a deliberate campaign that was carried out with "certain political motives." According to the report, the incidents often included high-placed Rwandans belonging to the Network Zero.[24] On February 17 Swinnen had another meeting with President Habyarimana in which he discredited the many anti-Belgian incidents. Habyarimana promised to act against them.[25]

Mid-March, after an attack on MDR Minister Nsengiyaremye, Swinnen ascertained in a telex to the Ministry of Foreign Affairs that mainly politicians with sympathy for Belgium had been the victim of attacks.[26] The minutes of a coordination meeting between the Ministries of Foreign Affairs and Defense mentioned explicitly the increasing violence against UNAMIR.[27]

---

20 Fax of January 22, 1994, from Marchal to Evere. Annex Belgian Senate, p. 30.

21 Telex No. 70, January 25, 1994, from the Belgian embassy in Kigali to the Ministry of Foreign Affairs in Brussels. Annex Belgian Senate, p. 30.

22 Report January 23, 1994, of UNAMIR to the Belgian Intelligence Service, documents SGR No. 1715; Annex Belgian Senate, p. 23.

23 Translated from French into English. Original text: "Me fait craindre une volonté délibérée de déclencher des incidents avec les militaires du Det BE." Doc. SGR No. 2571, 2190; Annex Belgian Senate, p. 31, 32.

24 Annex Belgian Senate, p. 32.

25 The embassy informed the Ministry of this meeting on February 17. Documents of the Belgian Intelligence Service No. 2591. Annex Belgian Senate, p. 24.

26 Telex No. 205, March 14, 1994, of the Belgian embassy in Kigali to the Ministry of Foreign Affairs in Brussels. Annex Belgian Senate, p. 24.

27 Minutes of the coordination meeting between the Ministry of Foreign Affairs in Brussels and the Ministry of Defense of March 17, 1994. Annex Belgian Senate, p. 33.

12.4 RADIO BROADCASTS REINFORCE THE ANTI-BELGIAN CLIMATE

In Chapter 2 we dealt with the hate radio in Rwanda in general. In this section, our attention is focused on the hate radio's role in reinforcing the existing anti-Belgian feelings in Rwanda. From November 1993 the radio started to promote the hostile atmosphere against the Belgians more and more actively.[28] RTLMC not only broadcasted provocative editorials, the National Radio also broadcasted some pro-French speeches of Habyarimana, which were implicit criticisms of Belgium. From the documents sent between the Ministries of Defense, Foreign Affairs and the Belgian embassy, it appears that the Belgian institutions were well aware of the critical role of the radio.[29]

On November 25 Swinnen informed the Belgian Ministry of Foreign Affairs of his meeting with the Rwandan Minister of Information about the anti-Belgian announcements on RTLMC. Swinnen wrote that the minister argued that he was "powerless in the brutal game played by a minority that didn't agree with the Belgian participation in UNAMIR."[30]

Half way through December, Radio Rwanda broadcasted a speech of Habyarimana in which he was all in favor of the French and implicitly blamed the Belgians.[31] In January Habyarimana gave an interview on the National Radio. He praised France and did not say anything about the Belgian partici-

---

[28] Annex Belgian Senate, p. 20.

[29] It was not only the radio which had a negative influence, the written press also dealt with the anti-Belgian atmosphere. In November one of the first anti-Belgian articles was published: the MRND-paper *Kamarampaka* published an article giving open criticism to the Belgians. On November 30 the article was sent from the Belgian embassy in Kigali to the Ministry of Foreign Affairs in Brussels. Telex No. 1196, November 30, 1993. A press article titled "Merci la France" mentioned that certain Rwandan areas were against the Belgian presence in UNAMIR. On November 27 the military technical cooperation sent the article to the general intelligence service. See Document General intelligence service of the Ministry of Defense, Doc. No. 657. Annex Belgian Senate, p. 20. On November 27 UNAMIR sent three press articles to Evere that showed the aversion and hostility towards the Belgians. Documents intelligence service of the Belgian Ministry of Defense. Nos. 590 and 917 and documents of Evere No. 7278. Annex Belgian Senate, p. 21. In a briefing sent from the Belgian Intelligence Service to Evere it is stated that the origin of the anti-Belgian atmosphere lay at the Office d'Information du Rwanda, which was responsible for the radio broadcasts. Document No. 7265 from the Belgian Intelligence Service. Annex Belgian Senate, p. 21.

[30] Telex No. 1180, November 25, 1993, from the Belgian embassy in Kigali to the Ministry of Foreign Affairs in Brussels. Annex Belgian Senate, p. 20.

[31] Habyarimana's words about the French were: "The true, the true friends who haven't abandoned Rwanda in the most difficult times." Translated from French into English. Original text: "Les vrais, les vrais amis qui n'ont pas abandonné le Rwanda dans les moments les plus difficiles."

pation in UNAMIR. The Belgian embassy reported both incidents with the President to the Ministry in Brussels.[32]

In January the Belgian intelligence service informed Evere that RTLMC was broadcasting anti-Belgian editions: "RTLMC, who take a malicious pleasure in disseminating false information, or in heavily emphasizing real incidents which implicated the Belgian soldiers . . . we can conclude that the campaign of anti-Belgian indoctrination is being renewed."[33] On January 27 Lieutenant Nees informed the commander of KIBAT, Lieutenant Colonel Leroy, commanding officer of the first Belgian paracommando battalion, that RTLMC was broadcasting that the Tutsi had killed Hutu with the help of the Belgians and that the radio questioned what other reason there was for the Belgian presence, besides helping the Inkontanyi to power.[34]

After an incident on the night of January 30–31, whereby a Belgian soldier threw stones at the house of Jean-Bosco Barayagwiza, the leader of the CDR, RTLMC and Radio Rwanda both broadcasted that Belgian soldiers had tried to kill him. The following day, RTLMC broadcasted that "the time has come to take aim at Belgian targets."[35] A few days later, the embassy informed the Ministry that the incident of the blue helmets at the house of Barayagwiza had led to broadcasts of RTLMC in which the radio encouraged the plundering of Belgian property.[36] On February 1 the embassy informed the Ministry of Foreign Affairs that the expanding broadcasts of RTLMC indicated a further expanding anti-Belgian feeling. The fax noted that RTLMC was broadcasting that Belgian soldiers were part of RPF murder squads.[37]

The Ad Hoc Group found relatively few documents dealing with the provocative role of RTLMC sent between the Belgian Ministry institutions in February but more at the end of March.

---

32 Telex No. 1261, December 21, 1993, from the Belgian embassy in Kigali to the Ministry of Foreign Affairs in Brussels; Telex No. 64, January 23, 1994, from the Belgian embassy in Kigali to the Ministry of Foreign Affairs in Brussels. Annex Belgian Senate, p. 22.

33 Translated from French into English. Original text: "RTLMC qui prend un malin plaisir à diffuser de fausses Info, ou à insister lourdement sur les incidents réels impliquant des Mil (BE) . . . On peut conclure que la campagne d'intoxication anti-belge est à nouveau en pleine recrudescence." Documents of the Belgian Intelligence Service No. 7338; Annex Belgian Senate (Findings Ad Hoc Group), p. 23.

34 Report of January 27 from Lieutenant Nees to the Commander of KIBAT, Leroy. Annex Belgian Senate, p. 31.

35 Des Forges, p. 159, note 74; Document 16, Belgian Military Intelligence, February 1, 1994 (confidential source).

36 Telex No. 92, February 3, 1994 from the Belgian embassy to the Ministry of Foreign Affairs in Brussels. Annex Belgian Senate, p. 23.

37 Telex No. 91, February 1, 1994, sent form the Belgian embassy in Kigali to the Ministry of Foreign Affairs in Brussels. Annex Belgian Senate (Findings Ad Hoc Group), pp. 23, 3. That same day Lieutenant Nees informed the commander of KIBAT, Leroy, of several broadcasts of RTLMC. Annex Belgian Senate, p. 23.

On March 22 the Belgian embassy in Kigali informed the Ministry of two new editorials from RTLMC in which the Belgian government was accused of colonialism, paternalism and of acting as an accomplice to the RPF. The radio blamed the Belgians "for Arusha." Furthermore, the radio announced that the Belgians wanted to force Rwanda "into a government of bandits and killers." The radio threatened the Belgians that the war would be without compassion. "The friendship has transformed into hatred without mercy." In a briefing on March 23, 1994, the Belgian intelligence service informed Evere of these new anti-Belgian broadcasts on RTLMC.[38]

On March 24 the Belgian intelligence service noted that RTLMC had broadcasted that Ambassador Swinnen was planning a coup.[39] A few days later, the embassy sent another report to the Ministry about anti-Belgian broadcasts on RTLMC.[40] On March 31 the embassy informed the Ministry that the editorials broadcast on RTLMC were "extremely disturbing for Belgium."

The Belgian Minister of Foreign Affairs was very aware of the danger and influence of RTLMC. On April 1 he sent a telegram to Ambassador Swinnen saying: "Given all that we are doing for Rwanda, it is incomprehensible that this radio station RTLMC, and we are well aware where the finance for this station comes from . . . is conducting a scandalous anti-Belgian campaign."[41]

12.5 ANTI-BELGIAN INCIDENTS

These anti-Belgian feelings resulted in some incidents against the Belgians at the end of January, the end of February and the beginning of April. The most important incidents will be set out below.[42]

On January 24 Belgian peace-keepers guarding Booh Booh's residence were shot at.[43] Two days later a Belgian UNAMIR patrol was fired upon.[44]

---

38 Documents of the intelligence service, No. 3352; Annex Belgian Senate, p. 24.

39 Noted by the Belgian Intelligence Service on March 24; Annex Belgian Senate, p. 24.

40 Telex No. 256, March 29, 1994.

41 Sénat de Belgique, Commission d'Enquête parlementaire concernant les événements au Rwanda, Sénat de Belgique, session de 1997–1998, 6 décembre 1997, Rapport fait au nom de la commission d'enquête par MM Mahoux et Verhofstadt, p. 595 (hereinafter Belgian Senate).

42 Two anti-Belgian incidents took place as early as November: A Belgian Red Cross truck was hit deliberately by a mine and two missionaries were harassed because they were thought to be Belgian.

43 According to Melvern, it was January 26. Linda Melvern, A People Betrayed. The Role of the West in Rwanda's Genocide, p. 96 (2000). UNAMIR informed Evere of the attack. Documents Evere, No. 1759. Annex Belgian Senate, pp. 25, 26.

44 The patrol was attacked on January 26. Annex Belgian Senate, p. 26. On

During the MRD meeting of February 20 Belgian peace-keepers who were protecting Madame Agathe, were stoned by a crowd. The blue helmets had to fire 63 shots in the air in order to free themselves.[45] On February 22 Belgian peace-keepers, escorting an RPF convoy, were attacked. One civilian and one RPF soldier were killed in the ambush, and a UNAMIR observer was wounded. According to the technical service, the Belgian school was closed in light of the violent circumstances these days in February.[46] On February 23 Belgian peace-keepers, who wanted to free a Rwandese judge, were shot at and had to shoot 20 times to free themselves.[47] The following day, UNAMIR informed Evere that there was a fire battle between Belgian troops and armed civilians in Gikonda.[48] The same report noted that the violence between the civilians and towards UNAMIR was increasing.

12.6 BELGIAN PEACE-KEEPERS: AN EASY TARGET

It must be said that the first contingent of Flemish Belgian peace-keepers misbehaved in the city and in the pubs. In an interview with Brent Beardsley, he stated that the first Flemish battalion provoked the Rwandans all the time. There was not a week that went by that there was not a major disciplinary incident in that unit. They were drunk in the streets and in the bars. They flew planes very low over Kigali. They broke into the house of the CDR leader Barigazira, beat him in front of his family and threatened to kill him. They did not salute African officers. Beardsley told us:[49]

> I have never experienced in my life white racism as it was with this contingent. . . . They were very provocative against the population. The situation was so serious that in February 1994 when the commander of the Belgian army, came to visit us, Dallaire took them into a room and said that he did not want to have this unit any longer and if the next unit, arriving in March, does not have strong leadership and dis-

January 30 an assailant threw a grenade at UNAMIR headquarters. Sénat de Belgique, Rapport du Groupe Ad Hoc Rwanda A La Commission des Affairs Etrangeres, Sénat de Belgique, 7 janvier 1997 p. 38 (hereinafter Belgian Ad Hoc Group). On the night of January 30–31 a Belgian soldier threw stones and broke windows of Barayagwiza's house. Des Forges, p. 159, note 74: Document 16, Belgian Military Intelligence, February 1, 1994 (confidential source).

45 Belgian Ad Hoc Group, p. 38.

46 Annex Belgian Senate, p. 26

47 Sitrep from KIBAT to Evere on February 24. Annex Belgian Senate, p. 33.

48 Sitrep form UNAMIR to the Belgian Intelligence Service. Annex Belgian Senate, p. 32.

49 Interview with B. Beardsley, June 6, 2005.

> cipline he would take the unprecedented step of going back to New York and asking for the full withdrawal of the Belgian contingent. I have never heard of that being done, but Dallaire was deadly serious, because he said these guys were becoming an operation deficiency, they were causing too many problems with the Rwandans. They were giving the extremists reload. Anyhow the behavior of the first contingent made them an easy target to offend feelings in Rwanda. . . . In March that unit left Rwanda, the next unit arrived and it was composed of Walloon thus only French speaking, and they were excellent. It shows the difference in leadership, we had no disciplinary problems with that entire second unit. Unfortunately they were the ones that were there on the 7th of April, and it were these soldiers that were killed.

The anti-Belgian feelings were prevalent amongst the extremists. For instance, President Habyarimana was also outspokenly pro-French and anti-Belgian. When he visited Brussels in 1994, he asked the King of Belgium to withdraw the Belgian Ambassador Swinnen from Kigali. The King became furious and vehemently rejected this request.[50] King Boudewijn made it clear to Habyarimana that the only way was reconciliation and the deployment of the Arusha Accords. Although the relationship between King Boudewijn and Habyarimana was good and close, both Claes and Boudewijn realized during this meeting how much influence the extremists had on the opinion of the President of Rwanda.[51] The impact of the anti-Belgian feelings, and in particular the propaganda from the radio, was enormous. The Belgians were aware of this, and they realized that the Belgian peace-keepers could become an easy target.

We may conclude that prolonging UNAMIR's mission for six months was presented as a routine decision. Although this time UNAMIR had to be put on the agenda, the members of the Security Council were not informed by Boutros-Ghali of the deteriorating situation in Rwanda, and not the slightest attention was given to the requests to strengthen and broaden the mandate of the force itself. Another way of undermining UNAMIR was the anti-Belgian smear campaign in Rwanda that was deliberately started by the media on behalf of the extremists in order to get rid of the peace-keepers. In particular, the Belgian peace-keepers were an easy target, because they were racist and behaved badly. The Interahamwe intended to start a civil war, and they played on this Belgian animosity. Even the Rwandan President supported these anti-Belgian feelings.

---

50 Interview with W. Claes, January 13, 2006.

51 *Id.*

CHAPTER 13

THE START OF THE GENOCIDE

13.1 INDIFFERENCE AS TO WHO SHOT THE PLANE DOWN

On April 6, at 8:23 in the evening, the plane carrying President Habyarimana was shot down. Habyarimana had been returning from Dar es Salaam where he had attended a meeting of the heads of state about the installment of the Rwandan transitional government.[1] All passengers were killed. People who had been on board besides Habyarimana were Cyprien Ntaryamira, the President of Burundi, Déogratias Nsabimana, the chief of staff of the Rwandan army and three French crew members.[2]

The attack, which led to the outbreak of the Rwandan genocide, remains largely uninvestigated. To this day, the killers have still not been identified.[3] Reyntjens, describing the first three days of the genocide, set out four hypotheses in his book:[4]

(1) Reyntjens' first hypothesis consists of the theory that the extremists of Habyarimana's own circle committed the attack. A variant to this hypothesis is that the French shot down the plane on behalf of the extremists.

(2) The second hypothesis is that the Burundian President was the target of the attack. This option seems very unlikely, however, because the Burundian President decided only at the very last moment to get on board.

(3) The third hypothesis entails the story of a failed *Coup d'Etat* by the Prime Minister and several officers. Their plan would have

1 Filip Reyntjens, L'Afrique des Grands Lacs, en crise: Rwanda, Burundi: 1988–1994, pp. 44–45 (1994) (hereinafter Reyntjens).

2 Reyntjens, pp. 44–45; NRC, *Le Monde onthult Frans onderzoek: President Rwanda doodde voorganger*, (Translated: NRC, Le Monde exposes French research: President Rwanda killed predecessor), March 10, 2004; NRC, *Een explosief Rwanda-rapport* (Translated: An Explosive Rwanda Report), March 11, 2004.

3 Reyntjens, pp. 44–45; Libération, Stephen Smith, *Deux missiles abattent l'avion du président Habyarimana*, April 6–7, 1994.

4 Reyntjens, pp. 44–45.

been to kill the President to create more leeway for an interim government and the implementation of Arusha.

(4) Reyntjens' last hypothesis consists of the theory that the attack was committed by the RPF. A variant to this theory is that the attack was committed with help from the Belgians.[5]

It is highly remarkable that there has never been any interest in starting an inquiry into the question of who committed the attack, although it was the plane crash that instigated or at least stimulated the eruption of the genocide. In Chapter 1 we called the plane crash the "trigger" for the genocidal developments but not the cause of the genocide. According to Reyntjens, the smokescreen about who shot the plane down seemed to suit all parties. At the national level, nobody was interested in investigating the issue; the RPF was not interested, nor was the MRND, nor were the other political parties. At the international level, nobody was interested either; the United Nations was not interested, nor were Belgium and France. This lack of interest is highly remarkable.

The most widely believed theory is the first hypothesis, that the Hutu extremists shot down the airplane to prevent the Arusha Accords from being implemented and to use Habyarimana's assassination as a pretext to start their planned genocide.[6] Controversially, Reyntjens argued on the basis of *"un faisceau d'indices"* (a bundle of indicators) in his investigation of 1994 that the attack was committed by the RPF.[7] Ten years later, Reyntjens' theory received endorsement from the French anti-terror division, DNAT. The research by the DNAT was conducted over a period of six years. This long research was made at the request of relatives of the French crew killed in the plane.[8] In March 2004 a DNAT investigation report, which dealt with the issue, was leaked to the press. The report argued that Major General Paul Kagame himself had ordered the attack. According to the French investigation report, it was an elite-group of ten RPF officers who received direct orders from Kagame.[9] The French report

---

5 Reyntjens, pp. 44–45. The question of who shot the plane down became even more intriguing when Reyntjens tried to find out who had been able to possess the two Russian SAM rockets. According to Reyntjens, none of the parties involved was able to do so.

6 Reyntjens, pp. 44–45; Alison Des Forges, Leave None to Tell the Story, Genocide in Rwanda p. 185 (1999) (hereinafter Des Forges).

7 Reyntjens, pp. 44–45.

8 NRC, *Le Monde onthult Frans onderzoek: President Rwanda doodde voorganger*, March 10, 2004.

9 *Id.;* NRC, *Een explosief Rwanda-rapport*, March 11, 2004. Despite the fact that it was a French airplane that had crashed and that three Frenchmen had been killed, France was not interested in investigating the issue. The investigation that became public in 2004 was done after repeated requests by the families of the French crew who had been on board the plane.

did not receive a lot of international attention, although it contained some serious accusations.

The United Nations—according to this French report—had undermined any investigation into the possible attackers of the plane, and the black box of the plane was stolen by the United Nations and transported to their headquarters in New York.[10] Kofi Annan said he was "amazed" by this report, because the French had not done any research at the United Nations.[11] However, within one day, the United Nations made public that the black box, after ten years, had been found at their headquarters in New York![12] Again, for the second time that week, Annan had to react; now he was "surprised" that he had the black box under his control. The U.N. spokesman, Eckhard, clarified that this black box had been put into a filing cabinet of the department of "Air Safety," but because this black box was totally intact, they did not believe it to have originated from the crashed plane.[13] It is at least very remarkable that within one day, the black box was found, whereas the U.N. inquiry resulting in the Carlsson Report was unaware of this. Annan announced another inquiry, but neither the results of this inquiry nor the contents of the black box have ever been made public.[14]

The accusation that the RPF was responsible for the attack is based on reports of hundreds of witnesses, including many dissidents from the revolting RPF movement. In their view, forwarded by *Le Monde*, the Tutsi leader in exile, Paul Kagame, planned the attack in order to get into power, although he was aware that killing the President would lead to massacres of the Tutsis in Rwanda.[15] These revelations are made in the inquiry report under the direction of examining magistrate Jean-Louis Bruguière. This outcome means that the RPF may be considered to be the instigators of the genocide, whereas the perpetrators of the genocide are and remain the Hutu extremists. Some will make use of this report to attempt to confuse and reverse the roles of the perpetrators and victims, as has so often been done in history through the so-called "blaming the victims behavior" afterwards.[16] The reaction to these accusations from Rwanda was put forward by the chief of the army James Kabarebe, who stated that only the French had the intelligence information of the flight and the military control over the area from where the missiles were launched, so it was therefore

---

10 NRC, *Le Monde onthult Frans onderzoek: President Rwanda doodde voorganger*, March 10, 2004.

11 *Id.*

12 NRC, *VN hadden "zwarte doos" toch in bezit*, (Translated: U.N. possessed "black box" nevertheless), March 13, 2004. Based on press release of Thursday, March 11, 2004.

13 *Id.*

14 See also Section 18.3.

15 NRC, *President offerde Tutsi's voor macht*, (Translated: President sacrificed Tutsis for power), March 10, 2004.

16 See also the article by Jeroen Corduwener in NRC, *Een explosief Rwanda-rapport*, March 11, 2004.

the French themselves who must have made the attack on the plane.[17] The government of Rwanda has, for a long time, accused the French government of having consistently supported the Hutu regime and the Hutu extremists during the genocide. However, the accusation that France had collaborated in the genocide has been refuted by the French Parliamentary Inquiry Commission of 1998.[18]

The most remarkable aspect, in our view, is that no national or international actor was interested in the question of who fired the missiles at the plane. Perhaps all actors were in some way involved in the attack, which caused their lack of interest in knowing the truth of who the attackers were. The general feeling directly after the attack, however, was that this was planned by the Hutu extremists, but it was the Rwandan government during the genocide who denied any responsibility. Not only the Hutu's but also the French believed that the RPF of Kagame attacked the plane. Even when this latest opinion turns out to be the truth, these Tutsi cannot be made into accomplices in a genocide aimed at the Tutsi population in Rwanda. The trigger in this case is not the same as the cause. The causes of the genocide have already been made clear in our previous chapters. The trigger was the crash of the plane—just as the trigger for the Kristallnacht ("Night of Broken Glass," i.e., progrom of November 9–10, 1938) in Germany was the shooting of the German diplomat Ernst vom Rath in Paris by Herschel Feibel on November 7, 1938. Preventing the trigger is almost impossible, but preventing the genocide is not the same as preventing the trigger. Only by taking all early warnings seriously could genocide have possibly been prevented.[19]

13.2 THE FIRST 12 HOURS FOLLOWING THE PLANE CRASH

13.2.1 A Denial of Prime Minister Agathe Uwilingiyamana's Authority

An hour after the plane crash, the Presidential Guard set up roadblocks throughout the city.[20] There were no people on the streets, no cars, only military vehicles. There was sporadic gunfire and explosions of grenades.[21]

---

[17] NRC, *Le Monde onthult Frans onderzoek: President Rwanda doodde voorganger*, March 10, 2004.

[18] See Section 18.3.

[19] See chapter 1.

[20] Des Forges, p. 187. Linda Melvern, A People Betrayed. The Role of the West in Rwanda's Genocide, p. 116 (2000) (hereinafter Melvern, 2000); United Nations, Report of the Independent Inquiry into the Actions of the United Nations during the 1994 Genocide in Rwanda, December 15, 1999, Ingvar Carlsson, Han, Sung-Joo, Rufus, M. Kupolati, U.N. Doc. S/1999/1257, p. 15 (hereinafter Carlsson Report, S/1999/1257).

[21] Des Forges, p. 183; Luc Marchal, Aan de poorten van de Rwandese hel:

The panic was evident; UNAMIR was overwhelmed by people calling for information.[22]

With Habyarimana's death, Prime Minister Agathe Uwilingiyamana had become the head of the government. As soon as Madame Agathe received the news, she tried to get her cabinet together. But in the hour after the crash, all hard-line ministers had disappeared; they seemed to have been evacuated by the Presidential Guard. Some of the moderate ministers had fled their homes to find a hiding place. Other ministers were too afraid to leave their homes.[23] The Prime Minister was advised to flee as well, but she refused. She felt that it was her responsibility to take charge and order the people to stay calm. She stayed at home with her husband and five children and decided to speak on the national radio the next morning.[24]

At 10 o'clock in the evening, one and a half hours after the crash, Roméo Dallaire was invited to attend a meeting of a Crisis Committee at the FAR headquarters. Before leaving, Dallaire informed Iqbal Riza by telephone of what was going on.[25] The Crisis Committee consisted of senior staff members of the Rwandan army and the *gendarmerie*. Because the President and the chief of staff of the army were both dead, Colonel Théoneste Bagosora, the Chef de Cabinet of the Ministry of Defense, took charge of the meeting.[26]

Bagosora immediately started arguing that the military needed to take control over the government. Dallaire replied that any military takeover would result in a withdrawal of UNAMIR. Dallaire stated that Rwanda still had a government, which was now headed by Prime Minister Agatha Uwilingiyimana.[27] Dallaire urged the officers several times to contact Madame Agathe to arrange a "legitimate continuation of the political authority," but Bagosora firmly refused.[28] Dallaire ordered the officers to make sure that the Presidential Guard, who were out on the streets, returned to their barracks.[29]

Because of the political aspects of the crisis, Dallaire decided to call the Special Representative of the Secretary-General, Jacques Roger Booh Booh. It was around midnight when Dallaire's phone call woke Booh Booh up. Dallaire

---

Getuigenis van een peacekeeper, pp. 171, 172 (2001) (hereinafter Marchal); Melvern, 2000 p. 116.

22 Roméo Dallaire, Shake Hands with the Devil, The Failure of Humanity in Rwanda, pp. 221, 222 (2004) (hereinafter Dallaire); Carlsson Report, S/1999/1257, p. 16.

23 Dallaire, pp. 221–222, 227; Des Forges, p. 183.

24 Melvern, 2000 pp. 116–117.

25 Dallaire, p. 222; Carlsson Report, S/1999/1257, p. 15. See Section 13.2.4.

26 Dallaire, pp. 222–224; Marchal, pp. 172–173; Carlsson Report, S/1999/1257, p. 15.

27 Dallaire, p. 222–223; Marchal, pp. 172–173.

28 Des Forges, p. 186, note 22: Human Rights Watch/FIDH interview, Plainsboro, N.J., June 14, 1996; Commission d'enquête, *Report*, pp. 420–421.

29 Marchal, p. 173; Dallaire, pp. 222–223.

briefed him on what had happened and they agreed to meet together with Bagosora at Booh Booh's residence.[30] The Special Representative of the Secretary-General repeated to Bagosora that Madame Agathe was the legitimate head of government. Bagosora protested again, saying that "the military would not accept her" and that "her own government and the Rwandan people had rejected her."[31]

Driving back to UNAMIR's headquarters, the peace and quiet in the streets of Kigali was striking. The usual explosions and gunfire were not heard.[32] Back at UNAMIR's headquarters, around 3:00 a.m., Dallaire called New York and was told by Riza: "UNAMIR is not, repeat not, to fire unless fired upon." Dallaire reminded Riza that "the rules of engagement allowed UNAMIR to intervene and use an escalation of force up to and including the use of deadly force to prevent crimes against humanity."[33] Riza repeated that UNAMIR was not to fire unless fired upon, that they had to negotiate and, above all else, avoid conflict. Riza stated that he "fully appreciated the crisis they were in but that they must not create any incident that could be exploited." Dallaire was not able to persuade him.[34]

13.2.2 UNAMIR Fails to Protect Madame Agathe

Just after 2:00 a.m., ten Belgian paratroops were sent out to Madame Agathe's house to escort her to the radio station, where she was going to speak at 5:30 the next morning. The paramilitary commandos had great difficulties in reaching her house, because the military had sealed the entire city-center through strategic roadblocks. The peace-keepers needed three hours to cover a distance usually traversed in fifteen minutes.[35]

At 5:20 the paramilitary commandos finally arrived at the Prime Minister's house. They met the five Ghanaian peace-keepers who were on night duty at Agathe's gate. The situation was very threatening. The sound of gunfire and explosions of grenades was heard in the street, an armored car of the Presidential Guard was standing close to Agathe's house and armed men were crouching on

---

30 Dallaire, p. 225; Marchal, p. 174; Carlsson Report, S/1999/1257, p. 16.

31 The meeting ended with the agreement that they would meet the following morning at the U.S. embassy with the French, Belgian and American diplomats. The meeting would never take place. After Bagosora and Dallaire had left, Booh-Booh informed Madame Agathe, at 1:00 a.m. that the military refused to give her the authority. Agathe refused to flee. Reyntjens, p. 54; Dallaire, p. 227.

32 Marchal, p. 174; Dallaire, pp. 227–228; Melvern, 2000 p. 118.

33 Paragraph 17 of the Rules of Engagement, see Section 4.5.1.

34 Dallaire, p. 229. See Section 13.2.4.

35 Carlsson Report, p. 16; Des Forges, p. 188.

rooftops. In these circumstances, Madame Agathe did not want to leave. She called for reinforcements of the escort.[36]

At 7 o'clock her house was surrounded by 20 heavily armed Rwandan soldiers and Presidential Guards on the roofs. The armored car of the Presidential Guard was still standing close, and a tank was parked in the road to Agathe's house. Lieutenant Thierry Lotin, the Belgian peace-keeper and leader of UNAMIR in Kigali, who was in charge of the U.N. escort, radioed U.N. headquarters saying that Madame's house was surrounded by 20 soldiers armed with guns and grenades. At 8:17 Lotin radioed again saying: "They have weapons we do not have, grenades, . . . bombs, . . . we will never hold out."[37] A few minutes later there was a sudden explosion. Madame Agathe together with her husband and children fled to their neighbor's house, an American diplomat. They tried to climb over the wall but failed. Then they fled to the home of a U.N. employee. But Madame Agathe and her husband were found at their hiding place, the house of a relative, and were both brutally killed.[38] Their five children were rescued by a U.N. Development Program employee and a military observer.[39]

13.2.3 The Killings Start with a Politicide

The relatively quiet night was followed by grave violence.[40] Very early in the morning of April 7 UNAMIR learned that whole families were being wiped out. Phone calls to UNAMIR reported that the Presidential Guard, the army, the *gendarmerie* and the Interahamwe were going from house to house with lists of names. The phone at UNAMIR headquarters continuously rang, with people pleading for help. Their pleadings were followed by the sound of screaming, then shooting and then deathly silence. The only answer that UNAMIR could give to the people on the phone was that help was forthcoming, knowing that the help was almost always too late.[41] Major Robbert van Putten, the Dutch assistant of Dallaire in Rwanda, recalled, in an interview in 2006, the morning of April 8 with many phone calls from threatened people requesting help: "I could not do anything direct from UNAMIR headquarters but I was able to forward the information to the operational patrols and ask to go to these spots."[42] In his book, Luc

36 Melvern, 2000 p. 119; Des Forges, p. 188.

37 Melvern, 2000 p. 120.

38 *Id.*; Des Forges p. 190; Carlsson Report, S/1999/1257, p. 16. Madame Agathe was found nearly naked with her face half blown away and a beer bottle in her vagina.

39 Melvern, 2000 p. 123; Des Forges, p. 191.

40 Marchal, pp. 177–185.

41 Marchal, p. 177; Carlsson Report, S/1999/1257, pp. 18–19.

42 Interview with Robbert van Putten by Jurgen Maas (IKON radio), broadcast on March 26, 2006, from 7.00–7.30 a.m. at Radio 1 in the Netherlands.

Marchal describes receiving a phone call from the Canadian wife of the Vice-President of the Liberal Party and Minister of Labor and Social Affairs, Mr. Landoald Ndasingwa. She pleaded for troops to be sent immediately to reinforce the troops already present, because the Presidential Guards were standing ready to attack them. Then Ndasingwa got on the phone himself and said to Marchal: "If you don't intervene immediately, me and my family will be killed." His words were followed by the sound of automatic rifles and exploding grenades. The last words he spoke to Marchal were: "It is already too late."[43]

Before Dallaire left headquarters around 10 o'clock that morning, he called Riza to inform him of what was happening.[44] The Force Commander told Riza that moderates were being targeted and that people under protection of UNAMIR had been attacked. Dallaire added that it was difficult to get through the roadblocks and that they soon might need to use force. Once again Riza instructed Dallaire not to use fire until fired upon.[45]

Des Forges writes that by midday on April 7, the Presidential Guard, with the help of soldiers, "had eliminated those leaders who could have legitimately governed."[46]

That morning, Félicien Ngango, a member of the PSD, Judge Joseph Kavaruganda, President of the Constitutional Court and, as stated above, Prime Minister Agathe and Minister Landoald Ndasingwa were all killed. Furthermore, Boniface Ngulinzira, the Minister of Foreign Affairs during the Arusha negotiations and his family were attacked and fled their homes.[47] All of these persons belonged to the moderate political elite of the country. It is clear, at this moment, that these people were killed because of their political position and power in Rwanda, and they were not killed because of their ethnicity. In other words, the start of the violence and the atrocities were at that moment not the beginning of a genocide but the start of a politicide to get rid of all political opponents. It was PIOOM scale 4 (orange) and not yet PIOOM scale 5 (red) that characterized the situation at that moment. It is important to realize that the trigger of the plane crash led directly—the following day—to a politicide, and, indeed, at that moment, a genocide could yet have been prevented.[48]

---

43 Marchal, p. 185; Carlsson Report, S/1999/1257, p. 18.

44 Dallaire, p. 233; Carlsson Report, S/1999/1257, p. 16. According to the Carlsson Report, Dallaire called Riza at 9:20. See Section 13.2.4.

45 Dallaire, p. 233; Carlsson Report, S/1999/1257, p. 16. According to Carlsson, Dallaire called saying that he might need to use fire to protect Madame Agathe, to which Riza replied not to use fire until fired upon. See Section 13.2.4.

46 Des Forges, p. 191.

47 Boniface Ngulinzira would be killed during the genocide. Des Forges, p. 191. Carlsson Report, S/1999/1257, pp. 18, 19.

48 See Section 1.3.1.

13.2.4 Contact Between Riza and Dallaire in the First Hours After the Crash

As seen above, in the first 14 hours following the crash of April 6, at 8:23 p.m., Dallaire spoke to Riza three times. In the last two phone calls, Riza made it very clear to Dallaire that he was not allowed to use fire. Dallaire, furious about this reaction, tried to persuade him but did not succeed. We will now briefly recapitulate the three endeavors of Dallaire:

(1) April 6, around 10 p.m., one and a half hours after the crash, Force Commander Dallaire informed Riza of what had happened.[49]

(2) April 7, around 3 a.m. (on the night between the 6th and the 7th), Dallaire informed Riza by telephone of the current situation. Riza replied firmly that UNAMIR was not allowed to use fire, unless they were fired upon. Dallaire argued that the rules of engagement allowed UNAMIR to intervene and use an escalation of force up to and including the use of deadly force to prevent crimes against humanity. However, Riza repeated that they were not to use fire and added that they had to negotiate and, above all else, avoid conflict.[50]

(3) April 7, around 10 a.m., Dallaire called Riza again. Dallaire told Riza that moderates were being targeted and that people under protection of UNAMIR had been attacked. Dallaire added that it was difficult to get through the roadblocks and that they soon might need to use force. Once again Riza instructed Dallaire not to use fire until being fired upon.[51]

After these three phone calls in 24 hours without any approval from New York to act in order to counter the atrocities, Dallaire decided to write a cable to U.N. headquarters in which he repeated his request. On April 8 Dallaire sent a cable with the first detailed assessment of the situation in Rwanda to New York. The cable stated that the terror was well-planned and organized; roadblocks isolated his Belgian soldiers; they had no supplies or power; ten peacekeepers were dead, and there was fear for the rest; they were short of ammunition and medical supplies; roadblocks prevented movements; Kigali was in a state of war. Dallaire thought this could be a military coup eliminating all opposing powers. He wrote that he might need a different mandate, when the peace-keepers were going to have to move the civilians out. Subsequently the question was asked whether the mandate was still viable.[52] The reply coming from Department

---

49 Dallaire, p. 222; Carlsson Report, S/1999/1257, p. 15. See Section13.2.1.

50 Dallaire, p. 229. See Section 13.2.1.

51 Carlsson Report, S/1999/1257, p. 16; Dallaire, p. 233. According to the Carlsson Report, Dallaire called at 9:20 to say that he might need to use fire to protect Madame Agathe, to which Riza replied not to use fire until fired upon. See Section 13.2.3.

52 Sénat de Belgique, Commission d'Enquête parlementaire concernant les événe-

of Peace-Keeping Operations (DPKO) stated that Dallaire had to negotiate a ceasefire and should not risk further losses or action that could result in reprisals.[53]

13.3 DEATH OF TEN BELGIAN PEACE-KEEPERS

13.3.1 Jean Pierre's Prediction Becomes Reality

The five Ghanaian and ten Belgian peace-keepers who were at Madame Agathe's house were taken prisoner by the Presidential Guard right after the Prime Minister and her family had fled.[54]

The peace-keepers had to give up all weapons and were brought to Camp Kigali, which hosted more than 1,000 Rwandan soldiers. Upon arrival, the five Ghanaian peace-keepers were brought into safety, but the ten Belgian peace-keepers were left at the hands of an enraged crowd of soldiers who were told that these Belgians were responsible for the assassination of Habyarimana. From Camp Kigali, Lotin was able to reach Jo Dewez, the Belgian commanding officer of the Belgian paramilitary commandos, through a Motorola radio. He told Dewez that he did not know where he was, but he thought they were going to be lynched. Dewez asked whether Lotin was not exaggerating a little.[55] Dewez called Marchal and told him that Belgian paramilitary commandos had been taken captive. Marchal called several senior officers of the FAR and demanded their release.[56] Most of the Belgian paramilitary commandos were beaten to death almost immediately after their arrival. According to Des Forges, the rest of the paramilitary commandos were able to defend themselves "for several more hours," thanks to a weapon they had been able to get hold of.[57] "Several hours" appears to actually have been six hours. It is very strange—to say the least—that no intervention was made by UNAMIR to rescue the peace-keep-

ments au Rwanda, Sénat de Belgique, session de 1997–1998, 6 décembre 1997, Rapport fait au nom de la commission d'enquête par MM Mahoux et Verhofstadt, pp. 508–515 (publication of the cable); Melvern, 2000 p. 130. According to Melvern, Dallaire wrote the cable and according to the Belgian Senate, Booh Booh sent the cable. It is likely that Dallaire was the one who wrote the cable, and it was signed off by the political man, Booh Booh, to DPKO.

[53] Melvern, 2000 pp. 130, 131. Booh Booh subsequently informed Annan that he was consulting a crisis committee about the security situation.

[54] Reyntjens, pp. 67–69; Carlsson Report, S/1999/1257, p. 17; Des Forges, p. 189.

[55] Annex Belgian Senate, p. 437; Melvern, 2000 p. 121; Marchal, p. 183.

[56] Melvern, 2000 p. 121; Marchal, pp. 182–183; Belgian Senate, pp. 429–457.

[57] Reyntjens, pp. 67–69; Des Forges, p. 189, note 32: Dewez, "Chronique;" Dallaire, "Answers to Questions;" Alexandre Goffin, 10 Commandos Vont Mourir (Editions Luc Pire, n.p. n.d.), pp. 63–65, 73–77.

ers.[58] They were captured at 9:00 a.m. and the dead bodies were found at 11:25 p.m., more than 14 hours later. Moreover, during that day, Dallaire was in close proximity to his captured peace-keepers, because when Dallaire passed Camp Kigali around 10 o'clock in the morning, he saw several Belgian blue-helmets. Dallaire describes in his book:

> I got a glimpse of what looked like two Belgian soldiers lying on the ground, it was a brutal shock. How had they been captured? I ordered the major to stop the car, telling him I thought I had seen some of my own soldiers on the ground. Instead he sped around the corner and drove directly into the college parking lot. . . . The major told me emphatically that I could not go into Camp Kigali, the troops inside the camp were out of control.[59]

From a Togoleze UNAMIR observer Dallaire heard that a number of Belgian peace-keepers were held in the camp and had been beaten up.[60] During the FAR meeting, Dallaire did not raise the question of the UNAMIR soldiers at the camp.[61] When the meeting ended around noon, Dallaire then asked Augustin Ndindiliyimana, the chief of staff of the *gendarmerie*, to intervene and to rescue them. Ndindiliyimana replied that Bagosora would take care of the problem.[62] The Carlsson Report indicates that Dallaire testified before the Belgian Senate that an armed operation to rescue the Belgian peace-keepers was not feasible, because the risk of casualties for those intervening would be too high. According to Dallaire, UNAMIR was a peace-keeping operation and "not equipped, trained, or staffed to conduct intervention operations."[63] Dallaire was of the opinion that his troops and resources were too limited to rescue the peace-keepers. He said to the Belgian Senate Commission:

> Had either Colonel Marchal or Lt. Col. Dewez requested authority from me to conduct an assault on Camp Kigali to rescue the detained

---

58 Informal interview with F. Reyntjens, February 21, 2006 in Antwerp.

59 Dallaire, pp. 236, 237; Annex Belgian Senate, pp. 407–408, 423.

60 Dallaire pp. 236, 237; Annex Belgian Senate, p. 423.

61 Dallaire, pp.239–244; Annex Belgian Senate, p. 423.

62 The rest of the day, Dallaire tried several times to get permission to enter the camp, but Bagosora refused. Before the Belgian Senate Dallaire stated that his troops and resources were too limited to get into the camp and rescue the peace-keepers: "The UNAMIR mission was a peacekeeping mission. It was not equipped, trained or staffed to conduct intervention operations." Carlsson Report, p. 17; Dallaire, pp. 239–244; Belgian Senate, pp. 422–425; Des Forges, p. 190, note 34: Dallaire, "Answers to Questions;" Alexandre Goffin, 10 Commandos Vont Mourir (Editions Luc Pire, n.p. n.d.) pp. 63–65, 73–77.

63 Carlsson Report, S/1999/1257, p. 17. For more information, see Belgian Senate, pp. 422–425.

> group under the conditions of that time, my response would have been an outright refusal for such an armed intervention. The only solution reasonably available to us at that time was to continue to negotiate as a neutral force.[64]

The Carlsson Report reflects Dallaire's view that UNAMIR was merely a peace-keeping force.

Dallaire found the ten Belgian peace-keepers at 11:15 on the evening of April 7 in the courtyard of the Kigali hospital.[65] It was a horrific sight. The men were piled on top of each other; Dallaire and his men were not even able to see how many people there were. They counted eleven, though it would turn out to be ten.[66] Robbert van Putten accompanied Dallaire and took photographs of the bodies. He had heard earlier that day on the radio that three peace-keepers had been killed. He was shocked, and seeing these ten bodies perplexed him.[67] So it came that, just as Jean Pierre had predicted, ten Belgian peace-keepers were killed. According to Jean Pierre, the aim of these killings was to guarantee a Belgian withdrawal, and on the day that the Belgians were killed, both Bagosora and Ndindiliyimana told Dallaire that, in the light of the death of the Belgian peace-keepers, it might be best for the Belgian troops to leave Rwanda.[68]

13.3.2 New York's First Response upon the Death of the Ten Belgian Paramilitary Commandos

After Dallaire found the ten Belgian peace-keepers, he went back to UNAMIR's headquarters to call New York.[69] His phone call reached New York around 4 o'clock in the afternoon of April 7. Dallaire spoke to Kofi Annan, Iqbal Riza and Hedi Annabi. He informed them of the death of the Belgian paramilitary commandos, the killings of the moderate political leaders, the sys-

---

64 Annex Belgian Senate, pp. 424–425.

65 Dallaire, p. 255; Annex Belgian Senate, p. 409. Dallaire does not specify at what time in the evening of April 7 he found the Belgian soldiers, but he does describe that he went together with General Ndindiliyimana to the Kigali hospital where they found the bodies. The Belgian Senate subsequently states that Ndindiliyimana found the bodies at 11:15. For this reason, we conclude that Dallaire found the bodies at 11:15.

66 Melvern, 2000 p. 125; Dallaire, p. 255.

67 Interview with Robbert van Putten by Jurgen Maas (IKON radio), broadcast on March 26, 2006, from 7.00–7.30 a.m. on Radio 1 in the Netherlands. Van Putten was the witness *à décharge* in Arusha in March 2006 to testify in the case of Bagosora, who—according to van Putten—had not killed the peace-keepers.

68 Dallaire, pp. 251, 258.

69 *Id.*, p. 259.

tematic killings, the failed political meeting and Bagosora's actions.[70] The three men from U.N. headquarters—Annan, Annabi and Riza—told Dallaire "not to risk UNAMIR troops, to help with the security of all U.N. civilians and dependants, to keep in close contact with the expatriate and diplomatic communities and to update the withdrawal plan and be ready to implement it." Upon hanging up, Dallaire felt angry, empty and in moral and ethical conflict.[71]

13.3.3 Marchal and Dewez Heavily Criticized in Belgium

The killings were followed by great anger in Belgium.[72] Marchal and Dewez, the two most senior Belgian officers in UNAMIR, were heavily criticized. Marchal was put through a court martial. He was accused of not taking adequate precautions. His trial ended in a total acquittal; he had not even known that the ten Belgian peace-keepers were in trouble.[73]

Marchal writes in his book that if he had been aware of the drama that was taking place in Camp Kigali, he would have intervened. There was no intervention, because, according to Marchal, nobody assessed the situation as dramatic, as a reason to intervene.[74] Dewez, the man who asked Lotin whether he was exaggerating when he said they were going to be lynched, testified in Marchal's trial: "If we had had the slightest indication of what was about to happen we would have intervened."[75] Dewez never even considered an armed intervention; he wanted to negotiate.[76] During Marchal's trial, a Belgian officer stated: "Given the events in Kigali that morning, although the problems encountered by Lotin were serious we did not think them exceptional, given what was happening elsewhere."[77]

With the death of the ten Belgian peace-keepers on April 7, the day after the plane crash, the situation changed dramatically. This change was particularly evident with regard to the involvement of international bystanders. The deliberate and well-organized plan to kill some peace-keepers was carefully

---

70 *Id.*, p. 260.

71 *Id.*

72 Melvern, 2000 p. 126.

73 Marchal, pp. 188, 189.

74 Marchal, p. 189. Marchal's statement confirmed by Dewez; see Belgian Senate, p. 430. For more information, see Belgian Senate, pp. 457–461.

75 Marchal, p. 188.

76 Before the Belgian Senate Dewez said that he had no idea of the drama that was going on. The fact that his men were taken prisoner by the Rwandan army assured him that they were safe. Belgian Senate, p. 451; Marchal, p. 181. For more information, see Belgian Senate pp. 429–457.

77 Melvern, 2000 p. 121, note 18: Testimony of Major Timsonet during the courts martial of Luc Marchal (unpublished).

designed to bring about a withdrawal of all international interference. Moreover, as will be elaborated on in the following chapters, it was very effective.

13.4 CONCLUSION

The plane crash was the trigger for the following dramatic events. It is remarkable that no one is, or was, very interested in the question of who the killers were. After ten years, for instance, the United Nations found the plane's black box completely by surprise in their office in New York. Opening the black box seems to be too dangerous for all parties involved. The killings started directly with all political adversaries of the extremists, which meant that the moderate Hutu leaders were also killed during the first days. At the early stages, this was only considered a politicide and not yet a genocide. It is important to realize that the more important and disappointing aspect was the reaction from New York. Dallaire phoned U.N. top civil servants, Annan and Riza, five times a day. They always reacted according to the "organizational process model," as it was a routine decisionmaking. New York prohibited the use of force by UNAMIR every time, even to give safety to the ministers of the government. During these first days the Prime Minister and many other moderate governmental officials were killed. Dallaire informed New York of the well-planned and organized terror in Kigali. The only reaction from Annan, Annabi and Riza to these alarming messages was to keep in close contact with the expatriates and diplomats. From the start, U.N. headquarters' priority was to save the foreigners in Rwanda and not the Rwandan people. As was predicted months before, on the first day following the plane crash, ten Belgian peace-keepers were deliberately murdered in order to prompt the withdrawal of the peace-keepers. This was the result of a deliberate and well-organized plan to kill some peace-keepers. It was carefully designed to bring about a withdrawal of all international interference. In other words, turning the bystanders into direct victims, counting on the world's indifference towards the other victims on the ground, precluded any solidarity from the outsiders with the real victims. In these circumstances, the perpetrators needed freedom of maneuver and, hence, no foreign actors were accepted. The *genocidaires* planned shrewdly and were helped by others outside Rwanda to fulfill their genocidal aims.

CHAPTER 14

EVACUATION

14.1 U.S. REACTION TO THE CRASH

Prudence Bushnell, the U.S. Assistant Secretary for African Affairs, was sitting at her desk when Kevin Aiston, the desk officer for Rwanda, came in and told her that the airplane with the Presidents of Rwanda and Burundi had crashed. She responded in disbelief and denial. Her first reaction to Aiston was: "No, it can't be. It just can't be. Go and get in touch with David Rawson [U.S. ambassador in Kigali] and check your facts. Please, this certainly can't be."[1] Bushnell, who had visited Rwanda in March, knew immediately that it was very bad news. The only thing that she did not know was whether it was worse for Rwanda or Burundi.[2]

Bushnell sent a memorandum, through the Under Secretary for Political Affairs, Peter Tarnoff, to the Secretary of State, Warren Christopher, titled: "Death of Rwandan and Burundian Presidents in Plane Crash outside Kigali."[3] She informed Tarnoff and Christopher of the information available: "The military intended to take power temporarily" and "there is an increase in sporadic gunfire and grenade explosions" in Kigali. Furthermore, she warned that "widespread violence could break out in either of both countries, particularly if it is confirmed that the plane was shot down."[4] During the day, Rawson informed Washington that it looked like the plane had indeed been shot down.[5] That same day, President William (Bill) Clinton issued a statement: "[I am] shocked and deeply saddened . . . horrified that elements of the Rwandan security forces

---

1 Frontline interview with Bushnell, September 30, 2003.

2 Interview with P. Bushnell, May 27, 2005.

3 U.S. Department of State, Bureau of African Affairs, Memorandum from Deputy Assistant Secretary of State Prudence Bushnell to the Secretary through Under Secretary for Political Affairs Peter Tarnoff, "Death of Rwandan and Burundian Presidents in Plane Crash Outside Kigali," April 6, 1994, *available at* http://www.gwu.edu/~nsarchiv/NSAEBB/NSAEBB53/rw040694.pdf.

4 *Id.* There was no response to her memo, but it was an "information memo." Frontline Interview Bushnell, September 30, 2003.

5 Interview with D. Rawson, October 5, 2003.

have sought out and murdered Rwandan officials . . . extend my condolences . . . condemn these actions and I call on all parties to cease any such actions immediately"[6] In the Frontline interview, Rawson stated that at that moment, his opinion was that the United Nations needed a stronger mandate and equipment to carry out that mandate if, "indeed, they were going to be able to hold—what I didn't realize was how very difficult that process is."[7] He indicated, however, that he was not aware of the very serious consequences the plane crash was to have. He admitted that he underestimated the situation.[8]

In the morning of April 7, U.S. time, the Central Intelligence Agency (CIA) produced the highly sensitive National Intelligence Daily (NID), which was titled: "Rwanda-Burundi: Presidential Deaths Likely to Renew Fighting." The NID, which was sent to top policymakers at the White House, the State Department, the Defense Department and other agencies, predicted that the shooting down of the plane would cause "Hutus in Rwanda to seek revenge on Tutsis" and predicted that "the civil war may resume and could spill over to Burundi."[9] That same morning the "Secretary Morning Summary," a State Department report of important intelligence items, was delivered to the Secretary of State and senior Department of State officials.[10] The Summary stated that the plane was reportedly shot down and that it was still unknown who the perpetrators were—whether it was "hard-line Hutu soldiers, former rebels of the RPF, or others seeking to fan Hutu-Tutsi tensions." Furthermore, the report indicated that the crash could "also spark an upsurge of violence in Burundi."

At 8:45 U.S. time, the first SPOT report was received. SPOT reports are intelligence reports written "on-the-spot," aimed at "flagging" severe problems for senior Department of State officials. The SPOT report stated that, according to the information of Ambassador Rawson, "rogue Hutu elements of the military, possibly the elite presidential guard, had shot the plane." The report continued by saying that: "Military elements had killed the Prime Minister and several other Rwandan cabinet officials, including senior ranking Tutsi."[11]

---

6 Frontline, 100 days of slaughter, A chronology of U.S./U.N. actions, *available at* http://www.pbs.org/wgbh/pages/frontline/shows/evil/etc/slaughter.html.

7 Interview with D. Rawson, October 5, 2003.

8 *Id.*

9 The NID has now been succeeded by the Senior Executive Intelligence Brief. CIA, "Rwanda-Burundi: Presidential Deaths Likely to Renew Fighting," Excerpt from Central Intelligence Agency, National Intelligence Daily, April 7, 1994, *available at* http://www2.gwu.edu/~nsarchiv/NSAEBB/NSAEBB119/Rw3.pdf.

10 The "Secretary Morning Summary," a summary report of important intelligence items from the Bureau of Intelligence and Research of the State Department, *available at* http://www2.gwu.edu/~nsarchiv/NSAEBB/NSAEBB119/index.htm. U.S. State Department, "Burundi/Rwanda: Presidents Killed," Excerpt from U.S. Department of State, Bureau of Intelligence and Research, Secretary's Morning Summary, April 7, 1994, *available at* http://www2.gwu.edu/~nsarchiv/NSAEBB/NSAEBB119/Rw2.pdf.

11 U.S. State Department, "Rwanda/Burundi: Turmoil in Rwanda," April 7, 1994,

Lieutenant Colonel Charles Vuckovic, who, besides his responsibilities at the U.S. embassy in Cameroon, also had responsibilities for Rwanda and Burundi, had coincidentally arrived in Rwanda one day before the crash.[12] On April 7, at 1 p.m. U.S. time, he wrote a SPOT report titled "Rwanda/Burundi: Violence Update, No. 2." The report stated that the Presidential Guards were "out of control on the streets of Kigali," while all other military units remained in their barracks. According to Vuckovic, the Presidential Guards were the key perpetrators of the violence.[13]

On that same day President Clinton made a statement in which he expressed his shock at the deaths of President Habyarimana and President Ntaryamira. Furthermore, he stated that he strongly condemned the murders of Rwandan officials, including the Prime Minister, by elements of the Rwandan security forces. He called upon all parties to cease any such actions immediately.[14]

From the foregoing, it becomes clear that, upon hearing of the plane crash, the United States immediately realized that this could lead to grave violence in both Rwanda and Burundi. The memo's and reports sent around show that within several hours the United States was aware of the situation in Rwanda. They were informed that the plane had been shot down, presumably by elite units of the Presidential Guard, they were aware of the killings of Rwandan officials, including the Prime Minister, and they were aware of the key role of the Presidential Guard in this violence. These events, in combination with the numerous early warning signals of the previous months, were threatening enough for the United States to decide upon an evacuation.

14.2 EVACUATION BY THE AMERICAN MILITARY

By midday on April 7, barely 24 hours after the plane crash, the United States decided to evacuate its nationals and to close down the embassy.

The U.S. decision to evacuate was made by the Secretary of State, Warren Christopher, who signed the decision memorandum. According to Bushnell,

---

Bureau of Intelligence and Research, SPOT Intelligence Report as of 08:45 EDT April 7, 1994, *available at* http://www.gwu.edu/~nsarchiv/NSAEBB/NSAEBB119/Rw4.pdf.

12 Linda Melvern, A People Betrayed. The Role of the West in Rwanda's Genocide, p. 140 (2000) (hereinafter Melvern, 2000).

13 U.S. State Department, "Rwanda/Burundi: Violence Update," No. 2, April 7, 1994, Bureau of Intelligence and Research, SPOT Intelligence Report as of 13:00 EDT, April 7, 1994, *available at* http://www.gwu.edu/~nsarchiv/NSAEBB/NSAEBB119/Rw5.pdf.

14 The White House, Office of the Press Secretary, Statement by the President: "The Deaths of the Presidents of Rwanda and Burundi," April 7, 1994, *available at* http://www.clintonfoundation.org/legacy/040794-presidential-statement-on-deaths-of-rwanda-and-burundi-presidents.htm.

President Clinton had spoken to both the Secretary of State and the Secretary of Defense saying that he wanted "all Americans out alive."[15] George Moose, the U.S. Assistant Secretary of State for African Affairs, said: "I'm sure it [the memo] was eventually signed off by the secretary. I'm not clear whether it was a top-down [decision]. No, I don't think so. I think it was understood by us that we did not wish to leave our people in that situation."[16] Everyone in the American administration was determined to rescue their own nationals from Rwanda, and in Washington that objective got the highest priority—and the only one—in the first days following the crash.[17]

At 1 p.m. U.S. time, Warren Christopher established a 24-hour inter-agency Task Force to coordinate the evacuation. Prudence Bushnell was appointed as head of the Task Force.[18] It was her duty to serve as the communication line between the agencies, the Secretary of State, the President and the U.S. nationals in Rwanda and Burundi.[19] Bushnell: "The Task Force was involved in information gathering, decision-making, getting organized and getting the convoys out."[20] The United States informed Brussels and asked whether they could pressure the Security Council for the Belgian troops to protect all foreign nationals in Rwanda, including the 240 U.S. nationals.[21]

Rawson received a phone-call from Washington about the decision to evacuate. When the ambassador received this call, he had already started to "sense that there was something systematic about the events happening in Rwanda." First of all, the extremists were going after the leadership of the opposition rather systematically, and secondly, the soldiers were going from house to house killing all people in areas where opponents of the government were living or where Tutsi were living.[22] Rawson proposed to Washington that a part of the embassy should stay in place to try to push for the Arusha peace process. This attitude now seems remarkable, but it confirms his opinion that he was not aware of the extremely serious consequences that the plane crash would have.

---

15 Frontline interview with Bushnell, September 30, 2003.

16 *Id.*; Frontline interview with Moose, November 21, 2003.

17 Frontline interviews with Bushnell, September 30, 2003, Lake, December 15, 2003, Shattuck, December 16, 2003.

18 Interview with P. Bushnell, May 27, 2005; Frontline interview with Bushnell, September 30, 2003; U.S. Department of State, "WGRW01: Working Group Formation to Deal with the Situation in Kigali and Bujumbura," April 8, 1994, Telegram State 092008, *available at* http://www2.gwu.edu/~nsarchiv/NSAEBB/NSAEBB119/Rw8.pdf.

19 Frontline interview with Bushnell, September 30, 2003.

20 Interview with P. Bushnell, May 27, 2005.

21 Sénat de Belgique, Commission d'Enquête parlementaire concernant les événements au Rwanda, Sénat de Belgique, session de 1997–1998, 6 décembre 1997, Rapport fait au nom de la commission d'enquête par MM Mahoux et Verhofstadt, p. 519; Melvern, 2000 pp. 139–140. For this Belgian pressure on the Security Council to fulfill a role in protecting the foreigners, see Section 15.2.

22 Frontline interview with Rawson, October 5, 2003.

Moreover, this also underlines that the United States, as well as the United Nations, had been totally focused on the implementation of the Arusha Accords in the preceding months, neglecting the emerging genocide. However, Rawson was ordered on April 7 by Washington to close down the embassy, to evacuate all American embassy personnel and to inform other Americans of the operation. He followed the orders received.[23]

On April 8 Rawson informed Luc Marchal that the Americans were going to leave Rwanda over land with the protection of some U.N. military observers. Marchal showed his concern about traveling over land, but Rawson answered that the United States had 250 rangers and helicopters on stand-by in Bujumbura (capital of Burundi).[24] Marchal was astonished: "It was the 8th of April. For the military to be operational you have to be in place at least 8 to 10 days in advance." "For me that was a sign that the U.S. was informed. It was no coincidence that they were in Bujumbura exactly at that moment to protect the evacuation."[25]

The first U.S. convoy left Rwanda on April 8.[26] Melvern writes that the American military officer, colonel Vuckovic, arrived six hours before the presidential plane was shot down in Kigali: "His mission was successful; Vuckovic got all Americans citizens out of Rwanda by Saturday, April 9. The civilian U.N. employees, some 150 people, who left in forty-two vehicles, got out first. The Americans traveled in a convoy of cars to Burundi protected by an armed escort of U.N. peacekeepers."[27] After the first convoy, others followed with 240 American civilians and lastly the embassy staff. The U.S. military in Bujumbura never left the airport.[28]

During the days following the crash, hundreds of Rwandans came to find sanctuary at the American embassy. Rawson allowed them to hide at the American residence. They were staying inside as well as outside. At a certain moment, one of the attacking forces got up in a tree and shot at the people hiding in the compound, killing a baby and wounding several others. Rawson describes: "When we got ready to evacuate, I went out and told [them] that we weren't going to be there any longer; that when we left, the United States flag would come down, and they were going to have to make their own decisions about what to do."[29] Rawson then got on the last convoy that left Rwanda.

---

23 Frontline interviews with Bushnell, September 30, 2003 and Rawson, October 5, 2003.

24 Interview with L. Marchal, January 21, 2005; Luc Marchal, Aan de poorten van de Rwandese hel: Getuigenis van een peacekeeper, p. 195 (2001) (hereinafter Marchal).

25 Interview with L. Marchal, January 21, 2005.

26 The American Lieutenant Colonel Vuckovic, who had arrived from Cameroon on April 6, also had brought an evacuation plan. Melvern, 2000 pp. 139–140); Frontline interview with Rawson, October 5, 2003.

27 Melvern, 2000 p. 140; Frontline interview with Rawson October 5, 2003.

28 Interview with P. Bushnell, May 27, 2005.

29 Frontline interview with Rawson, October 5, 2003.

In all the convoys that left Rwanda during the American evacuation, there was only one Rwandan family, and this family had American children.[30] Bushnell stated: "When we evacuate, we leave our poor national colleagues behind. It is not something I apologize for; it is a reality that is part of the searing and wrenching aspect of being a Foreign Service officer. You try your best to take care of them in terms of maintaining some kind of contact, in terms of keeping salary and benefits up. But when a situation becomes dangerous, we look after our own."[31]

The Task Force managed to get all people out safely within eight days. Its work was concluded on April 15. The Force had been focused exclusively on the evacuation. According to Bushnell: "There was never thought given to doing something else, never ever, not before, not during. Never."[32]

14.3 EVACUATION BY THE FRENCH MILITARY

In the evening of April 8 General Jose Charlier, chief of staff of the Belgian army, told Marchal that a French-Belgian coordinated evacuation operation was on its way. According to Charlier, the French would arrive early the next morning, followed by the Belgians one day later. It was in fact only three hours after his talk with Charlier that Marchal saw the first French planes—a Transal C-160—coming in, immediately followed by two others.[33]

To Marchal's great astonishment, he was at that moment ordered by Brussels to place the Belgian contingent at the airport under the command of the French Colonel, who would be the one giving the orders. As a direct consequence, the Belgian vehicles with the U.N. symbol would be used by the French paramilitary commandos.[34]

A phone call from Maurice Baril in New York informed Brent Beardsley and Roméo Dallaire only one hour before that the French were coming in. Baril gave Dallaire the order to "hold the airport." Dallaire rapidly made a call to the UNAMIR liaison with the RPF and the FAR to say "Don't shoot!" The runway which had been blocked with trucks since the President's plane crash was cleared.[35]

---

30 According to Rawson, taking Rwandans along in the convoy was not attempted, but regarding the many checkpoints it would probably have been impossible. Frontline interview with Rawson, October 5, 2003.

31 Frontline interview with Bushnell, September 30, 2003.

32 Interview with P. Bushnell, May 27, 2005.

33 Marchal, p. 194.

34 Interviews with L. Marchal, January 21, 2005, and B. Beardsley, June 6, 2005; Melvern, 2000 pp. 140–141; Marchal, p. 184.

35 Interview with B. Beardsley, June 6, 2005.

The first two planes carried 590 French soldiers between them; the third plane appeared to be filled with weapons. The ammunition was delivered directly to the FAR, which were at that moment in control of the airport.[36] Collette Braeckman stated that the French arms export not only continued until the genocide, but even during the genocide with the transport of arms at the Kigali airport during the evacuation operation (Opération Amaryllis) and continued in May, with sending ammunition and communication material in order to keep contact with the French army.[37] This information is neither denied nor confirmed by the French parliamentary inquiry commission. According to Marchal, the way these weapons were handed over to the FAR showed that the delivery had been organized in advance.[38] Upon arrival, the French immediately took control of the airport: "They had no problems gaining control."[39]

On April 9, as soon as the sun was rising, the French started their evacuation operation. The French had no problems getting around in Kigali and, except for the use of UNAMIR vehicles, they led a completely autonomous operation. According to Beardsley, the way the French were able to do the job showed that "the whole operation between the [French and the FAR] was well coordinated."

Remarkably, the first people being evacuated by the French that morning were not French nationals but members of the presidential family, together with several Akazu members.[40]

14.4 EVACUATION BY THE BELGIAN MILITARY

The following morning, on April 10, 500 Belgian paramilitary commandos arrived in Kigali.[41] Upon their arrival, Marchal was placed under the command of the Belgian Colonel Jean-Pierre Roman. As a UNAMIR-officer, he now had to act as a Belgian soldier.[42] Marchal was angry about the decision. In January he had requested regulations in case of an emergency or evacuation

---

36 Marchal, p. 194; Interview with L. Marchal, January 21, 2005; see also Organization of African Unity, The Preventable Genocide of the International Panel of Eminent Personalities to Investigate the 1994 Genocide in Rwanda and Surrounding Events, 2000, paragraph 15.58.

37 Collette Braeckman, Rwanda, l'enquête inachevée (translated: Rwanda, the unfinished inquiry), *Le Monde*, December 9, 2005; see Section 18.3.

38 Melvern, 2000 p. 141.

39 Melvern, 2000 p. 141; Interviews with L. Marchal, January 21, 2005 and B. Beardsley, June 6, 2005.

40 Roméo Dallaire, Shake Hands with the Devil, The Failure of Humanity in Rwanda, p. 282 (2004) (hereinafter Dallaire); Marchal, p. 194.

41 Another 500 paramilitary commandos would be staying in Nairobi to serve as a back up. Marchal, p. 196.

42 Interviews with L. Marchal, January 21, 2005 and B. Beardsley, June 6, 2005; Melvern, 2000 pp. 140–14.

situation. He had asked Evere: "Am I obliged to follow U.N. orders or do I have to take a Belgian position and evacuate nationals? (Under the Belgian hat instead of blue) I urgently ask for answers. Situation could escalate. Clear regulations!"[43] He never received an answer. Now, when the Belgians arrived for the evacuation, he was placed under the Belgian command. Marchal: "It was a very difficult situation, what should I do as the commander of the sector Kigali? I needed to have honesty regarding Dallaire." According to Beardsley, "placing Marchal under Belgian orders was a major problem; luckily Marchal knew how to play both sides. He did what Dallaire needed and he did what he had to do under the Belgian rules of engagement."[44]

According to the Belgian Minister of Foreign Affairs, Willy Claes, it was very logical to place Marchal under Belgian command. Claes: "We had withdrawn our troops, which means that they [Belgian troops] did not fall under the U.N. Statute anymore. Legally this is evident."[45] This reasoning might have been evident in Brussels where the withdrawal of UNAMIR was already a fact, but in Rwanda the Belgian withdrawal was not yet known. To put it more clearly: upon arrival of the evacuation troops, Dallaire thought that these troops were his long-requested reinforcements.[46]

Straight after the Belgian arrival, Roman and Marchal tried to coordinate the evacuation with the French. It was decided that the Belgians, who had trouble going out on the streets in Kigali because of the anti-Belgian climate, would secure the airport; the French, who had no problems going around in Kigali, would guard the assembly points and provide escorts; and UNAMIR would organize the convoys from and to the airport.[47] The coordinated evacuation operation was planned to start at 10 o'clock in the morning of April 11.

In reality, there was no coordinated operation at all. Marchal: "We [the Belgians] tried to make it a coordinated operation. . . . There was no cooperation whatsoever between Belgium and the French. . . . We were almost enemies. . . . It was two national operations."[48] It soon became clear that the French continued their own "autonomous" operation.[49]

According to Claes, this lack of cooperation was already shown at the moment the Belgians wanted to land in Kigali. Claes: "They [the Belgians] were arriving after the French, who were at that moment physically in the African territory. It took several hours before the French had cleaned the airport before

---

43 Report by L. Marchal to Evere on January 15. Interview L. Marchal, January 21, 2005.

44 Interview with B. Beardsley, June 6, 2005; for Belgian decisionmaking after the plane crash, see Chapter 15.

45 Interview with W. Claes, January 13, 2006.

46 See Chapter 11.

47 Dallaire, p. 287.

48 Interview with L. Marchal, January 21, 2005.

49 *Id.*

the Belgian planes could land." Claes added: "That raised questions with me. What happened I do not know, but it's a fact that we lost time because we couldn't land."[50]

In the evening of April 13, the French troops left Rwanda, followed by the Belgian and Italian troops two days later.[51] The evacuation had been very successful in the way the troops had been able to evacuate more than 3,000 people—their own nationals—from Rwanda within one week, and only 12 foreigners died during this evacuation period.[52]

14.5 U.N. ROLE IN THE EVACUATION

There was also no cooperation between UNAMIR in Rwanda and New York on the evacuation. According to Marchal: "These two operations [evacuation operation and the UNAMIR mission] had no relation. This was an initiative from France, Belgium and Italy, without any coordination from New York."[53] Only an hour before the French evacuation troops were to arrive, Dallaire was informed by New York of their arrival. He was then ordered by Baril to keep the airport.[54]

General Dallaire did not agree with the evacuation because of the limited task in the mandate. On April 9, Dallaire spoke to Lieutenant Colonel Jo Dewez and prohibited the Belgian blue helmets from taking part in the evacuation operation if New York did not change and broaden the UNAMIR mandate. According to a telex from Dewez to Evere, Dallaire's words were:

> If New York doesn't modify the mandate, we cannot participate in this operation and we must therefore form part of the UNAMIR personnel being evacuated, and not those evacuating . . . the humiliation of having to respond endlessly to our compatriots that we could hardly do anything . . . I urge Belgium to contact New York to demand that they either change our mandate, or allow us to leave UNAMIR and to go again under Belgian control and to undertake operations with our French and Belgian colleagues.[55]

---

50 Interview with W. Claes, January 13, 2006.

51 The Italian forces arrived on April 13 and left together with the Belgians on April 15. Marchal, p. 194.

52 Marchal, p. 197.

53 Interview with L. Marchal, January 21, 2005.

54 Interview with B. Beardsley, June 6, 2005.

55 Translated from French into English. Original text: "Si New York ne modifie pas le mandat, nous ne pouvons participer à cette ops et devrons donc nous même faire partie du pers Minuar à évacuer et non des unités évacuant . . . l'humiliation de devoir répondre sans cesse aux compatriotes qu'on ne pouvait quasiment rien faire. . . . Je

However, on that same day, Dallaire received a cable from Kofi Annan, in which he was ordered to cooperate with the French and the Belgians. Annan made clear that the mandate was not broadened or changed. The cable stated:

> Cooperate with French and Belgian commanders to facilitate the evacuation of their nationals, and other foreign nationals requesting their evacuation. You may exchange liaison officers for this purpose. You should make every effort not to compromise your impartiality or to act beyond your mandate (sic FG,) but may exercise your discretion to do should this be essential for the evacuation of foreign nationals. This should not, repeat not, extend to participating in possible combat, except in self-defense.[56]

14.6 CONCLUSION ON THE POSSIBLE PREVENTATIVE ROLE OF THE EVACUATION FORCES

At the start of the evacuation operation, UNAMIR was still under the presumption that UNAMIR was going to be enforced. UNAMIR was told that even though Belgium had lost ten soldiers, they were lobbying for reinforcement.[57] Beardsley: "So when the French and the Belgian troops arrived, we said this is outstanding . . . We knew that there were U.S. marines in Bujumbura and we knew that there were Italian special forces coming and there was a rumor that there were even Canadian paratroopers coming as well. Dallaire thought he had finally got his long requested reinforcements."[58] However, it immediately became clear on April 9 that these troops were no reinforcements. Beardsley: "They were not coming to reinforce us, they had strictly come to evacuate their expatriates and would then leave."[59]

---

demande instamment que Belgique contacte New York pour demander soit de changer notre mandat, soit de nous permettre de quitter la Minuar et de repasser sous ctl BE et faire ops avec collègues FR en BE." Telex of the 9th of April from Dewez to Evere in which he reports about his conversation with Dallaire. Sénat de Belgique, Commission d'Enquête parlementaire concernant les événements au Rwanda, (Commission of parliamentary enquiry concerning the events in Rwanda), session de 1997–1998, 6 décembre 1997, Rapport fait au nom de la commission d'enquête par MM Mahoux et Verhofstadt, Annexes, p. 59 (hereinafter Annex Belgian Senate). Document Belgian Intelligent Service (SGR) 4530.

56 United Nations, Report of the Independent Inquiry into the Actions of the United Nations during the 1994 Genocide in Rwanda, December 15, 1999, Ingvar Carlsson, Han, Sung-Joo, Rufus, M. Kupolati, U.N. Doc. S/1999/1257, p. 19 (hereinafter Carlsson Report, S/1999/1257).

57 Interview with B. Beardsley, June 6, 2005.

58 *Id.*

59 *Id.*

During the period of evacuation, there were in total 1,700 well-equipped and trained troops available in the region. There were the French, Belgian and Italian troops on the ground in Kigali, there was a Belgian back-up based in Nairobi and there were U.S. troops stationed in Bujumbura. If these troops, all well-trained and equipped forces, had stayed, they would have been able to at least reduce the number of victims and possibly to prevent the genocide.[60] According to Claes: "In hindsight the military potential that had been brought together for the evacuation could have been enough to stop the genocide. I really do not know whether this force would have halted this, but crucial is that the issue was never discussed."[61] In all of our interviews, both with the military leaders and the political leaders and civil servants involved in the decision-making in this second week of April 1994, everybody agreed that the evacuation forces could have stopped the genocide, but it was never discussed.

The prospects for the remaining peace-keepers were grave, because on the April 12 Dallaire received a phone call from Chinmaya Gharekhan, the special assistant to Boutros-Ghali, who told him that the Belgian government had just decided to withdraw its peace-keepers from Rwanda.

If these 1,700 well-armed and trained elite troops had been added to the 2,500 UNAMIR soldiers, the total number would have been 4,200, and that is exactly the number of soldiers all Rwandan parties of the Arusha Peace Accords asked for in 1993, and that was the number that was considered realistic by the military who prepared the peace-keeping mission.[62]

We may conclude this chapter by stating that the plane crash and the possible consequences were taken very seriously. Consequently, Western countries immediately organized a strong, heavily equipped military force to evacuate their own nationals. This was the top priority, and so even UNAMIR peace-keepers were ordered by their governments to become subordinated to the national hierarchical command structure. The UNAMIR Force Commander resisted this change of command structure somewhat, but Annan made it clear to him immediately that he must cooperate with Belgium and France to facilitate the evacuation of the foreigners. If necessary he could act for this purpose—and only for the objective of the evacuation—beyond his mandate in using force if essential. Maybe the peace-keepers in Rwanda were naïve in thinking that the arrival of the troops of the evacuation force would reinforce UNAMIR to stop the hostilities. The situation in Rwanda was very serious and precarious in the days in which these troops were in Rwanda from April 8 until April 15. The important signal was that they were only interested in the safety of their own nationals. The *genocidaires* could conclude that no deterrent force or counterforce would obstruct their intentions. We have concluded that in the

---

60 Alison Des Forges, Leave None to Tell the Story, Genocide in Rwanda (1999) p. 606 (hereinafter Des Forges), note 39: Commission d'enquête, *Rapport*, p. 558.

61 Interview with W. Claes, January 13, 2006.

62 See Section 5.1.

first day after the plane crash, a politicide took place and not yet a genocide. We cannot assess exactly at what date the politicide transformed in a genocide, but this must have been in the period between April 8–15. It is not said that a combination of the evacuation force with the UNAMIR peace-keepers, would have been able to stop the chaotic killings. The tragedy is that this option was not considered in any Western capital or at U.N. headquarters. In our definition at the start of this book we wrote that the third party, who will not act or will not attempt to act in solidarity with the victims of gross human rights violations, is the bystander who afterwards is evaluated as a collaborator.[63] The evacuation force illustrates this role.

63 See Section 1.2.

CHAPTER 15

BELGIAN DECISION TO WITHDRAW ITS TROOPS

15.1 INTRODUCTION

In the months before the plane crash, Belgium was the only country demanding an expansion of the UNAMIR mandate. The Belgian attitude showed great concern for the mission in Rwanda, but its role changed radically after the death of the Belgian peace-keepers. A few questions about the Belgian role, after the death of the peace-keepers, remain unanswered. In this chapter we will answer in particular the following questions:

(1) Did Belgium, after the death of the Belgian peace-keepers, continue its efforts to broaden the mandate in order to stop the unfolding genocide, or were these efforts only made in order to protect the Belgian nationals?
(2) When did Belgium decide to withdraw its troops? Was this decision made after it had become clear that the mandate would not be broadened (around April 15), or was this decision made immediately after the death of the peace-keepers, as early as April 7?
(3) Did Belgium, as often described in the literature, try to get a full withdrawal of UNAMIR in order to save face, or are the Belgian efforts in this context misinterpreted?

15.2 BELGIAN EFFORTS TO CHANGE THE MANDATE

15.2.1 Belgium Asks for an Explanation of the Mandate Immediately After the Plane Crash

On April 7 at 12:46 Belgian time, after the news of the plane crash and still before the news of the death of the peace-keepers, Belgian Foreign Minister Willy Claes sent a cable to New York and Washington in which he asked for a clarification of the mandate.[1]

1 Telex No. 452; Sénat de Belgique, Commission d'Enquête parlementaire con-

Claes stated:

> It is not excluded that the attack of the 6th of April on the plane with the presidents of Rwanda and Burundi on board, results in a military coup or in mass slaughter between several rivals. In case many deaths will follow the public opinion will not understand that UNAMIR will stay inactive, hiding behind a limited mandate. I would appreciate if Washington, New York and Paris would question the respective authorities about their view regarding the role of UNAMIR in such a hypothesis.

Furthermore, the Belgian Minister asked for instructions in the situation that Belgians in Rwanda asked for protection from Belgian U.N. peace-keepers. Claes: "I would like to have the opinion of the U.N. regarding the possibility of Belgium to, in a bilateral way, appeal to Belgian blue helmets to, outside UNAMIR, if necessary, provide help to Belgians and other foreigners in need, for example in case of evacuation."[2] In other words, immediately after the crash, the Belgian Minister of Foreign Affairs asked, by way of his ambassadors, both the top officials in the U.N. Secretariat and the U.S. government what role could be envisaged for the peace-keepers. He asked for a more active role for the peace-keepers in case of mass slaughter and asked in case of conflict for a role in protecting the foreigners, including the Belgians, in Rwanda. Both a stronger, more forceful role for UNAMIR and an evacuation force were put on the international agenda by Belgium.

Following Claes' cable, the Belgian representative to the United Nations, Paul Noterdaeme, conducted a meeting with both Iqbal Riza, the Assistant Secretary-General, DPKO and Kofi Annan, the U.N. Under Secretary-General in charge of peace-keeping operations. In the meantime, Riza had been in contact with Roméo Dallaire who had informed him of the death of several Belgian peace-keepers.[3]

At 5:29 Belgian time, Noterdaeme replied to Claes by fax. Noterdaeme stated that:

> According to Dallaire at least three Belgian soldiers of UNAMIR are said to have been killed (general Dallaire has seen their corpses). Ten other Belgian soldiers of UNAMIR are still in the hands (unarmed) of the Presidential Guard, who are responsible for the murder of the three Belgian soldiers. Dallaire did not get permission to get in contact with the other 10 Belgian soldiers. The Prime Minister's protection is fore-

---

cernant les événements au Rwanda, Sénat de Belgique, session de 1997–1998, 6 décembre 1997, Rapport fait au nom de la commission d'enquête par MM Mahoux et Verhofstadt, pp. 525, 526 (hereinafter Belgian Senate).

2 Telex No. 452; Belgian Senate, pp. 525, 526.

3 Telex No. 623; Belgian Senate, p. 526.

> seen by 13 Belgian soldiers, who are also said to have been killed (though that is not confirmed yet).[4]

After informing Belgium of this horrific news, Noterdaeme gave a description of the security situation in Rwanda and then continued by answering Claes' requests. Regarding the stronger and more forceful role of UNAMIR, Noterdaeme wrote that Annan had answered that this could contain two types of decisions:

> An expansion of the UNAMIR troops to be able to stand the new situation and a change of mandate through which a more offensive position becomes possible. Such an expansion would require days, because it demands a decision of the Security Council. It should not be forgotten that it is not easy to move over to an operation in the framework of Chapter VII. Such a decision would mean a complete change of the original operation for which the Americans, British, and Russians could only bring in a moderate enthusiasm and for which only defensive means were made appropriate.[5]

Concerning the protection of Belgian nationals in Rwanda, Noterdaeme wrote that Annan had underlined that a decision on whether or not protection could be given to Belgian nationals had to be made by Dallaire. Noterdaeme added that Annan had emphasized that all actions had to be in accordance with the existing rules of engagement: "As in the case with all peacekeeping operations that are resorted under Chapter VI, it is on the basis of those ROE only allowed to use fire in the case of self-defense. An offensive operation to save Belgians is therefore, for the blue helmets, not possible except if they themselves are being threatened."[6] This answer from Annan did not reflect a decision made in case of crisis but a routine answer that is, in theories of international relations, called the organizational process model, explained by Allisson as: "Less as deliberate choices and more as outputs of large organizations functioning according to standard patterns of behavior."[7]

---

[4] Telex No. 623; Belgian Senate, pp. 526–527. This shows that the first cable, which informed Belgium of the death of Belgian peace-keepers spoke of three dead men. At what moment Belgium was told that ten Belgians had been killed is unknown. This was probably communicated to Belgium by telephone.

[5] Telex No. 623; Belgian Senate, p. 528.

[6] Telex No. 623; Belgian Senate, pp. 527–528.

[7] Graham T. Allison, Essence of Decision, Explaining the Cuba Missile Crisis, p. 67 (1999).

15.2.2 Belgium Requests a Change of the Mandate After the Death of the Ten Paramilitary Commandos

The Belgian Minister of Foreign Affairs, Willy Claes, was about to go on stage to direct an orchestra in Bucharest, when the news of the Belgian casualties came in. Those close to Claes decided not to inform him directly but to wait until after his performance. When he had finished conducting the orchestra, Claes was immediately informed of the news. It was clear: he had to get back to Brussels as soon as possible. He would fly back early the next morning.[8] Not only was the Minister of Foreign Affairs absent from Brussels at this crucial moment, Prime Minister Jean-Luc Dehaene was also abroad.[9] Despite their absence, an emergency meeting of the Cabinet was conducted, under the presidency of the Vice Prime Minister Herman Van Rompuy, at 9:30 that evening.[10] The decisions that were taken show that the Council of Ministers was, at that moment, most concerned with the security of the Belgian nationals in Rwanda.[11] The Cabinet Council adopted three decisions on the evening of April 7:

(1) The Minister of Defense has to take care of all necessary measures for a possible departure of Belgian soldiers to Rwanda. These soldiers could be sent should the lives of Belgian nationals be threatened.
(2) Minister Claes is mandated to "immediately intervene at the U.N." to the effect that the "Belgian troops in Rwanda could intervene to warrant the safety of the Belgian nationals."
(3) The commander of the Belgian U.N. troops is asked to prepare the assurance, to his best capacity, of the protection of the Belgians.[12]

It is important to underline that during this first meeting of the Belgian Cabinet after the killing of the Belgian peace-keepers they did not decide to withdraw, but all attention was focused on the safety of the Belgian nationals in Rwanda who should be protected by both Belgian UNAMIR soldiers and by Belgian soldiers to be sent to Rwanda for their protection.

At 6 a.m. Noterdaeme sent a telex to Claes.[13] He wrote that he had informed Riza of the Belgian position as concluded in the Cabinet Council. Noterdaeme

---

8 Interview with W. Claes, January 13, 2006.

9 *Id.*

10 Belgian Senate, p. 530; Interview with W. Claes, January 13, 2006.

11 Belgian Senate, p. 530.

12 Report Council of Ministers on April 7, 1994; Belgian Senate, p. 530.

13 Telex No. 628; Belgian Senate pp. 530–533. Whether this telex was forwarded to Bucharest or Claes was informed about it the next morning is unknown. Noterdaeme started his telex by explaining once more the position of the U.N. diplomats regarding peace-keeping operations in general. Noterdaeme wrote that the United Nations was

explained to Riza the "incomprehension that would be the consequence of insufficient protection by the Belgian blue helmets of the Belgian nationals." Riza understood the situation, but responded that "a one-way operation (outside the mandate) of the Belgian contingents (under the supervision of the U.N.) in order to repatriate co-nationals would be a serious problem." Riza had proposed to try to secure a change of the UNAMIR mandate. Noterdaeme wrote that he could approach members of the Security Council the following day about a "possible prioritized repatriation (when that would appear to be necessary) of all foreign communities." However, he added that several members of the Security Council had already told him that the Council would not change the "present UNAMIR mandate (peacekeeping)." Moreover, several Western countries had questioned whether it was useful to keep UNAMIR in place.[14]

On April 8 at 3 p.m., the Belgian Council of Ministers held another meeting. Prime Minister Dehaene, who had returned from abroad, chaired the meeting and Claes, who had returned from Bucharest, was also in attendance. The Secretary-General of the Ministry of Foreign Affairs, Frans Roelants, presented a note that discussed the possibilities for a Belgian intervention. The note set out three ways under which a Belgian intervention would be justified:[15]

(1) The first possibility would be an intervention following a request from the local authorities. This possibility did not seem plausible under the present circumstances and was according to the Ministry of Foreign Affairs not "opportune," because it would lead to an intervention in the Rwandan internal conflict.
(2) The second possibility was the "protection and evacuation on the basis of article 3a and 3c of the mandate."[16] But according to the Ministry of Foreign Affairs the United Nations had already made

involved in 17 peace-keeping operations involving 70,000 peace-keepers. Noterdaeme: "Except for several extremely rare cases" all mandates foresee peace-keeping operations in the framework of a "peace process recognized by the parties." Noterdaeme wrote that the United Nations had to maintain the "largest possible neutrality" and the UNAMIR mission had to be seen in this context.

14 Telex No. 628; Belgian Senate pp. 530–533.

15 Belgian Senate, pp. 532–533.

16 Point 3 of the Security Council Resolution 872, October 5, 1993, point 3, U.N. Doc. S/RES/872 (1993), stated:

> Decides that, drawing on the Secretary-General's recommendations, UNAMIR shall have the following mandate: (a) To contribute to the security of the city of Kigali inter alia within a weapons-secure area established by the parties in and around the city; (b) To monitor observance of the cease-fire agreement, which calls for the establishment of cantonment and assembly zones and the demarcation of the new demilitarized zone and demilitarization procedures; (c) To monitor the security situation during the final period of the transnational government's mandate, leading up to elections.

known that it was against a broad interpretation of the mandate and that a new mandate under Chapter VII would take a lot of time, and the Security Council was reluctant.

(3) The third option was a humanitarian action by Belgian troops together with other countries and separate from the United Nations.

The second Cabinet Meeting was also focused on rescuing their own nationals, but, again, an intervention force to protect the Rwandan population, as well, was not excluded in any of these three options. Moreover, a decision was not made on Belgian withdrawal of UNAMIR.

After discussing the three options, the Council of Ministers decided in favor of option three: "A separate evacuation operation."[17] Prime Minister Dehaene summarized the outcome of the meeting in the Cabinet as follows:

> The following has to be communicated to the U.N.: Because of the death of the ten Belgian paras the Belgian public opinion is traumatized to such a degree that the continuation of the Belgian participation in UNAMIR is being questioned. Prolongation depends on the possibility of the U.N. to defend itself better. For this reason Belgium requests qualitative improvement (more weapons) and an expansion of the mandate. Undoubtedly Belgium cannot agree with a reinforcement of Belgian soldiers in UNAMIR. Belgium will execute an evacuation that is totally separate from the Belgian participation in UNAMIR.[18]

From this explanation of the second Cabinet meeting, we become aware that the Belgian presence in UNAMIR was discussed. Any reinforcement with Belgian troops was excluded. However, withdrawal was not the automatic choice at that moment. On the contrary, the Belgian government once again asked the United Nations for a more forceful mandate for their peace-keepers. The second day, an urgent second request was sent to the top of the United Nations for a stronger and more forceful UNAMIR mandate.

After the Council meeting, Minister Claes sent a telex to the Belgian delegation at the United Nations. The telex would function as the basis for a meeting with the Secretariat.[19] Claes stated that when the disorder continued and more Belgians were victimized: "It is not acceptable for the Belgian public opinion that the U.N. contingent and especially the Belgian troops, will passively observe." The Minister argued: "The least that in such case could be expected is that the contingent would try to protect the foreigners in a non-

[17] Belgian Senate, p. 534.

[18] Report of the Council of Ministers of April 8, 1994; Belgian Senate, p. 534.

[19] Telex No. 306; Belgian Senate, pp. 533–534.

aggressive manner." Claes added that if the situation should worsen, "we have not excluded that the Belgian commander, in order to protect Belgians, should receive his orders directly from the government."[20]

On the morning of April 9, the first seven C130 planes departed in the direction of Rwanda to evacuate the Belgian nationals.[21]

15.2.3 Sincerity of the Belgian Requests for a Broader Mandate

In some ways, we are now somewhat puzzled as to the real intentions of the Belgians in these two days in April. It is clear that their main concern was a rescue operation for their own nationals. In this regard, they do not differ from the policies of the Italians, French and Americans. In all of these countries, their main concern was how to evacuate their citizens from Rwanda. In these countries no reinforcement of UNAMIR was discussed. These countries did not participate in UNAMIR. This is the only big difference with Belgium. The decisions made by the Council of Ministers on the evening of April 7 discussed the possibility of sending more Belgian troops to "protect or evacuate Belgian nationals."

The fax sent by Noterdaeme to Claes at 6 a.m. on April 8 set out Noterdaeme's discussion with Riza about a broader mandate, but the fax made clear that they only discussed a broader mandate with the aim to "protect Belgian nationals and other foreigners in Rwanda." The note of the Ministry of Foreign Affairs that was discussed during the Council of Ministers on April 8, set out three ways to intervene in Rwanda but only spoke about an intervention to "protect and evacuate expats."

Only the summary of this Council of Ministers meeting, drawn up by Prime Minister Dehaene, spoke about an expansion of the mandate *without* adding that this expansion would be meant for an evacuation. But the summary stated as well that the prolongation of the Belgium participation in UNAMIR depended on this change of mandate and added that reinforcement would not contain Belgium troops.

The fax that Claes subsequently sent to the United Nations stated that if more people were victimized, the Belgian troops could not passively observe; he argued that the Belgian contingent would, in that case protect the foreigners in a non-aggressive manner. So, again, the efforts to be able to protect were made in the context of the protection of the foreigners.

The foregoing makes clear that the Belgian authorities only spoke about a change of mandate with the aim of protecting and evacuating Belgian nationals and other foreigners. This line of thinking is explicitly confirmed in several testimonies: The Belgian Vice-Permanent Representative to the United Nations, Alexis Brouhns, said in his hearing before the Belgian Senate: "When we spoke,

---

20 Telex No. 306; Belgian Senate, p. 535.

21 Belgian Senate, p. 520; see Section 14.4.

starting on April 7th or 8th, 1994, of a possible reinforcement of UNAMIR, as much in the instructions received from Brussels as in the discussions within the secretariat or in the Security Council, it concerned a reinforcement with a view to permitting evacuation."[22] In other words, in all instructions from Brussels and in all deliberations at U.N. headquarters, the reinforcement of UNAMIR was only meant to facilitate the evacuation. Alison des Forges agreed with Brouhns. She is convinced: "That the only aim of any request to broaden the mandate was to evacuate their own nationals and not to protect the people of Rwanda."[23] Brouhns added for the Senate:

> I took the initiative, because the question wasn't posed, to ask the secretariat and different members about the possibility of reinforcement of the mandate to be able to eventually turn to general protection, including the Rwandan population. The mission took the initiative to add to the two points asked by Brussels the question of a reinforcement of UNAMIR exceeding the framework of evacuation.[24]

Brouhns twice raised the issue of strengthening UNAMIR in order to protect the population of Rwanda at U.N. headquarters, although he was not instructed to ask these questions. Minister Claes told the Senate that he pleaded for reinforcement of the mandate "mainly with the objective of the security of

---

22 Hearing Brouhns, POR, Senate, 1996–1997, May 25, 1997, pp. 2F/35, 2/10 to 2/13; Belgian Senate, pp. 535–536. Translated from French into English. Original text: "Lorsqu'on a parlé, a partir du 7 ou 8 avril 1994, d'un renforcement possible de la MINUAR, tant dans les instructions reçues de Bruxelles que dans les discussions au sein du secrétariat ou en marge du Conseil de sécurité, il s'agissait d'un renforcement en vue de permettre l'évacuation."

23 Hearing Des Forges, POR, Senate, May 16, 1997, p. 15/15; Belgian Senate, p. 535. Original text: "Maintenant, je suis convaincue que la discussion à cette époque, sur l'élargissement du mandat a eu lieu pour justifier la collaboration de la MINUAR dans l'opération d'évacuation des étrangers. Il ne s'agissait pas d'élargir le mandat pour protéger les Rwandais. La question était plutôt: est-il nécessaire d'élargir le mandat pour évacuer plus vite nos propres ressortissants?" Prime Minister Dehaene said: "What we envisaged at one point was to know if the Belgian troops within UNAMIR could be available to organise a Belgian evacuation." Translated from French into English. Original text: "Ce que nous avons envisagé à un moment c'est de savoir si les troupes belges au sein de l'UNAMIR pouvaient être disponible pour organiser une évacuation du coté belge." Hearing Dehaene, POR, Senaat, PV, p. 1F/11; Belgian Senate, p. 536.

24 Hearing Brouhns, POR, Senate, 1996–1997, May 25, 1997, pp. 2F/35, 2/10 to 2/13; Belgian Senate, p. 536. Translated from French into English. Original text: "J'ai pris l'initiative—car la question n'était pas posée—d'interroger le secrétariat et différents membres sur la possibilité du renforcement du mandat pour pouvoir faire éventuellement face à une protection générale, population rwandaise incluse. La mission a pris l'initiative d'ajouter aux deux points demandés par Bruxelles la question d'un renforcement de la MINUAR dépassant le cadre de l'évacuation."

Belgian nationals and for our own troops, as well as to guarantee the security of Rwandan actors."[25]

The previous paragraph showed that the official Belgian instructions to broaden the mandate were mainly made in the context of the protection of Belgian nationals and other foreigners and not with the aim of protecting the Rwandan nationals and putting a halt to the developing genocide.

15.3 BELGIAN PARTICIPATION AT STAKE AFTER THE KILLINGS OF THE BELGIAN PARAMILITARY COMMANDOS

Claes told us that the Cabinet decided to withdraw the Belgian troops immediately after the death of the peace-keepers had become known. According to Claes, the decision was taken during the Council of Ministers meeting on the evening of April 7 in the absence of himself and Prime Minister Dehaene.[26] Claes: "When I arrived [back in Brussels, returning from Bucharest] the Cabinet had already come together under the presidency of the Vice Prime Minister and had already decided to withdraw, in the absence of Dehaene and myself." In his memory—in retrospect—the public opinion was vehemently against any continuation of Belgian troops in UNAMIR; therefore the only thing the Cabinet could do was to decide to withdraw. The three decisions, however, that were made by the Cabinet that evening did not say anything about the Belgian withdrawal.[27] As seen above, all three decisions dealt with the protection of the Belgian nationals. It has been reconfirmed to us that only these three decisions were made on April 7 by the Cabinet of Belgium.[28] Nonetheless, the Belgian withdrawal seems to have been an important issue during that meeting of the Cabinet. Minister Leo Delcroix said before the Belgian Senate: "When we, on the evening of the 7th, started to get an insight into the situation, it was the ultimate concern of the government to withdraw the troops." Delcroix added: "The decision to withdraw was made only on the 15th of April."[29]

In the meeting of April 8 the Council of Ministers made a decision again only upon the Belgian evacuation, but the summary of the meeting also mentioned the possibility of a Belgian withdrawal.[30] The summary stated that the continuation of the Belgian participation in UNAMIR was being questioned, and that prolongation depended on the possibility of the United Nations defend-

---

25 Hearing Claes, POR, Senate, PV, p. 24/1–2; Belgian Senate, p. 536.

26 Interview with W. Claes, January 13, 2006. Claes himself was still in Bucharest at that moment.

27 Report of the Council of Ministers of April 7, 1994; Belgian Senate, p. 530.

28 *Id.*

29 Belgian Senate, p. 540; Hearing with Delcroix, POR, Senate, June 18, 1997, PV, (BV, p. 809).

30 Belgian Senate, p. 534.

ing itself better.[31] Prime Minister Dehaene said that on April 10 there was an intention to withdraw the troops.[32]

The foregoing shows that the decision to withdraw had not yet been made on April 7 nor on April 8. Belgium started after that point to move in the direction of a withdrawal. The intention to withdraw was clear for the Prime Minister on April 10. The final decision to withdraw was made on April 15.[33]

15.4 BELGIUM DECIDES TO WITHDRAW

15.4.1 The Belgian Cabinet Prepares for the Meeting of Minister Claes with the U.N. Secretary-General

On April 12 Minister Claes was going to discuss the future of UNAMIR with Boutros-Ghali, who was making a trip through Europe.

In preparation of Claes' meeting with Boutros-Ghali, the Cabinet met on the afternoon of April 12.[34] According to Claes, the considerations that were mentioned during this Cabinet meeting were the following: The Arusha Accords were broken; the general conditions to accept a peace-keeping mission were no longer fulfilled; there was a plausible danger of new fatalities, particularly amongst the Belgian blue helmets; it was known, also through the *démarches* of Noterdaeme, that the mandate would not be changed from a Chapter VI to a Chapter VII mandate; the peace-keepers were unable to get the situation under control.[35] According to Claes, these arguments led to the Belgian conclusion that it was best to apply "the Angolan formula," which meant bringing the mandate back to a normal observation post.[36]

The Cabinet decision that was subsequently taken stated:

> The Minister of Foreign Affairs is ordered to question further participation of the Belgian troops to UNAMIR because of the disrespect of the Arusha Accords and [because] the general conditions of a U.N. operation are no longer fulfilled. Minister Claes has to ask Boutros Ghali formally to report to the U.N. on the evolution of the situation

---

31 Report of the Council of Ministers of April 8, 1994; Belgian Senate, p. 533.

32 Before the Senate: "Our intention (withdrawal of the Belgian blue helmets) was clearly formulated two days before the meeting (the meeting of Minister Claes with Boutros Ghali) of Bonn." Minister Claes would meet Boutros-Ghali on April 12, which would imply that Dehaene meant April 10.

33 See Section 15.5.

34 Belgian Senate, p. 540.

35 Belgian Senate, p. 541; Hearing Claes, POR, Senate, June 24, 1997, PV, pp. 18/8, 18/9, 19/1, 19/2 and 19/3 (BV, p. 838).

36 *Id.*

as requested in Resolution 909. UNAMIR is now a useless operation and an enforcement of the mandate and the troops are barely realistic options. The U.N. should, awaiting better times, limit its role to an observation post."[37] According to Claes, this decision meant that he had "to inform Ghali of the Belgian withdrawal."[38]

After the Council of Ministers meeting Claes, sent a telex to the Belgian embassy in Washington. He wrote that he was of the opinion that the Arusha Accords had definitely failed, and because they were the essence of UNAMIR, the mission had become pointless.[39] Claes argued furthermore that only a limited presence of the United Nations was now acceptable and that he wanted to withdraw his troops:

> Belgium wished all the more to remove its contingent of blue helmets from Rwanda because these troops have been severely hit by these events (the killing of 10 soldiers) and because as a result of the propaganda of an extremist political faction, the Belgian citizens are particularly threatened at present. All increase of the death toll of Belgians could preclude all participation of our country in peace-keeping operations for a very long time.[40]

15.4.2 Minister Claes Meets the U.N. Secretary-General on April 12 in Bonn

After the Cabinet meeting, Claes drove to Bonn, and he was waiting in a hotel for a long time for a meeting with the U.N. Secretary-General, Boutros Boutros-Ghali.[41] When the Secretary-General arrived, Claes briefed him on the situation in Rwanda, and he realized that Boutros-Ghali was not accurately

---

37 Report of the Council of Ministers of April 12, 1994.

38 Interview with W. Claes, January 13, 2006.

39 Telex No. 181; Belgian Senate, pp. 541–542.

40 *Id.* Translated from French into English. Original text: "Pour sa part, la Belgique souhaite d'autant plus retirer son contingent de Casques bleus du Rwanda que celui-ci a été durement touché par les événements (massacre de 10 soldats) et qu'en raison de la propaganda d'une faction politique extrémiste, les ressortissants belges sont à présent particulièrement menacés. Toute aggravation du bilan des pertes belges pourrait éloigner pour très longtemps notre pays de toute participation à des OMP."

In September 2006 Belgium decided to participate for the first time since Rwanda in the peace-keeping force UNIFIL in Lebanon. Belgium was very conscious that this military force was robust enough, as was exposed in the parliamentary debate.

41 Interview with W. Claes, January 13, 2006.

informed. Five days after the start of the genocide, the Secretary-General was not aware of the unfolding mass slaughter in Rwanda.[42]

After giving Boutros-Ghali an "apocalyptic description of the situation," Claes informed him of the Belgian position: "I have come with the mandate of the Belgian government that in the current situation we have to withdraw. I remind you that for months we have been requesting you to broaden the mandate."[43]

In response, Boutros-Ghali started speaking about the war in Yugoslavia. Claes: "He told me: "Mon ami, c'est la guère des riches en Yougoslavie, mais je manque l'argent à ce moment ci, je n'ai aucune chance au conseil de sécurité, aucune aucune."[44] I give you the consideration: Stay." Claes: "I said: In the current circumstances? I am not crazy. I am not going to risk my political head in Belgium. If nothing changes there will be a withdrawal. That has already been made known [to the parliament]. The only thing you can still do is to enforce the mandate. That is a possibility."[45]

Not only did Claes inform Boutros-Ghali of the Belgian withdrawal, the Minister also told the Secretary-General that Belgium was of the opinion that it was best "to withdraw all UNAMIR troops before more people got victimized."[46] In fact, he advised Boutros-Ghali, because any reinforcement of UNAMIR was not feasible, to withdraw all troops from UNAMIR in order to prevent more casualties among the soldiers.[47]

---

42 *Id.*

43 *Id.*

44 *Id.* Translation: "My friend it is the war of the rich in Yugoslavia but I miss the money now. I have no chance at all at the Security Council, not at all, in no way."

45 *Id.*

46 Belgian Senate, p. 543; Hearing of Claes, POR, Senate, June 24, 1997, PV, pp. 21/13, 21/14, 22/1, 22/2, 22/3, 22/4, 22/5, 22/6 and 22/7 (BV, p. 840); Report of the Council of Ministers of April 12, 1994; United Nations, Report of the Independent Inquiry into the Actions of the United Nations during the 1994 Genocide in Rwanda, December 15, 1999, Ingvar Carlsson, Han, Sung-Joo, Rufus, M. Kupolati, U.N. Doc. S/1999/1257, p. 19 (hereinafter Carlsson Report, S/1999/1257).

47 About his conversation with Boutros-Ghali, Claes told the Belgian Senate during his hearing: "Ik heb de heer Boutros Boutros Ghali gezegd: 'U weet beter dan ik dat een versterking van het mandaat er niet in zit. Het is ons oordeel dat u er beter aan doet alle UNAMIR-troepen wijselijk terug te trekken, vooraleer er nieuwe slachtoffers vallen. In elk geval, dat moet ik u melden in naam van de Belgische regering, kunnen de Belgische troepen niet blijven. Wij overwegen een terugtrekking via Tanzania over de grond omdat de risico's van een luchtevacuatie veel te groot zijn.'" Translated into English: "I told mister Boutros Boutros Ghali: 'You know better than I that an enforcement of the mandate is not feasible. It is our judgment that it is better for you to wisely withdraw all UNAMIR troops, before more people get victimized. In any case, I have to tell you in name of the Belgian government, the Belgian troops cannot stay. We consider a withdrawal via Tanzania by ground because the risks of an evacuation by air are too big.'" Belgian Senate, p. 543; Hearing of Claes, POR, Senate, June 24, 1997.

Boutros-Ghali told Claes that he did not know enough about the situation, so he would inform himself and call the Belgian minister the following day, and their meeting was ended. According to Claes: "The only conclusion of the meeting was that I said 'We withdraw if the situation does not change drastically' and Ghali had replied 'Consider again just to stay.'"

That following day, Boutros-Ghali called Claes to say that, now that he was fully informed, he was of the opinion that Claes had pictured the situation to be far worse than it was in reality. Claes answered in very strong words: "Secretary General, I confirm the analysis that I have given to you."[48] They agreed to stay in contact, but there has never been any contact since.

That same day, Boutros-Ghali sent a letter to the Security Council in which he informed the Council about his meeting with Minister Claes. In his letter, the Secretary-General was very clear about the consequences of a Belgian withdrawal. He wrote:

> He [Claes] informed me that the Government of Belgium has decided to withdraw its contingent serving with UNAMIR at the earliest possible date. In the light of the decision by the Government of Belgium, it is my assessment that it will be extremely difficult for UNAMIR to carry out its tasks effectively. The continued discharge by UNAMIR of its mandate will become untenable unless the Belgian contingent is replaced by another equally well equipped contingent or unless the Government of Belgium reconsiders its decision to withdraw its contingent. In these circumstances, I have asked my Special Representative and the Force Commander to prepare plans for the withdrawal of UNAMIR, should this prove necessary, and send their recommendations to me in this regard.[49]

15.5 BELGIUM STARTS CAMPAIGNING FOR A TOTAL WITHDRAWAL OF UNAMIR

15.5.1 Telling the World that UNAMIR Has Become Pointless

On April 13 Minister Claes sent a telex to the Belgian delegation in New York in which he described his meeting with Boutros-Ghali. Besides that, the telex stated that the embassies in member countries of the Security Council and

---

48 Translated from French into English. Original text: "Secretaire General, je confirme l'analyse, que je vous avez fait."

49 Letter of April 13, 1994 of Boutros-Ghali to the President of the Security Council; United Nations, The United Nations and Rwanda, 1993–1996 p. 259 (1996) (hereinafter United Nations, The United Nations and Rwanda); Carlsson Report, S/1999/1257, p. 20.

in troop-contributing states had to inform their interlocutors of the withdrawal "so that they could help to make the U.N. decide, as soon as possible, upon the withdrawal of UNAMIR."[50]

That same day, the Belgian Cabinet came together and decided, in the absence of Minister Claes, that:

> In expectation of the next meeting of the Security Council the diplomatic efforts to get an adjournment of UNAMIR are intensified. The government holds to its position that against the background of the existing mandate (Resolution nr. 909), the current mission is pointless and there is definitely no role for Belgium in the dispatch. The final position of Belgium will be made in the light of the developments of the meetings in the U.N.[51]

Brouhns declared before the Belgian Senate that there was a meeting of troop-contributing states on April 13 in New York, during which Noterdaeme intervened to set out the Belgian position.[52] In the light of the previous meetings and communications in which Belgium had set out its position, it can be expected that Noterdaeme repeated that, in the view of Belgium, the mission had become pointless.[53]

Also on April 13, Noterdaeme sent a letter to the Security Council about the Belgian evacuation. He used this letter to underline once more that Belgium was of the opinion that the continuation of UNAMIR was pointless. Noterdaeme wrote:

> It is obvious that under these conditions [widespread massacres and chaos] the continuation of the UNAMIR operation has become pointless within the terms of its present mandate. In any event, the continued presence of the Belgian contingent would expose it to unacceptable risks. . . . In conclusion the Belgian Government is of the opinion that it is imperative to suspend the activities of UNAMIR forces without delay.[54]

---

50 Belgian Senate, p. 547. Why Cleas sent the order, which was directed to the embassies in member countries of the SC and to troop-contributing states, to the Belgian delegation to the United Nations is unknown. Possibly the embassies themselves were already informed, or the embassy in New York had to forward the order to the relative embassies.

51 Belgian Senate, p. 549: "Decisions of the Cabinet of April 13, 1994."

52 Belgian Senate, p. 547: "Hearing Brouhns on June 25, 1997."

53 The previous meetings and communications (the Cabinet meeting of April 12, the telex from Claes to the Belgian delegation in New York on April 12, Claes' meeting with Ghali, the telex from Claes to the Belgian delegation in New York on April 13, the meeting of the Cabinet on April 13) all spoke of the Belgian position that it was best to withdraw all UNAMIR troops.

54 S/1994/430; Letter of the Belgium Permanent Representative at the U.N. to

During the Cabinet meeting on April 14 it was repeated that "diplomatic efforts" had to be continued to "get the Angolan option accepted."[55] On April 15 the Cabinet ordered Claes to get in contact with the Secretary-General, the members of the Security Council and the troop-contributing states by letter, to inform them that Belgium was of the opinion that the mandate had become pointless and that Belgium could no longer participate in UNAMIR.[56] The Cabinet decided furthermore to make a *démarche* to the Secretary-General, the members of the Security Council and troop-contributing states, explaining that the "U.N.-mandate had become politically useless and militarily untenable."[57] Despite the fact that there was still no consensus in the Security Council, the Cabinet concluded that the Belgian blue helmets had to get ready to leave Rwanda and that Luc Marchal had to be instructed to start preparing the Belgian withdrawal.[58]

That same day, on April 15, Claes sent a letter to the President of the Security Council and to Boutros-Ghali. In both letters he conveyed the decision of Belgium to withdraw and wrote: "All the information at our disposal reinforces our fear that UNAMIR as a whole may be exposed to very serious risks and be powerless in the face of the worsening situation. That is why my Government again recommends that the UNAMIR mission be suspended."[59]

The following day—April 16—Noterdaeme informed the Security Council that the Belgian blue helmets would be withdrawn whatever the Security Council decided.[60]

In short, after April 11 all meetings of the Council of Ministers, telexes and letters repeated that Belgium was of the opinion that the mandate of UNAMIR had become pointless and/or that it was best if all UNAMIR troops would be withdrawn. Here follows an overview of the different communications:

(1) The cabinet meeting preparing for Claes' meeting with Boutros-Ghali on April 12 decided: "UNAMIR is now a useless operation and an enforcement of the mandate and the troops are barely realistic options. The U.N. should, awaiting better times, limit its role to an observation post."[61]

(2) The telex from Claes to the Belgian delegation in New York on April 12 stated that Claes was of the opinion that: The Arusha Accords had definitely failed, and because they were the essence of UNAMIR, the

---

the President of the Security Council, April 13, 1994; United Nations, The United Nations and Rwanda, p. 258.

55 Belgian Senate, p. 550.

56 Report of the Cabinet of April 15, 1994; Belgian Senate p. 550.

57 *Id.*

58 Belgian Senate, p. 547.

59 S/1994/446; United Nations, The United Nations and Rwanda, p. 261.

60 Telex No. 691; Belgian Senate, p. 550.

61 Report of the Council of Ministers of April 12, 1994; Belgian Senate, pp. 541–542; see Section 15.4.1.

mission had become pointless, only a limited presence of the United Nations was now acceptable.[62]

(3) Claes in his meeting with the Secretary-General on April 12 advised Boutros-Ghali, because any reinforcement of UNAMIR was not feasible, to withdraw all troops from UNAMIR in order to prevent more casualties among the soldiers.[63]

(4) The telex sent from Claes to the Belgian delegation in New York on April 13 ordered the Belgian embassies in member countries of the Security Council and in troop-contributing states to inform their interlocutors of the withdrawal so that they could help to make the United Nations decide, as soon as possible, upon the withdrawal of UNAMIR.[64]

(5) The meeting of the Cabinet on April 13 decided that: "The diplomatic efforts to get an adjournment of UNAMIR will be intensified . . . against the background of the existing mandate (Resolution No. 909) the current mission is pointless and there is definitely no role for Belgium in the dispatch."[65]

(6) The letter from Noterdaeme to the Security Council on April 13 stated: "It is obvious that under these conditions the continuation of the UNAMIR operation has become pointless within the terms of its present mandate."[66]

(7) The Cabinet on th April 14 repeated: "Diplomatic efforts" have to be continued to "get the Angolan option accepted."[67]

(8) The Cabinet on April 15 ordered Claes to get in contact with the Secretary-General, the members of the Security Council and the troop-contributing states to inform them that Belgium was of the opinion

---

62 Telex No. 181; Belgian Senate, pp. 541–542; see Section 15.4.1.

63 About his conversation with Boutros-Ghali, Claes told the Belgian Senate during his hearing: "Ik heb de heer Boutros Boutros Ghali gezegd: 'U weet beter dan ik dat een versterking van het mandaat er niet in zit. Het is ons oordeel dat u er beter aan doet alle UNAMIR-troepen wijselijk terug te trekken, vooraleer er nieuwe slachtoffers vallen. In elk geval, dat moet ik u melden in naam van de Belgische regering, kunnen de Belgische troepen niet blijven. Wij overwegen een terugtrekking via Tanzania over de grond omdat de risico's van een luchtevacuatie veel te groot zijn.'" Belgian Senate, p. 543; Hearing of Claes, POR, Senate, June 24, 1997.

64 Belgian Senate, p. 547. Why Claes sent the order, which was directed to the embassies in member countries of the SC and to troop-contributing states, to the Belgian delegation to the United Nations is unknown. Possibly the embassies themselves were already informed, or the embassy in New York had to forward the order to the relative embassies.

65 Belgian Senate, p. 549: "Decisions of the Cabinet of 13 April 1994."

66 U.N. Doc. S/1994/430. Letter of the Belgium Permanent Representative at the U.N. to the President of the Security Council, April 13, 1994; United Nations, The United Nations and Rwanda, p. 258.

67 Belgian Senate, p. 550.

that the mandate had become pointless and that Belgium could no longer participate in UNAMIR.[68] The Cabinet decided to make a *démarche* to the Secretary-General, the members of the Security Council and troop contributing states, explaining that the "U.N.-mandate had become politically useless and militarily untenable."[69]

(9) Letter from Claes to the Security Council and to Boutros-Ghali said: "All the information at our disposal reinforces our fear that UNAMIR as a whole may be exposed to very serious risks and be powerless in the face of the worsening situation. That is why my Government again recommends that the UNAMIR mission be suspended."[70]

15.5.2 The Belgian Explanation for Its Efforts to Get a Total Withdrawal

The issue is whether the Belgian withdrawal was accompanied by a Belgian campaign to get a total withdrawal of UNAMIR in an attempt to save face.[71] Minister Claes had phoned all Ministers of Foreign Affairs of the Security Council members to inform them of the Belgian withdrawal and he said to them: "You have only one alternative: Enforce the mandate or withdraw, but nothing in between." Claes: "I never said walk away. No no. I said very clearly, you are underestimating the situation. There is not much choice: Either a stronger mandate, or a withdrawal, one of the two. That was my message."[72]

But when the Belgian Senate asked Claes why he made so much effort to promote a full withdrawal of UNAMIR he answered that "fear of a loss of face" definitely played a role.[73] According to Claes, this fear especially played a role

---

68 Report of the Cabinet of April 15, 1994; Belgian Senate p. 550.

69 *Id.*

70 U.N. Doc. S/1994/446, Letter dated April 15, 1994, from the Permanent Representative of Belgium to the United Nationals addressed to the President of the Security Council. United Nations, The United Nations and Rwanda, p. 261.

71 Interview with W. Claes, January 13, 2006; Interview with A. Destexhe, April 22, 2005; Interview with A. Lake, May 21, 2005; Belgian Senate, pp. 546–548; Michael Barnett, Eyewitness to a Genocide: The United Nations and Rwanda, p. 104 (2002); Linda Melvern, Conspiracy to Murder. The Rwandan Genocide, p. 179 (2004) (hereinafter Melvern, 2004); Alison Des Forges, Leave None to Tell the Story, Genocide in Rwanda (1999) (hereinafter Des Forges) paragraph: "The Security of UNAMIR." According to Des Forges: "The Americans were interested in saving money, the Belgians were interested in saving face, and the French were interested in saving their ally, the genocidal government." See BBC, World: Africa Rwanda slaughter "could have been prevented," March 31 1999.

72 Interview with W. Claes, January 13, 2006.

73 Hearing Claes, POR, Senate, June 24, 1997, PV, 24/9; Belgian Senate pp. 548, 549.

as a result of the letter from the Secretary-General to the Security Council on April13 in which the withdrawal of UNAMIR was argued to be caused only by the Belgian decision to withdraw. Claes: "The fact that that letter was written and known has obliged us psychologically to point out how weak the position of UNAMIR had become and how little ground there still was to fulfill any useful task."[74]

It is too simple and not fair to state merely that the Belgians brought the final blow to UNAMIR by urging a total withdrawal. One should take into account the many efforts from Belgium to achieve enforcement for the peace-keepers. Moreover, it did not withdraw its troops immediately after the killings of the Belgians. On the other hand, it did not use all possible diplomatic power to persuade the other states of the need to change policy with regard to the role of UNAMIR in Rwanda. Only once did Belgium make use of its diplomatic means at the highest echelons: That was to defend the Belgian decision to withdraw. Moreover, at that late stage in its defense, Belgium was arguing that without any enforcement, all troops should withdraw. This is not a very convincing plea for enforcement but more an advocacy for total withdrawal. Many authors,[75] political[76] and military leaders indeed have interpreted the Belgian role in this way with some disgust, making Belgium the easy scapegoat for a world-wide failure to prevent the genocide in Rwanda.

15.6 CONCLUSION

We are now able to draw some conclusions with respect to the Belgian policy on the withdrawal of its troops in the period from April 6 until April 16. It took ten days after the crash (April 6) or nine days after the killing of the Belgian soldiers (April 7) until Belgium made the decision to withdraw its troops public (April 16). The Belgian decision to withdraw was made on April 15 and thus not immediately after the news of the death of the Belgian peace-keepers. During

---

[74] *Id.*

[75] Des Forges, paragraph: "The Security of UNAMIR;" Interview with A. Destexhe, April 22, 2005; Linda Melvern, A People Betrayed. The Role of the West in Rwanda's Genocide, pp. 158–163, pp. 196–197 (2000) (hereinafter Melvern, 2000); According to Des Forges: "The Americans were interested in saving money, the Belgians were interested in saving face, and the French were interested in saving their ally, the genocidal government." See BBC, World: Africa Rwanda slaughter "could have been prevented," March 31, 1999.

[76] Interview with A. Lake, May 21, 2005; Frontline Interview with Moose, November 21, 2003, "But quite clearly the Belgians wanted to have a cover of having others leave as well, and we yielded to that request." Fronline interview with Bushnell, September 30, 2003: "There was a strong sense that the Belgians wanted to withdraw unilaterally if UNAMIR was not withdrawn as a collective. The decision was made to withdraw UNAMIR as a collective."

these ten days, the situation in Rwanda degenerated dramatically—from a cease-fire situation to a war situation in combination with a politicide, which developed within these ten days into a genocide. The deteriorating situation was totally underestimated, particularly at U.N. headquarters. The Secretary-General was hardly informed, even after a week, and was not willing or able to take firm action in order to change the situation by proposing mandatory measures to the Security Council.

Belgium was primarily concerned about the security of its own nationals, and it did its utmost to achieve a rescue operation. The Belgian efforts to broaden the mandate after the death of the Belgian peace-keepers were mainly made in the context of the protection of Belgian nationals and other foreigners and not primarily with the aim of protecting the Rwandan nationals and putting a halt to the developing genocide.

In the preceding months, however, Belgium had asked the United Nations for a more forceful mandate for UNAMIR. Belgium was fully aware of the seriousness of the situation at the brink of a war situation. All these requests were rejected by New York, which presented an unrealistic, rosy picture of the situation. Even after the crash and also after the killing of the Belgian peace-keepers, Belgium asked again for a strengthening of UNAMIR, mainly to secure the evacuation of their own nationals. It did not influence or pressure the members of the Security Council, and it hardly tried to influence others with diplomatic means. It did not threaten to withdraw without any enforcement. It also did not make its decision dependent on any U.N. decision with regard to UNAMIR. The Belgian decision to withdraw was not dependent on the authorization to broaden the mandate. In fact, it made little use of political and power leverage to influence international politics.

In Belgium, particularly within the government, the discussion of a withdrawal continued, and during these ten days the outcome developed increasingly in the direction of a total Belgian withdrawal. We have not observed any opposition in Belgium towards this position. Nor have we observed a direct mass appeal through public opinion for a direct withdrawal after the killing of the Belgian peace-keepers. Even if this pressure had been activated, it took eight days before the Belgian government acceded to these pressures. Moreover, we have not observed much pressure—apart from one comment from Boutros-Ghali during his meeting with Claes—encouraging Belgium to continue its participation in UNAMIR.

The Belgian Minister of Foreign Affairs only phoned all his colleagues from the member states of the Security Council once. This had never been done to strengthen the UNAMIR mandate, but it was done to explain the Belgian withdrawal. In explaining the Belgian withdrawal, Claes made it clear that any continuation of UNAMIR in the current situation with the limited mandate was useless. This active role of Claes on the international scene is remarkable. It is to be understood as a reaction to the letter of the Secretary-General to the Security Council in which he blamed Belgium in particular, because Boutros-

Ghali made his decision to stop UNAMIR in relation to the Belgian withdrawal.[77] It is in this context that many observers understood this Belgian activity as a plea for a withdrawal of all troops. Such a plea was seen by many as a face-saving gesture by the Belgians, so they would not be held solely responsible for the emerging disaster in Rwanda.

77 See Section 16.2.2.

CHAPTER 16

THE RESPONSE OF THE SECURITY COUNCIL

16.1 INTRODUCTION

After the plane crash, the Security Council was continually in secret sessions, sometimes twice a day and even during the night.[1] Normally the meetings would have remained secret, but an informant of the council provided Linda Melvern with a 155-page document.[2] This leak revealed some hideous details. According to Melvern, throughout the first four weeks of the genocide, the Security Council did not once debate the large-scale massacres, the systematic slaughter of Tutsi. The Council was silent about the killing of thousands of civilians and the thousands of refugees. The Council did not discuss the option of stopping the killings through the use of enforcement forces. Despite General Roméo Dallaire's daily reports about the mass murders, the priority in the Security Council was the so-called resumed civil war and the need to establish a ceasefire.[3]

Describing the meetings of the Security Council, the Ambassador of the Czech Republic, Karel Kovanda, said: "No one was sure what, if anything, needed to be done. Into this absolutely bizarre situation came the big powers . . . who said they could do nothing."[4] Kovanda: "Thousands and thousands of people were being killed, and yet 80 per cent of the Security Council's time was spent discussing the possibility of a ceasefire in the renewed civil war and the rest of the time deciding what to do about the peacekeepers in the U.N. assistance mission in Rwanda, UNAMIR."[5]

---

1 Linda Melvern, A People Betrayed. The Role of the West in Rwanda's Genocide, p. 152 (2000) (hereinafter Melvern, 2000).

2 Melvern, 2000 pp. 152–153.

3 Melvern, 2000 p. 152.

4 Melvern, 2000 p. 152, note 2: Interview Melvern with Karel Kovanda, June 2, 1994.

5 Melvern's briefing speech at the United States Holocaust Memorial Museum (Washington), March 11, 2002, *available at* http://www.ushmm.org/.

16.2 THE SECRETARY-GENERAL'S RESPONSE ON THE DEATH OF THE PEACE-KEEPERS AND THE BELGIAN WITHDRAWAL

The Secretary-General's response after the plane crash, the death of the Belgian peace-keepers and the news of the Belgian withdrawal had been understood as a preference for a withdrawal of UNAMIR. Boutros-Ghali himself, however, disagreed with this analysis, and argued that he had been misunderstood.[6]

16.2.1 The Secretary-General's April 8 Letter to the Security Council

On April 8, responding to the plane crash and the death of the peace-keepers, the Secretary-General sent a letter from Geneva to the Security Council.[7] It must be noted that there are two versions of this letter. The first version is a copy of the original, which was given to Linda Melvern by Colin Keating, the permanent representative of New Zealand and the President of the Security Council during the Rwandan genocide. In this version, Ghali suggested a withdrawal of UNAMIR. He is quoted to have stated:

> It is quite possible that the evacuation of UNAMIR and other U.N. personnel might become unavoidable, in which event UNAMIR would be hindered in providing assistance under its present mandate and rules of engagement. The members of the Security Council might wish to give this matter their urgent attention. Should UNAMIR be required to effect such an evacuation, the Force Commander estimates that he would require two or three additional battalions for that purpose.[8]

The second version, which is printed in the U.N. Blue Book Series, does not mention the evacuation of UNAMIR. The letter stated: "It is quite possible that the evacuation of civilian staff from the U.N. system as well as other foreign nationals might become unavoidable in which event UNAMIR would be hindered in providing assistance under its present mandate and rules of engagement."[9]

The words "It is quite possible that the evacuation of UNAMIR . . . might become unavoidable," mentioned in the original version, show that the Secretary-General was already inclined to withdraw UNAMIR on April 8.

---

6 Melvern, 2000 p. 159, note: 18: Boutros Boutros-Ghali, unvanquished. A U.S.-U.N. Saga. Londen: IB Tauris, 1999, p. 132.

7 Melvern, 2000 p. 139; United Nations, The United Nations and Rwanda, 1993–1996, p. 255 (1996) (hereinafter United Nations, The United Nations and Rwanda).

8 Melvern, 2000 pp. 139 149, note 10.

9 Melvern, 2000 pp. 139 149, note 10; United Nations, The United Nations and Rwanda, p. 255.

16.2.2 Boutros-Ghali's Response to the Security Council After His Meeting with Minister Claes

Four days after Boutros-Ghali sent this letter to the Council, he had his meeting with Minister Claes in Bonn. Boutros-Ghali's response to the news of the Belgian withdrawal during this meeting is disputed.

According to a Belgian telex, sent on April 13 to the Belgian delegation in New York, Boutros-Ghali agreed with the Belgian position as set out by Claes. The telex noted that Boutros-Ghali had responded with the words: "Je partage votre analyse."[10] The Secretary-General argued however that he did not agree with the Belgian position. In his report of the meeting he said: "I voiced my disagreement and asked that the Belgian troops at least leave their heavy weapons in Rwanda so that they could be used by other UNAMIR contingents."[11]

The day after their meeting, the Secretary-General communicated very clearly to the Security Council what the results of a Belgian withdrawal would be for UNAMIR. Boutros-Ghali wrote on April 13, with the Belgian withdrawal "it will be extremely difficult for UNAMIR to carry out its tasks effectively. The continued discharge by UNAMIR of its mandate will become untenable unless the Belgian contingent is replaced by another equally well equipped contingent or unless the Government of Belgium reconsiders its decision to withdraw its contingent." Furthermore, the Secretary-General added: "In these circumstances, I have asked my Special Representative and the Force Commander to prepare plans for the withdrawal of UNAMIR, should this prove necessary, and send their recommendations to me in this regard."[12]

These words seem to show again the Secretary-General's preference for the withdrawal of UNAMIR. Years later, however, Boutros-Ghali argued that this letter, sent on April 13, was misunderstood. According to the Secretary-General, he had written his letter in these words in order to put pressure on the

---

10 Telex of April 13 from the Ministry of Foreign Affairs to the Belgian delegation to the United Nations in New York. In the telex, it is unclear whether these words meant that he agreed with the Belgian decision to withdraw, with the Belgian view that all UNAMIR troops should be withdrawn or with the Belgian analysis regarding the chaotic situation in Rwanda. Sénat de Belgique, Commission d'Enquête parlementaire concernant les événements au Rwanda, Sénat de Belgique, session de 1997–1998, 6 décembre 1997, Rapport fait au nom de la commission d'enquête par MM Mahoux et Verhofstadt, p. 543 (hereinafter Belgian Senate).

11 United Nations, The United Nations and Rwanda, p. 38.

12 U.N. Doc. S/1994/430, Letter of April 13, 1994, from Boutros-Ghali to the President of the Security Council; United Nations, The United Nations and Rwanda, p. 259; United Nations, Report of the Independent Inquiry into the Actions of the United Nations during the 1994 Genocide in Rwanda, December 15, 1999, Ingvar Carlsson, Han, Sung-Joo, Rufus, M. Kupolati, UN Doc. S/1999/1257, p. 20 (hereinafter Carlsson Report, S/1999/1257).

Security Council, so that the Council would authorize enforcement.[13] As will be seen below, Boutros-Ghali's letter of April 13 was indeed not understood by the Council as a call for reinforcement but as an announcement of the withdrawal. Boutros-Ghali has never asked the Security Council for any enforcement force in Rwanda.

16.3 THE SECURITY COUNCIL: WHAT TO DO AFTER THE BELGIAN WITHDRAWAL

16.3.1 April 13: A Meeting of Troop-Contributing States and an Informal Security Council Meeting

On April 13, following the meeting in Bonn, the troop-contributing states met to discuss the situation in Rwanda. Colin Keating, the President of the Security Council, had decided upon this meeting to obtain an insight into the views of the troop-contributing states.[14] The most important announcement of the President was that of the Belgian decision to withdraw. Furthermore, Keating noted the worsening situation in Rwanda and emphasized that the Council could not abandon Rwanda, nor could they take intolerable risks. He added that U.N. personnel should not be "exposed to unnecessary danger." Keating told the troop-contributing states that the Security Council would support the Secretary-General, regardless of the decision taken by him. After Keating's words, a discussion followed in which Canada asked whether UNAMIR should stay or withdraw fully. Keating answered that the United Nations was protecting 20,000 people, and at the same time people were being evacuated, but the situation was described as "tolerable."[15]

After the meeting of the troop-contributing states, the Security Council gathered to discuss the situation in Rwanda. The meeting started with the letter of the Secretary-General concerning the Belgian decision to withdraw and the possible consequences for UNAMIR. The Council was informed of Boutros-Ghali's view that the Belgian contingent had to be replaced by an equally well-equipped contingent, otherwise UNAMIR had to withdraw.[16] The members of

---

13 Melvern, 2000 p. 15, note 18: Boutros Boutros-Ghali, unvanquished. A U.S.-U.N. Saga. Londen: IB Tauris, 1999, p. 132.

14 Dutch Ministry of Foreign Affairs, File DPV, 00214, Code: nyvi 382/698, April 5, 14, 1994.

15 *Id.*

16 U.N. Doc. S/1994/430. Letter of April 13, 1994, of Boutros-Ghali to the President of the Security Council; United Nations, The United Nations and Rwanda, p. 259.

the Council were annoyed by the letter, which was understood as an announcement of the withdrawal of UNAMIR.[17]

According to Melvern, the representatives at the United Nations gave the following responses.[18] The French representative wondered why Boutros-Ghali had assumed that a Belgian withdrawal would mean a total withdrawal of UNAMIR. France understood why Belgium wanted to withdraw, but if all troops were to be withdrawn, the situation would deteriorate further. A delegate from the United States said that it was "unfortunate" that the Secretary-General "seemed to blame" Belgium for a total withdrawal. The delegation reminded the Council of Somalia and said it would be best to withdraw all troops leaving a small group behind. The United Kingdom argued that the letter was "far from adequate" and "unfortunate," because the Secretary-General suggested that if Belgium were to stay, the situation would be "well," but these troops would not be able to protect the civilians either. The representative added that if at least a small UNAMIR presence were to be left, this could offer encouragement for the parties to get back to the peace agreements.[19]

Following the discussion, Iqbal Riza gave the Council an update of the current situation in Rwanda. He said that General Dallaire was trying to get a cease-fire, but that the RPF was against it; he said that the situation was deteriorating; he spoke about an estimated 14,000 refugees who were sheltering at the U.N. compound and explained that the mission was lacking the resources to protect these people.[20] This outline was followed by a question from Riza whether it was the task of a peace-keeping operation to protect civilians. Riza: "The Council should consider whether PKO [peace-keeping operations] should be assigned such tasks."[21] The Nigerian Ambassador Ibrahim Gambari then asked if Africa was not of a moral concern anymore.[22]

In the name of the Non-Aligned Caucus members, Nigeria had drawn up a draft resolution in which a mandate for an enforcement of UNAMIR was requested. The draft resolution suggested that the peace-keepers should be allowed to "enforce public order and the rule of law and create temporary state institutions." The resolution was discussed, but never formally tabled.[23] Nigeria

---

17 Dutch Ministry of Foreign Affairs. File: DPV, 00214, Code: nyvi384/6987, April 14, 1994; Melvern, 2000 p. 158.

18 Melvern, 2000 pp. 158–159.

19 Melvern, 2000 pp. 158–159; Dutch Ministry of Foreign Affairs. File: DPV, 00214, Code: Nyvi391/7071, April 15, 1994.

20 Melvern, 2000 p. 159.

21 Roméo Dallaire, Shake Hands with the Devil, The Failure of Humanity in Rwanda, p. 295 (2004) (hereinafter Dallaire); Melvern, 2000 pp. 159–160.

22 Melvern, 2000 p. 159. That same meeting, Augustin Bizimana, the Rwandan Ambassador, passed a letter of the Interim Government Minister of Foreign Affairs, Jérome Bicamumpaka, saying that the situation was improving and the presence of the United Nations was helping to stabilize. Melvern, 2000 pp. 159–160.

23 Carlsson Report, p. 20; Melvern, 2000 p. 159; Organization of African Unity,

also pointed out that the Council should not be focused only on the security of foreigners but also on the protection of Rwandan civilians.[24]

According to Barnett, it was not a draft resolution but a non-paper on intervention that Nigeria circulated among the non-permanent members. The non-paper was a record of all Nigerian oral presentations and should be "a focus for a strategy for intervention." Barnett writes that the Nigerian Ambassador told him that the non-paper was not circulated to the entire Council because of "tremendous pressure to achieve a consensus."[25]

During the discussion, the U.S. representative, Karl Inderfurth, said that the United States was of the opinion that peace-keeping was not appropriate for Rwanda. According to Melvern, he added that the United States would not push for a total withdrawal, "but the whole Council should give consideration to the future of the mission."[26] China disagreed and argued that there was no direct danger for the "remaining U.N. peacekeepers" in Rwanda.[27]

In the following discussion, the members of the SC were all of the opinion that there had to be some presence of UNAMIR. The more extreme options, such as a total withdrawal, on the one hand, or a peace enforcement mission, on the other hand, were turned down.[28]

16.3.2 April 14: An Informal Security Council Meeting: Three Options Are Presented to the Council

On April 14 another informal Council meeting would take place to discuss the future of UNAMIR. For this reason, DPKO sent two draft options, on April 13, to the Secretary-General and Dallaire and asked them for comments.[29]

The first option was to keep UNAMIR, minus the Belgian contingent, in place for a period of three weeks. The conditions for this option were an "effective cease-fire," "declaring Kigali a neutral territory" and "concentrating UNAMIR at the airport." If the agreement of an effective ceasefire was not secured by May 6, UNAMIR would withdraw. The second option involved

---

The Preventable Genocide of the International Panel of Eminent Personalities to Investigate the 1994 Genocide in Rwanda and Surrounding Events, paragraph 15.11 (hereinafter OAU Report); Dutch Ministry of Foreign Affairs, File: DPV, 00214, Code: nyvi384/6987, April 14, 1994.

24 OAU Report, paragraph 15.11, note 10: "A knowledgeable observer."

25 Michael Barnett, Eyewitness to a Genocide: The United Nations and Rwanda, pp. 106, 107 (2002) (hereinafter Barnett), note: 11: interview Barnett with Gambari.

26 Melvern, 2000 p. 159.

27 *Id.*, p. 159.

28 Dutch Ministry of Foreign Affairs. File: DPV, 00214, Code: nyvi384/6987, April 14, 1994.

29 Carlsson Report, p. 20.

UNAMIR being immediately reduced to just a small political presence of the special representative, some military observers, advisers and a small security force of about 250 troops.[30]

Dallaire responded that he was in favor of the first option. The Senior Political Advisor to the Secretary-General, Gharekhan, sent a cable to Annan stating that Boutros-Ghali also preferred option one. However, he added that this option had to be under the condition that, if no progress was achieved, they would proceed to the second option.[31] In that same cable, Gharekhan referred to the letters sent from Boutros-Ghali to the Council on April 8 and 13. Gharekhan wrote that Boutros-Ghali had "at no stage" favored a withdrawal of UNAMIR. He added: "Abrupt, total withdrawal is not feasible, nor desirable, or wise."[32]

On April 14, before the start of the Council meeting, the troop-contributing states gathered for a meeting.[33] Riza, who was in charge of the meeting, showed himself to be very aware of the gravity of the events in Rwanda. He stated that the situation was "already worse than in Somalia." Nevertheless, he told the troop-contributing states that the Council had to decide upon the future of UNAMIR and that an enforcement force would not be discussed in the Council meeting. He added that a total withdrawal would not be discussed that day either.[34]

After the meeting of troop-contributing states, the Security Council came together for its informal meeting. The Assistant Secretary-General in the Department of Political Affairs, Alvaro de Soto, discussed the Council's criticisms concerning the April 13 letter of the Secretary-General. De Soto noted that the Council had been wrong to respond in this manner. It was never the intention of the Secretary-General to abruptly withdraw UNAMIR; he was not in favor of a withdrawal: an abrupt withdrawal was "not feasible, not advisable, or wise." But, as De Soto stated, the problem was that the peace-keepers were not able to carry out their mandate.[35] Furthermore, he argued that despite the fact that the Secretary-General was on tour in Europe, he was in constant contact with U.N. headquarters, Dallaire and Jacques Roger Booh Booh, the SRSG.[36]

Riza then orally presented the two DPKO options to the Council: Option one: keep UNAMIR in place minus the Belgian contingent. Option two:

---

30 *Id.*, p. 20; Dallaire, p. 295.

31 Carlsson Report, p. 20.

32 United Nations, The United Nations and Rwanda, p. 41; Carlsson Report, p. 20.

33 Dutch Ministry of Foreign Affairs. File: DPV, 00214, Code: nyvi388/7068, April 15, 1994.

34 *Id.*

35 United Nations, The United Nations and Rwanda, p. 41; Belgian Senate, p. 545; Dutch Ministry of Foreign Affairs. File: DPV, 00214, Code: Nyvi391/7071, April 15, 1994.

36 Melvern, 2000 p. 161; Carlsson Report, p. 69.

UNAMIR would be reduced to a small political presence.[37] Both options were explained to be predicated on a ceasefire.[38] Furthermore, a third option was presented. This option was a combination of the other two and was communicated to the Council as Boutros-Ghali's favorite.[39]

The Council members responded very disparately to the three options, and not all of the members took a position.[40] Oman responded with a request for written proposals.[41] Spain asked why there was no option to change the mandate.[42] France stated a preference for option 1, on the condition that UNAMIR could operate in safety and with a clear objective.[43] France added that they were of the opinion that any mission in Rwanda would serve some purpose.[44] More countries then raised the problem that the three options did not discuss the mandate of UNAMIR, but De Soto did not clarify the issue.[45]

The United Kingdom supported the second option and asked the Secretariat to be more precise about the number of peace-keepers that would be left in Rwanda.[46] Russia supported the second option as well. The United States argued that they would only accept a total withdrawal of the mission, because they believed there was no peace-keeping role under the present circumstances.[47] Later in the discussion, the United States stated that they could also accept option two.[48] According to Dallaire and the Dutch Ministry of Foreign Affairs, Nigeria, speaking for the non-aligned countries, said that none of the options was good and wanted more time for a proposal.[49] According to the Carlsson Report, however, Nigeria favored option one.[50]

---

37 Melvern, 2000 p. 161; Carlsson Report pp. 20, 69. According to the Dutch Ministry of Foreign Affairs, it was De Soto who set out the three options. Dutch Ministry of Foreign Affairs. File: DPV, 00214, Code: Nyvi391/7071, April 15, 1994.

38 Carlsson Report, pp. 20, 69.

39 *Id.*, p. 20. The Carlsson Report does not say more than that this third option was "a combination" of the other two.

40 Melvern, 2000 p. 161. Dutch Ministry of Foreign Affairs. File: DPV, 00214, Code: Nyvi391/7071, April 15, 1994.

41 Melvern, 2000 p. 161.

42 *Id.*, p. 161.

43 Dutch Ministry of Foreign Affairs. File: DPV, 00214, Code: Nyvi391/7071, April 15, 1994.

44 Melvern, 2000 p. 161.

45 Dutch Ministry of Foreign Affairs. File: DPV, 00214, Code: Nyvi391/7071, April 15, 1994.

46 Carlsson Report, p. 21; Melvern, 2000 p. 161.

47 *Id.*

48 Carlsson Report, p. 21.

49 Dutch Ministry of Foreign Affairs. File: DPV, 00214, Code: Nyvi391/7071, April 15, 1994; Dallaire, p. 298. According to Dallaire, this response of Nigeria was written in a fax that he received at 4:30 on the morning of April 15 in Kigali. At that time it was the evening of April 14 in New York. This means that the cable dealt with the Council meeting of April 14.

50 Carlsson Report, p. 20.

Only the President of the Security Council, Colin Keating, said that the United States should "increase the strength of UNAMIR . . . and revise its mandate to enable it to contribute to the restoration of law and order and the establishment of transitional institutions within the framework of the Arusha peace-agreement."[51]

16.3.3 April 15: Another Informal Security Council Meeting: A Decision Without Saying "No"

Before the informal Council meeting on April 15, Colin Keating had a private meeting with the Nigerian Ambassador, Gambari, who told him to pay special attention to the views of Dallaire.[52] Gambari argued furthermore that the Belgian reaction was a bit "hysterical." After this talk with Gambari, Keating had another private meeting, this time with Paul Noterdaeme, the Belgian representative to the United Nations. Keating told Noterdaeme that the Belgian withdrawal would lead to a bloodbath.[53]

During the Council meeting, the non-aligned countries, together with China, Argentina and France opted for option one.[54] Several countries, including the United Kingdom and New Zealand attempted to convince the non-aligned countries, through Gambari, to accept option two, but they received no response.[55] Instead, Gambari pleaded for reinforcements; he argued that the Belgian advice was important, but that no other state had decided to withdraw its troops yet.[56] According to documents of the Dutch Ministry of Foreign Affairs, the Secretariat also declared that it favored option 1.[57]

---

51 According to Dallaire, this response of Keating was written in a fax that he received on 4:30 in the morning of April 15 in Kigali. At that time it was in the evening of April 14 in New York. This means that the cable dealt with the Council meeting of April 14. Dallaire, p. 298.

52 Melvern, 2000 p. 163. As seen above, it was April 15 when Belgium officially decided that the Belgian blue helmets would have to leave Rwanda. Melvern, 2000 p. 162, note 25: The letter is dated April 15, 1994 (reference S.1168). In the possession of Melvern. Belgian Senate, p. 547; Telex No. 691; Belgian Senate, p. 550. Melvern describes that during the day of April 15, a disagreement followed between officials of DPKO and the Belgian diplomats. Kofi Annan was against a complete pull-out, he argued that a withdrawal would only make the humanitarian situation worse. Dallaire sent a list of needed equipment, which was seen by a Belgian, who joked about Dallaire's optimism. Melvern, 2000 p. 162.

53 Melvern, 2000 p. 163.

54 Dallaire, p. 301.

55 Dutch Ministry of Foreign Affairs. File: DPV, 00214, Code: 16/04/94, nyvi394/7171.

56 Melvern, 2000 p. 163.

57 Dutch Ministry of Foreign Affairs. File: DPV, 00214, Code: 16/04/94, nyvi394/7171.

According to Melvern, the United States would only accept a resolution in which all peace-keepers were withdrawn.[58] Melvern writes that the United Kingdom put themselves in line with the United States but added that a compromise could be reached in which a small number of troops could be left behind. The United States stated that if a vote had to be taken, they would have to decide that there was no role for the peace-keepers.[59] Ghana and Bangladesh told the Council that they were planning to keep their troops in Rwanda for now.

Because of the different opinions, the Council meeting ended without a decision. The result of the meeting was seen as "a decision without saying no." It was Friday, April 15, and the discussion would not be resumed until Monday, April 18.[60] Hearing of the failure to come to a decision, Dallaire wondered "how many thousands of Rwandans would die that weekend."[61]

That same day, the President of the Security Council gave a statement to the press. Keating stated that the immediate priority was to achieve a ceasefire between the government forces and the RPF. The Security Council demanded that the parties agree upon a ceasefire and return to the negotiation table. Not a word was devoted to the ongoing massacres.[62]

16.4 DPKO SUDDENLY WANTS A TOTAL WITHDRAWAL

16.4.1 Information from Dallaire to New York

Dallaire sent a long and detailed cable to New York on April 17. He described his deep concern about the current situation in Rwanda and the consequences of the Belgian withdrawal. According to Melvern, Dallaire wrote that he was pessimistic about a ceasefire. Melvern quotes Dallaire: "The stopping of the massacres may become more and more difficult as the local groups/militia become seemingly bolder . . . the ethnic killings are continuing and in fact unconfirmed reports indicate it is even increasing in scale and scope in the

---

58 Melvern, 2000 p. 163. According to the documents of the Dutch Ministry of Foreign Affairs, however, the U.S.-position was unclear: A few days before, the U.S. had argued that a total withdrawal had to be prevented, after which it changed its position again and had stated that UNAMIR would be better to leave Rwanda, and now the U.S. took a middle position by saying that the American delegation could not accept any resolution at this moment. Dutch Ministry of Foreign Affairs. File: DPV, 00214, Code: 16/04/94, nyvi394/7171.

59 Melvern, 2000 p. 163.

60 Dutch Ministry of Foreign Affairs. File: DPV, 00214, Code: 16/04/94, nyvi394/7171.

61 Dallaire, p. 301.

62 Carlsson Report, p. 21.

areas just ahead of the RPF advance."[63] Melvern reveals in her book that Dallaire added that he was not aware of what was happening outside Kigali: "New York may very well know more about what is going on than UNAMIR with intelligence information (Satellite, EW etc.) from its members of the situation outside Kigali."[64]

Barnett, who is in possession of Dallaire's fax, quotes Dallaire:

> The FC [Force Commander] assesses the situation as being very difficult, dangerous, and explosive once one side or the other actually starts to smell victory. The force simply cannot continue to sit on the fence in the face of all these morally legitimate demands for assistance/protection, nor can it simply launch into Chapter VII type of operations without the proper authority, personnel, and equipment. It is thus anticipated that over the next 24 hours or so, the FC will either recommend a thinning out of the force down to a responsible level needed to ensure the security of the airfield for humanitarian relief efforts, the political/military process and the humanitarian support tasks. Thus a force of about 1,300 all ranks based on the preferred option of one large battalion of 800 men (instead of two small 450 men battalions with all their overheads) or the FC will recommend option B, i.e. the 250 man force just to keep the files going in a secure situation. Maintaining the status quo on manpower under these severe and adverse conditions is wasteful, dangerously casualty-causing and demoralizing to the troops. Either UNAMIR gets changes to its scope of work in order to get into the thick of things (with more resources), or it starts to thin out in order to avoid unnecessary losses and reduce the overheads and administrative burden to the negotiation process for a cease-fire and peace.[65]

---

63 Melvern, 2000 pp. 163–164.

64 *Id.*, p. 164.

65 Barnett, pp. 122–123, note 49: Document in possession of Barnett. Dallaire himself gives a shortened version of his fax:

> The force simply cannot continue to sit on the fence in the face of all these morally legitimate demands for assistance/protection, nor can it simply launch into Chapter VII-type operations without the proper authority, personnel, and equipment. It is thus anticipated that over the next 24 hours or so, the FC will either recommend a thinning out of the force down to a responsible level needed to ensure the security of the airfield for humanitarian relief efforts, the political/military process and the humanitarian support tasks . . . a force of 1,300 personnel, or the FC will recommend . . . the 250-man force.

Dallaire, p. 307. Melvern also gives a shorted version of Dallaire's fax, Melvern, 2000 pp. 165, 166.

16.4.2 Reverse Reaction from New York by Riza on Input from Dallaire

The fax from Dallaire was either misunderstood or deliberately wrongly explained by DPKO. On that same day, April 17, Dallaire received a reply from Riza saying:

> It should be impressed upon the RPF that without some quick agreement on a cease-fire—even a limited one—by Wednesday [the 20th of April] at the latest, the Security Council can be expected to decide to withdraw UNAMIR from Rwanda. At that time the RPF could be blamed for not accepting the cease-fire to allow discussions to begin . . . Please stress to them that without a cease-fire, humanitarian operations cannot begin.[66]

Riza continued by saying: "Your plans to start sharp reduction of UNAMIR personnel is approved. This also will demonstrate imminence of withdrawal of UNAMIR if cease-fire is not achieved."[67] With the remark "Your plans to start sharp reduction," Riza most likely referred to the words in Dallaire's fax: "The FC will either recommend a thinning out of the force down to a responsible level needed to ensure the security of the airfield for humanitarian relief efforts . . . a force of about 1300 all ranks . . . or the FC will recommend . . . the 250 man force just to keep the files going in a secure situation."

Reading Riza's fax, Dallaire was struck with amazement: this was absolutely not what he had intended to say in his fax.[68] Dallaire writes in his book: "I had given them an argument for pulling out and they jumped on it, though that hadn't been my intention . . . I felt helpless and frustrated by what I viewed . . . as my inability to make the horror sink into the minds and the souls of the people in DPKO, the Security Council, the Secretary-General's office, the world at large."[69]

16.4.3 Annan Favors Withdrawal

On April 18 Annan sent a cable to Dallaire, titled "Status of UNAMIR." The cable was signed off by Riza and stated that since there was no real prospect of a ceasefire, DPKO intended to report to the Security Council that a total withdrawal was envisaged rather than the two options that had been presented

---

66 Dallaire, pp. 307.

67 Dallaire, p. 308; Melvern, 2000 p. 166.

68 Dallaire, p. 308.

69 *Id.*, p. 308.

to the Council.[70] The cable asked Dallaire and Booh Booh for their final assessment of "the consequences of the withdrawal for those who had taken refuge at our sites."[71]

Dallaire was left without a choice. He had to conduct a risk assessment of the consequences of a total withdrawal. Before doing so, he had to find out what Booh Booh's opinion was. Together with Abdul Hamid Kabia, Acting Executive Director of UNAMIR, he went to see the Special Representative who appeared to be already aware of the content of the cable. Dallaire argued that a total withdrawal was out of the question; at least a small force had to stay on the ground. Dallaire: "We needed to keep the U.N. flag flying in Kigali, even if only to bear witnesses." Booh Booh replied that Dallaire "had to stop arguing and prepare to withdraw." Suddenly Booh Booh turned to Kabia and asked him for his position. Dallaire: "I suddenly saw that the future of UNAMIR hung totally on what Kabia would say." After a deathly silence, Kabia said that he fully supported Dallaire's proposal to leave a small force of 250 troops in Rwanda.[72]

In the evening of April 18 Dallaire sent the requested Military Assessment to DPKO in which he argued against a total withdrawal.[73] The assessment described the terrible situation and all tactical and moral reasons for keeping at least a skeleton of troops in Rwanda.[74] According to the Carlsson Report, Dallaire informed the Secretariat on April 19 that: "A wholesale withdrawal of UNAMIR would most certainly be interpreted as leaving the scene, if not even deserting a sinking ship."[75] According to Carlsson, Dallaire also indicated the consequences of a withdrawal. Carlsson quotes Dallaire: "The consequences of a withdrawal by UNAMIR will definitely have an adverse effect [sic] on the morale of the civil population, especially of the refugees who will feel that we are deserting them." We may observe that Dallaire was at the same time not very optimistic about the effective role UNAMIR could fulfill in these circumstances when he continues:

> However, in actual fact, there is a little that we are doing at the present time, except providing security, some food, and medicine, and presence. Humanitarian assistance has not really commenced . . . the refugees at locations like Hotel Mille Collines, the Red Cross, Sint Michels Cathedral, etc. in RGF [FAR] territory are in danger of mas-

---

70 Code Cable 1173; Dallaire, p. 312; Carlsson Report, p. 21.

71 Dallaire, p. 312; Carlsson Report, p. 21. The cable stated furthermore: "We feel that appropriate handover arrangements [of those who had taken refuge] should be negotiated with both sides." Dallaire was astonished that DPKO could believe that these Rwandans would be safe on either of the two sides. Dallaire, p. 312.

72 Dallaire, pp. 312–313.

73 Military Assessment of the Situation (MIR 19). Dallaire, p. 319.

74 Dallaire, p. 319.

75 Carlsson Report, p. 21.

sacre, but have been in this danger without result so far for the last week, even with UNAMIR on the ground.[76]

16.5 BOUTROS-GHALI SUDDENLY COMES UP WITH AN OPTION TO REINFORCE THE MISSION

It was only at the point when the DPKO wanted to inform the Council that a total withdrawal was being considered, that the Secretary-General suddenly came up with the option to *reinforce* the mission. Early on the morning of April 20, Dallaire received a code cable from DPKO. He was ordered to stop the withdrawal of his troops until further instructions, because the Secretary-General would present a report to the Council with three new options concerning the future of UNAMIR.[77]

The report of the Secretary-General, dated April 20, spoke of "widespread killings," "political and ethnic dimensions," "violence and mass killings." But the report, which was written two weeks after the start of the genocide, did not say anything about the planned killings of Tutsi and moderate Hutu.[78] The report included the following three new options for the future of UNAMIR:

(1) An immediate and massive reinforcement to stop the fighting and the massacres. This option would require several thousand additional troops and enforcement powers under Chapter VII.[79]
(2) Minimizing UNAMIR to about 270 troops, acting as an intermediary between the parties and seeking a ceasefire.[80]
(3) A complete withdrawal of UNAMIR.[81] With regard to this third option, the Secretary-General explicitly wrote in his report that he did not favor this option.[82]

According to the documents of the Dutch Ministry of Foreign Affairs, both the permanent representative from Rwanda and President Yoweri Museveni of Uganda had asked the Secretary-General to propose the first option to the

---

76 In Dallaire's book, p. 319, he speaks about an MIR sent on April 18 to DPKO in which he argued against a total withdrawal. The Carlsson Report states that Dallaire informed DPKO on April 19 that he was against a total withdrawal. With regard to the time difference, it is possible that Carlsson and Dallaire speak about the same communication.

77 Dallaire, p. 320.

78 Special Report of the Secretary-General on the United Nations Assistance mission for Rwanda. U.N. Doc. S/1994/470, April 20, 1994.

79 *Id.*, paragraphs 13–14.

80 *Id.*, paragraphs 15–18.

81 *Id.*, paragraph 19.

82 *Id.*, paragraph 19.

Security Council.[83] Dallaire suspects that option one for reinforcement "which would require several thousand troops" might only have been included for the archives, because when Dallaire cabled DPKO on April 21 and raised the reinforcement option, Maurice Baril, the Candian Military Adviser to the Secretary-General, responded that he should not expect anything from this reinforcement option; "it would never see the light of day."[84]

According to the Carlsson Report, Booh Booh "expressed full support" for option one, but added that he did not have problems with the amended option two. Regarding the last option, Booh Booh said that he had reservations about the remaining component being headed by the Force Commander. According to the Special Representative, both he and Dallaire should stay present.[85]

The Nigerian Ambassador Gambari met with the Secretary-General, who had returned to New York. Gambari asked the Secretary-General to prevent the Security Council from accepting a withdrawal. According to the Carlsson Report, the Secretary-General said to Gambari that he felt as though he was fighting alone and pressed Gambari "to encourage the African heads of state to rally behind his position and to write letters against a withdrawal."[86]

16.6 UNANIMOUS ADOPTION OF RESOLUTION 912: LEAVING A SYMBOLIC NUMBER OF PEACE-KEEPERS BEHIND

On April 20 the report of the Secretary-General was submitted to the Council.[87] Whether the Secretary-General gave his own preference for one of the three options is disputed.[88] Carlsson explains that according to Boutros-Ghali, his spokesman told the Council that he preferred option one and did not favor option three. Carlsson also reports that, on the other hand, several Council members complained that Boutros-Ghali did not state a preference of his own.[89]

Barnett agrees with this last opinion. He writes in his book that the Council asked the Secretariat repeatedly to present "contingency plans or to recommend options," but that the Secretariat's response was that "UNAMIR was unable to

---

83 Dutch Ministry of Foreign Affairs. File: DPV, 00214, Code: nyvi403/7516, April 22, 1994.

84 Dallaire, p. 322. Baril's response was given most likely by telephone, see Melvern, 2000 p. 173.

85 Carlsson Report, p. 22.

86 *Id.*, p. 22.

87 According to Carlsson, the report of the Secretary-General was submitted to the Council on April 20. Carlsson Report, p. 69. According to Melvern, 2000, however, the report was presented to the Council on April 21. Melvern, 2000 p. 171.

88 However, as stated above, the Secretary-General did write explicitly in his report that he did not favor the third option, a complete withdrawal. U.N. Doc. S/1994/470, paragraph 19.

89 Carlsson Report, pp. 22, 69.

present recommendations at this time." According to Barnett, in the Council's view, it was "very unusual and undesirable" to proceed without the input of the Secretariat, especially because "UNAMIR was the critical source of information" now that the diplomatic representatives had left the country.[90] Barnett concludes: "The Secretariat seemed to be in top bureaucratic and diplomatic form throughout the debate, minimally performing its roles and responsibilities and following the trade winds coming from the council."[91]

If Barnett is correct and the Secretariat indeed replied to the Council that they were not able to give their preference on the future of the mission, because "UNAMIR was unable to present recommendations at this time," then the Secretariat was deliberately withholding information.[92] As seen above, when DPKO sent two options to Dallaire on April 13, Dallaire replied that he favored the first option—keeping UNAMIR, minus the Belgian contingent, in place. Furthermore, in his fax of April 17, Dallaire gave a clear preference for a mission of "1,300 ranks." Barnett explains that the silence of the Secretariat increased the anxiety of the Council and enforced the opinion that it was "best to withdraw the mission before it would be too late."[93]

On April 21 the Security Council spent the whole day in informal sessions discussing the situation in Rwanda. These informal meetings had to lead to a Council vote on the future of UNAMIR at the end of the day. Unfortunately there are no formal records of the Council's sessions on April 21. For this reason, we have relied on the information collected by Melvern and the documents of the Dutch Ministry of Foreign Affairs.

In preparation for the decision, two letters were sent to the President of the Security Council. The letters were circulated among the members of the Council on April 21. One letter was sent by the permanent representative of Uganda, speaking on behalf of his President, Yoweri Museveni, and the other came from the permanent representative of Bangladesh. The representative of Uganda appealed to the Council to "maintain its presence in the war-torn neighboring country."[94] The representative from Bangladesh, also addressing his letter to the Secretary-General, declared that the government of Bangladesh was of the position that its contingent was "exposed to unnecessary risk to life and security." He stated that if the Secretary-General decided to keep the Bangladeshi troops in Rwanda, their "security and safety" had to be "ensured through political means."[95]

---

90 Barnett, p. 108.

91 *Id.*, p. 108.

92 *Id.*, pp. 108–109.

93 *Id.*, pp. 108–109.

94 U.N. Doc. S/1994/479, Letter dated April 21, 1994, from the Permanent Representative of Uganda to the United Nations addressed to the President of the Security Council.

95 U.N. Doc. S/1994/481, Letter dated April 21, 1994, from the Permanent

According to Melvern, the Council members gave the following response to the report of the Secretary-General. The British ambassador stated that he was disappointed because he had expected a choice of options based on the views of both Booh Booh and Dallaire. He argued that he was against the option to reinforce. The Council only had to "think back to Somalia and think about what you would ask these troops to do."[96] Melvern writes that in conclusion: "The U.K. opted for leaving a small force behind and urged a speedy decision, so did the U.S. delegate."[97]

Gambari responded that "none of the options responded to his government's approval. Instead it had to be found out what kind of force was needed to protect the 14,000 people presently sheltering under the U.N. flag." According to Gambari, the question was whether the United Nations was going to help the civilians.[98] What was the response of the other countries is unknown.

During a recess, Baril explained to the non-permanent members of the Council that the peace-keepers were living in horrific circumstances and that "there was not a military commander in the world who would leave a force exposed in such a way." The soldiers were "exhausted, confused and questioning the responsibility of their superiors." Furthermore, they were living in constant fear. Baril continued by saying that the situation was hopeless, some Bangladeshi soldiers had already deserted, the airport was the only lifeline, but its loss was becoming closer by the hour.[99]

It was now April 21, two weeks of deliberations had passed and the Council members still greatly differed upon the future of UNAMIR. Despite these differing opinions, however, a vote was going to be taken. On the evening of April 21, after a day of informal discussions, the Council started its formal meeting to finally come to a vote. The outcome was a unanimous vote for the adoption of Resolution 912, which stated that the majority of peace-keepers would withdraw, and a number of 270 would stay to mediate between the two parties and facilitate human relief.[100]

How was it possible that the Council members, who differed greatly in opinion, now unanimously adopted the second option? What happened to the countries, such as Nigeria and the non-aligned caucus members, arguing for enforcement? The Carlsson Report writes that Nigeria and the non-aligned caucus members were not able to support their preferred option one "because of

---

Representative of Bangladesh to the United Nations addressed to the President of the Security Council.

96 Melvern, 2000 p. 173, Carlsson Report, p. 22.

97 Melvern, 2000 p. 173.

98 *Id.*, p. 172.

99 *Id.*, pp. 172, 173.

100 U.N. Security Council Resolution 912, April 21, 1994, U.N. Doc. S/RES/912 (1994).

lack of political will."[101] Barnett's reasoning is that the countries that had been arguing for intervention "were resigned to the fact that with no troops on the horizon, a civil war raging, and a U.N. operation coming apart at the seams, the second best and only available option was a stripped down UNAMIR."[102] The OAU report concludes that "even Nigeria," which had been pressing for a broader protection that included the Rwandan civilians, decided "with western ambassadors pressing for a consensus" that its proposal was "a lost cause and did not pursue it."[103]

So it came that, on the evening of April 21, all Council members together decided to leave the Rwandan civilians to their fate. In the words of Barnett: "With this vote the council effectively decided that the "international community" would not disturb the killers. This was not an unintended consequence. . . . No Council member could feign ignorance or argue the fact that it was unaware of the implications of its decision. This action was premeditated."[104]

16.7 RESOLUTION 918: UNAMIR II, ENFORCEMENT UP TO 5,500 TROOPS

Only eight days after the Council's decision to withdraw, on April 29 Boutros-Ghali asked the Security Council to reconsider its decision and to decide on "more forceful action." On May 4 the Secretary-General publicly called the killings in Rwanda genocide. He warned that "the United Nations, if it did not act quickly, might later be accused of passivity."[105] Two days later the Security Council asked Boutros-Ghali "to prepare contingency plans to deliver humanitarian assistance and support of displaced persons, and indicated that the Council might later seek indications on logistics and financial implications of an expanded United Nations or international presence in Rwanda."[106]

On May 17 the Security Council unanimously adopted Resolution 918, which called for UNAMIR II, a mission of 5,500 troops. The resolution expanded UNAMIR's mandate to "contribute to the security and protection of refugees and civilians at risk." Under UNAMIR II, the troops were allowed to take "action in self-defense against persons or groups who threaten protected sites and populations, United Nations and other humanitarian personnel or the means of delivery and distribution of humanitarian relief."[107]

---

[101] Carlsson Report, p. 22. The report does not elaborate on what is meant exactly by the reasoning that they could not support it because of a lack of political will.

[102] Barnett, p. 127.

[103] OAU Report, paragraph 15.11, note 10: "A knowledgeable observer."

[104] Barnett, pp. 127–128.

[105] See http://www.un.org/Depts/dpko/dpko/co_mission/unamirFT.htm#APRIL; "Nightline," (ABC), May 4, 1994. Transcript 3378.

[106] See S/1994/546, May 6, 1994; http://www.un.org/Depts/dpko/dpko/co_mission/unamirFT.htm#APRIL.

[107] See http://www.un.org/Depts/dpko/dpko/co_mission/unamirFT.htm#APRIL.

The resolution called upon member states to "respond promptly" to the request for the resources required. However, no troops would become available. According to Colin Keating, ambassador of New Zealand and President of the Security Council, Resolution 918 was a "fiction;" indeed it would take up until October 1994 before the 5,500 troops of UNAMIR II would be fully employed.[108] In next chapter we will describe the refusal of the Netherlands to provide troops. UNAMIR I had not prevented the genocide; on the contrary, because with its withdrawal it facilitated the genocide. UNAMIR II did not stop or end the genocide. Although the decision to establish UNAMIR II was made during the genocide, its implementation took place more than three months after the genocide ended.

---

108 See http://www.un.org/Depts/dpko/dpko/co_mission/unamirFT.htm#APRIL.

CHAPTER 17

THE ROLE OF THE NETHERLANDS THROUGHOUT THE GENOCIDE

The role of a non-direct involved bystander state during the genocide will now be illustrated with the role of the Netherlands. The Netherlands had no specific ties with Rwanda from colonial history or in another way. The Netherlands was not represented in the Security Council during this period. There was very limited news coverage in the Netherlands on the situation in Rwanda. Political debates in the country and in parliament concerning the topic were scarce. In short, from the outside, the overall impression is that the Netherlands was in no way involved in the developments in Rwanda in the period 1993–1994. Since the 1970s Rwanda was however one of the countries that received development aid from the Netherlands, and the Netherlands even co-financed the negotiations in Arusha for a peace accord.[1] The Netherlands did not have an embassy in Rwanda, and the development aid was made by a Netherlands-based international development organization that hardly gave any political information to the Netherlands Minister for Development Cooperation, Jan Pronk. The plane crash and its consequences was a completely unexpected surprise for him. He had not been warned by his Belgian colleague, for instance, and in hindsight he considers his ignorance of the deteriorating situation in Rwanda as a failure.[2]

Some research into the archives of the Ministry of Foreign Affairs nevertheless showed that in the diplomatic field, the Netherlands was often asked to fulfill a role in the peace-keeping mission, and, as a result, it participated in the debates among the countries that might contribute soldiers to UNAMIR I and II. The Netherlands could have played a role, and it was informed in several ways on the developments and atrocities in Rwanda. The requests from the United Nations to the Netherlands were discussed at the highest decision-making echelon: the Cabinet. However, the government rejected all requests and was unwilling to send military material at all. The Netherlands was seen as a country with a rather high profile on human rights, and at that time, the government was composed of Ministers in Foreign Affairs, Defense and Development Cooperation with a strong and outspoken position in the promotion of human rights.

---

1 Interview with J. Pronk, August 21, 2006.

2 *Id.*

The Minister of Foreign Affairs, Peter Kooijmans, was for instance the former U.N. Rapporteur on Torture. As an expert professor in international public law, he also headed the delegation of the Netherlands at the Human Rights Commission in Geneva. The other two ministers belonged to the Labor Party, which had a more outspoken international orientation and was moreover a supporter of a strong U.N. role in the world. Jan Pronk, for instance was Deputy Secretary-General United Nations Conference on Trade and Development (UNCTAD, Assistant Secretary-General United Nations) in Geneva from 1980 to 1986, and had earlier been Minister for Development Cooperation in the Netherlands, in the period 1973–1977, a position that he continued in the period 1989–1998.[3] Since 2004 he has been the Special Representative of the Secretary-General of the United Nations in Khartoum in the Sudan. One may have expected that this government would be more willing to accept the U.N. invitation to play a role than it was in reality. Moreover, the failure of the Dutch peace-keepers in Srebrenica did not play a role at that moment, because the fall of Srebrenica took place one year later in July 1995. As we will show in this chapter, even a bystander state like the Netherlands was aware of what was happening but nonetheless made the decision at the highest level not to help the United Nations with military means to prevent or stop the mass murder in Rwanda.

On the other hand, we will pay particular attention to the role of the Minister of Development Cooperation, Jan Pronk, who was very involved and often made visits to the area. He made contact with Paul Kagame and other leaders during the genocide in Rwanda and did his best to mediate between countries surrounding Rwanda to promote a cessation to the warfare. He also did his best to obtain financial backing from the European Union for an African peace-keeping mission in the area. Our interview with Pronk reaffirmed that his endeavors were more personal initiatives, rather than being based on a firm Dutch policy position. He was not hindered in these activities by Parliament or by the other members of the Cabinet, and they all agreed to the continuing increase of development aid to this region, particularly for the refugees and displaced persons. On the other hand the other ministers in the Dutch government were unwilling to contribute with military means, a decision by which he had to abide.

17.1 THE DUTCH ROLE IN UNOMUR AND UNAMIR

The Netherlands was already asked to contribute at an early stage in the preparation of UNAMIR by UNOMUR. Parliament was informed in June 1993 of the U.N. request for assistance to UNOMUR from the Netherlands in a four-page letter from the Ministers of Defense and Foreign Affairs.[4] Dutch partici-

---

3 Http://www.janpronk.nl/index2.html.

4 Tweede Kamer, 1992–1993, 22 800 X, No. 63 on June 25, 1993.

pation was requested with UNOMUR observers in Ugandan territory to promote the ongoing negotiations on a peace agreement for Rwanda in Arusha following Security Council Resolution 846. The government was willing to react positively. The force would encompass 81 soldiers and 24 civil staff, and the Netherlands was asked for ten commissioned and non-commissioned officers including a lieutenant-colonel as the sector commander.[5] The budget for these ten soldiers for a period of four months was already reserved from the budget of peace-keeping operations of the Ministry of Defense.[6] For UNAMIR, the Netherlands was requested to participate with two Dutch military observers for four months. The government agreed to assist with one captain,[7] Captain Willem de Kant. He played an important role as the *aid-de-camp* of General Roméo Dallaire. He was the one who briefed the Force Commander first on the situation when Dallaire arrived on September 30, he lived together in the house with Dallaire and Brent Beardsley and he was, for instance, involved in the enquiry into the Interahamwe attack on the convoy of Belgian peace-keepers escorting the RPF on February 23.[8] De Kant was replaced by another Dutch captain, Robert van Putten, who was there at the moment of the plane crash on April 6 and during the onward course of events.[9] In particular, Van Putten was—with Dallaire—confronted at the hospital with the bodies of the murdered Belgian peace-keepers.[10] After these killings Van Putten was also withdrawn suddenly from Rwanda for his safety.[11] A deliberate decision in the Netherlands could not be observed in this research. What is nevertheless interesting is that the Netherlands, because of its role, was participating in the group of troop-contributing countries in New York. No remarkable role can however be disclosed.

17.2 MEETINGS DURING THE GENOCIDE WITHIN INTERNATIONAL ORGANIZATIONS AND THE EU

Searching in the archives of the Ministry of Foreign Affairs in the Netherlands, it is shocking to become aware, from discussions within the United Nations, that during the month of May, no efforts were made to stop the mass

---

5 *Id.*, p. 3.

6 *Id.*, pp. 3–4, the amount was 55,000 guilders.

7 Dutch Ministry of Foreign Affairs. File: DPVn02125, nyvi0322, October 22, 1993.

8 Roméo Dallaire, Shake Hands with the Devil, The Failure of Humanity in Rwanda, pp. 95, 97, 108, 192–193 (2004) (hereinafter Dallaire). For that attack on the convoy of February 23, see Section 10.3.

9 Dallaire pp. 218, 222–229, 234–235, 244–247, 255–256.

10 See Section 13.3.1; IKON Radio (Dutch radio), March 26, 2006, between 7:00–7:30 a.m., *Interview Robert van Putten by Jurgen Maas.*

11 Dutch Ministry of Foreign Affairs. File: DPVn02125, dpv-1000/94, May 8, 1994.

slaughter, although the United Nations was fully informed of the disastrous situation in Rwanda. The Human Rights Commissioner Lasso told the Dutch ambassador confidentially on May 13 that the fatalities exceeded 200,000.[12] Although this number may already have been doubled at that moment, the most incomprehensible aspect is that the proposals did not go beyond the regular diplomatic talks. For instance, the discussion focused on the question of whether or not a special human rights commission meeting in Geneva should be held. The argument was made that this would depend on pressure from Africa and on the feared loss of image for the Commission in Geneva. The postponement of decisions to act is most visible in the discussion of who would be sent to the area: a fact finding commission or a rapporteur, being a special rapporteur or a thematic rapporteur.[13] The outcome was a special rapporteur who was to investigate acts of genocide. The following resolution was the meager result of the decisions of the special meeting of the Commission in Geneva:

> Recalling that the killing of members of an ethnic group with the intention of destroying such a group in whole or in part constitutes crime of genocide, believing that genocide acts MAY have occurred in Rwanda. Also request the special rapporteur to gather and compile systematically information on possible violations of human rights and acts which may constitute breaches of international humanitarian law and crimes against humanity, including acts of genocide in Rwanda, and to make this information available to the Secretary General.[14]

At the end of May 1994, the killings could not be straightforwardly classified as genocide, because the British and others refused to accept this qualification at that moment when more than a half million people had been massacred. The outcome of the debates in Geneva was that the interim government of Rwanda—the *genocidaires*—must be told that they were violating international law.[15] In the discussions in New York, any interference was held to be dependent on the cooperation of the parties concerned in the situation at that time.[16] In Brussels, the European Union (EU) refused the request

---

[12] Dutch Ministry of Foreign Affairs. File: 00429 Ddi-DIO, Code: naii076/8584, May 13, 1994.

[13] Dutch Ministry of Foreign Affairs. File: 00429, Ddi-DIO, Codes: gevi314/8688, May 16, 1994, and Gevi322/8903, May 19, 1994, and gevu156/3309, May 24, 1994, and the Instruction to the Permanent Representative in Geneva from the Ministry of Foreign Affairs, subject: Special meeting of the HRC on Rwanda on May 24, 25, 1994.

[14] Dutch Ministry of Foreign Affairs. File: Ddi-dio, 00430, Code: gevi332/9233, May 26, 1994.

[15] Dutch Ministry of Foreign Affairs. File: 00429, Ddi-DIO, Code: naii076/8584, May 13, 1994.

[16] Dutch Ministry of Foreign Affairs. File: 00429, Ddi-DIO, Code: Nyvi474/8793, May 18, 1994.

from Jan Pronk to provide financial support to the African troops, but continued to state, in vague diplomatic language, that they hoped that the OAU would set up peace-keeping operations.[17]

17.3 RWANDA IN THE DUTCH PARLIAMENT

In our search for the role of parliament, we could not find any debates or documents on Rwanda in the period before the genocide and during the first month of the genocide. This means that the issue was given no parliamentary attention whatsoever, neither from members of parliament, who did not ask questions to the government, nor from the government, who did not inform parliament of the situation in Rwanda.

The first document from the government in 1994 on Rwanda was the letter from Pronk on May 24, in which he informed parliament of his trip to Rwanda from May 12–17.[18] He made clear that he was shocked by the total lack of protection for the population in a situation in which half million of people had already been killed, and he also estimated that between 1.5 and 2 million persons had already been displaced. He underlined to the journalists of Dutch newspapers the necessity of sending 8,000 military troops, because the remaining 450 peace-keepers could do little.[19] According to Pronk, the May 17 proposal and decision of the United Nations to send 5,500 troops was not enough. He was emotional and very aware of the systematic character of the mass murder.[20] Under U.N. escort, he visited sites where these mass murders had taken place in a church, a village and the stadium.[21] He upgraded the development aid enormously from 2 million guilders to 15 million guilders.[22] During Pronk's visit to Rwanda a Labor Party member of parliament asked the government to support within the EU (European Political Cooperation, which is the forerunner of the Common Foreign and Security Policy of the EU) a

---

17 Dutch Ministry of Foreign Affairs. File: 00429, Ddi-DIO, Code: brei162/8474, May 11, 1994.

18 Tweede Kamer, 1993–1994, 23727, No. 1.

19 *Algemeen Dagblad* (Dutch Newspaper), May 16, 1994.

20 *Het Parool* (Dutch Newspaper), May 16, 1994.

21 *NRC-Handelsblad* (Dutch Newspaper), May 16, 1994.

22 Since April 7, 7 million and, after his visit, an additional 2 million to the World Food Program, 5 million to direct food aid, 2 million to UNHCR, 0.5 million to UNICEF, 1.5 million to the Tanzanian and the International Red Cross and 4 million to local NGOs in order to remove the dead bodies from the river, for instance. The Dutch fund raising action "Rwanda bloedt" (Rwanda bleeds) also received money from the government. Tweede Kamer, 1993–1994, Appendix, 551 on June 10, 1994. Governmental answer of June 10, 1994.

strengthening of UNAMIR.[23] The Ministers for Foreign Affairs and Defense wrote a letter to parliament on May 30 in which they informed parliament of the mid-May U.N. request for Holland to participate with military police personnel, but the government decided, because of Yugoslavia, that 20 police officers were not available.[24] The request for a movement control unit for the Kigali airport was declined, as well, with the argument that the Dutch look very much like Belgians and so risked becoming victims.[25] The Ministry of Defense refused to be involved in Rwanda other than the evacuation of West-Europeans in the first days, for which Dutch Hercules planes were used with a Belgian crew. Again it is remarkable that the only military action in which the Dutch participated was the rescue of their own nationals.[26]

In the debate in parliament, the Minister of Foreign Affairs revealed that a discussion had taken place within his ministry, but that the outcome was a decision for no involvement in Rwanda because of the risks involved.[27] The Minister of Development Cooperation acknowledged that he should restrict the Dutch role to humanitarian aid. One member of parliament from the Labor Party, Josephine Verspaget, doubted that no *marechaussees* (military policemen) were available. After the genocide, the Netherlands was not prepared to give more support for UNAMIR or have no other involvement in Rwanda. Military activity was discussed by the Prime Minister, Ruud Lubbers, and the Minister of Defense, but the outcome was again negative. The only Dutch contribution was an extra 20 million guilders in aid, particularly for the refugees in Goma.[28] At the end of July, the Ministers of Defense and Foreign Affairs gave parliament an overview of the period since the end of May.[29] At the request of UNHCR and President Clinton, the Netherlands was willing to provide military material to deliver goods to the refugee camps in Zaire. Again a request for participation in UNAMIR was rejected, although abundant equipment could have been sent in August 1994 for use by Zambian soldiers. The members of parliament from the left (PvdA, D66, GroenLinks) and a small Calvinist orthodox party (RPF) were critical of the passive attitude of the government on July 28 both in bilateral relations and in its role as chair of the West European Union.[30] Only the Minister of Development Cooperation recognized that humanitarian

---

23 Tweede Kamer, 1993–1994, Appendix, 551 on June 10, 1994. Parliamentary question of May 16, 1994.

24 Tweede Kamer, 1993–1994, 23727, No. 2.

25 A.J. Klinghoffer, The International dimension of genocide in Rwanda, p. 89 (1998).

26 *Algemeen Dagblad* (Dutch Newspaper), April 11, 1994, and April 28, 1994.

27 Tweede Kamer, 1993–1994, 23727, No. 3.

28 Tweede Kamer, 1993–1994, 23727, No. 5.

29 Tweede Kamer, 1993–1994, 23727, No. 4.

30 Tweede Kamer, 1993–1994, 23727, No. 7. Tweede Kamer, 1993–1994, Appendix, 727 on August 16, 1994.

aid alone was not enough, but he had to abide by the Cabinet decision not to send military troops.[31] Only in his development aid to the World Food Program, was the condition made that the Hutu military received their food in exchange for their arms. As stated earlier, the only Dutch military activity in Rwanda was involvement in the evacuation of Europeans at the start of the genocide, and at the end they supported the medical assistance and food supply with military in Zaire in August and September.[32] As we have seen, the Netherlands was not willing to participate in UNAMIR II at the height of the genocide, although Pronk became aware of the need for such enforced military troops during his visit in May to Rwanda. The Secretary-General declared that it was a shame that he did not succeed in bringing together the needed 5,000 military troops and even, as he said explicitly, that the Netherlands refused to participate.[33] One year later, in 1995, Pronk took part in the ceremony in memory of the genocide in Kigali and he saw a billboard in front with the text "UNAMIR, where were you during the genocide?" It made an impact on Pronk: he made this known in a letter to parliament.[34] Pronk was the only Western leader who was invited to attend this memorial ceremony in 1995—even U.N. leaders were not invited—and Pronk explains his invitation was as a result of the good relationship he had with Kagame, which started at the height of the Genocide in May 1994.[35]

17.4 DUTCH NON-ROLE IN PEACE-KEEPING

With the change of mind of the Secretary-General on May 13, when he asked for a strong mandate with more (5,500) troops, the Netherlands was asked on May 12 and again on May 13 to contribute 20 civilian police (kmar) and 20 persons for a movement control unit (mcu).[36]

The Dutch government decided on Friday, May 20, to refuse any contribution to this peace-keeping force, UNAMIR II. Klinghoffer adds that "the Dutch cabinet decided not to send any peacekeepers to Rwanda as they could

---

31 It was also mentioned in the Dutch press, such as *Het Parool*, July 22 and 23, 1994. In an extra meeting between Pronk, Lubbers, Ter Beek and Koooijmans, it was decided that Dutch military would go to Zaire, although the decision not to participate in UNAMIR was maintained.

32 Tweede Kamer, 1993–1994, 23727, No. 6.

33 *Het Parool* (Dutch Newspaper), May 26, 1994.

34 Tweede Kamer, 1994–1995, 23727, No. 13.

35 Interview with J. Pronk, August 21, 2006.

36 Fax from Annan to permanent representative to the United Nations of the Netherlands, Dutch Ministry of Foreign Affairs, File: DPV, 00214: Codes: Fax No. 370-1954, Fax No. 963-4879 and nyvi457/8564, May 13, 1994, and May 17, 1994, nyv-4262 and May 20, 1994, nyvi494/8986.

be mistaken for Belgians." A request for a Hercules transport plane for personnel and humanitarian goods was also refused.[37] During this meeting in the Cabinet, Pronk was visiting Rwanda. He tried in vain many times to persuade the Ministry of Defense to contribute. He had been interim Minister of Defense a short time before, and he was well aware of the more ambitious plans for new Dutch defense strategy with involvement in many peace-keeping operations. Nonetheless, he was not able to overcome the strong resistance from the Ministry of Defense towards this risky operation in Africa.[38]

Even when the base for the air force was outside Rwanda, the Netherlands refused on May 27.[39] Almost one month later, on June 24, the United Nations once again asked the Netherlands for ten civilian police officers. Without any debate or putting this request on the agenda, the Dutch Minister of Foreign Affairs promptly refused in reference to the first Cabinet decision of May 20, as if nothing had happened since. The Dutch position was explained to the Secretary-General by Relus ter Beek on June 21 with the offer of an F27 plane to deliver medicine near the border of Rwanda, but this was an offer they did not need.[40] On June 28 Kofi Annan, addressing the "non-contributing" countries, could not mention any progress in attracting troops. He made clear one month later that only 500 to 600 men of the 5,500 troops were available at the end of July.[41] At the end of July, after the period of the genocide, the Netherlands was prepared, upon an American request from Deputy Secretary of State Strobe Talbott and asked by the U.S. Ambassador K. Terry Dornbush in The Hague to help to equip and deploy UNAMIR contingents, to deliver superfluous military material to the Zambian soldiers of UNAMIR II.[42] The Netherlands is thus only an example, among 190 other nations, of the overwhelming indifference towards the genocide in Rwanda.

---

37 Dutch Ministry of Foreign Affairs. May 18, 1994, dpv-1000/94 and Memo May 19, 1994, Dpv-1024/94 and Nyvu149/3277, May 20, 1994 and May 21, 1994, nyvi497/9053 and May 27, 1994, nyvu157/3435 and May 27, 1994, nyvi516/9286 and June 25, 1994, nyvi620/10944 and June 27, 1994, nyvu194/4063 and nh-563/94, July 11, 1994.

38 Interview J. Pronk, August 21, 2006.

39 Dutch Ministry of Foreign Affairs. File: DPV, Ara, 02125 Code: D84/290, August 11, 1994.

40 Dutch Ministry of Foreign Affairs. File: DPV, Ara, 02125 Code: June 25, 1994, nyvi620/10944 and June 27, 1994, nyvu194/4063 and File: DPV, Ara, 02125, Code: D84/290, August 11, 1994.

41 Dutch Ministry of Foreign Affairs. File: ARA, 02126, Code: nyvi561/9976 of June 9, 1994, June 29, 1994, nyvi631/11072 and Dutch Ministry of Foreign Affairs File: ARA, 02126, Code: June 29, 1994, nyvi631/11072. Only after an urgent request from the American Ambassador in The Hague, the Dutch government direct offered equipment to the Zambian contingent in UNAMIR on July 29.

42 Dutch Ministry of Foreign Affairs. File: DPV, Ara, 02126 Code: nyvi707/12381 of July 26, 1994, and wasu124/4692 of July 29, 1994.

17.5 PRONK'S VISITS TO RWANDA

The Minister for Development Cooperation, Jan Pronk, was active in the region during the period of genocide. During the month of May, Pronk went to Rwanda and surrounding countries twice to discuss the situation with the different parties. On May 1 he met the leaders of the RPF/RPA. The RPF was furious about the role of the United Nations and, in particular, the roles of Boutros-Ghali and Booh Booh with regard to the SC decisions on the limitation of UNAMIR, denying the genocide and not condemning the Rwandan government for the atrocities.[43] It was the first time Pronk met Paul Kagame, and from then on they developed a relationship of mutual trust.[44] The impressions of Pronk were at that moment that: (1) no party could win the war and (2) the mass slaughter continued. This was confirmed by many sources, for instance, the UNICEF spokesman, who after a visit to Rwanda said, in New York on May 4, this is "the worst of what I have ever seen and much worse than what is in the media about it."[45]

During his second visit (May 12–17) Pronk traveled alone without civil servants in Rwanda. He visited the stadium (containing 4,000 refugees) and the hospital (containing 3,000 refugees) under UNAMIR protection but in dramatically bad circumstances.[46] He was very much impressed and called it ethnic cleansing and supported the idea of a military attack by the United Nations on the hate radio station. This was, however, prohibited by headquarters in New York.[47] The Hutu interim government was blaming the Tutsis for the massacres, but this was not taken seriously by Pronk, the United Nations in Rwanda or surrounding countries, such as Tanzania.[48] Pronk tried to find some solutions in a situation where the RPF distrust of the United Nations was great and, for instance, Kagame refused to talk with Booh Booh.[49] During this visit, Pronk had a meeting with Booh Booh.[50] The RPF was in favor of the use of force for U.N. troops

43 Dutch Ministry of Foreign Affairs. File: DMP/2025 AIM: 01364, 127/1: Code: Minbuza, 16/05/1994, Naii077/8660 en File: DDI-DIO, 0049, Rwanda 1994, Code: Nyvi432/8023, May 2, 1994.

44 Interview with J. Pronk, August 21, 2006.

45 Dutch Ministry of Foreign Affairs. File: DDI-DIO, 0049, Rwanda 1994, Code: Nyvi434/8106, May 4, 1994

46 Dutch Ministry of Foreign Affairs. File: DMP/2025, AIM: 01364, 127/1, Code: Naii081/866, May 16, 1994. Interview with J. Pronk, August 21, 2006.

47 Dutch Ministry of Foreign Affairs. File: DDI-DIO, 0049, Rwanda 1994, Code: May 19, 1994, dari018/8935.

48 Dutch Ministry of Foreign Affairs. File: DMP/2025, AIM: 01364, 127/1, Code: Naii079/8661, May 16, 1994, and Code: May 19, 1994, dari018/8935.

49 Dutch Ministry of Foreign Affairs. File: DMP/2025, AIM: 01364, 127/1, Code: Naii 081/866, May 16, 1994.

50 Interview with J. Pronk, August 21, 2006.

in order to protect the refugees in places such as the stadium or the hotel *Milles Collines*, which was excluded in New York, because it went beyond the fixed mandate of ordinary peace-keepers. The RPF was, however, against a foreign intervention force.[51] Pronk did his best to spur the neighboring African countries into action and instigated a conference at the end of May in Tanzania. Moreover, he was willing to support the African solution financially and thus pleaded with the European Union to pay the OAU military force, a suggestion that was put forward to him by *Medecins sans Frontieres* (Doctors Without Borders) and which was forwarded by him to Brussels on the same day.[52] Brussels however rejected his proposal.[53]

17.6 EFFORTS TO ALLEVIATE THE REFUGEE PROBLEMS IN GOMA

In some way, the discussion within the Dutch Ministry of Foreign Affairs with regard to Operation Turquoise, a military enforcement action with the authorization of the Security Council of the United Nations under Chapter VII (Resolution 929, June 22, 1994), is interesting because it reveals the traditional Dutch-French antagonistic relationship in which the Dutch prefer to align themselves, in particular, with the United States, whereas France prefers an independent European role in world affairs.

The embassy in Nairobi stated that the French arguments for this military operation, precluding protection of the Tutsis in this genocide, were at least "bizarre,"[54] whereas the embassy in Dar es Salaam brought the message that French mercenaries fought on the side of the Rwandan army against the Tutsis.[55] The Netherlands Minister for Development Cooperation, Jan Pronk, mistrusted the French motivation for this military operation. They had their own political reasons to interfere at that moment, but, on the other hand, people needed to be saved, and that is why he had an ambivalent attitude. The Interahamwe had a dominant position in many camps in Goma, which was

---

51 Dutch Ministry of Foreign Affairs. File: DMP/2025, AIM: 01364, 127/1, Code Minbuza, May 16, 1994, Naii077/8660.

52 Dutch Ministry of Foreign Affairs. File: DDI-DIO, 0049, Code: Fm hag coreu, ref. pesc/com 180, April 27 and a Memo of a meeting of the Dutch Minister of Development Aid, Mr. Pronk with Mr. Empelen and Mr. Pieters of Doctors without Borders on April 27, 1994.

53 Dutch Ministry of Foreign Affairs. File: Map: DPV, 00214: Codes: Fax No. 370-1954, Fax. No. 963-4879 and nyvi457/8564 May 13, 1994, and May 17, 1994, nyv-4262 and May 20, 1994, nyvi494/8986.

54 Dutch Ministry of Foreign Affairs. File: Map: DAM, ARA, 00540Code: June 20, 1994, naii098/10599.

55 Dutch Ministry of Foreign Affairs. File: DpV, ARA, 02126, Code: June 22, 1994, dari025/10739.

seen by Kagame as a breeding place for his adversaries. An attack on these camps by the RPF/RPA was to be foreseen, and thus protection was needed.[56] The Dutch Prime Minister wrote to parliament that he welcomed the French military action, which saved many lives and which was in accordance with Security Council Resolution 929.[57]

The information from the embassy in Washington was that because the RPF was not against any humanitarian operation as long as the humanitarian operation would not enter the territory of Kigali, the United States would not vote in the Security Council against Resolution 929. The French supported the Hutu party, while the United States was more in favor of the Tutsis, which was reflected in their positions with regard to Operation Turquoise. Moreover, the French preferred to resort to this multilateral military operation under the aegis of the Western European Union (WEU).[58] The strengthening of this military branch of the European Union is a long-standing wish of the French. The Netherlands has been more in favor of a stronger NATO than a stronger WEU, but this Atlantic preference is stronger in the Ministry of Defense than in the Ministry of Foreign Affairs.[59] Some pressure within the Ministry of Foreign Affairs—in particular the political division on Africa and the Middle East—was therefore made encouraging participation in Operation Turquoise. It was also this division that was directly addressed by the French Ambassador in The Hague to participate.[60]

The government did not support any joint action by the EU that would be implemented by the WEU. However, the arguments in favor of the WEU and to improving bilateral relations with France were always bracketed together.[61] Therefore, although the Netherlands had held the chair of the WEU since July 1, 1994, no remarkable activity from the Netherlands in this forum could have been observed.

---

[56] Interview with J. Pronk, August 21, 2006.

[57] Tweede Kamer, 1993–1994, Appendix, 719, pp.1457–1458 on August 12, 2004.

[58] Information from Bonn and officially proposed on June 15 at the WEU meeting; see Dutch Ministry of Foreign Affaires. File: DAM, ARA, 00540, Code: ER, June 24–25, 1994, DAM/CN-m.l.

[59] In a confidential message from Brussels it is mentioned that the division with regard to participation in Turquoise was between the pro Christian Democratic (CVP) Minister of Defense and the anti-Socialist (SP) Minister of Foreign Affairs. See Ministry of Foreign Affaires. File: DAM, ARA, 00540, Code: May 7, 1994, brui081/11374. The latter, Willy Claes, became Secretary-General of NATO shortly afterwards.

[60] Dutch Ministry of Foreign Affairs. File: DAM, ARA, 00540, Memo, 113/94, July 4, 1994.

[61] Dutch Ministry of Foreign Affairs. File: DAM, ARA, 00540, Code: From Minister Foreign Affairs to department DGPZm, June 23, 1994.

CHAPTER 18

APOLOGIES FROM BYSTANDERS TEN YEARS LATER

In the period before and during the genocide, little attention was paid to the situation in Rwanda. It is remarkable that ten years later the attention was enormous, and it was almost unanimously accepted that states and international organizations failed tremendously by not acting to prevent or stop that genocide. Not only scholars, but political leaders all over the world now realized what happened and how the role they played as bystanders was miserable. By not acting and even withholding all instruments to stop or diminish the ongoing atrocities, the bystander states and bystander international organizations contributed to the killings by allowing the *genocidaires* to go on. In this chapter we will deal with this remorse and the subsequent apologies that were made by the leaders of some of these states and organizations. Moreover, we will pay attention to the more concrete lessons learned from the Rwandan tragedy.

18.1 APOLOGIES FROM BELGIUM

The Belgian Prime Minister, Guy Verhofstadt, made a speech on April 7, 2004, in the stadium of Kigali. Verhofstadt of the Liberal Party—which was not represented in the Belgian government in 1994—was the head of the parliamentary inquiry commission and made his excuses in public.[1] The Belgian delegation also consisted of the Ministers of Foreign Affairs (Louis Michel), Defense (André Flahaut) and Development Cooperation (Marc Verwilghen).[2] Verhofstadt was clear on his feelings in his speech: "I am moved because I can gauge the infinite sadness that your memories must still evoke. The memory of such an abominable tragedy cannot help but revive horrifying images. No words, no discussion, nothing can describe this sorrow."[3] He did not forget to

1 "Pour demander pardon au nom de mon pays;" see http://www.diplomatie.be/nl/press/speechdetails.asp?TEXTID=17615.

2 *Het Volk* (Belgian Newspaper), April 6, 2004.

3 See http://www.diplomatie.be/nl/press/speechdetails.asp?TEXTID=17615. Translated from French into English. Original text: "Je suis ému parce que je mesure bien l'infinie tristesse que vos souvenirs doivent encore réveiller. Le souvenir d'un drame aussi abominable ne peut que ramener des images horrifiées. Aucun mot, aucune parole, rien ne peut décrire cette douleur là."

mention the killed Belgian blue helmets: "The memory of our assassinated compatriots is intimately mixed in with the memory of the Rwandans who they tried in vain to protect. From now on all of these deaths are also and will always be our compatriots."[4]

He focused very strongly on his own responsibility, not just in a general way, because everyone is responsible, but stressed the failing: "We have all failed in our task, some because they didn't do enough, others because they remained indifferent. We also failed ourselves. We failed because rather than staying to assume our responsibility, we preferred to ignore the horror and the atrocity. We failed in our most elementary duty, the duty to intervene and the duty of fraternity."[5] It is important that he referred in these words to the indifference, which is characteristic of the bystander who does not act and does not want to act and therefore prefers not to know what is happening.[6] Indeed Verhofstadt was right when he said that the bystander prefers not to know but really is aware of everything that happens, and thus the bystander cannot pretend to be ignorant. Moreover, in this quotation, he is making "the duty to intervene" an international norm in these circumstances, a norm that legally did not exist but that is increasingly emerging in a moral sense. This norm may, as a result, be seen nowadays as an emerging norm of international law as well, as has been proposed by the international panel group some years later.[7]

18.2 APOLOGIES FROM THE UNITED STATES

The speech of President Bill Clinton was given four years after the genocide in 1998. It is seen as a statement of public remorse and "something of an apology," with the following words: "We in the United States and the world community did not do as much as we could have and should have done to try to limit what occurred."[8] On his own role, he said at the airport in Kigali: "All

---

4 *Id.* Translated from French into English. Original text: "Le souvenir de nos compatriotes assassinés se mêle intimement au souvenir des Rwandais qu'ils ont vainement essayé de protéger. Désormais tous ces morts-là aussi sont et pour toujours nos compatriots."

5 *Id.* Translated from French into English. Original text: "Tous, nous avons failli à notre tâche, les uns parce qu'ils n'ont pas fait assez, les autres parce qu'ils sont restés indifférents. Nous, nous avons échoué aussi. Nous avons échoué parce que plutôt que de rester pour assumer notre responsabilité, nous avons préféré ignorer l'horreur et l'atrocité. Nous avons failli à notre devoir le plus élémentaire, le devoir d'ingérence et de fraternité."

6 *Id.* Later in this speech, he repeated this rejection of an indifferent attitude: "Plus que jamais, nous plaidons pour l'abandon de l'indifférence, pour que cesse la diplomatie du silence."

7 See Section 18.7.

8 Samantha Power, A Problem from Hell: America and the Age of Genocide, p. 386 (2002).

over the world there were people like me sitting in offices who did not fully appreciate the depth and the speed with which you were being engulfed by this unimaginable terror."[9]

In hindsight, the American decisionmakers that were interviewed for this study underline that they never discussed and even never thought of the possibility of linking the evacuation force with a possible military force to halt the atrocities in Rwanda. Prudence Bushnell was convinced at the time that there was no way that the United States would send American troops for this purpose, and that is why it was not spoken of.[10] John Shattuck agrees and says that he does not remember the attachment of this evacuation force to UNAMIR ever having been an option. He now acknowledges that this is the best example of what could have been done to save lives.[11] Anthony Lake cannot find any memos or records of decision-making meetings he had with the President on the force in Rwanda. It was not discussed, and although he may not have been able to persuade Congress to support an intervention, afterwards he seems to have wished that he had at least tried. In his own words: "The point is that there should have been high-level decisions and there were not. This is not a case of an error of commission but of omission."[12] The silence was most remarkable. Kofi Annan, from his U.N. perspective, agrees with this view in hindsight, when he describes the Rwandan genocide to the BBC as a "sin of omission" ten years later.[13]

18.3 APOLOGIES FROM FRANCE

The French role has been increasingly seen as one of collaboration with the perpetrators rather than with the rescuers of the victims. The continuing support for the Habyarimana government against the RPF in the years before the genocide is no longer evaluated as support to stabilize the situation in Rwanda. Operation Turquoise, a military enforcement action with the authorization of the Security Council of the United Nations under Chapter VII, is no longer seen as just a protection force for the refugees who had to flee. This operation helped many Hutu militias to escape. During the genocide, France did not undertake any action to stop the atrocities or to strengthen UNAMIR. Moreover, France delivered weapons to one party even after the Arusha Agreement was made in order, to quote the French Ambassador in Rwanda, "to

---

9 Http://www.cnn.com/WORLD/9803/25/rwanda.clinton/.

10 Frontline interview with Bushnell, September 30, 2003.

11 Frontline interview with Shattuck, December 16, 2003.

12 Frontline interview with Lake, December 15, 2003.

13 Alex J. Bellamy, Reponsibility to Protect or Trojan Horse? The Crisis in Darfur and Humanitarian Intervention after Iraq, Ethics & International Affairs, 19 (2), 2005, p. 31, from BBC News World Edition, March 26, 2004, *available at* http://news.bbc.co.uk/1/hi/world/africa/3573229.stm.

prevent escalation of the situation."[14] The French parliamentary report criticizes this policy by stating that France was no longer supporting stability but, in training the army, training the militia as well, bearing in mind they were aware of the close links between the extremist elements—such as "reseau zero"—and Habyarimana. The parliamentary report concludes that France failed to appreciate the changing nature of the role of the army and other official bodies. The report perhaps gives the French governmental policy the benefit of the doubt, because we have observed in this study that France was very well aware of the changing situation in Rwanda but nevertheless did not change its policy. Patrick May accuses France not of helping the *genocidaires*—an accusation that was explicitly denied in the parliamentary report[15]—but of supporting those who orchestrated the genocide. Moreover, because of its position close to Habyarimana, France was in the best position to change the policy of Habyarimana and to prevent the genocide.[16] However, the French did not prevent nor stop the genocide. In the French documentary "Tuez les Tous" it is stated: "Defending French influence in Africa will have guided the actions of Paris throughout. The genocide and the need to halt it were never the priorities of the French state."[17] This fits well in our definition that afterwards a bystander will be evaluated as a collaborator if he, as the third party, will not act or will not attempt to act in solidarity with the victims.[18]

It is obvious that France was not welcome to attend the memorial ceremonies in 2004. In France a public debate on its role before and during the genocide is still going on. We will give some examples. In March 2004, the French examining magistrate Jean-Luis Bruguière made it public that the RPF leader and now President of Rwanda, Paul Kagame, was the person who ordered the shooting down of the plane on April 6, 1994. The plane crash was the trigger event for the genocide, and the RPF were hence given a role that was no longer the rescuer of the Tutsi victims but as the party that caused the atrocities. Even if the conclusion of the judge, whose report was based merely on witnesses from Rwandese outside the country, was correct, it not only confused cause and trigger but also tried to reverse the roles of victim and perpetrator.[19]

---

14 Assemblée Nationale du France, Rapport d'information, Mission d'information sur le Rwanda, No. 1271, le 15 décembre 1998, p. 357 ("de ne pas laisser déstabiliser le Rwanda").

15 *Id.*, pp. 368–371 under the sub title: "The absence of links with the militia" (L'absence des liens avec les milices).

16 Patrick May, Ce qui a manqué à l'opération "Turquoise," *Le Monde*, January 13, 2006 (What is missing in the operation "Turquoise").

17 Michel Hazanavicius and Arnaud Borges, Tuez les Tous (Kill them All), History of a genocide, A movie of Raphael Glucksmann, David Hazan, Pierre Mezerette, Production Dum Dum Films, Paris 2004.

18 See Section 1.2.

19 NRC, Le Monde onthult Frans onderzoek: President Rwanda doodde voorganger (Le Monde reveals French research: the President of Rwanda killed predeces-

In December 2005 and January 2006 the debate was revived in the French daily, *Le Monde*, after the book from Pierre Péan was published, in which he repeats the conclusion of Bruguière with regard to the attack on the plane. At the end of November 2006 the French examining magistrate, Bruguière, repeated his opinion that Kagame himself ordered the shooting down of the plane, and so he was responsible for killing Habyarimana. As a head of state, Kagame has immunity with regard to French criminal law, and so Bruguière advised prosecution of Kagame by the International Tribunal for Rwanda in Arusha. An anti-French demonstration of 25,000 people took place on November 24, 2006, in Kigali, and the Rwandese government called back their ambassador from Paris, whereas the French ambassador in Kigali and his diplomatic staff was expelled from the country immediately.[20] The book of Péan was described as being a revisionist study in order to defend the French role and was characterized as African colonialism.[21] Péan argues that the aim of Operation Turquoise was to save civilians, whereas Collette Braeckman asks him, in response, why France did then not send trucks, ambulances and nurses but military planes, helicopters and commander troops.[22] Moreover, in December 2005 France was accused of complicity with the genocide and crimes against humanity in Rwanda at a military tribunal in Paris because of its conduct during Operation Turquoise. The witness Auréa Mukakalisa stated in court: "Hutu militia entered the camp and pointed to Tutsi's who were forced by the French military to leave the camp. Outside the camp the Tutsi's were killed by the militia . . . I have seen French soldier who killed soldiers with big shining knives."[23]

The French commander of Operation Turquoise, General Jean-Claude Lafourcade, defends the military enforcement action, because it saved ten thousand lives by stopping the massacres and preventing cholera, by burying thousands of cadavers and protecting Hutu displaced persons in safe zones in

---

sor), March 10, 2004; NRC, Een explosief Rwanda-rapport, March 11, 2004 (An explosive Rwanda report).

20 NRC-Handelsblad, November 25, 2006, "Diplomatieke rel Rwanda-Frankrijk" (Diplomatic clash Rwanda-France).

21 Jean-Pierre Chrétien, Un pamphlet teinté d'africanisme colonial, *Le Monde*, December 9, 2005 (A pamphlet colored by African colonialism); (Pierre Péan, Noires fureurs, blancs menteurs (Angered black people, lying white people), ed. Mille et une nuits, 2005). In *Le Monde*, January 13, 2006, Pierre Péan (Une lettre de Pierre Péan) reacts on this criticism.

22 Colette Braeckman, Rwanda, l'enquête inachevée, *Le Monde*, December 9, 2005 (The incomplete research).

23 Deux rescapés accusent la France de complicité de génocide au Rwanda, *Le Monde*, December 25–26, 2005 (original text of the quote is: "des miliciens hutus entraient dans le camp et désignaient des tutsis que les militaires français obligeaient à sortir du camp. J'ai vu les miliciens tuer les Tutsis qui étaient sortis du camp. Je dis, et c'est la vérité, avoir vu des militaires français tuer eux-mêmes des Tutsis en utilisant des couteaux brillants d'une grande dimension.")

Rwanda.[24] In response, Patrick May underlines that France intervened at the moment the Tutsi won the war, and France had nothing done during the genocide but had voted, for instance, in favor of withdrawing UNAMIR on April 21, 1994. In his view, France should have vetoed Security Council Resolution 912, and Operation Turquoise should have started at the end of April instead of the end of June.[25]

18.4 APOLOGIES FROM THE EUROPEAN UNION

The European Union delivered a statement from the presidency on April 8, 2004, under the title "NEVER AGAIN."[26] It was not a very outspoken statement but more in general terms, such as:

> The lessons of the genocide in Rwanda must never be forgotten. This fact will continue to inspire and motivate the European Union as it works, both through its own instruments and with its international partners, for improved collective action in the areas of conflict prevention, early warning and defense of human rights. Continuing human rights abuses and humanitarian crises across the world need our concerted attention.[27]

The role of the failing bystander during the genocide in Rwanda was addressed with the following words:

> It is clear that tragic mistakes were made by the international community before and during the genocide. The international community's response to the genocide came too late and proved insufficient. The challenge to never again fail to prevent such horrors lies at the heart of the European Union's policy. The European Union is ambitious in its objective to avoid the recurrence of genocide anywhere in the world, yet humble in knowing that whatever it does, it may not be enough.[28]

There is no deep regret, however, for the role of the European Union itself during the genocide but only the very vague reference to the so-called "interna-

---

24 Jean-Claude Lafourcade, L'honneur des soldats de l'opération "Turquoise," *Le Monde*, January 5, 2006 (The honor of the soldiers of Operation "Turquoise").

25 Patrick May, Ce qui a manqué à l'opération "Turquoise," *Le Monde*, January 13, 2006.

26 European Commission, Press Releases P/04/45, 8219/1/04 (Presse 102) See http://europa.eu.int/rapid/pressReleasesAction.do?reference=PESC/04/45&format=HTML&aged=1&language=EN&guiLanguage=en.

27 *Id.*

28 *Id.*

tional community." The European Union will nevertheless support the U.N. proposals:

> The EU welcomes the decision by the U.N. Secretary-General to appoint a Special Advisor on the Prevention of Genocide. The EU will support the Special Advisor, and will make full use of the advice and information generated. The European Union itself is also increasing its work to prevent genocide, through its program on the prevention of armed conflict, its support to the International Criminal Court, its development co-operation, its commitment to human rights, as well as by other means. The EU has also been working hard to take on board the lessons deriving from the experience of the 1994 genocide, through improving its capacities to react quickly to crisis situations.[29]

At this point, the EU proudly refers to its action—Operation Artemis—in Summer 2003 in Ituri in the Democratic Republic of Congo (DRC), which is "considered the first case where the European Union effectively helped to prevent acts of genocide taking place. The European Union will continue its efforts to improve its capacities in the area of early warning and conflict prevention."[30] The EU was asked by Kofi Annan to take action in the situation when the situation in Ituri got out of hand. Annan feared at that moment a repetition of the genocide in Rwanda. He did his best to prevent this and pleaded for an operation under a European flag in a combined EU-U.N. operation. France, as has been shown in this study, was persona non grata in Rwanda and, therefore, the EU participation was needed instead of a French operation in cooperation with the United Nations. Some lessons were learned by the EU, but no explicit reference is, however, made in the EU statements on its own role in 1994 or on the roles of its member states.

18.5 APOLOGIES FROM THE AFRICAN UNION

In a report consisting of 293 pages, the inquiry commission of the African Union (AU) reported on their investigations on the role of the Organization of African Unity (OAU) during the genocide in Rwanda.[31] Although its Secretary-

---

29 *Id.*

30 *Id.*

31 Organization of African Unity, The Preventable Genocide of the International Panel of Eminent Personalities to Investigate the 1994 Genocide in Rwanda and Surrounding Events (2000) (hereinafter OAU Report). In 2002 the African Union replaced the Organization of African Unity. See http://www.visiontv.ca/RememberRwanda/Report.pdf.

General, Salim Ahmed Salim, condemned the killings of the Prime Minister and the peace-keepers in Rwanda and tried to prevent the withdrawal of UNAMIR, the AU was not able to have a similar common policy from African countries in the Security Council.[32] In addition, Nigeria and Djibouti, for instance, voted in favor of the reduction of the troops to 270 men in Resolution 912. We quote the following clear paragraph to illustrate its critical attitude towards the OAU:[33]

> But the OAU's reluctance to take sides in the Rwandan conflict continued to result in practices that this Panel finds unacceptable. It was bad enough that the genocide was never condemned outright. But this failure was seriously compounded at the regular Summit meeting of OAU Heads of State in Tunis in June, where the delegation of the genocidaire government under interim President Sindikubwabo was welcomed and treated as a full and equal member of the OAU, ostensibly representing and speaking for Rwandan citizens. If it was intolerable, as so many have angrily said, for this government to be allowed to keep its temporary seat on the Security Council in New York throughout the genocide, and for its ministers to be welcomed at the French presidential palace, how much more offensive for it to have been treated at Tunis with the same respect and the full paraphernalia of protocol as other legitimate African governments?

A very touching conclusion was made at the end of the report:

> There are reasons why Africa has been marginalized, why the world is indifferent, why there seems to be a double standard when it comes to Africa. Events in recent years make inescapable the conclusion that an implicit racism is at work here, a sense that African lives are not valued as highly as other lives. Nowhere was this demonstrated more flagrantly than when UNAMIR was instructed by New York in the first days of the genocide to give priority to helping expatriates flee Rwanda, and if necessary to go beyond its narrow mandate to achieve this end.[34]

For the future, the African Inquiry Commission acknowledged that the energy invested in conflict resolution initiatives in the past decade illustrates that this lesson from the genocide in Rwanda is being learned.[35]

---

32 *Id.*, 15.89 and 15.90.

33 *Id.*, 15.92.

34 *Id.*, 21.15.

35 *Id.*, 21.16.

18.6 APOLOGIES FROM THE UNITED NATIONS

The Secretary-General of the United Nations, Kofi Annan, also held a speech on April 7, 2004. He made his speech to the Commission on Human Rights at a special meeting to observe the International Day of Reflection on the 1994 Genocide in Rwanda in Geneva. It was a strong speech in which he apologized frankly for the U.N. role, which includes his personal role at DPKO in New York, ten years ago. He said:

> First, we must all acknowledge our responsibility for not having done more to prevent or stop the genocide. Neither the United Nations Secretariat, nor the Security Council, nor member states in general, nor the international media, paid enough attention to the gathering signs of disaster. Still less did we take timely action. . . . No one can claim ignorance. All who were playing any part in world affairs at that time should ask, what more could I have done? How would I react next time—and what am I doing now to make it less likely there will be a next time?[36]

He acknowledged that there was enough information to act and he did not deny that there were early warnings. He openly underlined that the United Nations should have done more to prevent or stop the genocide. No timely action was taken, although that was possible. Moreover, he not only reflected on the past but also made a plan in his speech in order to be better equipped to react in future. In his own words: "The only fitting memorial the United Nations can offer to those whom its inaction in 1994 condemned to die, and as recommended in 1999 by the Independent Inquiry into the actions of the United Nations during the genocide in Rwanda, I wish today to launch an Action Plan to Prevent Genocide, involving the whole United Nations system."[37] The first three points of his plan are rather general, and they encompass the orientation to prevent armed conflict (in addressing the roots of violence and genocide by strengthening local and regional capacities to prevent), to protect civilians in armed conflict (when prevention has failed by, for example, empowering peacekeepers whose mandate may include the protection of civilians), to end impunity to the *genocidaires* (in the Tribunals and International Criminal Court).

---

[36] Http://www2.unog.ch/news2/documents/newsen/sg04003e.htm, p.1; see also www.un.org/events/rwanda.

[37] *Id.*, p. 2.

18.6.1 Early and Clear Warning

The fourth point of Annan's plan is particularly important as a lesson from the failures we have addressed in this book. This point refers to early and clear warning. Annan said:

> One of the reasons for our failure in Rwanda was that beforehand we did not face the fact that genocide was a real possibility. And once it started, for too long we could not bring ourselves to recognize it, or call it by its name. If we are serious about preventing or stopping genocide in future, we must not be held back by legalistic arguments about whether a particular atrocity meets the definition of genocide or not. By the time we are certain, it may often be too late to act. We must recognize the signs of approaching or possible genocide, so that we can act in time to avert it.[38]

In this book, we have elaborated extensively on the top-level U.N. lack of perception of all early warnings as warnings for genocide, worrying only that the Arusha peace process was not being smoothly implemented. In all organs of the United Nations, the early warnings were not taken seriously, although the U.N. human rights system should have a special responsibility. Indeed Annan reminded the members of the Human Rights Commission that "your Special Rapporteur on Extrajudicial Killings described many warning signs in Rwanda the year before the genocide happened. Alas, no one paid attention."[39] He stated he would appoint someone in the new post of "Special Adviser on the Prevention of Genocide" who will report through the Secretary-General to the Security Council (as an early warning mechanism to them and to make recommendations on actions to prevent or halt genocide), the General Assembly and the Commission on Human Rights. The relationship of this post with the Security Council is particularly important, making the linkage between the two fields of U.N. concern—peace and security and human rights—stronger than before.

The fifth point of his plan is on "the need for swift and decisive action when, despite all our efforts, we learn that genocide is happening, or about to happen. Too often, even when there is abundant warning, we lack the political will to act."[40] Such a decisive action might be an enforcement action with the use of force. He asked for guidelines on when to act in order to "ensure that we have no excuse to ignore a real danger of genocide when it does arise. They would also provide greater clarity, and thus help to reduce the suspicion that allegations of genocide might be used as a pretext for aggression."[41] This pro-

38 *Id.*, pp. 3–4.

39 *Id.*, p. 4; see also Section 6.4.

40 *Id.*, p. 4.

41 *Id.*, p. 5.

posals made to the United Nations will be dealt with in the following section. At the end of his speech, he stressed again the need for prevention with the message: "Let us not wait until the only alternatives to military action are futile hand-wringing or callous indifference. Let us, Mr. Chairman, be serious about preventing genocide. Only so can we honor the victims whom we remember today. Only so can we save those who might be victims tomorrow."[42]

18.7 LESSONS LEARNED AT U.N. SUMMIT 2005

The responsibility to protect was put forward in 2001 by the International Commission on Intervention and State Sovereignty (ICISS).[43] They preferred to replace the concept of humanitarian intervention with the concept of responsibility to protect, which includes three stages: the responsibility to prevent, to act and to rebuild. They encompass in this the involvement of third parties before, during and after the atrocities take place. An important difference with the concept of humanitarian intervention is the change in focus: from the intervening state and the decision-making process in the intervening state towards the situation in the target country—where the intervention will take place. It is the latter that should be decisive for the intervening state to act, and more responsibility is placed on the third state in all stages, not only at the moment that the atrocities are already going on. Prevention is now much more heavily emphasized in the responsibility to protect than was the case with concept of humanitarian intervention. Alex Bellamy formulated this other approach as follows:

> Viewing humanitarian intervention as part of a wider set of relations raises important issues for the way that intervention relates to both conflict prevention and post-conflict rebuilding. In short, the idea that intervention is not a discrete act means that attempts to legitimize armed intervention on humanitarian grounds must go hand in hand with concerted efforts at conflict prevention and post-conflict rebuilding.[44]

In particular, the replacement of "the right of humanitarian intervention" with the new language of "responsibility to protect" is a victim-oriented approach. Moreover, the ICISS stated that the primary responsibility to protect civilians lies within the host state and that outside intervention is only possible "if the

---

42 *Id.*

43 The Responsibility to Protect, Report of the International Commission on Intervention and State Sovereignty (ICISS), Co-chairs Gareth Evans and Mohamed Sahnoun, Ottawa, December 2001, see http://www.iciss-ciise.gc.ca.

44 Alex J. Bellamy, Humanitarian Responsibilities and Interventionist Claims in International Society, Review of International Studies 29, pp. 321–340, p. 331 (2003).

state is unable or unwilling to fulfill this responsibility, or is itself the perpetrator."[45] The words "unable or unwilling" are very important, and they were repeated in the following report of the High Level Panel (2004), in paragraph 201. However, the outcome of the Summit Meeting (2005) was the replacement of these words with "manifest failure," with which they were raising the threshold to act and thus weakening the original idea. In paragraph 139, this was watered down all in the following formulation:

> We are prepared to take collective action, in a timely and decisive manner, through the Security Council, in accordance with the Charter, including Chapter VII, on a case-by-case basis and in cooperation with relevant regional organizations as appropriate, should peaceful means be inadequate and national authorities are manifestly failing to protect their populations from genocide, war crimes, ethnic cleansing and crimes against humanity.

Moreover, where, in previous proposals, the wording was "we recognize our shared responsibility," there is now merely the words "we are prepared." Bellamy concludes: "Thus, Annan's proposal that the international community had an "obligation" to take measures when the threshold was crossed, was rewritten as a "responsibility" to do so."[46]

In his speech of December 23, 2003, Kofi Annan spoke of the need "to begin a discussion on the criteria for an early authorization of coercive measures to address certain types of threats" and "to engage in serious discussions of the best way to respond to threats of genocide or other comparable massive violations of human rights."[47] Subsequently he installed an international advisory committee to the United Nations. They wrote: "A more Secure World: Our shared responsibility, Report of the High-level Panel on Threats, Challenges and Change."[48] We will now refer to the main relevant points that are put under the heading: "Chapter VII of the Charter of the United Nations, internal threats and the responsibility to protect." This is the most elaborated reaction to the atrocities in the past and the proposed lessons to be learned by the United Nations:

---

45 See ICISS report, p. 17.

46 Alex J. Bellamy, Whither the Responsibility to Protect? Humanitarian Intervention and the 2005 World Summit, Ethics & International Affairs, 20(2), pp. 143–169, and 165–166 (2006).

47 The Secretary-General Address to the General Assembly, New York, September 23, 2003.

48 U.N. Doc. A/59/565; A more Secure World: Our shared responsibility. Report of the High-level Panel on Threats, Challenges and Change; December 2, 2004. See http://www.un.org/secureworld/.

199. The Charter of the United Nations is not as clear as it could be when it comes to saving lives within countries in situations of mass atrocity. It "reaffirm(s) faith in fundamental human rights" but does not do much to protect them, and Article 2.7 prohibits intervention "in matters which are essentially within the jurisdiction of any state." There has been, as a result, a long-standing argument in the international community between those who insist on a "right to intervene" in man-made catastrophes and those who argue that the Security Council, for all its powers under Chapter VII to "maintain or restore international security," is prohibited from authorizing any coercive action against sovereign states for whatever happens within their borders.

200. Under the Convention on the Prevention and Punishment of the Crime of Genocide (Genocide Convention), states have agreed that genocide, whether committed in time of peace or in time of war, is a crime under international law which they undertake to prevent and punish. Since then it has been understood that genocide anywhere is a threat to the security of all and should never be tolerated. The principle of non-intervention in internal affairs cannot be used to protect genocidal acts or other atrocities, such as large-scale violations of international humanitarian law or large-scale ethnic cleansing, which can properly be considered a threat to international security and as such provoke action by the Security Council.

201. The successive humanitarian disasters in Somalia, Bosnia and Herzegovina, Rwanda, Kosovo and now Darfur, Sudan, have concentrated attention not on the immunities of sovereign Governments but their responsibilities, both to their own people and to the wider international community. There is a growing recognition that the issue is not the "right to intervene" of any state, but the "responsibility to protect" of *every* state when it comes to people suffering from avoidable catastrophe—mass murder and rape, ethnic cleansing by forcible expulsion and terror, and deliberate starvation and exposure to disease. And there is a growing acceptance that while sovereign Governments have the primary responsibility to protect their own citizens from such catastrophes, when they are unable or unwilling to do so that responsibility should be taken up by the wider international community—with it spanning a continuum involving prevention, response to violence, if necessary, and rebuilding shattered societies. The primary focus should be on assisting the cessation of violence through mediation and other tools and the protection of people through such measures as the dispatch of humanitarian, human rights and police missions. Force, if it needs to be used, should be deployed as a last resort.

202. The Security Council so far has been neither very consistent nor very effective in dealing with these cases, very often acting too late,

> too hesitantly or not at all. But step by step, the Council and the wider international community have come to accept that, under Chapter VII and in pursuit of the emerging norm of a collective international responsibility to protect, it can always authorize military action to redress catastrophic internal wrongs if it is prepared to declare that the situation is a "threat to international peace and security," not especially difficult when breaches of international law are involved.
>
> 203. We endorse the emerging norm that there is a collective international responsibility to protect, exercisable by the Security Council authorizing military intervention as a last resort, in the event of genocide and other large scale killing, ethnic cleansing or serious violations of international humanitarian law which sovereign Governments have proved powerless or unwilling to prevent.[49]

This advisory report formed the basis for the proposals of the Secretary-General, Kofi Annan in his report of 2005: "In larger Freedom: Towards development, security and human rights for all."[50] He starts with the observation that the member states disagree whether they have the right—or perhaps the obligation—to use force protectively to rescue the citizens of other states from genocide or comparable crimes.[51] Then he states:

> Where threats are not imminent but latent, the Charter gives full authority to the Security Council to use military force, including preventively, to preserve international peace and security. As to genocide, ethnic cleansing and other such crimes against humanity, are they not also threats to international peace and security, against which humanity should be able to look to the Security Council for protection?[52]

In putting the question in this way, he is responding to it in the affirmative. He furthermore proposes the formulation of criteria that can be used in the decisionmaking in future in concrete cases:

> The task is not to find alternatives to the Security Council as a source of authority but to make it work better. When considering whether to authorize or endorse the use of military force, the Council should come to a common view on how to weigh the seriousness of the threat; the proper purpose of the proposed military action; whether means short

49 *Id.*, Nos. 199-203, pp. 56–57.

50 U.N. Doc. A/59/2005; In Larger Freedom: Towards development, security and human rights for all. Report of the Secretary-General, March 21, 2005. See http://www.un.org/largerfreedom/.

51 *Id.*, No. 122.

52 *Id.*, No. 125.

> of the use of force might plausibly succeed in stopping the threat; whether the military option is proportional to the threat at hand; and whether there is a reasonable chance of success. By undertaking to make the case for military action in this way, the Council would add transparency to its deliberations and make its decisions more likely to be respected, by both Governments and world public opinion. I therefore recommend that the Security Council adopt a resolution setting out these principles and expressing its intention to be guided by them when deciding whether to authorize or mandate the use of force.[53]

This proposal from Annan was more fully adopted by world leaders at the summit of 2005 than many other proposals for reform. The final outcome from this World Summit of September 2005 is put under the heading "Responsibility to protect populations from genocide, war crimes, ethnic cleansing and crimes against humanity:"[54]

> 138. Each individual state has the responsibility to protect its populations from genocide, war crimes, ethnic cleansing and crimes against humanity. This responsibility entails the prevention of such crimes, including their incitement, through appropriate and necessary means. We accept that responsibility and will act in accordance with it. The international community should, as appropriate, encourage and help states to exercise this responsibility and support the United Nations in establishing an early warning capability.
>
> 139. The international community, through the United Nations, also has the responsibility to use appropriate diplomatic, humanitarian and other peaceful means, in accordance with Chapters VI and VIII of the Charter, to help to protect populations from genocide, war crimes, ethnic cleansing and crimes against humanity. In this context, we are prepared to take collective action, in a timely and decisive manner, through the Security Council, in accordance with the Charter, including Chapter VII, on a case-by-case basis and in cooperation with relevant regional organizations as appropriate, should peaceful means be inadequate and national authorities are manifestly failing to protect their populations from genocide, war crimes, ethnic cleansing and crimes against humanity. We stress the need for the General Assembly to continue consideration of the responsibility to protect populations from genocide, war crimes, ethnic cleansing and crimes against humanity and its implica-

---

[53] *Id.*, No. 126.

[54] U.N. Doc. A/RES/60/1; Resolution adopted by the General Assembly 60/1. 2005 World Summit Outcome. October 24, 2005. See http://www.un.org/Depts/dhl/resguide/r60.htm, Nos. 138-140, p. 30.

> tions, bearing in mind the principles of the Charter and international law. We also intend to commit ourselves, as necessary and appropriate, to helping states build capacity to protect their populations from genocide, war crimes, ethnic cleansing and crimes against humanity and to assisting those which are under stress before crises and conflicts break out.
>
> 140. We fully support the mission of the Special Adviser of the Secretary-General on the Prevention of Genocide."

A position was created by Annan, after the memorial ceremony in Rwanda of 2004, which is now fulfilled on a part-time basis by Juan Mendez, with support from two civil servants and a secretary, and meant mainly to advise the Secretary-General, the Security Council and the different divisions within the Secretariat at the New York headquarters.

The final question to be raised in this context is whether the genocide in Rwanda would have been prevented or halted, had the "the responsibility to protect" been in place in 1994. Both decisionmakers and scholars are rather pessimistic in their answers to this question. For instance, Bellamy argues that although activist Security Council members, such as New Zealand and the Czech Republic, the media and public opinion in 1994 "might have shamed powerful states into action by prohibiting them from plausibly justifying inaction by reference to the responsibility to protect norm . . . there is little evidence to suggest that states intervene emergencies because they are in some sense morally shamed into doing so by either domestics or global public opinion."[55] In our view, however, a strong domestic public opinion, particularly in Western democracies, may make the difference and bring inactive states towards active policy behavior. In particular, many foreign policy changes in the United States and Western Europe were the results of domestic influences. The obstacle in this respect is that the wordings of the responsibility to protect are formulated in such a way that both supporters of intervention in humanitarian emergencies and those who take an anti-interventionist stance can legitimize arguments from it. This was demonstrated in research on the case of Darfur in 2004 and 2005. At the end, it is concluded by Bellamy: "Responsibility to protect language was used by both advocates and opponents of intervention to legitimize their actions by reference to the prevailing normative order."[56]

The first impression from these documents and from the reports of the inquiry commissions on both Rwanda and Srebrenica was that the United Nations was prepared to learn lessons from their failures in the past. However, when

---

55 *Id.*, pp. 150–151.

56 Alex J. Bellamy, Reponsibility to Protect or Trojan Horse? The Crisis in Darfur and Humanitarian Intervention after Iraq, Ethics & International Affairs, 20(2), pp. 31–53, and 52 (2005).

the reports and final outcome at the summit meeting are scrutinized, the opinion is less optimistic. Moreover, when persons within the U.N. who are involved in this field are asked, an even less positive impression comes into being. The rapporteur of the inquiry commission on Srebrenica, David Hartland, now head of the DPKO in New York, gave the impression that there was hardly any debate in the United Nations after his report was published. Jan Pronk—the Special Representative of the Secretary-General in Sudan in 2004–2006—is also very skeptical of the possible change of policy based on the verbal agreements after adopting resolutions on the right to protect, which are interpreted by many as a duty to protect in times of genocide.[57]

On the other hand, we should acknowledge that nowadays most peace-keeping resolutions are adopted with a reference to Chapter VII, allowing for the possibility of the use force if needed. Stronger rules of engagement have also been made since 1994. Moreover, the awareness of the relationship between human rights and peace and security is now more underlined than before. Human rights are now incorporated in all U.N. departments and are part of any decisionmaking in New York, as told in an interview by an insider with a very long experience in this field.[58] Moreover, according to Bacré Waly Ndiaye, the lack of information on Rwanda sent to the Security Council in 1993–1994 would not happen today because of the direct reporting of the Special Representatives of the Secretary-General on, for instance, Darfur to the Security Council nowadays. A more transparent communication and decisionmaking can thus now be observed. Realizing that this greater transparency needs not to lead to better results in the prevention of genocide or other gross human rights violations, it is nevertheless an improvement in comparison with the situation in our study of 1994, because awareness is a necessary condition for any policy in this field.

---

57 Interview with D. Hartland, June 2, 2005. In fact Hartland only said that he did not know about the reception of the inquiry report because, at the moment that the report was presented to the Security Council, he was in East Timor. He acknowledged that within the U.N. system, no consequences with regard to the positions of persons in the Secretariat has been made, although many failed terribly, for instance, in giving the right information at the appropriate time to the members of the Security Council. Interview with J. Pronk, August 21, 2006.

58 Interview with B.W. Ndiaye, May 25, 2005.

CHAPTER 19

CONCLUSIONS

The failure to prevent the genocide in Rwanda in 1994 is the topic of this book. In particular, the research focused on why the early warnings of an emerging genocide were not translated into early preventative action. The warnings were well documented by the most authoritative sources and sent to the leading political civil servants in New York. The communications and the decision-making processes are scrutinized in this book, i.e., who received what messages at what time, to whom the messages were forwarded and which (non-)decisions were taken in response to the alarming reports of weapon deliveries and atrocities. It is made clear that this genocide could have been prevented by third parties. Third parties at the state and international level are the focal point for the prevention of gross human rights violations, because the perpetrator is unwilling and the victim is unable to prevent or stop the atrocities. This brings us to the conceptualization of the third party, the bystander. Therefore, we have developed a working definition for the bystander as: the third party that will not act or that will not attempt to act in solidarity with the victims of gross human rights violations. This means that this bystander will be evaluated afterwards as a collaborator. However, there is an alternative, and that is to act or to attempt to act in solidarity with the victims of the gross human rights violations. In this case, they will be considered afterwards as the rescuers.

From previous research, we found many models for early warnings in which the main root causes and immediate causes were investigated and measured by indicators. These indicators became more and more developed and, with hindsight, researchers were able to indicate that enough signals had been available to constitute a warning. However, in almost all these situations, these early warnings were not translated into early action or any action. In short, the main question remains: why did states and international organizations not intervene to stop the escalation? This question takes into account the realization that early warning—in any form, whether it is simple or very sophisticated—is not enough, because it will not automatically generate the spill-over effect from early warning to (early) action. That is why we have focused our research on this point: The bridge or gap between early warning and early action. This is also why we analyze the decisionmaking precisely before the genocide in Rwanda, took place in order to analyze the lack of prevention, and how the decisionmaking was conducted during the genocide, in order to analyze the passivity that did not lead to action to stop the genocide.

The International Criminal Tribunal for Rwanda was the first international tribunal in history to convict someone for genocide. The hate speeches broadcasted on the radio and printed in newspapers were also addressed during the trials. It was concluded that the people responsible for hate propaganda broadcasted or published *prior* to the genocide, which are an incentive to genocide, must be held responsible for genocide. Such incitements to hate and to kill an ethnic group were clear indications of the genocide that followed, and, in retrospect, these radio broadcasts and newspaper articles have been qualified as such. The judgment makes clear that these incitements are punishable as genocide. Though at the time they were neglected by the bystanders, after the genocide they were taken extremely seriously by the court as being genocide.

On August 4, 1993, the Arusha Peace Accords between the Rwandan government and the RPF were signed. After one year of negotiations and three years of war, the parties agreed upon the power-sharing agreement and made explicit demands for an international force under the responsibility and command of the United Nations. This peace-keeping operation was foreseen as a rather simple operation to implement the agreement and to install the interim government. The Arusha Peace Accords asked for a force to guarantee the overall security of the country and assist in the tracking of arms caches. The U.N. mandate for the peace-keeping force that was sent, UNAMIR, only stated that UNAMIR would contribute to the security of the city. Thus, the Security Council devalued the mandate. While the Arusha agreement asked for a force that would *guarantee* the security of the *country*, the force was now limited to the security of *Kigali*, inter alia, *within a weapons-secure area established by the parties in and around the city*. In addition, the UNAMIR mandate did not provide for the possibility to search for arms, while Arusha had asked for a force that would *assist in the tracking of arms caches*. In the operational procedures, it was stated that UNAMIR could be led to organizing a search operation with a view to searching for arms, munitions and explosives, though a preliminary authorization from the headquarters of UNAMIR would be necessary to execute such an operation. This operation would be done in liaison with the *gendarmerie* and the local police and should be done with sufficient forces and funds. However, in the rules of engagement, the Force Commander General Roméo Dallaire deliberately included paragraph 17, which widened the scope to make use of military force in cases of crimes against humanity. This paragraph was never approved by New York; in fact, they did not react at all towards the proposed rules of engagement, which in the end were never put into practice, because any use of force was prohibited by New York. There could have been some leeway, had the rules been subjected to a broad interpretation, but the rules were interpreted very strictly. In creating the Weapons Secure Area, UNAMIR was restricted to "helping," "participating" and "cooperating with the local authorities." UNAMIR was not allowed to act alone in dismantling the arms caches, a limitation that would prove to be a great hindrance in carrying out the mandate. One important factor in the failure to prevent genocide in Rwanda was therefore already made in the making of a far weaker mandate, lacking the use of force instruction that was requested, needed and proposed by the Rwandan parties of the peace agreement. Moreover, with regard to the strength of the installed peace-keeping mission, it was in all aspects too weak. Four thousand, two-hundred and sixty troops were requested by the Rwandan parties concerned, and the U.N. specialists of the reconnaissance mission agreed that at least 5,000 were needed, yet only 2,500 troops were authorized by the Security Council. These soldiers were very badly equipped, and only the Belgians were well trained and had good equipment available. However, the Belgians, because of their colonial history and the bad behavior of the Belgian soldiers, were hated among the population. In this way, getting rid off the peace-keepers was thus facilitated and contributed to the genocide.

The German and Belgian colonial rule reinforced the dominant position of the Tutsi minority in Rwanda. Because of this colonial rule, they maintained political power. This was reversed after the *coup d'état* and independence in the 1960s. The superiority of the Tutsis ended after the independence of Rwanda. After the independence, many Tutsis were killed and forced to flee to neighboring countries. A huge Tutsi population lived outside the country (particularly in Uganda) and aimed to recover their position of power in Rwanda. The period between 1991 and 1993 were the years in which Hutu extremism laid the foundations for the genocide in 1994. In 1993, after the Arusha Agreement was concluded, many warnings from divergent sources with clear, very serious signals of a worsening situation with a possibility of consequential atrocities were made in the years preceding the genocide. Various NGOs, such as Amnesty International, Human Rights Watch and also an International Commission of Human Rights Organizations were very clear, concrete and outspoken. The same can be said of the Special Rapporteur of the United Nations; he clearly concluded that not politicide but genocide was already taking place in 1993. No one paid attention inside and outside the United Nations to his very reliable report. Moreover ambassadors, ministers and other diplomats from Canada, the United States, France and Belgium made these serious early warnings public. No one reacted to these outspoken warnings. State and non-state actors informed others, but no action for any prevention was undertaken. The situation was deteriorating at the end of 1993. No progress was made with the implementation of the peace agreement, whereas the installation of the transitional government was postponed. The massacre in the neighboring country Burundi and the continuing and increasing scale of killings in Rwanda worsened the situation. In particular, the elaborated plans to assassinate the political opposition and to provoke unrest in combination with the distribution of weapons were alarming signals. Many early warnings by states and NGOs were forwarded, and these messages were received on almost a daily basis at the Belgian Ministry of Foreign Affairs.

On January 11, 1994, the Force Commander Dallaire sent a cable to the U.N. headquarters with the alarming information, from a trainer of the

Interahamwe militia, that Belgian troops were to be provoked, and if Belgian soldiers resorted to force, a number of them were to be killed, thus guaranteeing Belgian withdrawal from Rwanda. The cable continued by saying that the Interahamwe had trained 1,700 men in the camps of the FAR, split into groups of 40 throughout Kigali. The informant had been ordered to register all Tutsis in Kigali, which he expected to be for their extermination. He argued that his personnel were able to kill 1,000 Tutsi in 20 minutes. The informant was prepared to identify major arms caches throughout Rwanda, containing at least 135 weapons. Force Commander Dallaire wrote that he intended to take action within 36 hours. However the prompt answer from the top civil servants, Kofi Annan and Hedi Annabi, in New York was the prohibition of any action by the peace-keepers. The request to seize the arms caches was repeated many times by cable and phone but rejected every time by New York. The top officials decided on their own without informing the Secretary-General of the United Nations, Boutros Boutros-Ghali, or the U.N. Security Council. This fax, which entailed this clear warning of the emerging extermination of the Tutsis, should have been shared with both the Security Council and Secretary-General *immediately*. This fax should not be considered as simply one of many alarming signals, because speaking about killing 1,000 people every 20 minutes makes this fax unique. In hindsight, Iqbal Riza has admitted that the wording of this fax was different than others, acknowledging, "there are number of cables that we get of this nature, but not of this magnitude, not with such dire predictions."

Not only the wording of the fax, but also the highly tense political and security situation in Rwanda, should have triggered the Secretariat to act. The Secretariat should have interpreted the fax in the light of the pre-existing warnings and intelligence that corresponded with Dallaire's fax. The explicit and serious warning set out in the fax, together with highly tense political and security situation in Rwanda, should have led to a far more adequate response from the U.N. headquarters. Instead, the Security Council was not even informed of this early warning, no decision-making process based upon it could therefore follow and early action to prevent the genocide was precluded. It is important not to concentrate on just one moment in assessing the reaction from New York to the events in Rwanda. It was not only this fax but also the repeated requests based upon the increasing tensions in Rwanda, which were all turned down by the U.N. political leadership—Riza, Annan and Annabi. They have been condemned in the report of the U.N. inquiry commission because of the pattern of neglecting all these requests. Indeed, the continuing refusal of Annan, Riza and Annabi to approve any early action to prevent the atrocities is extremely alarming. The signals from UNAMIR in Rwanda were not ignored, but the early warnings that were received were not translated into any early action, nor were the signals and requests for action forwarded to the U.N. Security Council. The withholding of this information from the members of the Security Council by the U.N. bureaucracy precluded any Security Council decision in this field.

The inadequate response from New York on the warning fax was that Dallaire and Jacques Roger Booh Booh had to make a *démarche* to President Habyarimana, in which he was informed of the information received and asked to take action within 48 hours. Furthermore, they had to inform the heads of the missions of the United States, Belgium and France and ask them to make a similar *démarche*. This shows that New York fully trusted the President, and this line of thinking is in accordance with an expected smooth progress of the peace process. This trust however was not justified, as we made clear in the description of the deteriorating security situation in the first three months of 1994. No progress was made in the political negotiations to install a moderate cabinet. Extremists gathered more and more influence and destabilized the situation both on the political and security fields. Violence between both ethnic groups led to killings in February. UNAMIR was hardly able to act and was deliberately provoked. The RPF leader, Paul Kagame, concluded, following an incident of February 23, that he could no longer count on the peace-keepers for the safety of his Tutsi people. On the other hand, the mitigating effect of UNAMIR on the violent atmosphere was floored by the top U.N. officials in New York when they underlined every time that UNAMIR could be withdrawn when Habyarimana did not stop the unrest in the country. The changing attitude of Habyarimana—increasingly under the influence of extremists—was not observed, and he was thus trusted too much. The reaction from New York towards these events in this period was a continuing compulsion to proceed with the peace process; all pressure from New York was placed directly on President Habyarimana. The ultimate threat given by New York to Habyarimana was a possible withdrawal of UNAMIR. All interactions between the Rwandan President and New York were characterized by two aspects. The first aspect was the trust in the head of the Rwandan government, holding him accountable for the situation in the country. The second aspect was the trust in the progress of the peace process. Everything was based on both the Arusha agreement and the classic peace-keeping force, UNAMIR, which was the only means of achieving the implementation of the Accords. From this perspective, the U.N.'s reluctance to act is easy to understand. A change of perception, which could have been prompted by all alarming early warnings, was not achieved.

In this research, the continuing behavior, as if nothing had changed on the ground since the signing of the peace agreement, was exposed obviously in the New York reaction towards the requests from UNAMIR to act. In the three months preceding the genocide, the UNAMIR Commander asked at least six times for a stronger mandate to seize the hidden arms. All these requests were rejected. This would be understandable had the Security Council concluded, for example, that a broadening of the mandate would have endangered the peace-keeping force or the situation in the country. However, this was not the case, because none of these requests and none of these rejections were tabled on the agenda of the Security Council. The members of the Security Council were never informed of these requests from the peace-keeping force, and they had no opportunity to decide whether to act. The top officials—Annan, Annabi and Riza, lacking any democratic legitimization—deliberately kept the members of the Security Council ignorant. We do not know whether the Security Council members would have taken decisions, and, if they had, what kind of decisions these would have been. Instead they missed the opportunity to react on the alarming signals. It is this pattern of negligence by these top U.N. officials of the very serious warnings from the very trustful source, their own UNAMIR Peace-Keeping Force Commander, which is the most horrifying aspect of this period before the genocide.

Belgium was fully informed of the deteriorating situation and requested the strengthening of the mandate. It was Belgium that acted and asked the Secretary-General urgently to allow UNAMIR to undertake firmer action. Five messages followed this request in February. The message from Minister Willy Claes to Secretary-General Boutros-Ghali on February 11, was that a strong deterrent force was needed to stop the increasingly dangerous situation. Dallaire was asked by New York to write a response to Claes in Brussels. Dallaire appreciated very much that at least some diplomatic support was given to his request. He wrote a reply, but the answer that was sent to Brussels via Booh Booh was a distortion of his original reply, emphasizing the limitations of the mission and downplaying the information on illegal weapons distribution and the recruitment and training of the militias. The original letter, without the distortion, was sent by Booh Booh only to New York, where Annan again answered that UNAMIR was not allowed to undertake firmer action.

At the end of the month of February, after a visit to Rwanda during which Claes witnessed the very bad situation, he again made an appeal to Boutros-Ghali to raise the profile of UNAMIR, with more power in order not to "remain passive witnesses to genocide." This message was also not forwarded to the Security Council members. The top officials of the United Nations only answered that the United Kingdom and the United States would oppose any enlargement. The top officials of the United Nations are to blame for their behavior in not forwarding all these requests to the authoritative organ of the United Nations and basing themselves on their own anticipatory expectations in their rejections.

On April 5 the Security Council had to decide on the prolongation of UNAMIR for another six months. Although this time UNAMIR had to be put on the agenda, the members of the Security Council were not informed by Boutros-Ghali of the deteriorating situation in Rwanda, and not the slightest attention was given to the requests to strengthen and broaden the mandate of the force itself. The prolongation was presented as a routine decision. Another way of undermining UNAMIR was the anti-Belgian smear campaign in Rwanda that was deliberately started by the media on behalf of the extremists in order to get rid of the peace-keepers. In particular, the Belgian peace-keepers were an easy target because they were racist and behaved extremely badly. The

Interahamwe intended to start a civil war, and they played on this Belgian animosity. Even the Rwandan President supported these anti-Belgian feelings.

The plane crash of April 6 was the trigger for the following dramatic events. It is remarkable that no one has been very interested in the question of who the killers were. After ten years, for instance, the United Nations found the black box of the plane in their office in New York as a complete surprise. Opening the black box seems to be too dangerous for all involved parties. The political adversaries of the extremists were the first to be killed immediately after the plane crash, which meant that the moderate Hutu leaders were also killed during the first days. These killings can be qualified as a politicide, however, not yet as a genocide. It is important to realize this, but the more important and disappointing aspect is again the reaction from New York. Dallaire phoned top U.N. civil servants, Annan and Riza, five times a day. They always reacted according to the "organizational process model," as it was a routine decision. New York prohibited the use of force by UNAMIR every time, even to give safety to the ministers of the government. During these first days, the Prime Minister and many other moderate governmental officials were killed. Dallaire informed New York of the well-planned and organized terror in Kigali. The only reaction from Annan, Annabi and Riza to these alarming messages was to keep in close contact with the expatriates and diplomats. From the start, U.N. headquarters' priority was to save the foreigners in Rwanda and not the Rwandan people. As was predicted months before, on the first day following the plane crash, ten Belgian peace-keepers were deliberately murdered in order to prompt the withdrawal of the peace-keepers. This was based on a deliberate and well-organized plan to kill some peace-keepers. It was carefully designed to bring about a withdrawal of all international interference. In other words, turning the bystanders into direct victims, counting on the world's indifference towards the other victims on the ground, precluded any solidarity from the outsiders with the real victims. In these circumstances the perpetrators needed freedom of maneuver, and hence no foreign actors were accepted. The *genocidaires* planned shrewdly and were helped by others outside Rwanda to fulfill their genocidal aims.

The plane crash and the possible consequences were taken very seriously. Consequently, Western countries immediately organized a strong, heavily equipped military force to evacuate their own nationals. This was the top priority, and so even UNAMIR peace-keepers were ordered by their governments to become subordinated to the national hierarchical command structure. The UNAMIR Force Commander resisted this change of command structure somewhat, but Annan made it clear to him immediately that he must cooperate with Belgium and France to facilitate the evacuation of the foreigners. If necessary, he could act for this purpose—and only for the objective of the evacuation—beyond his mandate in using force if essential. Perhaps the peace-keepers in Rwanda were naïve in thinking that the arrival of the troops of the evacuation force would reinforce UNAMIR to stop the hostilities. The situation in Rwanda was very serious and precarious in the days in which these troops were in Rwanda, from April 8 until April 15. The important signal was that they were only interested in the safety of their own nationals. The *genocidaires* could then conclude that no deterrent force or counter-force would obstruct their intentions. We have concluded that in the first day after the plane crash, a politicide took place and not yet a genocide. We cannot assess exactly at what date the politicide transformed into genocide, but this must have been in the period between April 8 and 15. It is not said that a combination of the evacuation force with the UNAMIR peace-keepers would have been able to stop the chaotic killings. The tragedy is that this option was not considered in any Western capital or at U.N. headquarters. In our definition at the start of this book, we wrote that the third party, which will not act or will not attempt to act in solidarity with the victims of gross human rights violations, is the bystander that will afterwards be evaluated as a collaborator. The evacuation force illustrates this role.

We were very interested in the Belgian role after ten Belgian peace-keepers were killed, because Belgium was the only country that often asked for a strengthening and broadening of both the mandate and the troop strength of UNAMIR. In the end, Belgium withdrew its troops. It took ten days after the crash (April 6) or nine days after the killing of the Belgian soldiers (April 7) until Belgium made the decision to withdraw its troops public (April 16). The Belgian decision to withdraw was made on April 15 and thus not immediately after the news of the death of the Belgian peace-keepers. During these ten days, the situation in Rwanda degenerated dramatically—from a ceasefire situation to a war situation in combination with a politicide, which developed within these ten days into a genocide. The deteriorating situation was totally underestimated, particularly at U.N. headquarters. The Secretary-General was hardly informed, even after a week, and not willing or able to take firm action in order to change the situation by proposing mandatory measures to the Security Council.

Belgium was primarily concerned about the security of its own nationals, and it did its utmost to achieve a rescue operation. The Belgian efforts to broaden the mandate after the death of the Belgian peace-keepers were mainly made in the context of the protection of Belgian nationals and other foreigners and not primarily with the aim of protecting the Rwandan nationals and putting a halt to the developing genocide. In the preceding months, however, Belgium had asked the United Nations for a more forceful mandate for UNAMIR. It was fully aware of the seriousness of the situation at the brink of a war situation. All these requests were rejected by New York, which presented an unrealistic, rosy picture of the situation. Even after the crash and also after the killing of the Belgian peace-keepers, Belgium asked again for a strengthening of UNAMIR, mainly to secure the evacuation of their own nationals. Belgium did not influence or pressure the members of the Security Council, and it hardly tried to influence others with diplomatic means. It did not threaten to withdraw without any enforcement. It also did not make its decision dependent on any U.N. decision with regard to UNAMIR. The Belgian decision to withdraw was not dependent on the authorization to broaden the mandate. In fact, it made little use of political and power leverage to influence international politics.

In Belgium, particularly within the government, the discussion of a withdrawal continued, and during these ten days, the outcome developed increasingly in the direction of a total Belgian withdrawal. We have not observed any opposition in Belgium towards this position, nor have we observed a direct mass appeal through public opinion for a direct withdrawal after the killing of the Belgian peace-keepers. Even if this pressure had been activated, it took eight days before the Belgian government acceded to these pressures. Moreover, we have not observed much pressure—apart from one comment from Boutros-Ghali during his meeting with Claes—on Belgium to continue its participation in UNAMIR.

The Belgian Minister of Foreign Affairs only phoned all his colleagues from the member-states of the Security Council once. This had never been done to strengthen the UNAMIR mandate, but it was done to explain the Belgian withdrawal. In explaining the Belgian withdrawal, Claes made it clear that any continuation of UNAMIR in the current situation with the limited mandate was useless. This active role of Claes on the international scene is remarkable. It is to be understood as a reaction to the letter of the Secretary-General to the Security Council in which he blamed Belgium in particular, because he made his decision to stop UNAMIR in relation to the Belgian withdrawal. It is in this context that many observers understood this Belgian activity as a plea for a withdrawal of all troops. Such a plea was seen by many as a face-saving gesture by the Belgians so that they would not be held solely responsible for the emerging disaster in Rwanda. It is too simple and unfair to state merely that the Belgians brought the final blow to UNAMIR by pushing for a total withdrawal. One should take into account the many efforts from Belgium to achieve enforcement for the peace-keepers. Moreover, it did not withdraw its troops immediately after the killings of the Belgians. On the other hand, it did not use all possible diplomatic power to persuade the other states of the need to change policy with regard the role of UNAMIR in Rwanda. Only once did it make use of its diplomatic means at the highest echelons, and that was to defend the Belgian decision to withdraw. Moreover, at that late stage in its defense, Belgium was arguing that without any enforcement, all troops should withdraw. This is not a very convincing plea for enforcement but more an advocacy for total withdrawal. With this plea, it was rather easy to make Belgium the scapegoat for a world-wide failure to prevent the genocide in Rwanda.

The response of the Security Council and of the Secretary-General to both the start of the genocide and the Belgian withdrawal of its troops came on April 21, with a total withdrawal of UNAMIR from Rwanda, except 270 men to act as an intermediary between the parties and to facilitate humanitarian relief. It is again remarkable and in line with our earlier findings in this research—as had been demonstrated with an installment of a force that was far too weak, with the prohibition of seizure of weapons and use of force—that not all possible options were presented by the top civil servants of U.N. headquarters to the members of the Security Council. For instance, at a meeting of the troop-contributing countries on April 14, Riza stated that a proposal for an enforcement force would not be presented as an option to the members of the Security Council that same day. Riza was already very much aware of the dramatic situation at that moment—nine days after the crash with still the evacuation force on the ground—a situation that he described as already worse than Somalia. It is again their (U.N. Secretariat) determination on the feasibility—based on the reserved attitude that had resulted from the failure of the peace-keepers in Somalia—which was the overwhelming concern in the agenda setting. Boutros-Ghali was traveling in Europe in these days and showed himself to be ill-informed on what was going on in Rwanda in a meeting with Claes on the evening of April 12. The Security Council ended on April 15 without a decision, but only a Presidential statement in which they demanded that the parties agree upon a ceasefire and return to the negotiation table. We repeat that even at the start of the genocide, all attention was still focused on the implementation of the Arusha Peace Accords, though the situation had changed dramatically into massacres on a huge scale. On April 20 the Secretary-General sent a report to the Security Council in which he now included the option of a massive reinforcement of the troops with an enforcement mandate under Chapter VII. On the evening of April 21 the Security Council voted unanimously for the force reduction to 270 persons. The comment of an involved researcher, Barnett, was that with this vote, the SC effectively decided that the "international community" would not disturb the killers. This was not an unintended consequence, and no Security Council member could feign ignorance or argue the fact that it was unaware of the implications of its decision. This action was premeditated.

In order to get an insight into the behavior and attitude of other states outside the Security Council or states not as directly involved as Belgium, we did a comparative study into the role of the Netherlands during the genocide. Although the Netherlands were financially supporting the meetings in Arusha to achieve a peace accord and were involved with military in the first observer mission in UNOMUR on the Ugandan side of the border, and one high-ranking soldier assisted the Force Commander in UNAMIR, they were not well informed on the deteriorating situation in Rwanda, and the massacres after the plane crash were a completely unexpected surprise for the Dutch Minister of Development Cooperation. He, Jan Pronk, directly made many visits to the area and tried in vain to get support for African mediation or European financial help for an African peace-keeping force. The Dutch government was asked by the United Nations, at the end of May, to contribute to UNAMIR II with soldiers, but they declined this request. The Netherlands was not willing to participate in UNAMIR II at the height of the genocide, although Pronk became aware of the need for such enforced military troops during his visit to Rwanda in May. The Secretary-General declared that it was a shame that he did not succeed in bringing together the needed 5,000 military troops and even, as he said explicitly, that the Netherlands refused to participate. One year later, in 1995, Pronk took part in the ceremony in memory of the genocide in Kigali and he saw a billboard in front with the text "UNAMIR, where were you during the genocide?" It made an impact on Pronk, because he made this known in a letter to parliament. The Netherlands was aware of the situation on the ground during the genocide and, as one of the troop-contributing countries, was not excluded from the decision-making process in New York when the UNAMIR withdrawal was discussed. The Netherlands increased the development aid for the refugees and displaced persons, but the Dutch government, influenced by the Minister of Defense in particular, refused to be involved in Rwanda other than in the evacuation of West-Europeans in the first days, for which Dutch Hercules planes were used with a Belgian crew. Again, it is remarkable that the only military action in which the Dutch participated was for the rescue of their own nationals.

The Netherlands is thus only an example, among the 190 other nations, of the overwhelming indifference towards the genocide in Rwanda.

Ten years later, many apologies concerning their role were made by many states and international organizations. Some of these had been pushed to establish inquiry commissions to reveal the truth of what happened and what their particular role was. These inquiry commissions on Belgium, France, the African Union and the United Nations have presented reports of their research. These are interesting and sometimes very frank and critical concerning their own role, but no personal consequences resulted from these. Only the perpetrators were convicted at international, national and local tribunals. The bystanders were shielded. Some lessons were learned, however. It was precisely on the day of the memorial ceremonies for Rwanda in 2004 that Annan, the Secretary-General of the United Nations launched his plan for early warning and early action with the following words:

> One of the reasons for our failure in Rwanda was that beforehand we did not face the fact that genocide was a real possibility. And once it started, for too long we could not bring ourselves to recognize it, or call it by its name. If we are serious about preventing or stopping genocide in the future, we must not be held back by legalistic arguments about whether a particular atrocity meets the definition of genocide or not. By the time we are certain, it may often be too late to act. We must recognize the signs of approaching or possible genocide, so that we can act in time to avert it.

He realizes very well—and maybe more than anyone else in the Secretariat—the need for swift and decisive action when, despite all our efforts, we learn that genocide is happening, or about to happen. Too often, even when there is abundant warning, we lack the political will to act. Such decisive action might be an enforcement action with the use of force. He is asking for guidelines concerning when to act in order to ensure that we have no excuse to ignore a real danger of genocide when it does arise. His plan has eventually resulted in the following paragraph in the declaration at the summit of the United Nations in September 2005.

> The international community, through the United Nations, also has the responsibility to use appropriate diplomatic, humanitarian and other peaceful means, in accordance with Chapters VI and VIII of the Charter, to help to protect populations from genocide, war crimes, ethnic cleansing and crimes against humanity. In this context, we are prepared to take collective action, in a timely and decisive manner, through the Security Council, in accordance with the Charter, including Chapter VII, on a case-by-case basis and in cooperation with relevant regional organizations as appropriate, should peaceful means be inadequate and national authorities are manifestly failing to protect their populations from genocide, war crimes, ethnic cleansing and crimes against humanity.

In scrutinizing the documents that have led to this summit outcome with the "right to protect," our conclusion is that the original ideas have been watered down. The original ideas started with the realization to prevent in future new Rwandas. What started as a duty to protect victims from gross human rights violations by third parties, when their own state was not able or willing to act or in case the state was itself the main perpetrator of these gross human rights violations, ended in a preparedness to take action when national authorities are manifestly failing to protect their own population. The threshold was put higher to intervene, and, moreover, this language could be used very well by both supporters of intervention in humanitarian emergencies and those who take an anti-interventionist stance and can legitimize arguments from it.

The final question to be raised in this context is whether the genocide in Rwanda would have been prevented or halted, had "the responsibility to protect" been in place in 1994. Both decisionmakers and scholars are rather pessimistic in their answers to this question. On the other hand, the involvement of the Security Council with human rights has increased tremendously. The transparency in the communication has increased, and a lack of information as happened in 1994 is no longer taking place in comparison with the information available on Darfur today.

The way of changing minds is, however, more complicated as we have shown in this study where all attention was focused on the implementation of the peace agreement. That is also why no heavy military means were allowed to be used. However, a neutral peace-keeping force is no longer tenable, when genocide is on the brink. Often it is said that no military means are available to act when it is needed. In the 1994 case of Rwanda, we have demonstrated that military means could have been employed and strengthened.

The military people that we interviewed were particularly convinced that with military means, the genocide could have been halted. Robbert Van Putten underlined the missing equipment, arms and broadened mandate that were needed in order to stop the atrocities.[1] Brent Beardsley underlines that it was the strong message that no intervention would take place that strengthened all parties in Rwanda, allowing them to fight in order either to win the war or to continue in the genocide. This was most clearly demonstrated with the evacuation force but also before this point. Beardsley believes that if this evacuation force had stayed, they could have stabilized the situation, and the genocide may not have happened.[2] Luc Marchal explains the plane crash as a result of the success of UNAMIR. In his view, UNAMIR was achieving its objectives, but because some parties did not want this successful implementation of the Arusha Accords, they deliberately started the genocide. In the vision of Beardsley, his messages from Rwanda to New York—he was very familiar with the key players in New York because he has worked in their DPKO department for three months—were not underestimated. Headquarters was just hoping that diplomacy would be the answer and they therefore believed in the no-use-of-force option. In the end, it is this belief among the decisionmakers in New York in continuing the promotion of the peace agreements, and the lack of a shift towards thinking in terms of gross human rights violations, for which other means were needed, which can be seen as a very important factor in why the genocide in Rwanda was not prevented. Even so, we have demonstrated that the warnings were clear and reliable and that the means were at their disposal or could have been attached to them. Moreover, afterwards all involved regret that no other choices were made in the decisionmaking to prevent or stop the genocide in 1993–1994. The bystanders at the state level and at the international level did not act in solidarity with the victims. They did not attempt to rescue the victims by preventing or halting the genocide. Evaluating afterwards, we may conclude that these bystanders turned into collaborators who facilitated the *genocidaires* by not acting against continuing atrocities.

---

[1] Interview with R. Van Putten by Jurgen Maas, IKON Radio (Dutch radio), March 26, 2006, between 7:00–7:30 a.m.

[2] Interview with B. Beardsley, June 6, 2005.

ANNEX 1

SCHEME "HURIVIC," HUMAN RIGHTS VIOLATIONS AND CONFLICT

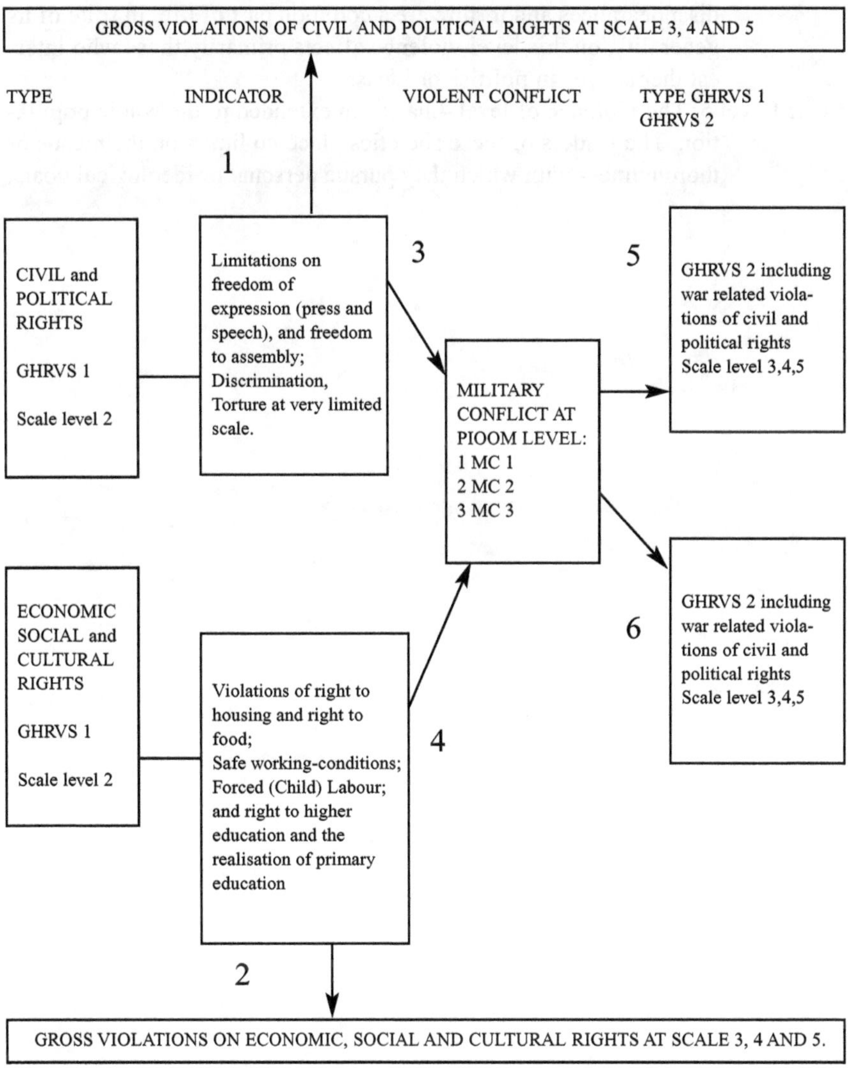

Scale Level 1: Countries live under a secure rule of law, people are not imprisoned for their views and torture is rare or exceptional. Political murders are extremely rare.

Scale Level 2: There is a limited amount of imprisonment for non-violent political activity. However, few persons are affected, torture and beatings are exceptional. Political murder is rare.

Scale Level 3: There is extensive political imprisonment or a recent history of such imprisonment. Executions or political murders and brutality may be common. Unlimited detention, with or without trial, for political views is accepted.

Scale Level 4: The practices of level 3 are expanded to larger numbers. Murders, disappearances and torture are a common part of life. In spite of its generality, on this level violence affects primarily those who interest themselves in politics or ideas.

Scale Level 5: The violence of level 4 has been extended to the whole population. The leaders of these societies place no limits on the means or thoroughness with which they pursue personal or ideological goals.

ANNEX 2

ORGANIZATION AND COMPOSITION OF UNAMIR[1]

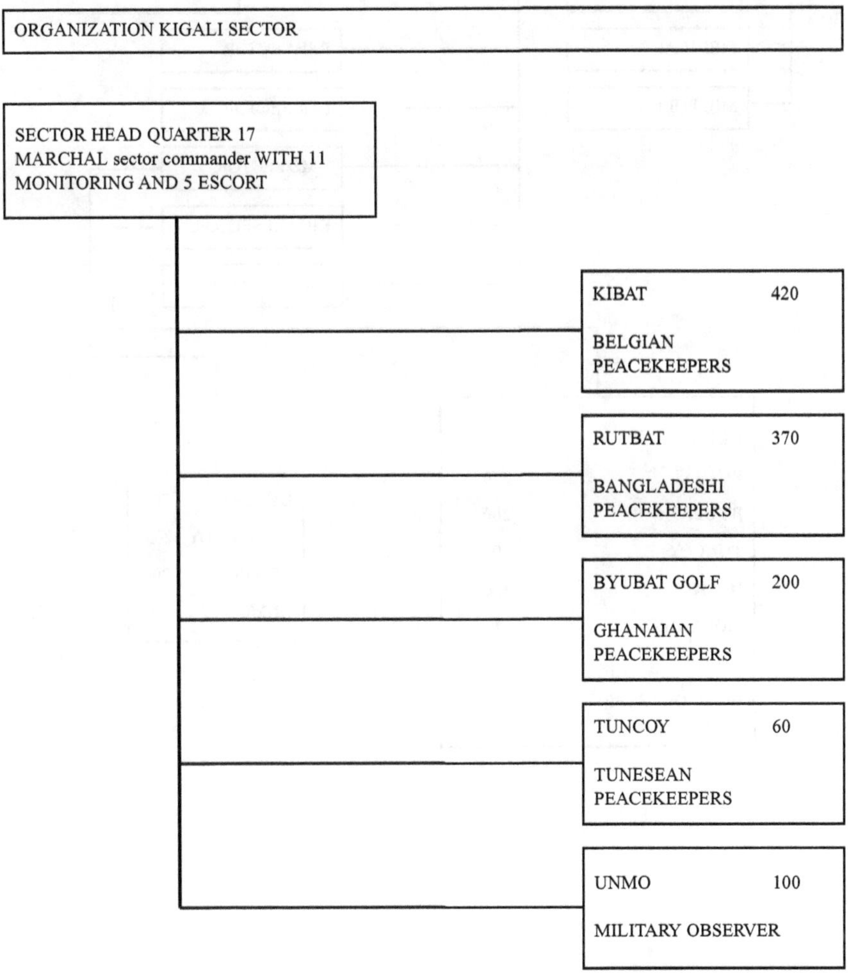

[1] Luc Marchal, Aan de poorten van de Rwandese hel: Getuigenis van een peacekeeper, pp. 256–257 (2001).

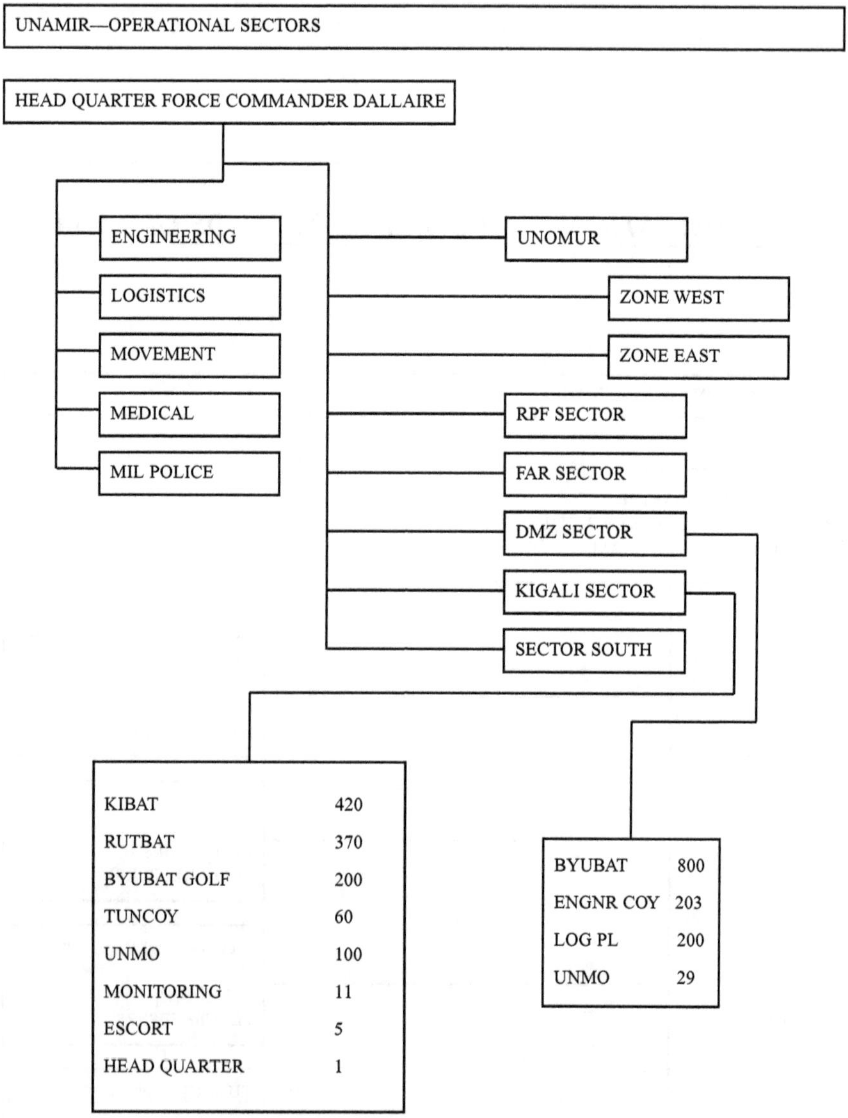
UNAMIR—OPERATIONAL SECTORS
HEAD QUARTER FORCE COMMANDER DALLAIRE
ENGINEERING
LOGISTICS
MOVEMENT
MEDICAL
MIL POLICE
UNOMUR
ZONE WEST
ZONE EAST
RPF SECTOR
FAR SECTOR
DMZ SECTOR
KIGALI SECTOR
SECTOR SOUTH
KIBAT 420
RUTBAT 370
BYUBAT GOLF 200
TUNCOY 60
UNMO 100
MONITORING 11
ESCORT 5
HEAD QUARTER 1
BYUBAT 800
ENGNR COY 203
LOG PL 200
UNMO 29

ANNEX 3

FAX DALLAIRE [1]

TO: BARIL/DPKO/UNATIONS NEW YORK

FROM: DALLAIRE/UNAMIR/KIGALI

FAX NO: MOST IMMEDIATE-CODE CABLE-212-xxx-xxxx
FAX NO: 011-xxx-xxxxx

INMARSAT:

SUBJECT: REQUEST FOR PROTECTION OF INFORMANT

ATTN: MGEN BARIL

ROOM NO: 2052

TOTAL NUMBER OF TRANSMITTED PAGES INCLUDING THIS ONE: 2

1. Force commander put in contact with informant by very very important government politician. Informant is a top level trainer in the cadre of Interahamwe-armed militia of MRND.

2. He informed us he was in charge of last Saturdays demonstrations which aims were to target deputies of opposition parties coming to ceremonies and Belgian soldiers. They hoped to provoke the RPF BN to engage (being fired upon) the demonstrators and provoke a civil war. Deputies were to be assassinated upon entry or exit from Parliament. Belgian troops were to be provoked and if Belgians soldiers restored to force a number of them were to be killed and thus guarantee Belgian withdrawal from Rwanda.

3. Informant confirmed 48 RGF PARA CDO and a few members of the gendarmerie participated in demonstrations in plain clothes. Also at least one Minister of the MRND and the sous-prefect of Kigali were in the demonstration. RGF and Interahamwe provided radio communications.

4. Informant is a former security member of the president. He also stated he is paid RF150,000 per month by the MRND party to train Interahamwe. Direct link is to chief of staff RGF and president of the MRND for financial and material support.

---

1 Http://www.pbs.org/wgbh/pages/frontline/shows/evil/warning/cable.html.

5. Interahamwe has trained 1,700 men in RGF military camps outside the capital. The 1,700 are scattered in groups of 40 throughout Kigali. Since UNAMIR deployed he has trained 300 personnel in three week training sessions at RGF camps. Training focus was discipline, weapons, explosives, close combat and tactics.

6. *Principal aim of Interahamwe in the past was to protect Kigali from RPF. Since UNAMIR mandate he has been ordered to register all Tutsi in Kigali. He suspects it is for their extermination. Example he gave was that in 20 minutes his personnel could kill up to 1,000 Tutsis.*

7. Informant states he disagrees with anti-Tutsi extermination. He supports opposition to RPF but cannot support killing of innocent persons. He also stated that he believes the president does not have full control over all elements of his old party/faction.

8. *Informant is prepared to provide location of major weapons cache with at least 135 weapons*. He already has distributed 110 weapons including 35 with ammunition and can give us details of their location. Type of weapons are G3 and AK47 provided by RGF. He was ready to go to the arms cache tonight-if we gave him the following guarantee. He requests that he and his family (his wife and four children) be placed under *our* protection.

9. *It is our intention to take action within the next 36 hours* with a possible H HR of Wednesday at dawn (local). Informant states that hostilities may commence again if political deadlock ends. Violence could take place day of the ceremonies or the day after. Therefore Wednesday will give greatest chance of success and also be most timely to provide significant input to on-going political negotiations.

10. It is recommended that informant be granted protection and evacuated out of Rwanda. This HQ does not have previous U.N. experience in such matters and urgently requests guidance. No contact has as yet been made to any embassy in order to inquire if they are prepared to protect him for a period of time by granting diplomatic immunity in their embassy in Kigali before moving him and his family out of the country.

11. Force commander will be meeting with the very very important political person tomorrow morning in order to ensure that this individual is conscious of all parameters of his involvement. Force commander does have certain reservations on the suddenness of the change of heart of the informant to come clean with this information. Recce of armed cache and detailed planning of raid to go on late tomorrow. Possibility of a trap not fully excluded, as this may be a set-up against this very very important political person. Force commander to inform SRSG first thing in morning to ensure his support.

13. Peux Ce Que Veux. Allons-y.

ANNEX 4

LIST OF EARLY WARNINGS

December 1990

— Hutu paper *Kangura* published its "Ten Commandments of the Hutu," which composed what the Hutu would like to see imposed on the minority.[1]

February 1992

— Africa Watch, a Committee of Human Rights Watch, Talking Peace and Waging War: Human Rights since the October 1990 invasion, February 27, 1992 (Vol. IV, Issue No: 3): More than 10,000 Tutsi had been detained and 2,000 murdered since 1990; at least three major massacres of Tutsi, a possible genocide.

May 1992

— Amnesty International: Report "Rwanda, persecution of Tutsi minority and repression of government critics 1990–19992," (AI. Afr. 47/02/92) was published and talked about more than 1,000 extrajudicial executions and over 8,000 political prisoners following the October 1990 invasion by the RPF.

June 1993

— The hate radio, *Télévision Libre des Milles Collines* (RTLMC) started broadcasting.

— Human Rights Watch, Beyond the Rhetoric: Continuing Human Rights Abuses in Rwanda, Human Rights Watch, June 1993 (HRW, Index No: A507).

November 1993

— On November 17, 36 people were killed, all Hutu and members of the local authority and, on November 29 about 25 people got killed in Mothare.[2]

[1] Reprinted and translated in African Rights, *Rwanda: Death, Despair and Defiance,* in, Review of African Political Economy, 61, pp. 42–43 (1994).

[2] Linda Melvern, A People Betrayed. The Role of the West in Rwanda's Genocide, p 88 (2000) (hereinafter Melvern); see also HRW, Fédération Internationale des Ligues des Droits de l'Homme/Alison Des Forges, Leave None to Tell the Story, part Warnings, p. 2 (March 1999) (hereinafter HRW, Leave None to Tell the Story).

— At the end of November the extremist party CDR gave a press release that the majority population had to be ready to neutralize its enemies.[3]

— On November 26 the Belgian Ambassador in Kigali reported to his Ministry of Foreign Affairs that RTLMC had called for the assassination of Prime Minister Uwilingiyimana and of Prime Minister-designate Twagiramungu.[4]

— A Belgian Red Cross truck was deliberately targeted by government soldiers and blown up by a mine.[5]

— On November 29–30 assailants killed more than a dozen people in Mutura.[6]

December 1993

— A study by the CIA found that some 40 million tons of small arms had been transported from Poland, through Belgium, to Rwanda.[7]

— On December 1 CLADHO published a report about recent attacks on Tutsi, saying that the assailants "declare that this population is an accomplice of the Inkotanyi because it is mostly Tutsi and its extermination would be a good thing."[8]

— On December 2 assailants armed with machine guns fired on a UNAMIR patrol.[9]

— On December 3 an anonymous letter, coming from high-ranking military officers from the government, was sent to Dallaire and was copied to all diplomatic missions, which warned that Hutu militias were planning a massacre, starting in areas with large concentrations of Tutsi; politicians were going to be assassinated, two names were specified: the prime-minister designate under the Arusha Accords Faustin Twagiramungu and the head of the Parti Social Démocrate the head of the Parti Social Démocrate, Félicien Gatabazi.[10]

---

[3] Melvern, p. 89.

[4] HRW, Leave None to Tell the Story, part Warnings, p. 2.

[5] Sénat de Belgique, Commission d'Enquête parlementaire concernant les événements au Rwanda, session de 1997–1998, 6 décembre 1997, Rapport fait au nom de la commission d'enquête par MM Mahoux et Verhofstadt, p. 29 (hereinafter Belgian Senate).

[6] HRW, Interview with diplomat present in Kigali at the time, by telephone, Washington, January 13, 1997; see HRW, Leave None to Tell the Story, part Warnings, p. 2.

[7] Samantha Power, A problem from hell: America and the age of genocide, p. 338 (2003) (hereinafter Power).

[8] Belgian Senate, p. 70.

[9] Belgian Senate, p. 37.

[10] André Guichaoua, (ed.), Les Crisis Politiques au Burundi et au Rwanda, pp. 653–654 (1995).

— On December 8 CLADHO addressed a memo about killings throughout the country to UNAMIR and diplomatic missions in Kigali. CLADHO asked to disarm the militia.[11]

— At the end of the month the two-person cell, which reported to UNAMIR, received information that stocks of weapons were stored at the homes of militia leaders; the MRNDD leaders had a plan to undermine the credibility of the Belgian troops, using the Interahamwe.[12]

— On December 27 Belgian intelligence reported on a meeting of military commanding officers from December 22, stating: "The Interahamwe are armed to the teeth and on alert. Many of them have been trained at the military camp in Bugesera. Each of them has ammunition, grenades, mines and knives. They have been trained to use guns that are stockpiled with their respective chiefs. They are all just waiting for the right moment to act."[13]

January 1994

— Belgian Ambassador in Kigali informed the Foreign Ministry what he knew from the extremists involvement in the radio RTLMC. Swinnen wanted the broadcasts to be translated, but there was not enough embassy staff to do the job.[14]

— A minibus full of Belgian soldiers was surrounded by Interahamwe calling them Tutsi. A grenade was thrown in the office of Marchal's of headquarters.[15]

— Swinnen reminded his ministry about the distribution of weapons by supporters of the President.[16]

— On January 7 the Belgian contingent received information about a top-level meeting at the MRND headquarters where plans were made to avoid future seizures and to cause trouble between the Belgian battalion.[17]

— On January 8 there was a violent demonstration from the Interahamwe in Kigali. Marchal was told that there had been grenades and guns distrib-

---

11 CLADHO, Memorandum Adressé à la Minuar et aux Missions Diplomatiques en Rapport avec les Tueries en Cours dans le Pays, December 8, 1993; HRW, Leave None to Tell the Story, part Warnings, p. 3.

12 Melvern, pp. 91–93.

13 De Morgen, Walter de Bock, "Belgische Wijkagenten zagen voorbereiding genocide," November 4, 1995, p. 5; HRW, Leave None to Tell the Story, part warnings p. 3.

14 Belgian Senate, p. 607.

15 Melvern, p. 90.

16 HRW, Leave None to Tell the Story, Part Warnings, p. 4, note 28; Sénat de Belgique, Rapport du Groupe Ad Hoc Rwanda A La Commission des Affairs Etrangeres, Sénat de Belgique, 7 janvier 1997, pp. 61, 65 (hereinafter Belgian Ad Hoc Group).

17 HRW, Leave None to Tell the Story, p. 149.

uted among the crowd, and, when the Belgian soldiers would intervene, they would be killed.[18]

— On January 9 General Ndindiliyimana told Belgian UNAMIR officers that confrontations the day before "would inevitably lead to losses, especially when the population had many grenades."

— RTLMC broadcasted that UNAMIR was opposed to the Interahamwe and in favor of the RPF.[19]

— On January 10, Jean Pierre, Hutu, former member of the President's security guard, who worked as a chauffeur and was now a senior trainer of the Interahamwe, came forward. He told about the rapid arming and training of local militia; in 20 minutes his personnel could kill up to 1,000 Tutsi's; the militia first planned to murder Belgium peace-keepers in order to guarantee Belgian withdrawal from Rwanda; he was prepared to identify major arms caches throughout Rwanda, including at least 135 weapons.[20]

— On January 16 four to 5,000 MRND supporters, met at the Nyamirambo stadium in Kigali. Justin Mugenzi, leader of the Hutu Power faction of the Liberal Party, played on ethnic divisions. Two days later, UNAMIR officers found out arms were distributed at this meeting.[21]

— On January 22 a planeload of arms from France was confiscated by UNAMIR at Kigali airport.[22]

— RTLMC broadcasted a call for Hutu to defend themselves to the last man, there was propaganda against UNAMIR, the station asked the population to "take responsibility," because otherwise the Belgian soldiers would give Rwanda to the Tutsi.[23]

---

18 Melvern, p. 89.

19 HRW, Leave None to Tell the Story, Part Warnings, p. 4, note 35 and p. 36: Service de Police Judiciaire auprès de la Justice Militaire, En cause de Dewez Joseph and Marchal Luc, Annexe A/5 au PV No. 1210 du 6/11/95, Document 7, Belgian Military Intelligence, January 9, 1994 (confidential source).

20 Code Cable, January 11 1994, from Dallaire to Baril, Fax No. most immediate; Cable: 212-963-4652, Subject: request for protection for informant.

21 HRW, Leave None to Tell the Story, Part Warnings, p 8, note 55: Marchal, "Considerations relatives," p. 14; Annex A/7 au PV No. 1210 du 6/11/95 du Service de Police Judiciaire auprès de la Justice Militaire.

22 Howard Adelman and Astri Suhrke, Early warning and conflict management genocide in Rwanda, p. 27, (1995); Belgian Ad Hoc Group, pp. 44, 87, 133; Filip Reyntjens, Rwanda, trois jours qui on fait basculer l'histoire, p. 19 (1995).

23 HRW, Leave None to Tell the Story, Part Warnings, p. 9, note 71: Document 15, Belgian Military Intelligence, January 29, 1994 (confidential source) and note 72: Document 14, Belgian Military Intelligence, January 27, 1994 (confidential source).

— On January 26 shots were fired at Belgian peace-keepers at Booh Booh's residence.

— At the end of the month, HRW released the report: Arming Rwanda: The Arms Trade and Human Rights Abuses in the Rwandan War, Human Rights Watch, January 1994 (HRW Index No: A601) reporting that Habyarimana's regime had entered into arms deals with Egypt, South Africa and France. The report: "It is impossible to exaggerate the danger of providing automatic rifles to civilians, particularly in regions where residents, either encouraged or instructed by authorities, have slaughtered their neighbors. In light of the widespread and horrific abuses committed by Hutu civilian crowds and party militia armed primarily with machetes and spears, it is frightening to ponder the potential for abuses by large numbers of ill-trained civilians equipped with assault rifles."

— According to a confidential source, at the end of January, a U.S. government intelligence analyst estimated the potential loss of life should there be renewed conflict in Rwanda. He described three possibilities. The worst: The loss of one half million lives. A colleague of the analyst told Human Rights Watch that work of the analyst was usually highly regarded but that his superiors did not take this assessment seriously.[24]

— The CIA had given desk-level analyses to the State Department stating: if hostilities would resume, half a million people would die, the Arusha Accords would fail and massive violence would break out.[25]

February 1994

— On February 2 Belgian military intelligence summarized, in a 13-page memorandum on the Interahamwe, the knowledge of the militia. The information was reported to various Belgian authorities. The information: plan of the militia to attack Belgian UNAMIR troops to get Belgium to withdraw its soldiers from Rwanda, plans of the militia of targeting Tutsi and members of parties opposed to Habyarimana and their training and arming by the Rwandan army.[26]

— On February 3 Dallaire cabled New York that they could expect more frequent and more violent demonstrations and armed attack on ethnic and

---

24 HRW, Leave None to Tell the Story, Part Warnings, p. 9, note 77: Human Rights Watch interview, Washington, December 8, 1995; Organization of African Unity, The Preventable Genocide of the International Panel of Eminent Personalities to Investigate the 1994 Genocide in Rwanda and Surrounding Events, chapter 9, p. 5 (2000).

25 Melvern, p. 91.

26 HRW, Leave None to Tell the Story, Part Warnings, p 9, note 79: Major Hock, Service Générale du Renseignement et de la Sécurité, to Maison Militaire du Roi, Ministre de la Défense Nationale, and others, February 2, 1994.

political groups, more assassinations and possibly more outright attacks on UNAMIR. The message was in very strong words.[27]

— On February 3 Ambassador Swinnen reported to the Belgian Ministry of Foreign Affairs that UNAMIR was powerless, distribution of arms had to stop and UNAMIR had to eliminate the stocks that were already built up.[28]

— On February 17 Dallaire cabled New York about information of the killing of oppositions.[29]

— The Rwandan Minister of Defense requested authorization for the landing of three planes carrying arms (mid February); UNAMIR refused.[30]

— On February 20 six people died during a demonstration. Stones were thrown at Belgian soldiers when they protected the Prime Minister Uwilingiyamana during a meeting of the MDR. The Belgian peacekeepers needed 63 shots in the air to free themselves.[31]

— On February 21 extremist Hutu's blocked the city of Kigali and demonstrators burst into a government building where they took hostages. The prominent opposition leader, Minister of Publics Works, Félicien Gatabazi, was killed.

— On February 22 Martin Bucyana, the head of the hard-line Hutu Coalition pour la Defense de la République (CDR) was killed.[32]

— On the February 22 a convoy with the RPF leadership, protected by U.N. military observers and Belgian peace-keepers, was attacked by the Interahamwe and the Presidential Guard in civilian clothes. One person got killed and two were wounded. (It turned out that there was no RPF leadership in the convoy; none of the Belgians had responded.)[33]

— On February 23 Dallaire reported to New York[34] that all information was directing to death squad target lists.[35]

---

[27] This cable is General Dallaire to New York, Code-cable, MIR 267, February 3, 1964. See HRW, Leave None to Tell the Story, p. 160, note 81: General Dallaire to U.N., New York, Code Cable MIR 267, February 3, 1994 (confidential source).

[28] Belgian Ad Hoc Group, p. 71.

[29] Melvern, p. 100.

[30] HRW, Leave none to tell the story, Part Warnings, p. 11, note: 93 Human Rights Watch interview, General Romeo Dallaire, by telephone, Kigali, February 25, 1994.

[31] Belgian Ad Hoc Group, p. 38.

[32] Melvern, p. 100.

[33] Interview, Major-General Paul Kagame, Kigali, October 1997.

[34] U.N., Report of the Independent Inquiry into the Actions of the United Nations during the 1994 Genocide in Rwanda, December 15, 1999, Ingvar Carlsson, Han, Sung-Joo, Rufus, M. Kupolati, U.N. Doc. S/1999/1257, p. 12 (hereinafter Carlsson Report, S/1999/1257).

[35] Carlsson Report, S/1999/1257, p. 9.

— On February 24 Booh Booh wrote: "Reports had been circulating that the previous days' violence might have been ethnically motivated and directed against the Tutsi minority. . . . the possibility of ethnically motivated incidents is a constant threat, especially during moments of tension, fear and confusion."[36]

— February 22–26: Interahamwe killed some 70 people and destroyed property in Kigali. Belgian officers were limited by their mandate.[37]

— On February 25, according to informants, a meeting had taken place where Kajuga, head of the Interahamwe met local militia leaders: A system of communication was devised for the Interahamwe to keep in touch through telephones, whistles and runners.

— On the February 27 another meeting took place in the offices of the MRND. Here, compiling a list with Tutsi was discussed.[38]

— On February 27 Belgian intelligence reported on continuing arms deals for the Rwandan army.[39]

— African diplomats reported that CDR members told them that, in the future, there would be no Tutsi left in Rwanda.[40]

— The newspaper *Kangura* said that U.N. peace-keepers were there to help the RPF, and the RPF was planning to kill the President.[41]

— February 25–28: Tutsi started to seek shelter in religious centers and with U.N. employees. On February 28 the United Nations opened two centers, one near Amahoro stadium and another at the Magerwa storehouse, for Tutsi who were seeking protection.[42]

— Late February the second issue of *Kangura* for February talked of "The Final Attack" that the RPF was preparing to make on Kigali.[43]

---

36 Carlsson Report, S/1999/1257, part I A, under Political deadlock and a worsening of the security situation, I have not been able to find the original cable of Booh Booh in which he made this statement.

37 HRW, Leave none to tell the story, Part Warnings, p 12, note: 102: Tribunal de Première Instance de Bruxelles, Deposition de Témoin, dossier 57/95, September 18, 1995 (confidential source).

38 U.N. Commission on Human Rights, Report on the situation of human rights in Rwanda submitted by Mr. René Dégni-Séui, Special Rapporteur, under paragraph 20 of Resolution S-3/1 of May 25, 1994. (E/CN.4/1995/7), June 28, 1995, p. 9.

39 HRW, Leave None to Tell the Story, Part Warnings, p 13, note 111: Document 19, Belgian Military Intelligence, February 27, 1994 (confidential source).

40 Howard Adelman and Astri Suhrke, Early warning and conflict management genocide in Rwanda, p. 27 (1995); Melvern, p. 102.

41 Melvern, p. 102.

42 Belgian Ad Hoc Group, pp. 71–72.

43 *Kangura*, No. 57, février 1994, p. 4.

— Report of U.N. special rapporteur Ndiaye was tabled at the CHR; he warned explicitly of a possible genocide.[44]

March 1994

— On March 1 RTLMC was broadcasting inflammatory statements calling for the the extermination of the Tutsi.[45]

— On March 2 a MRND informant told Belgian intelligence that the MRND had a plan to exterminate all the Tutsi in Kigali if the RPF should dare to resume the war. The informant said "if things go badly, the Hutu will massacre them without pity."[46]

— On March 15 the sponsors of the International Commission on Human Rights Abuse in Rwanda (Human Rights Watch, the International Federation of Human Rights Leagues, the International Center for Human Rights and Democratic Development and the Inter-African Union of Human Rights) together with Amnesty International gave a declaration about the growing violence in Rwanda, the distribution of arms, the delays of the Arusha Accords.[47]

— Also on March 15 Ambassador Swinnen reported that UNAMIR had blocked the delivery of arms to the Rwandan army from the Mil-Tec Corporation of the United Kingdom and the Société Dyl-Invest of France.[48]

— On March 17 a "respected source" in the National Police (probably Chief of Staff Ndindiliyimana) told Belgian officers that UNAMIR's mandate should be strengthened so it could act more firmly. According to this source, the National Police was not able to carry out alone the role it had under the Arusha Accords.

— On March 22 a Belgian announcer (Georges Ruggiu) on RTLMC radio, warned that the Belgians wanted to "impose a RPF government of bandits and killers on Rwanda and that the Belgian ambassador had been plotting

---

44 Carlsson Report, S/199/1257, pp. 3–4. and United Nations, Report by B.W. Ndiaye, Special Rapporteur Extrajudicial, Summary of Arbitrary Executions on his mission to Rwanda, 8–17 April 1993, Geneva: United Nations 1990 (E/CN.4/1994/7/ Add. 1).

45 Belgian Ad Hoc Group, p. 78.

46 HRW, Leave None to Tell the Story, Part Warnings, p 13, note 116: Document 20, Belgian Military Intelligence, March 2, 1994 (confidential source).

47 Amnesty International, Human Rights Watch, Inter-African Union of Human Rights, International Center for Human Rights and Democratic Development, International Federation of Human Rights Leagues, "Declaration of Five International Human Rights Organizations Concerning the Delays in the Implementation of the Peace Agreements in Rwanda," March 15, 1994.

48 Belgian Ad Hoc Group, p. 133.

a coup. He told the Belgians to wake up and go home because, if not, they would face a fight without pity, hatred without mercy."[49]

— During the third week of March, the Officer in Charge of Intelligence for the Rwandan Army told a Belgian military advisers "if Arusha were implemented, they were ready to liquidate the Tutsi." (Si Arusha était exécuté, ils étaient prets a liquider les Tutsis.)[50]

— On March 26 Dallaire told New York that he needed plans in case an "extreme scenario takes place."[51]

— On March 30 CLADHO issued a declaration detailing attacks by soldiers, including the Presidential Guard and Interahamwe. It again demanded that the soldiers be disciplined and the militia be disarmed.[52]

— In the last days of March, RTLMC broadcast increasingly bitter attacks on UNAMIR, Dallaire, the Belgians, and some Rwandan political leaders.[53]

— At the end of March, the violence increased; assaults on civilians and murders took place.[54]

April 1994

— On April 2 RTLMC announced that military officers and the Prime Minister planned a coup against Habyarimana.[55]

— On April 3 RTLMC predicted that on April 3, 4 and 5 and from April 7 to 8 the RPF would do "a little something with bullets and grenades."[56]

— On April 4 during a celebration of the national day of Senegal, Bagosora said "the only plausible solution for Rwanda would be the elimination of the Tutsi." Dallaire, Booh-Booh, Marchal, and Shariyah Khan (adviser to Booh-Booh) were present.[57]

— April 6: The plane with President Habyarimana was shot down.

---

49 Belgian Ad Hoc Group, p. 91 and p. 49.

50 Belgian Senate, p. 334.

51 HRW, Leave None to Tell the Story, Part Warnings, p. 15, note 131 Human Rights Watch/FIDH interview, by telephone, October 25, 1997.

52 HRW, Leave none to tell the story, Part Warnings, p. 15, note 133: CLADHO, "Declaration sur les Violations Systematiques et Flagrantes des Droits de l'Homme en Cours dans le Pays Depuis Les Tentatives de Mise en Place des Institutions de Transition," March 30, 1994 (CLADHO).

53 HRW, Leave none to tell the story, Part Warnings, p. 15, note 134: Human Rights Watch/FIDH interview, by telephone, Brussels, July 24, 1998.

54 Melvern, p. 106.

55 HRW, Leave none to tell the story, Part Warnings, p. 15, note 135: Human Rights Watch/FIDH interview, Brussels, August 4, 1998.

56 HRW, Leave none to tell the story, Part Warnings, p. 15, note 137: RTLMC, April 3, 1994, recorded by Faustin Kagame (provided by Article 19).

57 Belgian Ad Hoc Group, p. 79.

BIBLIOGRAPHY

Literature

Ahrendt, Hannah. "What Is Authority." In *Between Past and Future: Eight Exercises in Political Thought*. New York: Penguin Books, 1993 (originally published 1954).

Albright, Madeleine. *Madam Secretary: A Memoir*. New York: Talk Miramax, 2003.

Allison, Graham T. *Essence of Decision, Explaining the Cuba Missile Crisis*. New York: Longman, 1999.

Ampleford, Susan. "Methodology Review, Discussion Paper Country Indicators for Foreign Policy." July 2000.

Austin, A. "Early Warning and the Field: A Cargo Cult Science?" In *Berghof Handbook for Conflict Transformation*. Berlin: Berghof Research Center for Constructive Conflict Management, 2003.

Barnett, Michael. *Eyewitness to a Genocide: The United Nations and Rwanda*. London: Cornell University Press, 2002.

Bellamy, Alex J. "Humanitarian Responsibilities and Interventionist Claims in International Society." In *Review of International Studies* 29 (2003): 321–40.

———. "Responsibility to Protect or Trojan Horse? The Crisis in Darfur and Humanitarian Intervention after Iraq." In *Ethics & International Affairs* 19, No. 2. 2005: 31–53.

———. "Whither the Responsibility to Protect? Humanitarian Intervention and the 2005 World Summit." In *Ethics & International Affairs* 20, No. 2, 2006: 143–69.

Boot, Machteld. *Genocide, Crimes against Humanity, War Crimes, Nullum Sine Lege and the Subject Matter Jurisdiction of the International Criminal Court*. New York: Intersentia, 2002.

Burkhalter, Holly J. "The Question of Genocide: The Clinton Administration and Rwanda." In *World Policy Journal* 11, no. 4 (1994–1995): 44–54.

Callaway R. L., and J. Harrelson-Stephens. "The Path from Trade to Human Rights: The Democracy and Development Detour." In *Understanding Human Rights*, edited by S. C. Carey and S. C. Poe. Aldershot: Ashgate Publishing, 2004.

Carey, S. C. "Domestic Treat and Repression: An Analysis of State Response to Different Forms of Dissent." In *Understanding Human Rights*, edited by S. C. Carey and S. C. Poe. Aldershot: Ashgate Publishing, 2004.

Castonguay, Jaques. *Les Casques Bleus au Rwanda*. Paris: Editions l'Harmattan, 1998.

Chrétien, J.-P. *Rwanda: Les Medias du Genocide*. Paris: Karthala, 1995.

———. *Le Défi de l'Ethnisme: Rwanda et Burundi, 1990–1996*. Paris: Karthala, 1997.

Clarke, J. N. "Early Warning Analysis for Humanitarian Preparedness and Conflict Prevention." In *Journal of Humanitarian Assistance* January 24, 2004. http://www.jha.ac/articles/a146.pdf.

Cohen, Stanley. *States of Denial, Knowing About Atrocities and Suffering*. Cambridge: Polity Press, 2001.

Coomans, Fons, Fred Grünfeld, Ingrid Westendorp, and Jan Willems, eds. "The Role of the Bystanders in Human Rights Violations." In *Rendering Justice to the Vulnerable. Liber Amicorum in Honour of Theo van Boven*. The Hague, London, Boston: Kluwer Law International, 2000.

Dallaire, Roméo. "End of Innocence: Rwanda 1994." In *Hard Choices: Moral Dilemmas in Humanitarian Interventions*, edited by Jonathan Moore, 55–70. Oxford: Roman and Littlefield, 1998.

———. *Shake Hands with the Devil, The Failure of Humanity in Rwanda*. London: Arrow Books, 2004 (originally published in Canada by Random House Canada 2003).

De Saint-Exupéry, Patrick. *L'inavouable, la France au Rwanda*. les Arenes, 2004.

Des Forges, Alison. *Leave None to Tell the Story, Genocide in Rwanda*. New York: Human Rights Watch, 1999.

Destexhe, Alain. *Rwanda and Genocide in the Twentieth Century*. New York: New York University Press, 1996.

Engel, Ulf, and Andreas Mehler. "Closing the Gap Between Early Warning and Early Action: Applying Political Science to Violent Conflicts in Africa." ULPA (University of Leipzig Papers on Africa), 2000.

Feinstein, L., and Slaughter, A.-M., "A Duty to Prevent." *Foreign Affairs* January/February 2004.

FEWER (Forum on Early Warning and Early Response). "Conflict Analysis and Response Definition, Abridged Methodology," April, 2001.

Gordon, Gregory S. "A War of Media, Words Newspapers, and Radio Stations: The ICTR Media, Trial Verdict and a New Chapter in the International Law of Hate Speech." In *Virginia Journal of International Law* 45 (2004):139–96.

Gourevitch, Philip. *We Wish to Inform You that Tomorrow We Will Be Killed With Our Families: Stories from Rwanda*. New York: Farrar Straus and Giroux, 1998.

Graaff de, Bob. (Inaugural speech, April 3, 2006, Universiteit Utrecht), Op de klippen door de vaargeul? De omgang van de historicus met (genocidaal) slachtofferschap, (Steering clear of dangerous rocks: History-writing and genocidal victimhood.). Amsterdam: Humanistic University Press, SWP, 2006.

Grünfeld, Fred. Vroegtijdig optreden van omstanders ter voorkoming van oorlogen en schendingen van de rechten van de mens, oratie (Early action of bystanders to prevent wars and gross human rights violations, inaugural lecture), Universiteit Utrecht, December 10, 2003.

———. Bookreview: Sabine C. Carey and Steven C. Poe (ed.). Understanding Human Rights Violations, New Systematic Studies. Ashgate: 2004. In *Netherlands Quarterly of Human Rights* 23 no. 3 (September 2005): 530–34.

Guichaoua, André, ed. *Les Crisis Politiques au Burundi et au Rwanda*. Lille: Université des Sciences et Technologies, 1995.

Harff, Barabara, and Ted Robert Gurr. "Systematic Early Warning of Humanitarian Emergencies." In *Journal of Peace Research* 35, no. 5 (1998): 551–80.

Hoefnagels, Marjo. *Repression and Repressive Violence*. Amsterdam, Lisse: Swets and Zeittinger, 1977.

Kimmerling, Baruch. *Politicide; Ariel Sharon's War Against the Palestinians*. London, New York: Verso, 2003.

Klinghoffer, A. J. *The International Dimension of Genocide in Rwanda*. New York: New York University Press, 1998.

Kuperman, Alan J. *The Limits of Humanitarian Intervention: Genocide in Rwanda* Washington, DC: Brookings Institution Press, 2001.

Laqueur, Walter, ed. *The Holocaust Encyclopedia*. New Haven, CT: Yale University Press, 2001.

Lema, Antoine. *African Divided: The Creation of Ethnic Groups*. Lund: Lund University Press, 1993.

Lemarchand, René. *Rwanda and Burundi*. New York: Praeger Publishers, 1970.

———. *Burundi: Ethnic Conflict and Genocide*. Cambridge: Cambridge University Press, 1995.

———. "The Rwanda Genocide." In *Century of Genocide: Eyewitness Testimonies and Critical Views*, edited by Samuel Totten et al., 408–23. New York: Garland Publishing, 1997.

Linden, Ian. "The Churches and Genocide: Lessons from Rwanda." *Month* 28 (1995): 256–63.

Marchal, Luc. *Aan de Poorten van de Rwandese Hel: Getuigenis van een Peacekeeper (At the Gates of Rwandan Hell, Witness from a Peacekeeper)*. Leuven: Van Halewyck, 2001.

Melvern, Linda. *A People Betrayed. The Role of the West in Rwanda's Genocide*. London: Zed Books, 2000.

———. *Conspiracy to Murder. The Rwandan Genocide*. New York: Verso, 2004.

———. "The Security Council: Behind the Scenes in the Rwanda Genocide." In *Genocide, War Crimes & the West: History and Complicity*, edited by Adam Jones. London: Zed Books, 2004.

Mettraux, Guémaël. *International Crimes and the Ad Hoc Tribunals*. New York: Oxford University Press, 2005.

Milner, W. T., et. al. "Providing Subsistence Rights: Do States Make A Difference?" In *Understanding Human Rights*, edited by S. C. Carey and S. C. Poe. Aldershot: Ashgate Publishing, 2004.

Peel, Quentin, "OSCE Minorities Chief Aims for Early Action." *Financial Times*, May 19, 2000. In *Quiet Diplomacy in Action: The HCNM*, edited by W. A. Kemp. Ashgate: Kluwer Law International, 2000.

Poe, S. C. "The Decision to Repress: An Integrative Theoretical Approach to the Research on Human Rights and Repression." In *Understanding Human Rights*, edited by S. C. Carey and S. C. Poe. Aldershot: Ashgate Publishing, 2004.

Power, Samantha. "Bystanders to Genocide: Why the United States Let the Rwandan Tragedy Happen." In *Atlantic Monthly* 288, no. 2 (2001): 84–108.

———. *Problem from Hell: America and the Age of Genocide*. New York: Perennial; London: Flamingo, 2002–2003.

Prunier, Gerard. *The Rwanda Crisis: History of a Genocide (1959–1994)*. London: Hurts and Company, 1995.

Reiding, Hilde. *The Netherlands and the Development of International Human Rights Instruments*. Antwerp, Oxford: Intersentia, 2007.

Reyntjens, Filip. *L'Afrique des Grands Lacs, en Crise: Rwanda, Burundi: 1988–1994*. Paris: Karthala, 1994.

———. *Rwanda, Trois Jours Qui on Fait Basculer l'Histoire*. Paris: L'Harmattan, 1995.

Rosner, Jeremy. *The New Tug-of-War. Congress, the Executive Branch and National Security*. Washington, DC: Carnegie Endowment, 1995.

Schabas, W. A. *Genocide in International Law, the Crimes of Crimes*. Cambridge: Cambridge University Press, 2000.

———. "The International Criminal Tribunal for Rwanda 1994–1999." In *Annotated Leading Cases of International Criminal Tribunals*, edited by André Klip and Göran Sluiter, 539–54. Antwerp: Intersentia, 2001.

Scheinin, Martin. "Improving the EU's Human Rights Country Assessment Through the Use of Indicators." Vienna: Ludwig Boltzmann Institute of Human Rights, 2006. Speech at the plenary session of the COST Workshop on the Occasion of the 7th annual conference of the Association of Human Rights Institutes (AHRI) on Indicators and Monitoring Systems Preventive Tools for Ensuring Peace and Security and Respect for Human Rights in External Policy-Making of the EU, September 8, 2006.

Shattuck, John. *Freedom on Fire: Human Rights Wars and America's Response*. Cambridge, MA: Harvard University Press, 2003.

Staub, E. *The Roots of Evil: The Origins of Genocide and Other Group Violence*. New York: Cambridge University Press, 1989.

Stettenheim, Joel. "The Arusha Accords and the Failure of International Intervention in Rwanda." In *Words over War: Mediation and Arbitration to Prevent Deadly Conflict*, edited by M. C. Greenberg, et al., 213–36. New York: Roman & Littlefield, 2002. http://wwics.si.edu/subsites/ccpdc/pubs/words/8.pdf.

Uvin, Peter *Aiding Violence, The Development Enterprise in Rwanda*. West Hartford, CT: Kumarian Press, 1998.

Verlinden, Peter. *Hutu en Tutsi, Eeuwen strijd (Hutu and Tutsi, Eternal Struggle)*. Leuven: Davidsfonds, 1995.

WANEP. Preventative Peacebuilding in West Africa—West Africa Early Warning and Response Network Training Module. Accra-Ghana: WANEP, 2000.

Wiesel, Elie. *Le Ville de la Chance*. Paris: Seuil, 1962. (Translated in English as: *The Town Beyond the Wall*. New York: Bergen Belsen Memorial Press, 1964. Translated in Dutch as: *De Stad van het Geluk*. Den Haag: BZZTôH, 1987).

———. *Un Juif, Aujourd-hui*. Paris: Seuil, 1977. (Translated in English as: A *Jew Today*. New York: Vintage, 1979. Translated in Dutch as: *Een Jood, Vandaag*. Hilversum: Gooi en Sticht, 1978).

Documents

Reports

African Rights. "Rwanda: Death, Despair and Defiance." In *Review of African Political Economy* 61 (1994): 471–72.

Africa Watch. A Committee of Human Rights Watch, "Talking Peace and Waging War: Human Rights since the October 1990 Invasion," 4, no. 3, February 27, 1992.

Africa Watch. "Beyond the Rhetoric: Continuing Human Rights Abuses in Rwanda," A Human Rights Watch Short Report, 5, no. 7, June 1993.

Amnesty International. "Rwanda, Persecution of Tutsi Minority and Repression of Government Critics 1990–1992," May 1, 1992 (AI. Afr. 47/002/92).

Assemblée Nationale du France. Rapport d'Information, "Mission d'Information sur le Rwanda," No. 1271, December 15, 1998. http://www.assemblee-nationale.fr/11/dossiers/rwanda/telechar/telechar.asp.

Belgian Intelligence Service (SGR). "Note of September 28, 1993," Documents of the Belgian Intelligence Service No. 7260.

CIA National Intelligence Council (NIC). National Intelligence Estimates (NIE), Doc: NIE 93–36, October 1993. http://www2.gwu.edu/~nsarchiv/NSAEBB/NSAEBB117/Rw36.pdf.

CIA. "Rwanda-Burundi: Presidential Deaths Likely to Renew Fighting," Excerpt from Central Intelligence Agency, National Intelligence Daily, April 7, 1994. http://www2.gwu.edu/~nsarchiv/NSAEBB/NSAEBB119/Rw3.pdf.

European Commission. Press Releases P/04/45, 8219/1/04 (Presse 102). http://europa.eu.int/rapid/pressReleasesAction.do?reference=PESC/04/45&format=HTML&aged=1&language=EN&guiLanguage=en.

Federation of International des Droits de l'Homme. "Rapport sur la Commission d'Enquete sur les Violations des Droits de l'Homme au Rwanda Depuis le 1er October 1990," Paris, March 1996.

Frontline. "100 Days of Slaughter, A Chronology of U.S./U.N. Actions." http://www pbs.org/wgbh/pages/frontline/shows/evil/etc/slaughter.html.

Human Rights Watch. "Beyond the Rhetoric: Continuing Human Rights Abuses in Rwanda," June 1993 (HRW, Index No. A507).

Human Rights Watch. "Arming Rwanda: The Arms Trade and Human Rights Abuses in the Rwandan War," January 1994 (HRW Index No. A601).

Human Rights Watch. Fédération Internationale des Ligues des Droits de l'Homme. Alison Des Forges, "Leave None to Tell the Story: Genocide in Rwanda," March 1999 (HRW Index No. 1711).

International Commission on Intervention and State Sovereignty (ICISS). "The Responsibility to Protect," International Development Research Center, Ottawa, 2001.

Michelsen Institute. Bergen, Norway, Study 2: Howard Adelman and Astri Suhrke, "Early Warning and Conflict Management Genocide in Rwanda." Toronto, Canada: York University, September 1995.

Netherlands (Dutch) Ministry of Foreign Affairs, The Hague. Files on Rwanda in the Period 1993–1994 (exact source linked to the footnotes in the text).

Netherlands Parliamentary Reports, 1992–1993 and 1993–1994 on Rwanda:

Tweede Kamer 1992–1993, 22800 X, No. 63, June 25, 1993.

Tweede Kamer, 1993–1994, 23727, No. 1, 2, 3, 4, 5, 6, 7 and 13.

Tweede Kamer, 1993–1994, Appendix 551, June 10, 1994 Governmental answer, June 10, 1994.

Tweede Kamer, 1993–1994, Appendix 551, June 10, 1994. Parliamentary question, May 16, 1994.

Tweede Kamer, 1993–1994, Appendix 719, August 12, 2004, 1457–58.

Tweede Kamer, 1993–1994, Appendix 727, August 16, 1994.

The Nordic Africa Institute. Uppsala, Sweden, Study 1: Tor Sellström and Lennart Wohlgemuth, edited by David Millwood, "The International Response to Conflict and Genocide: Lessons from the Rwanda Experience;" Steering Committee of the

Joint Evaluation of Emergency Assistance to Rwanda, March 1996. http://www.reliefweb.int/library/nordic/.

Organization of African Unity. "The Preventable Genocide of the International Panel of Eminent Personalities to Investigate the 1994 Genocide in Rwanda and Surrounding Events," 2000. http://www.visiontv.ca/RememberRwanda/Report.pdf.

Sénat de Belgique. Commission d'Enquête Parlementaire Concernant les Événements au Rwanda (Commission of Parliamentary Enquiry Concerning the Events in Rwanda), session de 1997–1998, 6 décembre 1997, Rapport fait au Nom de la Commission d'Enquête par MM Mahoux et Verhofstadt. [Belgian Senate].

Sénat de Belgique. Commission d'Enquête Parlementaire Concernant les Événements au Rwanda (Commission of Parliamentary Enquiry Concerning the Events in Rwanda), session de 1997–1998, 6 décembre 1997, Rapport fait au Nom de la Commission d'Enquête par MM Mahoux et Verhofstadt, Annexes [Annex Belgian Senate].

Sénat de Belgique. Rapport du Groupe Ad Hoc Rwanda A La Commission des Affairs Etrangeres, Sénat de Belgique, 7 janvier 1997. [Belgian Ad Hoc Group].

UNHCR. "Fiche Pays: Rwanda," January 2006.

U.S. State Department. The Secretary Morning Summary, "Summary Report of Important Intelligence Items from the Bureau of Intelligence and Research." http://www2.gwu.edu/~nsarchiv/NSAEBB/NSAEBB119/index.htm.

U.S. State Department. "Burundi/Rwanda: Presidents Killed," Excerpt from U.S. Department of State, Bureau of Intelligence and Research, Secretary's Morning Summary, April 7, 1994. http://www2.gwu.edu/~nsarchiv/NSAEBB/NSAEBB119/Rw2.pdf .

U.S. State Department. "Rwanda/Burundi: Turmoil in Rwanda," April 7, 1994, Bureau of Intelligence and Research, SPOT Intelligence Report as of 08:45 EDT April 7, 1994. http://www.gwu.edu/~nsarchiv/NSAEBB/NSAEBB119/Rw4.pdf.

U.S. State Department. "Rwanda/Burundi: Violence Update," No. 2, April 7, 1994, Bureau of Intelligence and Research, SPOT Intelligence Report as of 13:00 EDT, April 7, 1994. http://www.gwu.edu/~nsarchiv/NSAEBB/NSAEBB119/Rw5.pdf.

U.S. Department of State. WGRW01: Working Group Formation to Deal with the Situation in Kigali and Bujumbura, April 8, 1994, Telegram State 092008. http://www2.gwu.edu/~nsarchiv/NSAEBB/NSAEBB119/Rw8.pdf.

The White House. Office of the Press Secretary, Statement by the President: "The Deaths of the Presidents of Rwanda and Burundi," April 7, 1994. http://www.clinton-foundation.org/legacy/040794-presidential-statement-on-deaths-of-rwanda-and-burundi-presidents.htm.

Faxes

Code Cable, January 11, 1994, from Dallaire to Baril, Fax No: Most immediate; Cable: 212-963-4652, Subject: Request for protection for informant.

U.S. Department of State, Bureau of African Affairs, Memorandum from Deputy Assistant Secretary of State Prudence Bushnell to The Secretary through Under Secretary for Political Affairs Peter Tarnoff, Death of Rwandan and Burundian Presidents in Plane Crash Outside Kigali, April 6, 1994. http://www.gwu.edu/~nsarchiv/NSAEBB/NSAEBB53/rw040694.pdf.

NIE 93–36, October 1993. http://www2.gwu.edu/~nsarchiv/NSAEBB/NSAEBB117/Rw36.pdf.

Kigali 01316, March 25, 1994, Subject: Bushnell meets Habyarimana and RPF. http://www2.gwu.edu/~nsarchiv/NSAEBB/NSAEBB117/Rw01.pdf.

Kigali 01458, April 1, 1994, From embassy Kigali, to embassy Kampala, from Rawson to Moose. http://www2.gwu.edu/~nsarchiv/NSAEBB/NSAEBB117/Rw02.pdf.

Conventions

Convention on the Prevention and Punishment of the Crime of Genocide, Adopted by Resolution 260 (III) A of the United Nations General Assembly on December 9, 1948, Entry into force: January 12, 1951.

U.N. Security Council Resolutions

SC Resolution 812, March 12, 1993, U.N. Doc. S/RES/812 (1993).

SC Resolution 846, June 22, 1993, U.N. Doc. S/RES/864 (1993).

SC Resolution 872, October 5, 1993, U.N. Doc. S/RES/872 (1993).

SC Resolution 893, January 6, 1994, U.N. Doc. S/RES/893 (1994).

SC Resolution 909, April 5, 1994, U.N. Doc. S/RES/909 (1994).

SC Resolution 912, April 21, 1994, U.N. Doc. S/RES/912 (1994).

SC Resolution 918, May 17, 1994, U.N. Doc. S/RES/918 (1994).

SC Resolution 929, June 22, 1994, U.N. Doc. S/RES/929 (1994).

SC Resolution 955, November 8, 1994, U.N. Doc. S/RES/955 (1994).

U.N. Documents

A/48/824—S/26915, December 23, 1993.

A/59/2005, In Larger Freedom: towards development, security and human rights for all. Report of the Secretary-General, March 21, 2005.

A/59/565, Report of the Secretary-General's high-level panel on threats, challenges and change, A more secure world: Our shared responsibility, December 2, 2004.

A/RES/60/1, Resolution adopted by the General Assembly 60/1. 2005 World Summit Outcome, October 24, 2005.

E/CN.4/1994/7, Extrajudicial, summary or arbitrary executions: report by the Special Rapporteur, Bacré Waly Ndiaye, submitted pursuant to Commission on Human Rights resolution 1993/71, July 13, 1993.

E/CN.4/1994/7/Add. 1, Extrajudicial, summary or arbitrary executions, addendum: report by the Special Rapporteur, Bacré Waly Ndiaye on his mission to Rwanda from April 8–17, 1993.

S/1994/44, Letter of April 15 from Claes to the president of the SC.

S/1994/360, Second progress report of the Secretary-General on UNAMIR for the period from December 30, 1993 to March 30, 1994.

S/1994/430, Letter from the Permanent Representative of Belgium to the United Nations addressed to the President of the Security Council, April 13, 1994.

S/1994/446, Letter from the Permanent Representative of Belgium to the United Nations addressed to the President of the Security Council, April 15, 1994.

S/1994/470, Special Report of the Secretary-General on the United Nations Assistance mission for Rwanda, April 20, 1994.

S/1994/479, Letter from the Permanent Representative of Uganda to the United Nations addressed to the President of the Security Council, April 21, 1994.

S/1994/481, Letter from the Permanent Representative of Bangladesh to the United Nations addressed to the President of the Security Council, April 21, 1994.

S/1994/546, Letter from the President of the Security Council addressed to the Secretary General, May 6, 1944

S/26488, Report of the Secretary-General on Rwanda, September 25, 1993. Presidential statement S/PRST/1994/8.

United Nations, Report of the Independent Inquiry into the Actions of the United Nations during the 1994 Genocide in Rwanda, December 15, 1999, United Nations, Ingvar Carlsson, Han, Sung-Joo, Rufus, M. Kupolati, U.N. Doc. S/1999/1257 (Carlsson Report, S/1999/1257).

United Nations Department of Public Information, The United Nations and Rwanda, 1993–1996, Blue Book Series, United Nations, New York: Department of Public Information, 1996.

ICTR

Press Release ICTR/INFO-9-2-510.EN. Arusha, January 19, 2007: Appeals Chamber Concludes Hearing in the Media Case.

Prosecutor v. Akayesu, (Case No. ICTR-96-4-T), Judgment and Sentence, September 2, 1998.

Prosecutor v. Kambanda (Case No. ICTR-997-23-S), Judgment and Sentence, September 4, 1998.

Prosecutor v. Nahimana, Barayagwiza, and Ngeze, Judgment and Sentence, (Case No. ICTR-99-52-T), Judgment, December 3, 2003.

"Recent Cases, U.N. Tribunal Finds that Mass Media Speech Constitutes Genocide, Incitement to Genocide and Crimes Against Humanity." In *Harvard Law Review*, 117 June 2004: 2769–76.

Media

BBC, World. "Africa Rwanda Slaughter Could Have Been Prevented," March 31 1999.

CNN. "U.N. Tribunal to Give First Verdict on Rwanda Genocide," September 1, 1998. http://www.cnn.com/WORLD/africa/9809/01/rwanda.tribunal/index.html.

Globe and Mail. Scott Straus, "Remember Rwanda, Dallaire Pleads," Toronto, February 27, 1998.

Hazanavicius, Michel and Arnaud Borges. "Tuez les Tous" (Kill them All), History of a genocide, A movie of Raphael Glucksmann, David Hazan, Pierre Mezerette, Production Dum Dum Films, Paris 2004.

IKON Radio (Dutch radio). Interview Robert van Putten by Jurgen Maas, March 26, 2006, between 7:00–7:30 a.m.

Israel Nieuwsbrief. Ronny Naftaniel, "Lessen uit het Verleden" ("Lessons from the Past"), March 17, 2005.

Libération. Stephen Smith, "6 Avril 1994: Deux Missiles Abattent l'Avion du Président Habyarimana," (Two missiles shoot down the plane of President Habyarimana) April 6–7, 1996.

La Libre Belgique. Marie-France Cros, "Rwanda: M. Kuypers Denounce l'Entourage du President," (Rwanda: M. Kuypers denounces President's entourage) December 1992, 3–4.

Le Monde. Patrick May, "Ce qui a Manqué à l'Opération 'Turquoise,'" ("What Is Missing in the Operation 'Turquoise'"), January 13, 2006.

Le Monde. Jean-Pierre Chrétien, "Un Pamphlet Teinté d'Africanisme Colonial," (A pamphlet colored by African colonialism) December 9, 2005.

Le Monde. Colette Braeckman, "Rwanda, l'Enquête Inachevée" ("Rwanda, the Incomplete Inquiry"), December 9, 2005.

Le Monde. "Deux Rescapés Accusent la France de Complicité de Génocide au Rwanda," (Two escapees accuse France of complicity in the genocide) December 25–26, 2005.

De Morgen. Walter de Bock and Gert van Langendonck, "Legerstaf wist Alles over Nakende Genocide Rwanda," (Chief of Army was aware of emerging genocide in Rwanda) November 4, 1995.

De Morgen. Walter de Bock, "Belgische Wijkagenten Zagen Voorbereiding Genocide," (Belgian police officers observed preparation of genocide) November 4, 1995.

The New Yorker. Philip Gourevitch, "The Genocide Fax," May 11, 1998, 43–46.

NRC. "*Le Monde* Onthult Frans Onderzoek: President Rwanda Doodde Voorganger" ("*Le Monde* Reveals French Research: the President of Rwanda Killed Predecessor"), March 10, 2004.

NRC. "Een Explosief Rwanda-Rapport" ("An Explosive Rwanda Report"), March 11, 2004.

NRC. "VN Hadden "Zwarte Doos" Toch in Bezit" ("U.N. Possessed 'Black Box' Nevertheless"), March 13, 2004.

NRC. "President Offerde Tutsi's Voor Macht" ("President Sacrificed Tutsis for Power"), March 10, 2004.

NRC. "Diplomatieke rel Rwanda-Frankrijk" (Diplomatic clash Rwanda-France), November 25, 2006.

Reuters. Jim Wold, "Clinton Moves to Limit U.N.Peacekeeping Role," May 5, 1994.

Interviews

Authors' Interviews

Interview with B. Beardsley, June 6, 2005 (Fred Grünfeld).

Interview with P. Bushnell, May 27, 2005 (Fred Grünfeld).

Interview with W. Claes, January 13, 2006 (Fred Grünfeld and Anke Huijboom).

Interview with A. Destexhe, April 22, 2005 (Fred Grünfeld and Anke Huijboom).

Interview with D. Hartland, June 2, 2005 (Fred Grünfeld).

Interview with A. Lake, May 21, 2005 (Fred Grünfeld).
Interview with L. Marchal, January 21, 2005 (Fred Grünfeld and Anke Huijboom).
Interview with B.W. Ndiaye, May 25, 2005 (Fred Grünfeld).
Interview with J. Pronk, August 21, 2006 (Fred Grünfeld and Anke Huijboom).
Interview with D. Rawson, May 26, 2005 (Fred Grünfeld).
Interview J. Shattuck, May 26, 2005 (Fred Grünfeld).

PBS Frontline Interviews

All these interviews have been taken from the Frontline website, at http://www.pbs.org/wgbh/pages/frontline/shows/ghosts/interviews/. and http://www.pbs.org/wgbh/pages/frontline/shows/evil/interviews/.

Interview with Madeleine Albright, February 25, 2004. http://www.pbs.org/wgbh/pages/frontline/shows/ghosts/interviews/albright.html.

Interview with Kofi Annan, February 17, 2004. http://www.pbs.org/wgbh/pages/frontline/shows/ghosts/interviews/annan.html.

Interview with Brent Beardsley, November 15, 2003. http://www.pbs.org/wgbh/pages/frontline/shows/ghosts/interviews/beardsley.html.

Interview with Prudence Bushnell, September 30, 2003. http://www.pbs.org/wgbh/pages/frontline/shows/ghosts/interviews/bushnell.html.

Interview with Roméo Dallaire, Autumn 2003. http://www.pbs.org/wgbh/pages/frontline/shows/ghosts/interviews/dallaire.html.

Interview with Boutros Boutros-Ghali, January 21, 2004. http://www.pbs.org/wgbh/pages/frontline/shows/ghosts/interviews/ghali.html.

Interview with Anthony Lake, December 15, 2003. http://www.pbs.org/wgbh/pages/frontline/shows/ghosts/interviews/lake.html.

Interview with Luc Marchal. http://www.pbs.org/wgbh/pages/frontline/shows/evil/interviews/marchal.html.

Interview with Tony Marley. http://www.pbs.org/wgbh/pages/frontline/shows/evil/interviews/marley.html.

Interview with George Moose, November 21, 2003. http://www.pbs.org/wgbh/pages/frontline/shows/ghosts/interviews/moose.html.

Interview with Samantha Power, December 16, 2003. http://www.pbs.org/wgbh/pages/frontline/shows/ghosts/interviews/power.html.

Interview with David Rawson, May 10, 2003. http://www.pbs.org/wgbh/pages/frontline/shows/ghosts/interviews/rawson.html.

Interview with Ibqal Riza. http://www.pbs.org/wgbh/pages/frontline/shows/evil/interviews/riza.html.

Interview with John Shattuck, December 16, 2003. http://www.pbs.org/wgbh/pages/frontline/shows/ghosts/interviews/shattuck.html.

Interview with James Woods. http://www.pbs.org/wgbh/pages/frontline/shows/evil/interviews/woods.html.

Hearings in Belgian Senate

Hearing Brouhns, POR, Senate, 1996–1997, May 25, 1997.
Hearing with Claes, BV, BCR, Senate, 1996–1997, April 18, 1997 and June 24, 1997.
Hearing Dehaene, POR, Senate, PV, 1996–1997, p. 1F/11.
Hearing with Delcroix, POR, Senate, 1996–1997, June 18, 1997.
Hearing Des Forges, POR, Senate, 1996–1997, May 16, 1997.
Hearing with Lieutenant Nees, BV, BCR, Senate, 1996–1997, March 7, 1997.
Hearing of Ambassador Swinnen, BV, BCR, Senate, 1996–1997, March 12, 1997.
Hearing with General-Major Uytterhoeven, BV, BCR, Senate, 1996–1997, April 25, 1997.

INDEX

www.ingramcontent.com/pod-product-compliance
Lightning Source LLC
LaVergne TN
LVHW020651300926
849161LV00004B/897